Enemies to Allies

ENEMIES TO ALLIES

Cold War Germany
and
American Memory

BRIAN C. ETHERIDGE

UNIVERSITY PRESS OF KENTUCKY

Editorial and Sales Offices: The University Press of Kentucky
663 South Limestone Street, Lexington, Kentucky 40508-4008
www.kentuckypress.com

Cataloging-in-Publication data is available from the Library of Congress.

ISBN 978-0-8131-6640-7 (hardcover : alk. paper)
ISBN 978-0-8131-6642-1 (epub)
ISBN 978-0-8131-6641-4 (pdf)

This book is printed on acid-free paper meeting
the requirements of the American National Standard
for Permanence in Paper for Printed Library Materials.

Manufactured in the United States of America.

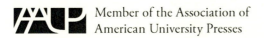 Member of the Association of
American University Presses

For Erica

Contents

Introduction

Answering the German Question

In the United States today, visitors can find almost as many memorials dedicated to the two most visible symbols of recent German history—the Holocaust and the Berlin Wall—as in Germany itself. Although both events happened thousands of miles away and neither directly involved the United States, American public and private officials have dedicated museums to the Holocaust and memorialized sections of the Berlin Wall in places throughout the country. Major Holocaust sites can be found in several cities, including Los Angeles, Albuquerque, Buffalo, and Miami. The Berlin Wall has been enshrined in locales ranging from the George Bush Presidential Library in College Station, Texas, to the men's bathroom at the Main Street Station Casino in Las Vegas. In many of these memorials, the Holocaust and the Berlin Wall reflect a positive narrative of the United States that affirms America's mission, ideals, and values in the world.

These American monuments to the Berlin Wall and the Holocaust suggest the visibility and importance of German history to American society. For much of the second half of the twentieth century, the "German Question" was a widely debated issue in the United States. Often framed in terms of how Americans should assess and address Germany's past, and thus its present and future, manifestations of the German Question saturated America's mass media, appearing in newspapers, magazines, journals, history books, novels, films, and television shows. At a basic level, then, the answers offered through these numerous monuments to the Berlin Wall and the Holocaust underscore a significant truth in post-war American history—for many Americans narratives of Germany have played an important role in defining domestic and international realities.

Although the proliferation of American monuments to Germany's past might seem natural and the meaning of them self-evident, this book argues that Germany's visibility in and significance to American life during the postwar period have been neither foreordained nor fixed. Since the end of World War II, various actors have tried to mobilize German representations for different ends. As a result, images of Germany have been manufactured, contested, and co-opted as rival narratives have competed for legitimacy and hegemony. In examining the history of German representations in America's mass media, this book tells the story of how these representations have been both produced by and subjected to different forms of diplomatic, political, social, and cultural power.

This book argues that the story of German representations in the United States is about far more than images of Nazis and Berliners in the American media. In its broadest telling, this work connects international and domestic, diplomatic and cultural, and German and American histories. It narrates not only the activities of American and West German government officials but also the efforts of journalists, public intellectuals, filmmakers, public relations experts, neo-Nazis, Jews, conservatives, and student radicals in shaping and articulating narratives of Germany's past and present. It also examines the fruits of their efforts in cultural products ranging from Fred Zinnemann's *The Search* to William Shirer's *The Rise and Fall of the Third Reich,* from CBS's *Hogan's Heroes* to George Lincoln Rockwell's *White Power.* This book ties these themes and more together to show that the story of German representations, conceived broadly, has been a central thread in the life of postwar America.

In contextualizing the cultural and political milieu in which these narratives were created and circulated, this book expands our understanding of the relationship between policymaking and meaning making.[1] Because most of the major works that have touched on the German Question are focused almost exclusively on foreign policy decisions, they have offered little beyond vague generalizations, citing the influence of events like the Berlin Blockade without consideration for how these events were shaped by interested actors or how they intersected with existing discourses about Germany. Often assuming that the beliefs of the American public simply followed the same trajectory as the country's policymakers, they ignore the struggle over German representations in the mass media and thus fail to appreciate the complex nature of American attitudes toward Germany. Moreover, the story of this struggle not only complicates our understanding of how representations of Germany circulated in America's media in the postwar period but also sheds light on larger issues involving state power, public diplomacy, and cultural reception.[2]

To integrate these different stories, I deploy a concept called *memory diplomacy,* which draws from the study of both public memory and public diplomacy. For years, scholars of foreign relations have been interested in the role of individual memory in shaping foreign policy, but they have been slower to take on the study of public memory, most likely because its relevance for policymaking is less clear. As numerous scholars have pointed out, modern conceptions of memory frame remembering as a presentist act of reconstruction dependent on social affirmation for articulation and solidification. In this sense, modern studies emphasize that the study of "forgetting" memories is equally as important and interesting as the study of "remembering" them. Maurice Halbwachs's notion of collective memory, which theorizes that every memory is shared and reinforced by the larger community, has emerged as the dominant framework for understanding and exploring memory historically. Building on Halbwachs's work, a number of studies have been written on how societies construct and interact with their pasts through commemoration, rituals, ceremonies, popular culture, works of history, and monuments.[3]

As Jérôme Bourdon has noted, the emphasis on "collective" has concentrated attention on "political-territorial entities, at the level of nation and below." Within whatever collectivity is being examined—nation-state, city, ethnic group—many studies focus on how different memory narratives vie for dominance. Some, such as John Bodnar, juxtapose "official" memories, narratives sanctioned by the state, with "vernacular" memories, stories or narratives nurtured and maintained by common people. Others, such as Marita Sturken, conceive of official history and memory as "entangled," with the distinctions between the two often blurred. Carol Gluck has developed the notion of "memory activists" to describe those individuals and organizations involved in pushing or spinning various narratives. Regardless of approach, however, all scholars of collective memory recognize and support the notion that collective memory is about more than the past: rather, building on the work of Benedict Anderson, they argue that the collective memory of an entity is directly tied to its identity or subjectivity.[4]

Diplomatic historians who have ventured into the study of public memory have contributed to the study of collective memory of war, exploring, for example, how specific narratives of World War II and Vietnam have played out in American collective memory. While these works demonstrate that foreign relations historians can do memory work as well as those trained in cultural history, they build upon existing work that examines how the various actors have sought to use memory narratives to foster support for or opposition to the state. In this sense, their work reinforces the dominant conceptualization of memory as a domestic phenomenon, in that they study *American* actors wrangling over *American* memories. Conceiving of memory in such a way prevents memory from connecting to the growing movement to internationalize foreign relations history and American history more broadly.[5]

But recent theorizing of memory offers ways in which international history, both in content and in practice, can be integrated in the study of memory. Some scholars have argued that, in the age of electronic mass media, the relationship between memory and the collective has become more complicated as traditional ways of passing on memory have been disrupted. "Instead of relating to the past through a shared sense of place or ancestry," George Lipsitz argues, "consumers of electronic mass media can experience a common heritage with a people they have never seen; they can acquire memories of a past to which they have no geographical or biological connection." For this reason, Alison Landsberg, in what is the most important work on this phenomenon, eschews the term *collective memory* for the twentieth century, opting instead for *prosthetic memory* in an effort to highlight the often fabricated or artificial nature of memory narratives. For Landsberg, modern technologies "can structure 'imagined communities' that are not necessarily geographically or nationally bounded and that do not presume any kind of affinity among community members." In an age of mass culture, "memories of the Holocaust do not belong only to Jews, nor do memories of slavery belong solely to African Americans." Prosthetic memories encourage subjects to adopt these "foreign" memories through mediated representations that collapse time and position viewers to identify with "others" from the past. Memories thus can be prosthetic and "transportable"; identities and subjectivities become more fluid.[6]

While Landsberg focuses primarily on the transformation of memory as a result of technological change and the onset of modernity, this book stresses how the notion of "prosthetic memory" opens up the study of memory in new ways for historians of foreign relations. Memory theorized as "collective" suggests an exclusively domestic focus; but memory conceived as prosthetic opens the realm for narratives and actors not "organically" tied to the community. Despite the oft-heard contention that no memory narrative is more historically accurate than another, the term *collective memory* still conveys some measure of authenticity on domestic narratives and actors because it conceives of memory work as an almost exclusively indigenous enterprise. Prosthetic memory implicitly moves these narratives away from the authenticity associated with their originators and thus fully liberates both the narratives and their activists from "authentic" trappings of nationality, blood, or ethnicity. Any actor can fashion and promote a memory narrative in a society; there is no requirement that the actor or the narrative have an organic relationship with the community.

When viewed in this light, it becomes apparent that the study of public diplomacy can serve as a model for analyzing and recognizing how prosthetic memories of other nations are promoted and understood. Alternately known as propaganda, cultural diplomacy, informational policy, and psychological warfare, public diplomacy denotes communication activities designed to shape, manipulate, or otherwise influence public opinion to achieve or facilitate the attainment of foreign policy objectives. Recent scholarship has expanded the concept of public diplomacy by emphasizing how private initiatives and actors can participate in, augment, and supplement state-sponsored public diplomacy initiatives. Building on these works, this book understands public diplomacy to involve any information work that targets the "public" for the purpose of affecting the "diplomacy," or the foreign relations, of the host country. Conceiving of memory as prosthetic enables work in public diplomacy to highlight how foreign agents (in league with indigenous state and non-state actors) can circulate memory narratives of their nation to encourage target peoples to adopt prosthetic memories of their homeland and, in the process, position them to sympathize, identify with, and ultimately support their foreign policies. At its most basic level, then, this book uses the concept of "memory diplomacy" to show how the *means* of public diplomacy can be used to carry out the *ends* of public memory work.[7]

I argue that two broad memory narratives dominated American thinking about Germany in the Cold War period. Depicting the German people as dedicated democrats standing firm on the front line of the Cold War, the Cold War narrative sought to train American attention on the present heroism of the Germans in supporting the United States and the West during the period. Involving government and nongovernment officials on both sides of the Atlantic, the memory coalition supporting this narrative portrayed the German people as Western or "Americanized," and thus facilitated the adoption of prosthetic memories of Germany by emphasizing the sameness of the two peoples. Memory actors routinely portrayed the East-West struggle as a war against totalitarianism, explicitly linking Nazi Germany with the Soviet Union. When addressing Germany's past, members of this coalition built upon World War II understandings of the conflict that differentiated between Nazis and Germans, arguing that most Germans were not only innocent of the horrors of World War II but had been fighting the Nazis (and hence totalitarianism) with the Americans from the beginning. Most popular, however, was the invocation of Berlin as the symbol of the Cold War, which fostered the identity of West Berliners, and by extension all West Germans, as foot soldiers on the front line in this common struggle against totalitarianism.

Supporters of the world war narrative, on the other hand, urged Americans to reject this prosthetic memory, encouraging them instead to maintain more organic memories (American-centered) of the First and Second World Wars. Rooted in America's experience with Germany in the first half of the decade, their narrative supported the notion of collective guilt and warned against German revanchism. Comprised primarily of liberals and Jews wary of a renewed Germany, this memory coalition depicted the German people as nascent Nazis still bent on world domination. Their strategy lay primarily in maintaining difference between Americans and Germans. They regularly drew attention to vestiges of Nazism in West German government and society, and often used terms like *Nazis* and *Pan-Germans* to refer to all Germans. Both were intended to recall Germany's past aggression and encourage Americans to think of Germans as the "other."

Just as scholars of public diplomacy have acknowledged that they must go beyond simply chronicling the activities of states in formulating and carrying out their policies, tracing and detailing the activities of these memory activists do not provide a complete picture. An equally important part of the study of memory diplomacy is looking at how "communities of memory" (to borrow from Stanley Fish's notion of interpretive communities) formed around these narratives. Often disparate and hard-to-generalize groups of people came together around common understandings of the German people, and these communities of memory often interpreted the messages and narratives in unintended or unexpected ways.[8]

In exploring the memory diplomacy associated with Germany during the Cold War, I emphasize five themes. Above all, perhaps, the use of memory diplomacy shows how these conflicts over and through German representations serve as a window for understanding the changing nature of American identity and state power in the postwar world. This is the *first* theme—the evolving power of the American state in framing American identity during this period. I conceptualize foreign policy as more than just an effort to reconcile geopolitical aims and means. The articulation of foreign policy involves the mobilization of public opinion, and as such, intimately involves questions of national identity. Through the politics of affiliation and disaffiliation, a nation's foreign policy defines friends and enemies, allies and adversaries, constructing what a people are for and what a people are against. Challenges to long-standing foreign policy traditions, such as the period right after World War II or during the Vietnam War, have necessitated a reorientation of public attitudes if the policy is to be supported. In this case, how the American government framed Germany in the early Cold War period, how these definitions later changed, and how effectively these framings were resisted or contested says much about who wields power and how it is exercised in American society.

The U.S. government was not the only actor interested in shaping narratives of Germany. The new Federal Republic of Germany had an even greater interest in mobilizing American public opinion on its behalf. Telling the story of West German public diplomacy in the United States, the *second* theme, illustrates the many benefits that can be gained from dislodging the privileged place of Americanization in the study of public diplomacy and intercultural relationships. Exploring the efforts of West

Germany in the United States enables students of intercultural relationships, and especially of America's place in the world, to revisit some of the
assumptions that the study of Americanization has brought to the analysis
of these cultural relations. More specifically, it complicates conventional
understandings drawn from Americanization studies on the relationship
between power and method, highlighting the different imperatives and
strategies of states on the cultural periphery attempting to influence the
cultural core. In this sense, West Germany's public diplomacy program in
the United States was different in both degree and kind from the imperial strategies of the United States in West Germany and of Wilhelmine
and Nazi Germany in the United States. When compared with American
public diplomacy in Germany and with previous German public diplomacy in America, West Germany's public diplomacy efforts in the United
States show how and why such efforts from the cultural margins matter
to the study of intercultural relationships.

Both governments found themselves joined by other, nonstate actors
interested in shaping narratives of Germany in the United States, such as
the Society for the Prevention of World War III (SPWWIII), the American Council on Germany (ACG), and a number of Jewish organizations, including the American Jewish Committee (AJC), the American
Jewish Congress (AJ Congress), the Anti-Defamation League of B'nai
B'rith (ADL), and the Jewish War Veterans (JWV). The political relations
among these state and nonstate actors reveals the different strategies and
tactics pursued in the formulation and execution of effective public relations campaigns. More important, the story of their interaction, the *third*
theme, highlights the evolving ability of the American state in coercing
consent and containing dissent among national organizations.

Because of their unique relationship with Germany's past, the positions of Jewish organizations and their constituents are especially noteworthy. Unlike the positions of the SPWWIII, which was implacably
opposed to the German people, and the ACG, which was founded to
propagandize on behalf of the new West German government, those of
Jewish organizations were neither clear-cut nor uniform. This intra-Jew-
ish conflict and its significance for the growth of Holocaust consciousness in the United States represent the *fourth* theme. During the 1940s
and 1950s, all Jewish organizations worried about developments in Germany and viewed the Federal Republic against the backdrop of the Third

Reich and the Holocaust. But while an overwhelming majority of Jews favored a hard peace for the German people in the postwar period, Jewish organizations did not agree on the extent to which this should be supported, as some Jewish leaders worried that a vengeful approach would place them outside the developing Cold War consensus. Also, local Jewish officials and members often disagreed with national Jewish organizations that sought to accommodate the American state, continuing, in several instances, to criticize Germans and Germany despite admonitions and instructions against such behavior. These incidents of resistance suggest an oppositional Jewish "community of memory" that provided validation for contesting state-sponsored narratives.

The multiplicity of meanings for Germany and the Holocaust in the Jewish community underscores the importance of exploring how these narratives circulated in American society. Examining narratives of Germany in the mainstream and underground media show how these narratives were replicated, contested, and rejected. This story of cultural circulation, the *fifth* theme, is especially important because it illuminates another realm of conflict. Whereas the study of institutional interactions tells of the political struggle among national and international organizations, the study of representations in American culture examines how that same conflict continued in entertainment, informational, and political discourse—sometimes with unexpected results. Studying the circulation of these media texts is also important because it demonstrates that many policymakers and opinion makers often misunderstood or mischaracterized the impact of their efforts to shape public opinion. In these ways, I argue that examining the diplomatic, political, and cultural aspects of German representations in the United States offers both a more complicated and a more complete picture of the exercise of and the resistance to different forms of state power.

I begin by establishing how Germans, in many ways, have served as America's "other" since the founding of the English colonies in the seventeenth century; they were a people upon whom Americans projected both their fears about and their aspirations for themselves and their society. For the first half of American history, Americans largely interpreted Germany and Germanness through the waves of German settlers coming to the New World. As the largest non-Anglo ethnic group before the Great War, German Americans served as a convenient point of contrast for understanding Americans and Americanism. During the colonial period, Anglos admired the work ethic of their German neighbors but feared their clannishness and potential for subversion. After the founding of the American Republic, German Americans became part of the larger story of the American democratic experiment, as Americans unfavorably contrasted a perceived lack of restraint and potential for self-government among Germans with an American propensity for liberty. After the establishment of the German empire, mainstream Americans looked to the German nation for a better understanding of Germans and Germanness and were impressed with German culture, education, efficiency, and productivity during much of this time period. At the same time, however, as the emerging foil against the United States in both world wars, the German nation furthered America's continued conception of itself as the defender of freedom against militarism and authoritarianism. I show how the arrogant public diplomacy of the Wilhelmine and Nazi regimes failed to capitalize on the former impressions and often reinforced the latter. Still, the ongoing debate during the Second World War as to the nature of the German people failed to arrive at a clear consensus by the end of the war.

With the disruption of long-standing foreign policy traditions, the immediate post–World War II era represented a moment of malleability for the American government. At the center of this important moment lay Germany. After the war ended, the Truman administration settled on an occupation policy that sought to rehabilitate Germany for a variety of reasons, including historical understandings of Germany within the administration itself. Once decided upon this course of action, the American government in the early Cold War period had a vested interest in promoting a specific narrative of Germany that legitimized America's struggle against the Soviet Union. American officials relied heavily on the notion of totalitarianism to frame both World War II and the Cold War—with Germany as the critical linchpin. In this sense, then, the American state sought to utilize both Nazis *and* Berliners in its representation of Germany's past to justify American foreign and domestic policies.

The state aggressively leveraged its power to promote this narrative and manufacture consent at various levels of American society. With the prestige and stature that the American government enjoyed after victory in World War II, the dawning of a new ideological struggle with the Soviet Union, and a widespread fear of communist subversion, an era of consensus settled in that discouraged dissent. While some actors, such as the Federal Republic of Germany and the American Council on Germany, promoted a different Cold War narrative based on their respective self-interests, major Jewish groups like the American Jewish Committee and the Anti-Defamation League offered their support, or at least refused to dissent, out of fear of being labeled as anti-American or sympathetic to Bolshevism. The only organization that remained faithful to the world war narrative and resolved to stand against the power of the state was the Society for the Prevention of World War III. It was marginalized in the larger society and abandoned by its erstwhile allies.

The hegemony of the Cold War narrative was replicated in the mainstream American media. In a time of consensus, government endorsement naturalized the Cold War narrative and gave it the veneer of commonsense reality. Mainstream discourse reproduced the Cold War narrative in both content and form. Conventional publications not only absolved most ordinary Germans from responsibility for the Third Reich and praised postwar progress in West Germany but did so by "Americanizing" Germans—and thus positioned Americans to adopt prosthetic memories of the German people. The hegemony of the Cold War narrative contributed to the state's larger aims of including the Federal Republic of Germany in the Western world and employing Germany to differentiate between the East and West. In the process, the Cold War narrative legitimated American domestic and foreign policy in the era by trumpeting the superiority of American civilization.

Americans also spontaneously endorsed this narrative because it both reflected and contributed to the emerging consensus on the Cold War in general. The Cold War, the clash between the United States and the Soviet Union in Germany, and particularly the struggle in Berlin, helped Americans conceive of Germany as a battleground between capitalism and communism, a place where these different systems could be contrasted for the rest of the world to see. The concept of totalitarianism, and Nazi Germany's pivotal role in that concept, encouraged many Americans to view the Cold War as a conflict of ideologies, a struggle between democracy and totalitarianism, a struggle that Americans had been engaged in for centuries. Postwar images of a German landscape dominated by rubble and fräuleins furthered the notion that the Nazis, and not the German people, were responsible for the Third Reich.

During the late 1950s and early 1960s, a number of factors changed the landscape both abroad and at home. Under the Kennedy and the Johnson administrations, the U.S.-German relationship became strained for a variety of reasons related to conflicting national interests but also because the new American regimes subscribed to a more critical historical understanding of Germany. Although this opened up space for critical discussion of Germany among mainstream organizations, the rhetoric of the Democratic administrations did not differ significantly from that of previous administrations. Especially by the mid-1960s, with the war in Vietnam intensifying, the civil rights movement fragmenting, and campuses in open revolt, Johnson deployed the Cold War narrative to legitimize his foreign and domestic policies. Thus, while Johnson was critical of the Germans in private, he often evoked Cold War victories in Germany and described current American foreign policy as spanning from "West Berlin to Vietnam."

The modified posture of the American government had an effect on the position of interested organizations. Aware of the strained relationship with the U.S. government, West German officials sought to combat what they perceived as an "anti-German wave" of material in the American mass media by intensifying their public activities, primarily through the creation of the German Information Center (GIC). Fearful and critical of the tension between the American and West German governments, the American Council on Germany similarly sought to strengthen the alliance and attack those who trafficked in anti-German ideas. The rift between the two governments, along with a series of international events that cast West Germany in a bad light, led Jewish organizations to reassess their stance on the German Question. Still, while they became more critical, they, like the Kennedy and Johnson administrations, refrained from an open break with the West German government.

Although most West German officials believed that the apparent "anti-German wave" signified an upsurge in anti-German feeling, an examination of the constituent parts of the wave as well as of the discourse of the time period reveals that the story was far more complex. Events taking place in and about Germany—the swastika daubings of late 1959, the Eichmann trial, the publication of William Shirer's *The Rise and Fall of the Third Reich*—offered a new set of symbols for Americans to use in discussing their current and future foreign and domestic policies.

Most important, with the fragmentation of the postwar consensus in light of civil rights activism, increasingly violent riots, open dissent against American foreign policy, and outright cultural rebellion, the state's ability both to contain alternative narratives of Germany and maintain a media monopoly on Germany's meaning for America faltered. Conjuring the Cold War narrative failed to persuade many Americans to stay within the fold. Although the state-sanctioned narrative endured and remained evident in mainstream products such as *The Battle of the Bulge, 36 Hours, The Great Escape, Hogan's Heroes,* and *Combat!* Germany was remembered and deployed by different groups to critique the Cold War consensus itself.

I conclude by observing how the first two decades of the postwar period established patterns for understanding Germany and Germanness that endured for the rest of the twentieth century. As the Berlin Wall and the Holocaust emerged as the primary symbols of Germany during the latter half of that century, familiar ways of understanding Germany and its meaning for Americans continued to shape how Americans made sense of themselves and the world around them. In the long history of America's encounter with Germany, then, interpretations formed in the early Cold War period remained an important foundation upon which Americans based their worldview.

1

"Tomorrow the World"

Images of Germany before the Cold War

On 2 May 1863, the Eleventh Corps of the Army of the Potomac, a unit dominated by soldiers of German descent, was routed in a surprise flanking maneuver executed by Lieutenant General Thomas "Stonewall" Jackson during the American Civil War. Four days later, the Union army was forced to retreat in what became known as the battle of Chancellorsville. While in hindsight General Robert E. Lee's victory at Chancellorsville is often seen as his greatest—a testament to his bold, daring, and audacious military style—at the time the losing side laid the blame squarely on the Eleventh Corps, and particularly at the feet of its predominantly German troops. Before a Joint Committee on the Conduct of the War, Union army leaders faulted the cowardice of German troops for their losses. When asked if the Eleventh Corps put up "reasonable resistance," Major General David Birney exemplified the response when he replied: "Portions of it may have fought, but the flight, stampede of artillery, transportation, officers and men, has been described to me, by officers who saw it, as disgraceful in the extreme." Fellow soldiers likewise held the German performance in complete disdain; one Ohio soldier wrote to his son that "every Dutchman was making for the river . . . trying to save his own cowardly body." The Anglo press picked up the theme; the *New York Times* reported: "Threats, entreaties, and orders of commanders were of no avail. Thousands of these cowards threw down their guns and soon streamed down the road toward the headquarters. . . . General Howard, with all his daring and resolution and vigor, could not stem the tide of the retreating and cowardly poltroons." Writing about the incident and the reaction it engendered, one historian concludes that blaming German cowardice for the loss simultaneously "set the stage for the strongest nativist and anti-German backlash since the rise of the Know Nothing Party in the previous decade" and restored the overall morale of the Army of the Potomac "at the expense of its ethnically German element."[1]

These images of cowardly Germans from the Civil War era stand in stark contrast to the stereotypes that Americans have become familiar with since World War II. While Americans in the last sixty years have fought vigorously over the meaning of Germany—indeed, these representations and conversations form the heart of this book—they nevertheless have shared a general understanding of Germans rooted in narratives of power and strength. Few Americans in the post–World War II period would recognize the view of Germans offered by Major General Birney in the report cited above. And yet recovering images of Germans from the pre–Cold War period, many of which, like those associated with Chancellorsville, would be unexpected in modern times, is an essential starting point for fully understanding the relationship between these representations and the larger culture in which they have been manufactured and received. When they are viewed against the backdrop of American interactions with Germans in the last three hundred years, it becomes clear that representations of Germans in the last century have not been natural or foreordained—they have been, like those before them, contingent upon historical circumstance. Moreover, throughout American history, narratives of Germans and Germany have been instrumental in the construction of American identity—but the role cast for Germans in the story of America has varied significantly in different eras. Like Americans in the post–World War II period, Americans in earlier eras formed these impressions as they attempted to define themselves in the context of both their German American neighbors and a globalizing world. And because narratives of Germany have been contingent upon their historical context, certain stereotypes endured because they remained useful, while others disappeared because they became less relevant. Throughout all of this, Germans have been most effective in defining themselves when they have understood the contours of the story in which they have been cast and found relevant ways to present themselves and manage their own representations. Along these lines, this chapter provides a necessary backdrop for understanding the issues and debates of the Cold War period, while at the same time foreshadowing a number of themes that will reappear repeatedly in subsequent chapters.

From the first waves of German settlement in British North America in the late seventeenth century to the Allied invasion of Germany almost 350 years later, narratives about Germans, Germany, and Germanness (*Deutschtum*) played a crucial role in the formation and evolution of American identity. More specifically, Germans often functioned as the "other," a people upon whom Anglos and later Americans projected both their fears and their ambitions. In the period before the establishment of the German Empire, a time when most Americans formed their impressions based on their German neighbors in the New World, many Americans incorporated Germans in American narratives of self-sufficiency, democracy, manliness, and loyalty. After the formation of the German Empire and the emergence of a formidable rival, Americans both admired and feared the power unleashed by an organized—and ultimately dangerous—authoritarian regime. With the advent of World War II, these shifting tropes of Germans become modernized and crystallized but not resolved. In the last days of the war, as American troops entered Nazi-held territory, Americans still debated the nature of Germans and, flowing from that, what should be done with them once the war was finally won.

"The Most Ignorant Stupid Sort of Their Own Nation"

In contrast to the ways that Germanness is typically understood in the modern period, that is, principally through the nation-state of Germany and its citizens, it is important to note that before the late nineteenth century, almost all American knowledge of and interaction with Germans took place in North America. During the American colonial period, the only way that British colonists gained knowledge of and formed impressions of Germans was through the immigrants they encountered. The first German in the American colonies was Dr. Johannes Fleischer Jr., who came to Jamestown in 1607, but sustained American exposure to Germans and German culture came only with the founding of Germantown in Pennsylvania in 1683 and the ensuing wave of German immigration that brought approximately one hundred thousand Germans to British

North America before the Revolutionary War. Attracted by the promise of land, religious tolerance, and freedom from oppression, Germans became the single largest immigrant group in the eighteenth century. Living, in the words of one historian, "in highly visible ethnic enclaves in largely segregated, rural landscapes," they made a significant, although by no means uniform, impression on their neighbors. Because the notion of a unified "Germany" was far from a reality during the eighteenth century, English colonists struggled to define these strange immigrants, offering various misnomers from "Palatines" to "Dutch." But as many Americans understood and, in many cases, feared Germans as inhabitants of separate enclaves, others, primarily British officials responsible for managing German immigrants, engaged more closely with their German neighbors. And because they dealt with them in a more intimate way, their impressions became more complex as they tried to reconcile their own need for labor with the German desire for land and political and cultural autonomy. Because for most of this period British colonists still viewed themselves as British, not as distinctly American, the Germans were often treated as "others" whose acceptance was often predicated on their usefulness—their tractability and industry. Despite their concerns about their German neighbors, colonists generally agreed that the Germans were a hardworking people—a stereotype that would endure through the twentieth century.[2]

In many ways, the first significant German enclave in America foreshadowed the major elements of the American encounter with Germans during the colonial period. The initial wave of Germans relocated to the British colonies to flee religious persecution. Led by Francis Daniel Pastorius, Johannes Kelpius, and Daniel Falkner, they headed to Pennsylvania, drawn by William Penn's utopian vision. Although small in number (perhaps three hundred), they exerted a major influence, establishing and solidifying the first permanent German presence in the colonies. Over time, the tide of German immigrants to Pennsylvania generated sharply conflicting impressions. On the one hand, the Germans were praised by their neighbors for their industry and practicality. On the other, they were feared for their numbers, clannishness, and ignorance. In 1723, for example, Governor William Keith, desiring their labor, encouraged the relocation of German immigrants from New York to Pennsylvania. But the colonial assembly, responding to nativist fears, sought to ban all immigration. When that failed, the assembly empowered local officials to assess the suitability of immigrants wishing to live in Philadelphia. In 1726, John Hughes referred to the idea of a multiethnic society as a "monstrous Hydra."[3]

These dueling impressions persisted and were best articulated by Benjamin Franklin. In the 1750s, Franklin supported the continued admission of Germans into the colony, observing that "their industry and frugality is exemplary; They are excellent husbandmen and contribute greatly to the improvement of a Country." At the same time, however, he referred to them as "the most ignorant Stupid Sort of their own Nation" who, "not being used to Liberty . . . know not how to make modest use of it." In 1751, Franklin worried, "Why should Pennsylvania, founded by the English, become a colony of aliens, who will shortly be so numerous as to Germanize us instead of Anglifying them"? Concerned that the colony would be overrun by inferior aliens, Franklin counseled that the German enclave should be broken up and distributed among the Anglo settlers.[4]

For their part, the Germans in Pennsylvania, while appreciative of the opportunities they encountered there, clearly found fault with their British neighbors. Accustomed to firm guidance in secular and religious affairs, Germans argued that the colony suffered from a lack of strong leadership. In 1742, a Moravian spokesman claimed that "the refusal of authority to maintain honesty and public standards of behavior" led to loose standards. The German settlers also chafed at the condescending efforts of the British to change German ways. One religious leader reacted strongly to allegations that "we were German boors and oxen, we did not know how to live, we had not the manners to associate with gentle folk etc."[5]

Present in Pennsylvania, then, were many of the elements indicative of the American encounter with Germans during the colonial period (and beyond): the German desire for land and a continuation of their ways; the English desire for German labor (in large part because of the perception that Germans were industrious); the attendant fear and negative reaction, when they came, that they were inassimilable and could overrun the area; and the bitter counterreaction from the Germans about their shoddy treatment.[6]

The story of German immigration to New York, in what is often thought of as the second major wave of German immigration into the

United States during this period, replicates many of these same contours. Similar to other migrants from German lands, the immigrants to New York were lured by stories of free passage and land across the ocean in British North America. And here, too, the German focus on acquiring land and autonomy inspired diverse reactions. Throughout their experience in migrating to and settling in the New World, their handlers interpreted the Germans in relation to their tractability and cooperativeness. But thanks to work by Phil Otterness, we have a better sense of the Germans' own agency in this process. In examining how the Germans responded to the impressions of others, we gain a clearer sense of how they manipulated them to their own advantage.[7]

The dynamics involved asserted themselves even before the Germans came to America, as they huddled together in London in preparation for the ocean voyage. Whigs, like Daniel Defoe, who supported immigration because they equated the strength of the nation with a high population, crafted enduring narratives of the German immigrants to support their position. In a persuasive piece of propaganda on their behalf, "A Brief History of the Poor Palatine Refugees," Defoe claimed that the immigrants were ideal for settling the hinterlands of Britain because they were "laborious and skillfull—Industrious to Labour, and ingenious in working, and exceeding willing to be employ'd in anything—In a word, They every way recommend themselves as a People, that shall bring a Blessing, and not a Curse to any Place that shall receive them." To generate sympathy for their plight and to link their story with that of another group favorably viewed by the British public, the Huguenots, he framed all of the "refugees" as Protestants fleeing "the Oppression of Popish persecution." In lumping them together as Palatines and Protestants and arguing for their utility in settling undesirable areas of Britain, he ignored both their diverse origins (many did not come from the Palatinate and some were Catholic) and their desire to continue on to America. For their part, the leaders of the immigrants embraced these images to achieve their own ends, namely, immediate assistance and eventual passage to America. They issued a petition, "The State of the Poor Palatines," in which they claimed their "utter Ruin was occasion'd by the merciless Cruelty of a Bloody Enemy, the French." They signed it "the poor distressed Protestants, The Palatines." It was immediately successful in jump-starting a charity drive on their behalf, although sympathy for their position rapidly dwindled as British citizens discovered that many of them were actually Catholic.[8]

After the Germans made it to America in 1710, however, British impressions soured further as the German colonists proved difficult to control. The crown decided to locate them in New York, where they could settle along the Hudson and make tar and pitch to support the British navy (and serve as a buffer against the nearby Native American tribes). Believing that they had been treated unfairly, many German colonists became sullen, uncooperative, and "threatened the social order by needling the colonial elite and by challenging conventions of proper behavior." Exasperated New York officials called the Germans "rascals" who were "worse than northern savages" and "liars and imposters"; at best, they were "a laborious and honest but a headstrong ignorant people." The Germans proved particularly stubborn and nettlesome in their relations with non-British residents of the colony. They consorted with slaves, opening their Lutheran churches to them. More troubling, they developed close relationships with Native American tribes, some going so far as to learn their language and customs. Their independence led one official to grumble that their attitude, "together with some words they now and then drop gives me some Reason to doubt their Fidelity." The clear disconnection between British and German expectations in New York set up understandable conflicts. The Germans took advantage of British stereotypes as far as they could to advance their interests. But the British insistence that the Germans serve the interests of the empire led to predictable resistance. These conflicts, and the perceived desire for German autonomy, colored colonial narratives of the Germans for much of the first half of the eighteenth century.[9]

Elsewhere in North America, colonists viewed Germans in very much the same ways. Georgia's founders had mixed views of the Germans, based on their assessment of German productivity and tractability. The captain of the ship who brought a large group of Palatines to Savannah in 1737 complained that it would be hard to find among the indentured servants "a more lazy, obstinate, and dissatisfyd people." Later that year, he charged that they were a "slothful and mutinous Crew, always complaining of too much Work, and too little Victuals, and that they were daily growing more and more troublesome." On the other hand, James Oglethorpe, founder of the colony, praised the industry of Georgia's German immigrants, observing that "the Germans seem to take more to Planting than English do." Another British leader marveled at their economic independence, writing that "the Palatines on the German Village of St. Simon's (being six or seven Families) have no other Dependence but the Produce of their Lands." Several officials reached the same conclusion that Franklin had in Pennsylvania: the Germans were most effective if they could be separated and handled individually.[10]

The French and Indian War and the ensuing American Revolutionary War resolved some of these tensions. Initially, however, the advent of the French and Indian War intensified these conflicts and pressures. Worried about the allegiance of their German colonists, British administrators and neighbors demanded their loyalty and assistance in the coming conflict. Overestimating their own autonomy, the Germans, for the most part, believed that they could remain independent and neutral; the German community in New York, for example, attempted to negotiate a separate peace with the Iroquois. But the attacks by French and Indian forces against German settlements in the late 1750s transformed the nature of the relationship between the Germans and British. The Germans understood that the protection of British forces was absolutely necessary for safeguarding their own interests. As a result, Germans in the colonies quickened the process of acculturation and assimilation by integrating into colonial political life, rediscovering a shared Anglo-Saxon history, and forging a common identity. This rapprochement strengthened throughout the war, so much so that by the time the revolution began in the colonies a decade later, the Germans had clearly cast in their lot with the upstart Americans. Baron von Steuben, the idealistic and generous (at least by initial appearances) drillmaster of Washington's army, became the symbol of German-American friendship, not the ruthless Hessians employed by the British on the other side.[11]

Although the events of the French and Indian War and the American Revolutionary War seemed to submerge past tensions, they never went fully away. More important perhaps were the lessons learned by both sides. Building on what they had learned in Pennsylvania, New York, Georgia, and elsewhere, Americans concluded that Americanized Germans could be loyal and useful but that Germans concentrated in areas and clinging to their ancestral ways could be a threat. For their part, German Americans understood that complete autonomy was not a viable option. What was yet to be resolved, however, was the degree to which they should give up their Germanness to be American.

"Emigrants from the Land of Kraut"

In the almost hundred years between the successful founding of the American Republic and the establishment of a unified German reich, most Americans continued to understand Germany and Germanness on the basis of their experiences with immigrants from German lands. And although the wave of German immigrants to the United States during the nineteenth century was much larger and more diverse, the German immigrants reaching American shores still encountered Americans who viewed and understood them through the prism of their own self-definition. Augmenting these native understandings was a stream of impressions formed by Americans visiting Europe. Because the worldview of Americans had shifted in the wake of the American Revolution, however, the roles cast for Germans changed. To be sure, Americans still remained concerned about German foreignness and clannishness. But in general, Americans during this period focused less on the German propensity for economic productivity, as had been the focus during the colonial period, and more on their own political experiment. As a result, Americans interpreted the Germans more in cultural and political terms, especially in light of their perceived potential for democracy. In all, Americans tended to take a negative view of the German proclivity for liberty in general and American democracy in particular. They often tied notions of vigor and individuality to their ideas of democracy, and in these they found the Germans generally wanting. As we will see, these concerns about the German potential for democracy would endure, although the causes for worry changed after the establishment of the German Empire. For its part, the growing German-American community struggled over the course of the nineteenth century with how to address these issues.

Although the nature of nineteenth-century German immigration differed from that of the colonial period, the Germans coming to America's cities and countryside after the American Revolution encountered many of the same dynamics. Historians estimate the number of German immigrants to the United States during the nineteenth century at 5.5 million and, as might be expected given its size, the character of this wave differed significantly from the patterns of the eighteenth century—the Germans coming to America now came from a larger array of areas and professions, migrated for a wider variety of reasons, took advantage of a broader range of German-American institutions in settling into their new lives, and relocated to a greater number of places in the United States. As a result of this massive relocation across the Atlantic, Germans constituted one-third of all foreign-born residents in the United States by 1860. Still, despite their significant numbers, German immigrants during the nineteenth century encountered a significant amount of discrimination.[12]

As had been true of the earlier wave of German immigration, the Germans pouring into midwestern states like Missouri, Indiana, Illinois, and Wisconsin, or southern cities such as Memphis and Nashville clumped together in ethnic enclaves, seeking to re-create as much of their European culture as possible. In bringing their customs, traditions, and institutions to the New World, and seemingly refusing to accommodate or acculturate to American ways, they, perhaps inevitably, invited unfavorable comparisons between American and German cultural norms and inflamed suspicions about their ultimate suitability for American-style democracy. In rural areas of the Midwest, where different ethnic groups lived in close proximity to each other on family farms, blanket assessment of races and ethnicities were often based on perceived differences among gender relations. In 1839, for example, Michel Chevalier wrote that "it is now a universal rule among the Anglo-Americans that the woman is exempt from all heavy work, and she is never seen, for instance, taking part in the labours of the field, nor in carrying burdens." As a result, Anglo-American women have "also escaped that hideous ugliness and repulsive coarseness of complexion which toil and privation every where else bring upon them." By contrast, women in the German parts of Pennsylvania performed hard labor "at least as much as the men" and therefore were "wretched objects, who are feminine only with the physiologist."[13]

Another personal indicator of the "backwardness" of German civilization was the apparent lack of love in German households. Herbert Quick, who grew up near Germans in Iowa, recalled a shocking, but in his mind representative, story:

> One of our neighbors, a German settler fresh from the old country, took his wife into the harvest field to help with the binding.

She took her baby along and parked it under a shade. One day
the man came to the house of a neighbor just as they were sitting
down to dinner. They invited him to join them and he accepted.
After eating heartily, he confided to them that his wife was sick.
"She vas vorkin in te field," said he, "an' a snake stung her in de
handt. Pretty soon she couldn't vork no more, and so she vent to
de house to git dinner; but ven I vent to dinner she didn't haf any
got. I was jungry too." . . . A man who could stick to his work
after his wife had been snakebit, send her to the house to get dinner after the virus in her veins had begun its deadly work, and
then calmly sit down and eat a meal before mentioning it to a
neighbor, stamped the entire class of immigrants in our rather
narrow minds as being of a low order of intelligence.[14]

While Americans held negative attitudes of their German neighbors,
Europeans in rural areas reciprocated, finding fault with old-stock Americans and their notions of progress. They labeled the American home a
place of languor and waste. A Dutchman reported, "The women of the
American people are terribly lazy."[15]

Americans traveling in Europe in the nineteenth century reached
conclusions similar to those of their less privileged countrymen. Although
drawn from a wide variety of backgrounds and motivated by a diverse set
of intentions, Americans abroad encountered Germans and Germany in
ways that resonated with the opinions of their less privileged compatriots
back home. Regardless of their point of origin or reason for travel, many
of the dozens of Americans who went to Germany during this time period
found themselves comparing Germans and Germany to their own democratic experiment back home—and noting that the Germans came up
woefully short. Visiting Americans saw their German hosts as indolent,
immoral, and politically immature. They were astonished at the languid
pace at which Germans consumed their beverages and meals; many New
Englanders simply marveled at the aptitude for Germans at wasting time.
Washington Irving complained that the sense of time in Germany was
completely different—everything happened at a much slower pace, even
travel. Many Americans also faulted the Germans for their sinful ways.
They were appalled at their addiction to alcohol and tobacco, shocked by
their lax observation of the Sabbath, and scandalized by their frank and

immoral behavior. Finally, many Americans were disappointed with the flawed German labor and political systems—the hardworking, immodest women offended their Victorian sensibilities (some even compared their plight to slaves), and their slavish obedience to a rigid, heavily regimented political and social structure outraged their democratic sensibilities. Rather than finding their worldviews challenged during their time on the continent, many Americans felt confirmed in them.[16]

These attitudes about Germans crystallized around two significant events of the nineteenth century, both of which challenged the nature of American democracy itself. The first was the European revolutions of 1848, which put a German face on the American ambivalence toward revolution. Since their country's inception, Americans had largely looked with favor on revolutionary movements abroad, seeing them as being inspired by their own struggle for liberty. Because of this tradition, Americans initially responded favorably to the European revolutions of 1848. Seeing in European calls for constitutional reform a direct link to their own revolution, President Millard Fillmore and many American opinion makers expressed support. Mainstream Americans joined in the enthusiastic reception of Germans and other ethnic groups to the news of the revolutions. Mayors and city officials rushed to join the spontaneous celebrations that erupted in major cities around the country—Baltimore, Boston, Cleveland, Cincinnati, Chicago, Detroit, Buffalo, Pittsburgh, New Orleans, St. Louis. In particular, Americans welcomed the Hungarian revolution against the Habsburgs, showering famed freedom fighter Louis Kossuth with praise and support during his visit to the United States. Some even urged the Fillmore administration to break with the American policy of nonintervention and become involved on behalf of the rebels.[17]

But when it became apparent that the aims of some of the revolutionary participants involved major social change and upheaval, and particularly after many of those participants relocated across the Atlantic and sought to apply those aims to American society, American reception of their ideas splintered. On the one hand, supporters of trade unions appreciated the passion of the so-called forty-eighters, German radicals who settled in American cities. Horace Greeley's *New York Daily Tribune* wrote that "no class of our population goes more effectively to work than our German artisans, who have held meetings nearly every evening during the past week, and have succeeded in uniting many of these trades into

Unions." Others, on the other hand, recoiled at their ideas and activities. Subscribing to the American notion of republicanism, which privileged the good of the whole and preached the importance of self-disinterestedness, many blanched at the thought of class-based struggle. Feeding this reaction also was a fear of internal subversion dating back to Loyalist sedition during the American Revolution and taking in the current context the specific manifestation of the specter of red socialism. A New York congressman railed against the "malcontents of the Old World, who hate monarchy, not because it is monarchy, but because it is restraint. They are such men as stood by the side of Robespierre." The *Cincinnati Daily Enquirer* faulted a convention of German Ohioans for focusing on a European instead of an American model of democracy: "The European idea of Democracy has always been essentially different from the American, and has never succeeded so well in actual trial. The former carries it to the point where it borders on anarchy and unbridled license."[18]

In a similar way, Germans found themselves targets in the political struggles surrounding the second major event of the mid-nineteenth century—the American Civil War. In associating Germans with European radicalism, the American response to the forty-eighters and the growing trade union movement built on and updated some long-held images of Germans: the foreign German ideology of socialism was seen as a threat to American society and democracy. Now, in the rise of sectionalism and the coming of the American Civil War, Germans and their culture were invoked by Southerners and Northerners alike, each for their own purposes. Southerners believed that the German lack of support for slavery was a danger to their way of life. Slaveholder and future governor of Missouri Claiborne Fox Jackson stated in 1857 "that men from Northern states and Germans seeking homes in Missouri should be met at the threshold, knocked on the head, and driven back." In a clear pitch to nativists, Senator Andrew Butler of South Carolina offered his opinion that slaves in Nebraska would be vastly preferable to "emigrants from the land of Kraut." In many ways, these Southern fears were not unfounded. Germans opposed the expansion of slavery. In a few instances, to the horror of their Anglo neighbors, Germans, who sometimes had difficulty integrating into mainstream culture, preferred to consort with slaves.[19]

But German Americans did not fare much better in the North. For years, the temperance movement had targeted German culture as a threat.

With the spike in immigration in the 1850s, which included a large number of Catholics from Ireland and Germany, xenophobic Americans
became politically active, eventually establishing the American (or Know-
Nothing) Party. After its meteoric rise, the party rapidly dissolved—but
the sentiments that fueled it remained. Many nativists then rallied to the
Republican banner, which complicated things enormously for Germans:
their own antislavery stance made them natural allies of the Republicans,
but many were put off by the attitudes of the party's xenophobic supporters. Although Lincoln openly courted Germans, in the end, the Republicans garnered less than half of the German vote in 1860.[20]

Their wariness toward the Republican Party did not stop Germans
from openly embracing the Northern war effort once hostilities began
after Fort Sumter. Indeed, Germans enlisted in numbers disproportion-
ately larger than their percentage of the population. These German soldiers became the darlings of an increasingly unified German American
population, which formed relief organizations intended exclusively for
German soldiers. The German American community was incensed when
Franz Sigel, a prominent German leader in the Union army, resigned after
being insulted by the general in chief. Moreover, many German Americans believed that the heroism of German troops in the early battles of
the war was not adequately appreciated in the Anglo-American press. It
should come as no surprise, then, that when the debacle at Chancellorsville was blamed on the cowardice of the predominantly German Eleventh
Corps, German Americans reacted strongly, attacking critical American
press outlets as nativists. The German-American experience during the
Civil War, represented in its most searing form by American criticism of
German cowardice in the battle of Chancellorsville, convinced many ethnic Germans that they should maintain a distinct German identity within
American society.[21]

The conclusions that the German community reached during the
Civil War represented the culmination of a long period of debate among
German Americans. As the community had grown throughout the nineteenth century, its members had engaged in a series of conversations about
how they should respond to their circumstances. Lamenting that earlier
German Americans had assimilated completely, German immigrants in
the 1840s argued that the Germans should maintain a strong sense of
their heritage and history. Despite coming from many different parts of

the German lands, Germans in the United States began to embrace a shared sense of Deutschtum (or Germanness). Subscribing to the superiority of German *Kultur,* they claimed that maintaining an affinity for their cultural ways was not incompatible with political allegiance to their new country. Although some advocated separatism, the dominant approach in the late 1850s centered on the idea of the melting pot, a concept that was advocated in the German American community a half century before it entered Anglo-American discourse. The idea that Germans would assimilate into American culture but change it in the process was abandoned after the Civil War, as German Americans came to believe that such a course would be ruinous. Instead, they advocated for a distinct German presence in American society.[22]

Although during the nineteenth century Americans focused on different things, namely, the German character and its penchant and potential for American-style democracy, they continued to interpret and understand Germanness in the same framework as their forebears, largely in terms of their German neighbors and the German lands abroad. Those neighbors, for the most part, struggled over the best way to integrate into American society, with most of them framing their dilemma along the same lines as their ancestors had done: namely, what parts of their cultural heritage should be maintained, understanding all along, of course, that they had left their German lands for good reason and that little connection could be, or should be, maintained with the present-day Fatherland, which was by and large an embarrassment. The contours of the debate, however, changed dramatically after 1871 in a way that would fundamentally alter the question, upset the uneasy balance between German Americans and their neighbors, and usher in a new period of understanding and debating Germanness.

"The Great Nation over the Sea"

The establishment of the German Empire on 18 January 1871, forever changed the way that Germanness was understood and debated in the United States. Up until this point, Americans largely witnessed and comprehended Germanness in the form of their German neighbors, whose numbers increased dramatically over the eighteenth and nineteenth centuries. And up to this time, German Americans primarily understood themselves and the debates over their culture in terms of integration into American society. But because of the demonstrated success and strength of its military and economy, the newly unified and powerful German nation shifted the focus of everyone in the United States, both Anglos and Germans, to Europe. For German Americans, this stimulated a greater sense of pride in, and therefore heightened identification with, the German homeland. For everybody else, it produced a highly ambiguous reaction: Americans both admired and feared the rising central European power. As a result, by the turn of the century, Germanness was increasingly defined not by German Americans but by the new German nation, and in the process many of the more modern stereotypes of Germany were formed. Most important of these, perhaps, was an emerging duality between the German people and their government; positive stereotypes of Germans as cultured and educated were increasingly juxtaposed against the autocratic actions of their representatives, particularly their emperor. Indeed, as the German Empire asserted itself on the world stage, its actions—and, more important, the actions of its primary symbol, William II—became more of a focal point for American ambitions and fears. Previous qualities and stereotypes associated with Germans became more aggressive and threatening viewed in the light of these new impressions—and, more pragmatically, as the empire itself threatened American interests. Officials of the German government were all too aware of the negative impact of their actions on American narratives of Germanness; as a result, this period witnessed the emergence of a powerful new voice articulating narratives of Germany: Germany's own public diplomacy. Seeking to capitalize on the perceived superiority of German Kultur, the empire tried a number of tactics to improve American perceptions of Germany but failed in the end.

Although the establishment of the German nation did not stem the flow of German immigration into the United States—indeed, from 1871 to 1885, 1.5 million Germans left the Fatherland, with over 95 percent coming to the United States—it did significantly affect how German Americans thought about themselves and their old home. When news of German unification broke in the United States in 1871, German Americans celebrated for days in the streets of major American cities such as Baltimore, Chicago, and Philadelphia. In particular, with the conclusion of the Franco-Prussian War that eventually brought about the new empire,

German Americans rediscovered and championed the perceived German traits of education, intelligence, and morality. In the triumphalist words of Gustav Koerner, Germans were "the most humane, the most just, the most genial and noble of all peoples." Germany was "the guide of civilization, the modern Hellas of art and science."[23]

In the years following unification, under the capable leadership of Otto von Bismarck, Germany was admired for its advances in technology, science, industry, and education. Embraced by the most recent immigrants and eventually washing over all but the hardcore forty-eighters (who never reconciled themselves to Bismarck, the Prussian military, or the wars of unification), a wave of pride in Germany and Germanness swept over German American life. German American newspapers and schools proliferated. German place-names spread across the country: Little Saxony, Germantown, Little Germany, Over the Rhine, dozens of versions of Humboldt (derived from the famous scientist), Berlin—hundreds of places, many in rural areas, seeking to identify with the new German state. Organizations such as the German-American Alliance were founded that promoted German Kultur. This chauvinism regarding German culture brought with it a stiffening against assimilation. These expressions of pride and demonstrations of superiority seemed to settle decisively the long-running debate among German Americans about how they should interact with the larger community—German Americans should be proud of and hold on to their Germanness.[24]

But while German Americans celebrated and identified with the newfound prowess associated with their homeland, other Americans had decidedly mixed views of the unified state. Much of the ambivalence came from the rapid changes happening in each country. The years right after the American Civil War and German unification represented the high point of cordial relations between the two countries. Beginning in the 1890s, however, friction emerged between the two rising powers. Both embarked on aggressive navy-building campaigns as they sought to join the contest for colonial empire—and the Americans increasingly saw the Germans as formidable rivals for the scraps that remained. German incursions in Latin America were particularly alarming, as the Germans' actions in Venezuela and elsewhere appeared to threaten the Monroe Doctrine, a policy that other European powers seemingly respected. These international disputes were linked directly to the booming economies of both countries which, it was widely believed, needed access to external markets. And of course all of these perceptions of threat, perceptions that likely would have existed anyway, given the natural grievances that would emerge between two growing and competing powers, were exacerbated by the perceived antidemocratic behavior of the new German regime.[25]

Balancing these concerns, however, were incredible stories of German progress, orderliness, technological innovation, and cultural contribution. As a result, the information about this paradoxical nation-state pouring into the United States through newspapers, literature, and travelogues did not offer a consistent narrative of Germany and Germanness. Further complicating these issues was that Americans, as in previous (and future) eras, interpreted these stories of Germany from different personal, institutional, and political perspectives.[26]

A good example of this ambiguity was the American response to German innovations in education. In general, American experts were impressed with German education. But unlike earlier American admirers of German education, who had sought inspiration for personal enlightenment and humanistic ideals, U.S. educators in the latter half of the nineteenth century were most impressed with how Germans used education to further the aims of the state. Educator William Torrey Harris, asserting that national education was an essential element of national competitiveness, argued that the Germans, as far back as Frederick the Great, had been the most effective at using public education to harness and develop the talents of its people for the state. The Standing Committee on Education of the National Association of Manufacturers agreed, worrying that the United States was falling far behind its German competitors. Frank Vanderlip articulated these concerns best: "On what does Germany rest her ability thus to compete with us even in the face of the prodigal aid which nature has given us and withheld with such niggardly hand from the great nation over the sea? . . . You know as does every manufacturer know, that Germany's superiority in international commerce rests almost wholly on Germany's superior school system. . . . It has put Germany, in spite of her natural disadvantages, in the forefront of commercial nations." As a result, a number of high-profile American educational experts visited Germany to study its elementary, secondary, and higher education systems. Most came away very impressed. And although the extent to which German models influenced or shaped American education has been debated, it is clear that many American experts highly respected what the Germans were doing.[27]

At the same time, the presence of authoritarian and antidemocratic tendencies in German society increasingly called into question the suitability of the German model for the United States. In 1892, in a study commissioned by the Massachusetts Board of Education, John Prince expressed concern about the German militaristic approach to patriotism and the severe discipline meted out by Prussian schoolmasters. As the nineteenth century drew to a close, American admiration and patronage of the German system of higher education dwindled, as a new generation of Americans became less fascinated with German universities and more concerned with German politics. The number of Americans studying in Germany steadily declined, dropping from 1,088 in 1880 to 338 in 1912. This suspicion even spread to scholars visiting the United States from the Fatherland; Hermann von Holst, a German historian of the United States, drew the scorn of his colleagues, who saw him as an apologist for the German emperor.[28]

For its part, the imperial government was aware of these negative attitudes. William II, in particular, understood the deleterious impact of these views on his broader *Weltpolitik*. When combined with the fact that Germany's fledgling efforts at public diplomacy lagged behind its European competitors, these unfavorable attitudes represented a significant obstacle to German ambitions. As the nation's European competitors understood, friendship with and influence in the powerful United States was becoming increasingly necessary. Unfortunately for the Germans, their efforts to stem the tide of these negative perceptions backfired and instead intensified these concerns.[29]

Much of what passed for German public diplomacy during this period consisted of private, academic, and religious initiatives. And much of it was based on assumptions of cultural and racial superiority. To German intellectuals (as well as to those of Britain and France), the United States, in the words of Jessica Gienow-Hecht, "represented a cultural wasteland ready to be civilized but also a convenient battlefield where the European powers would fight their last battle for global cultural preponderance." German professors, as a group one of the most visible agents of German cultural transfer, sought to enlighten Americans about their own primitiveness by trumpeting the superiority of the German model of higher education. This sense of superiority was most evident in the conduct of the kaiser. Frank Trommler has illustrated how William II "transformed [the German nation] into a mere appendage of an odd personality." With his help, the Germans became "arrogant," "power-mad," "militaristic and imperialistic," and "fond of vainglory and conquest" in the eyes of many Americans. Imperial gifts intended as tokens of friendship, such as William's present of a bronze statue of Frederick the Great, instead came across as ominous. (One historian pointed out that "the statue of Frederick the Great was hardly a statue of liberty.") The kaiser's frequent gaffes, such as when he urged German soldiers to "be as terrible as Attila's Huns" in putting down the Boxer Rebellion in China, did not help the cause. As a result, German cultural activities in the imperial period often did not solidify the latent respect that many Americans had for German culture and education. Many times, with the help of misguided public diplomacy, traditionally positive German characteristics such as "hardworking" and "efficient" took on terrifying militaristic dimensions. This was especially true after the outbreak of World War I. With the help of British propaganda, previous German initiatives appeared even more sinister.[30]

Still, despite the emperor's ham-handed efforts, American attitudes were by no means uniformly hostile to Germany on the eve of World War I. In a survey of American magazines and works of nonfiction from 1906 to 1914, one historian found that the Germans were portrayed favorably. Another looked at American textbooks and grammar books and found that German immigrants and nationals were generally seen in positive (diligent, trustworthy) terms. If language instruction is any indication of popularity, then Germany remained popular in the early twentieth century. Twenty-five percent of Americans took German in public high schools, and most of their German-language teachers stressed the "moral idealism of Wilhelmian Germany." Put simply, before the outbreak of hostilities in Europe, Americans were highly conflicted about Germans and Germanness.[31]

"Warfare against Mankind"

The outbreak of the Great War represented a watershed in the history of American understanding of Germany. Breaking with the past, and in the process establishing a precedent that would be followed by subsequent

presidents, Woodrow Wilson offered a clear interpretation of Germanness, one that played an essential element in his emerging understanding
of American identity and mission in the world. In a related and similarly
pathbreaking manner, the federal government subsequently engaged in
a deliberate propaganda campaign to persuade Americans to accept this
ideology. But unfortunately, both the president's rhetoric and the government's follow-up propaganda proved too nuanced for Americans to
understand; many were unable to resist ugly stereotypes, and a wave of
race-based violence and discrimination swept the country. Such violence
encouraged most German Americans to sever their identification with the
Fatherland, so much so that by the end of the war the German American
community ceased being a substantial source for understanding Germanness in the United States.

In the run-up to the Great War and during American involvement in
it, the president played a crucial role in shaping public discourse around
the Germans. As Jason Flanagan has demonstrated, the evolution of how
Woodrow Wilson conceived of and articulated America's participation in
the Great War was a defining moment both in America's self-definition
and in its image of Germany. For the first time, at least in foreign policy discourse, the two became linked—the notion of autocracy, as represented by the German imperial government, became the necessary foil to
the purpose and the ambitions of the United States on the world stage. In
Wilson's rhetoric during the First World War the United States was transformed from its traditional role as a passive beacon of liberty to a global
defender of human rights. This restructuring was necessitated by and
inextricably tied to the simultaneous transformation of Germany from
a morally ambiguous participant in a European conflict to an enemy of
human liberty across the earth.[32]

The impact of the Great War on official American understanding of
both itself and Germany can be seen clearly. At the beginning of the war,
Wilson defined America's stance in the conflict in the nation's long-standing tradition of neutrality. As the friend of all combatants, Wilson said,
"the test of friendship is not now sympathy with one side or the other, but
getting ready to help both sides when the struggle is over." In the beginning, he refused to assign blame for the outbreak of the war, seeing its
cause as the result of "great blind material forces." After the attack on the
Lusitania, however, Wilson began to make distinctions among the com-

batants. He characterized the attack, and the use of submarine warfare itself, as an evil act. Although he stopped short of holding the German government responsible—indeed, he offered an excuse for the kaiser and government by blaming independent and reckless German naval commanders for the loss of life and property—he nevertheless made distinctions over the next several months between the sins of the British, whose violations of neutrality entailed the loss of property, and those of the Germans, whose violations affected the rights of humankind, and most important the right to life. At the same time, he began asserting a more muscular role for America in defending these rights. The German attack on the British passenger vessel the *Sussex* in March 1916 crystallized these evolving changes. Asserting that submarine warfare involved "the most palpable violations of the dictates of right and humanity," Wilson laid the responsibility squarely on the shoulders of the imperial government, alleging that the attack was an example "of the spirit and method which the Imperial German Government has mistakenly adopted." In blaming the imperial government for such evil acts but professing continued friendship with the German people, Wilson further developed his framework for understanding the differences between democracy and autocracy—and in the process sharpened the differences between the United States as the democratic defender of liberty and the Second Reich as the autocratic enemy of human rights.[33]

After the German government announced that it would unleash its submarines on all ships bound for Britain, and the British intercepted and happily informed the Americans of the contents of the Zimmermann telegram, in which the German government promised to help Mexico reconquer large parts of the American Southwest in exchange for Mexican assistance in a future war against the United States, Wilson hardened and operationalized these ideological disparities. In his April 1917 declaration of war, Wilson bluntly asserted that "the present German submarine warfare against commerce is a warfare against mankind." In the face of such a threat, he claimed that "neutrality is no longer feasible or desirable where the peace of the world is involved and the freedom of its peoples, and the menace to that peace and freedom lies in the existence of autocratic governments backed by organized force which is controlled wholly by their will, not by the will of their people." He elaborated: "We are accepting this challenge of hostile purpose because we know that in such a Government, following such methods, we can never have a friend; and that in the presence of organized power, always lying in wait to accomplish we know not what purpose, there can be no assured security for the democratic governments of the world. . . . The world must be made safe for democracy." A few months later, Wilson accused Germany's leaders of global ambitions, arguing that "their plan was to throw a broad belt of German military power and political control across the very center of Europe and beyond the Mediterranean into the heart of Asia, and Austria-Hungary was to be as much their tool and pawn as Serbia or Bulgaria or Turkey or the ponderous states of the East. The dream had its heart in Berlin."[34]

Established to educate Americans about the war and the threat posed by an American loss to the Central Powers, the new Committee on Public Information (CPI) carefully followed Wilson's attempts to distinguish between the actions of the German government and the German people. The origins of the CPI can be found with George Creel, a national journalist and associate of the president who, after learning that many in the military favored a policy of strong censorship, encouraged Wilson to mount an aggressive public campaign on behalf of the war effort instead. Under Creel, the CPI's job was challenging—it had the task of generating support for the war without embittering and dividing an ethnically conscious population. Although the CPI made emotional appeals based on American patriotism, Creel was mindful to avoid stirring up hatred. His instructions to his volunteer army of Four-Minute Men, who stumped on behalf of the war effort throughout the country, stated, "No hymn of hate accompanies our message."[35]

Creel was especially sensitive about the position of German Americans, for obvious reasons: on the one hand, they were one of the largest ethnic groups in the country; on the other, most Americans, following their president, believed Germany had started the war. So the very identification that German Americans had been building with the reich over the last several years complicated the CPI's efforts considerably. The CPI sought to establish support among German Americans by encouraging the community's leaders to develop a loyalty league and then support it through "counsel, not commands." Along these lines, the American Friends of the German Republic, later the Friends of German Democracy, was founded by German American educators and businessmen. Its assistant secretary, Julius Koettgen, also served as director of the CPI's

German Bureau. The Friends of German Democracy served as a conduit for the CPI, translating its publications for German Americans. With the encouragement of the CPI, the German group also, according to its manifesto, sought in other ways "to unify the people of America in the common cause as well to arouse the people [of] Germany to a sense of their duty and their opportunity." One of the CPI's best efforts at wooing the German American population was a pamphlet entitled "American Loyalty by Citizens of German Descent," a collection of essays by famous German American citizens. One linked the revolutions of 1848 to the Great War in an effort to establish a continuity of German struggle for democracy.[36]

Despite the CPI's ethnic sensitivities, its overriding mandate to whip up support for the war effort often led to blanket condemnation of the German nation. For example, a speech from the January 1918 *Four Minute Bulletin* began: "While we are sitting here tonight enjoying a picture show, do you realize that thousands and thousands of Belgians, people just like ourselves are *languishing in slavery* under Prussian masters?" It went on to note that "Prussian 'Schrecklichkeit' (the deliberate policy of terrorism) leads to almost unbelievable besotten [*sic*] brutality." A number of posters drumming up support for Liberty Loans invoked the German stereotype of "Huns." One infamous example featured a bloody handprint accompanied by a simple description: "The Hun—his Mark, Blot it Out with Liberty Bonds."[37]

A number of the organization's pamphlets carried out the indictment against the German nation. Many of them, such as "Conquest and Kultur" and "The German War Code," sought to use the reich's own words against it. Perhaps the most sensational was historian John Tatlock's "Why America Fights Germany." Asserting that a "net of German intrigue had encompassed the world," Tatlock argued that if the United States did not help defeat Germany in Europe, then the Americans would one day face invasion from imperial Germany. To make his argument, he provided a graphic account of what this would look like. Near the end of his narrative he wrote: "By this time some of the soldiers have managed to get drunk; one of them discharges his gun accidentally, the cry goes up that the residents are firing on the troops, and then hell breaks loose. Robbery, murder, and outrage run riot. Fifty leading citizens are lined up against the First National Bank building and shot."[38]

Efforts such as these undercut the CPI's ambitions for a nuanced approach; instead, they fed a resurgent nativist movement. Americans interpreted these images in ways unintended by the government. In carrying out a campaign of 100 percent Americanism aimed at eliminating foreign influence, nativists drew on these narratives to discriminate against German Americans. Despite Wilson's pleas of neutrality at the outbreak of hostilities, the invasion of Belgium eliminated doubt in the minds of many Americans, convincing them that stereotypes of the Hun and Prussian soldiers were accurate. In response, hundreds of midwestern schools canceled German-language education. Iowa governor William Harding opined, "Let those who cannot speak or understand the English language conduct their religious worship in their home." Music by German composers was banned from concert halls. Public pressure forced German American owners to sell their businesses. The hysteria ranged from the silly—sauerkraut was infamously rechristened "liberty cabbage" and German measles "liberty measles"—to the deadly—German-born Robert Praeger was lynched by a mob in Illinois for allegedly making disloyal remarks.[39]

Officially, at least, the war period witnessed a provisional resolution to the conflicting images of Germans that had characterized German-American relations since the establishment of the German reich. The sense of pride and close identification of many German Americans with the newly established empire in 1871 served to transfer the source of mainstream impressions of Germans and Germanness from German Americans to the German reich. In the process, it made possible a duality between a view of Germans (as symbolized by Germans and German Americans) as educated and cultured and an estimation of the German government as authoritarian and dangerous, a nuanced view that Wilson tried to crystallize in his articulation of America's mission in the war and the world. But in practice, previous negative interpretations of Germans, rooted in enduring fears of foreigners, proved difficult to supplant, especially when they were aided by propaganda from both the American and British governments.

In response to this discrimination, German Americans rapidly abandoned a heritage that they had passionately embraced a generation earlier. Although some have argued that the war represented not so much a sea change in the German-American approach to their Anglo neighbors as an acceleration of acculturation that began before the war, brought about by a desire to become more "white" in an increasingly racialized worldview, it is clear that the end of the Great War brought with it an end to widespread conscious German-American identification with the homeland. No matter the plans of subsequent German governments, German Americans would never again constitute a significant force in shaping American understanding of Germanness.[40]

"Professional Soldiering Is Imbedded Deeply in the Teutonic Character"

More than any other period in American history, the years between the Great War and the Cold War loomed largest in defining the terms of Germanness in the United States during the Cold War era. Images of Germans from the 1930s and 1940s became the benchmark against which all subsequent German representations would be understood and measured. In part because of the immediacy and relevance of the period to the Cold War era but also because of the scale and scope of its impact on America's citizenry, the World War II experience came to hold a privileged place in the popular imagination. The war also helped order and solidify many of the conflicting images that had been swirling around in American society regarding Germans. Although many variations existed, interpretations of Germans during the war essentially fell along one of two pathways, and both centered on the relationship between Nazism and the German people: either the Nazi regime was the natural outgrowth of a defective German character, or the Nazi regime hijacked the nation and led it down a ruinous path. Both of these schools of thought built upon and synthesized previous interpretations of Germans, and they would endure, albeit in changed form, into the Cold War period. In both narratives, the German experiment with democracy during the 1920s, the Weimar Republic, was cast as the prelude to a sinister and cautionary tale. In this way, this period presented the dominant narratives of Germans and Germany that Americans and Germans would wrestle with over the rest of the century.

While the events of the 1930s and 1940s undoubtedly deserve the spotlight because of the influence they would have on subsequent understandings of Germans, it is important to note that the 1920s represented a rupture that offered an opportunity for Germans to significantly reshape American attitudes regarding the German people, an opportunity that German officials during the Weimar Republic tried to take advantage of. In the wake of what was often regarded as a pointless war, many Americans struggled to understand and articulate America's role in the world. Upset with the results of the conflict, many Americans rebelled against Wilson's eventual framing of the origins of the war and America's reasons for becoming involved. As a result, the 1920s witnessed a fertile reexamination of the roots and course of the conflict. To the extent that critics were willing to concede that European conditions warranted some level of American involvement in the conflict, these causes were couched in broader terms of European nationalism and militarism. Many critics cynically rejected Wilson's overarching war aims, seeing the Treaty of Versailles, and the war guilt clause in particular, as the true measure of the Allied struggle against Germany. Reverting to Wilson's early interpretation of the conflict, these critics saw the Germans as no more morally responsible for the conflagration that their British allies. Most liberals and revisionists, however, focused their ire at British propagandists and American munition makers and bankers. Americans blamed British propaganda for inflaming American emotions through distorting and publicizing incidents of German atrocities, and they blamed America's moneyed elite for deceiving the nation, dragging it into a conflict that only served to protect their narrow interests.[41]

The 1920s also represented a chance to break with World War I images of Germany because of the perception, whether it was real or imagined, that Weimar Germany was making significant steps toward a democratic and capitalist society in the mold of the United States. Although some critics found fault with the new republic over ideological issues, such as the failure of the regime to break up the Prussian state or to fulfill the social obligations promised by the new Weimar constitution, most Americans hailed the establishment of democracy in German lands. Many Americans rightly understood that the Germans had made a deliberate attempt to reconstruct their society along distinctly American lines. The *New York Times,* easily the most influential journalistic outlet of the time, consistently evinced faith in German democracy, especially after 1925. In 1927, the American ambassador to Germany boasted: "Never in our history have the political institutions and international ideals of Germany and the United States been as much in agreement as they are today. Both nations believe in government of the people, by the people, and for the people. Both are instinctively and unalterably opposed to dictators, no matter whether the dictator is an individual or a class." Indeed, building upon Wilson's understanding of America's democratizing mission, many saw it to be in the interests of the United States for Weimar Germany to develop along American lines.[42]

For their part, German diplomats in the United States tried to capitalize on the new circumstances to change the way Americans thought about Germany. Although almost all within the Weimar government believed that the Treaty of Versailles was an abominable hindrance to German rehabilitation and reintegration into the global order, and most agreed that the United States was the most likely effective partner in revising its terms, government officials disagreed over the manner in which public support in America should be enlisted in this effort. Over the course of the 1920s, German officials stationed in the United States consistently resisted pressure from the Foreign Office to revive German-American identification with the German nation, rally them to the cause of the Weimar Republic, or propagandize Americans in general about perceived injustices against the German nation. Claiming that such initiatives would be counterproductive, these German representatives argued that after their experiences during the Great War Americans had become distrustful and critical of foreign influences. What's more, German officials challenged the belief that German-American influence could have any significant impact on American politics. They repeatedly argued against any effort to galvanize German-American public opinion for short-term political gains. Instead, they urged efforts designed to bolster German American identification with and standing in American society, while informally and surreptitiously encouraging stronger cultural ties with the Fatherland through occasional visits and the German American press. Positive efforts along these lines included support for the Baron von Steuben Society, the Carl Schurz Society, and the German Academic Exchange Service, all of which nurtured goals for the rehabilitation of Germany's image.

The pitfalls of more immediate identification with the Fatherland were illustrated in the 1926 visit of the German naval vessel *Hamburg,* the first to come to the United States since World War I. Intended to revive a sense of ethnic pride, the visits of the ship to Hawaii and San Diego appeared to be successful. But in New Orleans, the ship's visit produced a more disruptive effect: Louisiana governor Huey Long insulted the German captain and consul by receiving them in his pajamas, leading to protests by local German Americans. In other ports, German sailors upset local police, and eventually State Department officials, by reacquainting Prohibition-era Americans with beer, selling it in many places for a "buck a bottle." The controversies surrounding the visits of the *Hamburg* validated the fears of German officials in the United States. Their sensitivities and concerns about activating unfavorable stereotypes prefigured the attitudes of future West German officials who sought to reestablish public diplomacy in the United States after World War II.[43]

On many levels, the rise of Hitler's murderous regime in 1933 signaled an end to this interregnum and ensured that, over time, many of these questions would be resolved in a way that would reintroduce Wilson's conceptualizations of America's mission in the world (and Germany's role as foil). But even here it is important to note that from the beginning Americans, including the new president, Franklin Roosevelt, were uncertain about the nature and extent of the threat. "To the very end of his life," Michaela Hoenicke Moore has written, "Roosevelt would hold to an ambiguous view of Germany where the Third Reich figured as the epitome of all that was repulsive about the country; its authoritarianism, militarism, and loss of religious values." At the same time, however, he believed that underneath "there was an older, healthy German culture that should be recovered." Roosevelt traveled to Europe extensively during his childhood, and he often marshaled his memories of Germany from these travels to support his views. As early as 1918, when he was assistant secretary to the navy, he claimed that his experiences led him to believe that the Germans were "a mistaken and misguided people . . . subjected to the rule of a military caste and prepared by years of false teachings." On a tour that year of German sites he remembered from his childhood that had been devastated during the war, Roosevelt drew on these views to support a policy of unconditional German surrender: "A drastic lesson against the Germans themselves on German soil will be necessary before any understanding can be hammered into the American mind." Once Roosevelt became president, these personal experiences, along with the reports he received from American officials and trusted confidants, led him to take a dim view of the Third Reich.[44]

But he did not, in public at least, form a coherent view of Hitler's regime. In the early years of the Nazi period, he held out hope that the Nazi hold on the German people was tenuous, and that the economic crisis would soon encourage the German people to rebel. Arguing that most "people of the world really want peace and disarmament," he cast the Nazis early on as part of a small group "headed in the opposite direction" who "block our efforts." At other times, however, he took a dark view of the relationship between the regime and its people. At a press conference in 1934, he related a number of personal stories that demonstrated the militaristic nature of Germans, concluding, "If I were a Frenchman, I would be scared, too." Over time, he developed the images of disease and gangsterism to resolve these tensions and describe the threat. These metaphors, which would endure and grow more powerful during wartime, served a number of useful functions, as Hoenicke Moore points out. Both metaphors helped link the Nazi phenomenon to a long German trajectory that stemmed from the rule of the landed elite and contributed to a "conspiratorial" view of the regime. At the same time, both implicitly differentiated Germans from Nazis, and cast Germans as the first victims of the Hitler regime. Finally, both metaphors performed a political function, enabling Roosevelt to stress the need for vigilance against subversion at home and, more specifically, to cast his political opponents as stooges of Hitler and Goebbels by linking them with Nazi apologist organizations in the United States (regrettably not the last time that Nazis were invoked to castigate political opponents). After American entry into the war, Roosevelt's use of these metaphors intensified.[45]

FDR's failure to resolve publicly the relationship between Hitler's regime and its people was echoed in the larger discourse. Indeed, many Americans greeted initial reports on the Third Reich with disbelief and scorn. Many, especially those who had visited and admired Germany's clean and, at least on the surface, orderly streets, scoffed at critical views of the Nazi Party. In the debate over American participation in the 1936 Olympic Games held in Munich, for example, many Americans dismissed stories of German anti-Semitism as unsubstantiated and errant. Journalists stationed in Germany, most of whom had come to understand the horrific nature of the Hitler regime, were often exasperated by such attitudes. And yet, journalists critical of Nazi Germany, such as Edgar Mowrer, William Shirer, and Dorothy Thompson, often "read" Germany in radically different ways. For Americans who turned to these respected journalists for guidance and information about Germany, these competing interpretations and assessments were of little help in helping them forge some consensus about the German threat. Often these journalists had difficulty convincing Americans about the dangerous events going on in Nazi Germany.[46]

For Americans alarmed about the nature of the new regime, help came from an unexpected source—Fritz Kuhn's German American Bund. The German American Bund was part of the Third Reich's effort to galvanize Germans in the diaspora. Recapturing and building upon previous attitudes developed during the imperial period, and brusquely casting aside the careful concerns of Weimar officials, Nazi administrators conceived of German Americans as a political bloc that could be activated in support of the reich. Noting that millions still spoke German as their primary language, and estimating that fully a quarter of the American population was of German blood, party leaders reasoned that the American population was as much German as it was English. The Nazi Party believed that these German elements in the United States remained "uncontaminated" by corruptive Jewish influences. Nazi race theorists went so far as to label the "melting pot" philosophy a "Jewish invention."[47]

Accordingly, the Nazi regime attempted to reawaken Deutschtum among German Americans. Reversing over time the efforts of Weimar officials, they sought to make German Americans aware of their racial heritage and encouraged them to think of themselves as Germans exclusively. One of the first things Goebbels did in the United States was hire an American public relations firm. The German government also disseminated information through more direct means, such as the German Library of Information and the German Railroads Information Office. The Nazi government supplied several indigenous American groups with pro-Nazi and anti-Semitic propaganda.[48]

The German American Bund was one of the Nazis' most important indigenous groups but was, by all accounts, a disaster. Its final leader, Fritz Kuhn, was also its most ambitious and, from the perspective of the Nazis, the most damaging. Kuhn liked to ape der Führer, and by the late 1930s, when the Nazi leadership realized that Deutschtum was not being revived, his antics were viewed as anathema. For many Americans, as historian Sander Diamond has noted, Kuhn "represented the essence of un-Americanism: his thick foreign accent, his Nazi-style uniform, his repeated statements of allegiance to Hitler, and above all, his apparent misuse of his recently acquired American citizenship." By 1937, Kuhn accomplished "what . . . a host of other Americans had failed to do in the years immediately following Hitler's consolidation of power: he made numerous Americans aware of the fascist challenge." Obsessed with Kuhn and his bund, fiction writers published stories about their activities, exaggerating the strength and popularity of the organization.[49]

The most effective narrative about the bund was the groundbreaking Warner Bros. movie *Confessions of a Nazi Spy*. The first anti-Nazi film produced in the United States, *Confessions of a Nazi Spy* was based on a 1938 court trial in New York in which four individuals were convicted of spying. Warner Bros., already well known for its antifascist sympathies, sent writer Milton Krims to cover the trial and write a screenplay based on its proceedings. The resulting film emphasized the involvement of a former bund leader in the spying activity. In suggesting that the bund was a Nazi instrument of domestic subversion in the United States, the film elided the fact that the German government eventually found the bund to be counterproductive to its aims of reawakening Germanness. Suggesting that Americans should heighten their awareness of "fifth column" activities in the United States, lest their country suffer the same fate as Austria and Czechoslovakia, the film was intended as a clarion call for ideological preparedness.

The reception of *Confessions of a Nazi Spy* illustrates how unsettled public opinion was about the Third Reich. Karl Lischka, an official of the Production Code Administration, concluded that "Hitler and his government are unfairly represented in this story." "To represent Hitler *only* as a screaming madman and a bloodthirsty persecutor, and *nothing else*," he believed, "is manifestly unfair, considering his phenomenal public career, his unchallenged political and social achievements, and his position as head of the most important continental European power." Others drew different meanings from the film. Some praised the "splendid use of factual material" and the film's "courage" in coming out "openly and boldly for the cause of patriotism and love of our country." Others went further, reviving the nativist anxiety expressed in earlier eras. Signing his letter "An American Born," one critic suggested to Warner Bros. that after this picture, "it would be suitable [for Warner Bros.] to follow with 'I am a

Communist' starring Eddie Cantor and a few other Communist Jews in order to let the public know what progress the Communists are making in this country, and who the people are who support these Reds." Many more balanced critics who wrote to Warner Bros. nevertheless evinced similar concerns about such "one-sided propaganda" that did not detail the dangers of communism. As one viewer pleaded sarcastically, "Let us now see 'Confessions of a Communist Spy,' or the 'Red Menace Exposed,' or 'Red Moscow and Satanic Utopia.'" In lumping Nazism and communism together, these critics revealed that many Americans were concerned about the dangers of all foreign ideologies to, as one critic termed it, "true American ideals." Because of the economic dislocations associated with the Great Depression, the 1930s were viewed as a decade ripe for subversion, with the doctrines of fascism and communism holding particularly popular appeal.[50]

Even after American entry in the war, many Americans still appeared to be unconvinced of the rightness of the country's participation. After the United States had been at war for almost half a year, government pollsters discovered some disturbing information: Americans did not display the requisite commitment to the fight; only half seemed to know what the war was even about. The Office of War Information (OWI) was established in the summer of 1942 to shape American attitudes on the war. Taking its cue from Roosevelt's utterances on the war, particularly his 1942 State of the Union address, OWI placed an emphasis on the Nazis as the primary culprits. The wisdom of this policy was confirmed by polls that found few Americans thought the German people were the enemy. OWI policy focused on abstract Nazis as the primary enemy but also suggested that the German people had been beaten and subordinated, thereby implying that simply removing the Nazi leaders would not be enough. At the same time, the OWI encouraged Americans to sympathize with the German victims of the regime, so that they might feel a greater sense of urgency in the need to fight the Nazis.[51]

Arguably the most popular government-sponsored representation of the German threat was not produced by the OWI, however. Under the supervision of Chief of Staff George Marshall, Frank Capra created a film series called *Why We Fight*. The goal was to explain to American troops the reasons for American involvement in the war. Inspired and intimidated by Leni Riefenstahl's *Triumph of the Will*, Capra sought to use as much authentic footage as possible to make his case. Capra and his team made a special effort to incorporate the enemy's own propaganda to demonstrate the oversized ambition of their adversaries. Focused on motivating America's young men to fight and kill, his series portrayed the enemy bluntly, making little distinction between Germans and Nazis. The series proved so effective among the troops that the government approved it for public distribution in 1943, thus complicating the official position on the nature of the threat even further.[52]

In discussing the German Question during the war, then, Americans concentrated on the relationship between Nazis and Germans. Put simply, was there any meaningful distinction between the two? Even during the lowest moments of the conflict, Americans debated this issue with an eye toward American influence over the postwar world. If all Germans were Nazis, then leniency could lead to disaster, for the Germans would take advantage of any weakness to make another attempt at world domination. If, however, the Nazis were indeed just a small portion of Germans who were able to come to power by taking advantage of desperate times, then excessive harshness would not only be unjust but unproductive. As it became clear that the Allies would win the war in Europe, this debate increased in ferocity.

There was no shortage of people convinced that the Germans bordered on irredeemable. Much of this argument was historical in nature; many portrayed German history as a succession of aggressive ventures. "The fact is that the Germans have been warriors for centuries," declared a columnist for the *American Mercury*. "Professional soldiering is imbedded deeply in the Teutonic character." He argued that the Germans would continue to fight as long as there was a "fifty-fifty chance of winning." Henry C. Wolfe, foreign correspondent, member of the Hoover Commission in the Soviet Union, specialist on Nazi Germany's foreign policy, and author of the alarmist tract *The German Octopus*, sounded a similar note of concern. "The Nazis have taken military defeat into their calculations," he warned. "In their long-range program for world domination, military defeat in World War II is provisional." To assume that killing Hitler and his fellow hierarchs would kill off Nazism would be a "tragic mistake." After the war, Wolfe foresaw, the Germans will "step in and say: 'Let's go to work at once. We have the plans. Not all our machinery was destroyed by bombs. Give us the manpower and the raw materials and we shall produce for the world markets.'" Any leniency, these authors believed, would be dangerous given Germany's long warlike history in international affairs. Even Thomas Mann, the famous exile from Germany, conceded that there was something fundamentally disturbing about the German character. Horrified at the brutality of his homeland, he referred to his country's deficiencies in terms of a "dark curse" rather than "crime and guilt." He argued that this curse was a product of Germany's excessive idealism and prerational nature. Such innocence, he claimed, could easily be taken advantage of by demagogues, as had happened with Hitler.[53]

Others were not so convinced that something intrinsic to the German culture, race, or nation led to Nazism. A columnist for the *New Republic,* for example, claimed that the argument that Nazism "is due to something inherent in the German character is silly—or worse, an inverted Goebbelism." Every "totalitarian regime," he opined, relied on a "deliberately puerile ideology" and the "methodical disruption of family life" to implement a fascist state. Dorothy Thompson, reporter and author of great reputation, emerged as the most powerful advocate for a lenient peace with the Germans. "It may be said," she argued, "that all this could not have happened in any other nation. It is my opinion that it could happen to any people if the continuity of all their traditions were so drastically broken by the convergence of many circumstances, as many of them fortuitous as designed." In short, she claimed, "we shall have to deal . . . with an abnormal people; not abnormal because their race made them so, or their history, or Bismarck, Nietzsche, Hegel and Fichte, but abnormal because they have led an abnormal life." Thompson believed that integration within a new Europe was the only means of keeping Germany peaceful and free from Soviet influence.[54]

The rest of the American population was just as uncertain. Reactions to Thompson's article, for example, revealed a deeply divided public. Some supported Thompson's ideas, with one even suggesting that she should work for the State Department. Others, however, expressed horror at Thompson's proposals. Public opinion polls reflected this uncertainty. Although in a late 1942 Gallup poll 74 percent of Americans claimed that their country was at war with the German government and not the German people, Americans were deeply divided over what should be done with the Germans after the war. In the results of a series of Gallup polls throughout the war, Americans vacillated between strict control of Germany following the war and destroying it as a political entity altogether.[55]

Given the rhetoric of the Third Reich, one group that paid particular attention to the developing German Question was America's Jewish community. Foreshadowing a story that will form a major theme of this book in subsequent chapters, American Jews understood and reacted in different ways to the Nazi threat. Rooted in a long history in the United States, in which European Jews migrated to the country and then rapidly assimilated, major Jewish publications such as the *National Jewish Monthly* (*NJM,* the journal of B'nai B'rith, the largest Jewish service fraternity) and *Commentary* (the journal of the American Jewish Committee) initially replicated the indecision found in the larger society regarding Germanness. Edward Grusd, editor of the *NJM,* for example, offered an essentially class-based interpretation of Nazism. Arguing that anti-Semitism was merely a disguise for the Nazis' true purpose, the concentration of wealth into the hands of a few, Grusd claimed that "a Fascist junta could use anything as a smokescreen: 'Negroes,' 'Quakers,' 'Catholics' or 'redheads.'" Eugene Tillinger, on the other hand, contended that Nazism was the natural outgrowth of German Prussianism. "It is this Prussian spirit that lay behind the five wars of aggression launched by Germany within the past century, first under Bismarck, then under William II, and finally under Adolf Hitler," he claimed. "It is Prussianism that has made the Germans the most warlike nation in the world." Not until the full extent of the Holocaust became known in the United States later in the war did American Jews begin to debate a separate Jewish interpretation and response to the question.[56]

Participation in the debate over what do with the Germans was broadened through Lester Cowan's 1944 film *Tomorrow, the World!* Adapted from a Broadway play of the same name, *Tomorrow, the World!* presented an allegorical tale in which the German people are represented by the Nazi Youth child Emil. In this film, Emil is sent to the United States to live with his uncle after his mother and father are killed in German concentration camps for speaking out against Hitler. His uncle Mike and his friends are excited about the arrival of Emil but are shocked at what has become of him under Hitler's rule. Emil causes problems with Mike's fiancée, a Jewish schoolteacher, and his housekeeper, a German who refuses to support the Third Reich. After repeated efforts to disrupt and destroy

Mike's life, Emil is finally humbled by an unexpected act of kindness from Mike's sister and breaks down, begging for forgiveness. Realizing that the boy is an innocent victim of the Nazis, Mike allows him to stay.

The main theme in *Tomorrow, the World!* revolves around the clash between the Nazi and American ways of life. By placing a Nazi youth in American society, the film enabled the viewer to draw distinctions between Nazism and democracy and come to conclusions about what should be done with Germans after the war. Urging moviegoers to engage in this debate, the marketing team for Cowan's film constructed its campaign around ways to underscore the difference between the two ways of life and celebrate American society. One of the major aims of the campaign would be to "highlight the social and political angle presenting the boy as a problem the world will have to face, 12 million strong, when Germany capitulates and its Nazi trained youth are thrust upon the world." The Cowan publicity team considered a number of stunts to emphasize these themes. One team member suggested the creation of an award for the film based on the judgment of New York nightclub chorus girls, with "the girls, of course, naming 'Tomorrow the World.'" "The idea of pretty chorus girls liking a play like 'Tomorrow the World,'" so the ploy went, gave "it a stamp of down-to-earth just-folks acceptability and approval." Even more suggestively, one member of Cowan's publicity team "proposed that we invite fifty people, representing all walks of life from corporation head to, let us say, boot-black, to meet at dinner and then see our picture." In being sure to include "the time-honored group, 'doctor, lawyer, Indian Chief, poor man, rich man, beggar, thief,'" such a gathering would "typify American democracy" and provide an "excellent photographic possibility."[57]

The most important effort, however, was providing funding for a study conducted by a group of school superintendents. The study asked high school students to answers questions on the differences between the American and Nazi ways of life, watch the film, and then take the same test again to see if their answers had changed. The intent of the study was to examine the effect of the film upon preexisting attitudes toward the Nazi way of living. Although Cowan's primary motive was almost surely publicity, the study was professionally conducted. Its results therefore are instructive in illustrating the ways in which the children interpreted and understood the film. Moreover, in order to get a broad sample

of responses, the organizers of the study questioned students from affluent areas (Beverly Hills) and disadvantaged districts (Willowbrook in Los
Angeles).[58]

One of the most striking findings, according to the authors of the
report, was that almost all of the students, regardless of socioeconomic
background, believed strongly and deeply in the American way of life.
This belief in the American dream was so strong in the disadvantaged
community that the educators worried that these children's views were
unrealistic and could lead them to major disappointment and disillusionment. The effect of this powerful belief in the righteousness of the American way of life was that expressed attitudes toward the Nazis were often
framed by favorable allusions to the United States.[59]

The most instructive part of the study for the purposes of this work is
the section of the exam asking students, immediately after they had watched
the film in a commercial theater, what they would do with Emil, the Nazi
youth who came to live with his American relatives, because it illustrates
their attitudes to Nazis and Germans. Like their parents, the children were
divided in their opinions of the Nazis, even within their own communities. Interpretive communities of the German people therefore cut across
racial and social lines. Some children, no matter what background they
came from—affluent white, disadvantaged African American, or Mexican—favored a forgiving embrace for Emil, while other members of each
ethnic community preferred a stern and unforgiving response to Emil's
mischief. Educators were able only to generalize about degrees of sophistica-
tion among the different school districts. The African Americans and Mexi-
cans from Willowbrook, the report noted, tended to voice simplistic "gang
methods" for dealing with Emil, while the students at Beverly Hills waxed
eloquent about the various possibilities for handling the child (with many
suggesting psychological counseling for the young boy). To the surprise of
the educators, the Jewish children were the most forgiving. Two-thirds of
that group supported the kindest possible course for Emil, while only 11
percent said they would reject him. As the responses to this film illustrate,
Americans near the end of the war had failed to make up their minds about
what should be done about the Nazi threat.[60]

One final point bears mentioning. During this debate, Americans
read Berlin no differently than Germany. Before the Cold War, Americans viewed Berlin as synonymous with Germany; Berlin, in fact, was

often viewed as the seat of a reich intended to last a thousand years. As a result, American readings of Berlin were as contested as those of Germany in general. Both the production and reception of the Warner Bros. 1945 film *Hotel Berlin* illustrate this fact. Based on Vicki Baum's novel of the same name, *Hotel Berlin* described, in the words of one reviewer, "the stinking mess the German capital has become under the combined impact of the Nazis and Allied air blows." It depicted the efforts of a German underground, the effects of Nazism on the German people, and the attitudes of the Nazi elite. In short, it spanned the entire range of opinions outsiders held of the German people. Several reviewers approved of its evenhanded treatment, while others balked at its sympathetic portrayal of several Germans. Like their reaction to the rest of Germany, Americans were divided on what to make of Berlin.[61]

During the war, then, Americans evinced an uncertainty about the German people. Drawing on the "lessons" of Germany's past, some Americans advocated a "hard" peace, determined to emasculate the Germans forever. Others, employing a comparative perspective that emphasized the provisional aspect of Nazi rule, favored a "soft" peace designed to reeducate Germany and reintegrate it into the family of civilized nations. As the Allies entered German territory in the winter of 1944, American contact with the Germans did not shed new light on this debate. Indeed, into the post–World War II era, Americans remained uncertain about what to do with Germany.

From the establishment of the British colonies in North America to the eve of America's emergence as the world's preeminent economic and military power in the Cold War, the American understanding of Germanness played a crucial role in the formation and evolution of American identity, figuring prominently in the country's narratives of self-sufficiency, democracy, industrialization, and national mission. But over this time period, both the sources for understanding Germanness and the roles it played in these narratives were not fixed; they changed depending on national and international events. Indeed, over the course of the evolution of American understanding of Germanness, a range of actors engaged in efforts to shape its trajectory, none more important than the Germans themselves, first represented informally by German immigrants and later, when the source for understanding Germanness had shifted toward the

German nation, by professional German diplomats. By the time of the Second World War, the historic cacophony of narratives and understandings of Germanness had been narrowed and sharpened by a number of critical debates that defined it in the context of its relationship to Nazism. Although the searing impact of the war reduced the number of German questions to one, that being the relationship of Nazism to Germanness, it did not provide a definitive answer. That would be left to the next period.

2

"Germany Belongs in the Western World"

Germany and Consensus Politics in America, 1945–1959

In late 1950, Hollywood screenwriter and producer Nunnally Johnson met with Henry Kellermann of the U.S. State Department to discuss Johnson's new project, *The Desert Fox*—a film based on British brigadier general Desmond Young's admiring biography of Nazi general Erwin Rommel. Concerned about potential political fallout, Kellermann sought to dissuade Johnson from pursuing the project any further, crafting his objections to appeal to Johnson's moral and patriotic sensibilities. Arguing that Rommel was a Nazi unworthy of rehabilitation, Kellermann pointed out that Rommel turned against Hitler only after defeat was inevitable. Moreover, Kellermann stressed that such a film would be seized by the Soviet Union as pro-German propaganda, and would cast further doubts in skeptical American circles about American resolve to prevent the rise of German militarism. On both counts, the screenwriter strongly disagreed, contending that his intent was "to demonstrate that there were good as well as bad Germans, an objective which he felt was in accord with State Department policy." Promising that the script would not "glorify Rommel but treat him objectively," Johnson ignored Kellermann's advice and proceeded with the production of the film.[1]

The State Department was not the only organization interested in

Johnson's film. Major Jewish groups monitored the film's progress through the office of John Stone, the Hollywood representative of the National Community Relations Advisory Council (NCRAC), the umbrella organization of American Jewish organizations. After reading the full script, Stone worried that Rommel emerged too sympathetic. Stone pointed out to Johnson that the film would antagonize Jews, veterans, and American allies from World War II. Undeterred, representatives from Twentieth Century-Fox maintained that the film served as a "warning to all who are enmeshed in totalitarian adventures." After previewing the film, all major Jewish organizations, with the exception of the American Jewish Committee, issued a joint press release: "There is only one major villain in this picture—Hitler. The audience is asked to believe that only he was evil; that the soldier, Rommel,—and other German generals—were military men, without 'political' aims or motivations, carrying out orders. This is to make a ghastly mockery of the lesson of history. . . . The world knows that totalitarianism infects the whole body politic of a nation, that neither fascism nor communism can be sustained except with the active collaboration in its depravity of politicians, diplomats, and generals— especially generals." Various veteran organizations, members of Congress, and the Society for the Prevention of World War III, an anti-German lobby group, joined in the protest, especially when it became known the following year that Twentieth Century-Fox intended to distribute the film in West Germany.[2]

Both the production and circulation of *The Desert Fox* revealed a wide-ranging struggle over German representations in the early Cold War period. The State Department, Jewish organizations, veterans' groups, and the filmmaker himself all understood that the German Question, regardless of any specific political or diplomatic manifestation, was rooted in historical understandings of German society and culture—in precisely the kind of narratives found and contested in films like *The Desert Fox*. Aware that these narratives framed American public opinion and therefore shaped long-term foreign policy considerations regarding Germany, different actors, state and nonstate, American and German, offered competing accounts of Germany's past. And like Johnson's film, many of these products functioned as media sites of memory, places where different memories of the Germans were revealed, constituted, and contested.

The story of *The Desert Fox* reveals how competing coalitions of inter-

James Mason as Field Marshall Erwin Rommel in *The Desert Fox* (1951). (Fox/Photofest © Fox)

ested actors sought to use the American media to influence thinking about Germany. These coalitions supported two broad, contradictory narratives of the German people: one I call the Cold War narrative, which focused on stories of German heroism in the face of Soviet totalitarianism, in an effort to rehabilitate Germany and anchor it firmly in the Western world; the other I call the world war narrative, which stressed tales of the enduring power of Nazism and fascism in postwar Germany, in the hopes of maintaining vigilance against a resurgence of German might.

The story of these competing coalitions—their ideas, their actions, and their agendas—in the early Cold War era establishes two interrelated themes that will be developed in subsequent chapters. First, it highlights the importance of the U.S. government in gathering allies and framing the parameters of debate. During this period of consensus, the prestige of the U.S. government, evident in its ability to define and mobilize support for the Cold War, gave it hegemonic power. Building on the ideas of Antonio Gramsci, T. J. Jackson Lears has defined such influence as "the power to help define the boundaries of common-sense 'reality' either by ignoring views outside those boundaries or by labeling deviant opinions 'tasteless or irresponsible.'" The state exercised this power most often through discourse on foreign policy in which it naturalized the Cold War narrative of the German people and, in the process, rhetorically structured the identity and "imagined community" of the United States. In this vein, Melanie McAlister has written that foreign policy "defines not only the boundaries of the nation but also its character, its interests, its allies, and its enemies." The state often translated its cultural influence to political power, using its legitimacy with the American population to privately negotiate, intimidate, marginalize, or otherwise dissuade dissenters from challenging its narratives. In this sense, the ebbing influence of the memory coalition that supported the world war narrative stemmed not so much from the increasing irrelevance of its interpretation or ideas but from the nature and power of its adversaries. Challenging state-sponsored narratives in a time of consensus was an enterprise fraught with peril and difficulties, as many Jewish leaders argued and as the only explicitly anti-German group, the Society for the Prevention of World War III, discovered. By the end of the 1950s, the coalition in support of the world war narrative was in disarray.[3]

Second, this story emphasizes that these behind-the-scenes machinations and political maneuverings decisively affected the kinds of cultural products in circulation. More specifically, it argues that much of the ostensibly "spontaneous" consent to the Cold War narrative was in fact authored, scripted, or heavily influenced by pro-German memory activists. The U.S. and West German governments, private journalists and, most important, the Roy Bernard Company, a public relations firm in the employ of the West German government, heavily regulated cultural production regarding Germany. In this way, this chapter complicates notions of cultural hegemony by highlighting the roles that institutions and organizations played in using and manipulating cultural products on Germany to "manufacture" the appearance of consent.[4]

For example, all of these actors fought over and sought to influence the reports of Drew Middleton, the *New York Times* reporter who gained fame for his frontline reportage of the European theater during World War II and later was assigned to Germany during the formative years of the Cold War and the Federal Republic. Members of the memory coalition in support of the Cold War narrative believed that many of Middleton's reports deliberately sought to dredge up memories of World War II by exaggerating the influence of former Nazis or the Nazi ideology on contemporary German society. They worried frequently about the tone and emphasis of Middleton's reports and sought to contain their influence by a variety of means, including complaints directly to his employer and public attempts to rebut his stories. By contrast, members of the coalition in favor of the world war narrative sought to draw attention to his writings and replicate his analysis in a number of venues in order to raise awareness of the persistence of Nazi influence in the country.[5]

Finally, this story takes place within the context of an evolving mass media landscape. The first fifteen years of the postwar period witnessed a remarkable transformation in this respect. At the end of the war, print, film, and radio all shared an uneasy understanding of American patronage of their respective industries. Print media, particularly newspapers, still represented the most trusted source of news. Forming perhaps a quarter of overall print consumers in America, Americans interested in national and international affairs subscribed to major dailies such as the *New York Times* and the *Chicago Tribune* and followed major stories in periodicals like *Time, Life,* and the *Saturday Evening Post.* Likewise, Americans were heavy consumers of film. During the war, the domestic box office in the United States increased threefold; this enhanced revenue also represented a dramatic influx of new patrons into America's eighteen thousand theaters: one study found that the percentage of Americans who regularly went to the movies more than doubled from 1935 to 1945. And finally, evidence suggests that radio had emerged as the most popular medium by the end of the war. A November 1945 poll found that, if forced to choose, 84 percent of respondents would pick radio over film and 62 percent would choose radio over their beloved daily. Memory activists interested in promoting narratives of Germany and Germanness engaged all of these media, albeit unevenly and according to their individual strengths.[6]

But all actors were caught flat-footed by the emergence of television. First offered for mass consumption in 1948, television came to dominate the mass media landscape with shocking quickness. With nine out of ten homes reportedly having a set by the end of the 1950s, newspaper circulation fell, some periodicals went out of business, and weekly movie attendance fell by almost half. Although the new medium of television achieved hegemony by the end of the decade, these memory activists proved unable to adjust adequately until much later.[7]

"I Dislike Making Plans for a Country Which We Do Not Yet Occupy"

The position of the U.S. government toward the German people was the most important in the postwar period. The American government was the most effective memory activist of the period, not so much because it proved to be the most active—far from it—but because its prestige in the first fifteen years of the Cold War significantly shaped the parameters of discussion about Germany. In a period of hyperpatriotism, official U.S. pronouncements served to demarcate the boundaries of acceptable and unacceptable discourse about Germany. Those actors who championed narratives different from the one supported by Washington ran the risk of marginalizing themselves within the larger society.

As leader of the successful fight against international fascism, the American government possessed incredible cultural power that had already become manifest in the latter years of the war; what was less clear was which narrative the government would ultimately support regarding Germany. During this period, the debates about Germany's society and culture within governmental circles suggest that competing historical narratives of Germany, along with economic and political factors, played an important part in determining American policy. Indeed, the primary factions vying for control over reconstruction policy in Germany subscribed to competing historical understandings of World War II and therefore drew very different conclusions about what should be done. As a result, in the last days of World War II, a struggle among historical narratives raged within this most important memory actor. Although the world war narrative, which stressed differences between the people of the United States and Germany, gained brief ascendancy in the executive branch during the last years of the Roosevelt administration, the advent of Harry Truman to the White House in 1945 brought to power those who subscribed to narratives that facilitated the rise of Germany, thus delivering the most important actor in the contest for shaping American thinking on Germany to the coalition in support of the Cold War narrative.[8]

The autumn of 1944 saw the height of the world war narrative's influence. Under the leadership of Henry Morgenthau, the Treasury Department supported a "hard" policy aimed at destroying the German state as an entity and demolishing the industrial capability of the German people. Based on a historical understanding of Germans as militaristic and authoritarian, Morgenthau believed that they must be reduced to a simpler state of existence whereby they could no longer have the power to cause trouble. As Morgenthau affirmed in a memorandum to Franklin Roosevelt: "The German people have the will to try it again; Programs for democracy, re-education and kindness cannot destroy this will within any brief time; Heavy industry is the core of Germany's warmaking potential." "Nearly all Americans grant the first point," Morgenthau declared. "A few, such as Dorothy Thompson, appear to disagree with the second; but all that we know and have learned recently—our experience with war prisoners, for instance—seems to argue against them."[9]

Staunch Wilsonians such as Secretary of State Cordell Hull and other State Department officials interpreted history differently. They argued that the Treaty of Versailles was ultimately responsible for World War II because its unjust provisions provided the opportunity for Hitler's rise to power. They believed that the best way to prevent German revanchism was to rebuild Germany in the American mold. Thus they supported a policy aimed at the reconstruction and rehabilitation of the German economy, based on the belief that German recovery was essential to European recovery and ultimately necessary for American prosperity. Also believing that World War II was a product of the failure of world leaders to follow Wilson's vision, Secretary of War Henry Stimson agreed with the State Department's assessment of Morgenthau's plan of "enforced poverty," which "destroys the spirit not only of the victim but debases the victor."[10]

As we have seen, President Roosevelt sent conflicting messages throughout the war. Toward the end of the war, he privately sympathized with Morgenthau's desire to partition and deindustrialize Germany. With victory in sight, the president did not want to starve the Germans, but he did want it "driven home" to them that their "whole nation has been engaged in a lawless conspiracy against the decencies of modern civilization." Morgenthau, invited to a conference between Roosevelt and Churchill at Quebec in September 1944, used the opportunity to further impress his views on the president and expand his influence to the British prime minister. Using the carrot of extended Lend-Lease, Morgenthau and Roosevelt secured Churchill's consent to what became known as the Morgenthau Plan: Churchill even added the memorable phrase that the aim was to remake Germany "as a country primarily agricultural and pastoral in . . . character."[11]

Although Roosevelt was sympathetic to Morgenthau's ideas, he publicly disavowed the Morgenthau Plan after news of the Quebec conference reached a critical American press. At the end of September, the president admitted to Stimson that he had "pulled a boner" in Quebec. Faced with public and private resistance to a "hard" peace with Germany, Roosevelt returned to a policy of vacillation, equivocation, and indetermination. In view of his desire to continue the Grand Alliance into the postwar period, Roosevelt saw no need to ruffle feathers needlessly. In other words, he stalled on occupation policy, saying, "I dislike making plans for a country which we do not yet occupy."[12]

The brief triumph of the Morgenthau Plan in 1944 represented the zenith of the world war narrative's influence in American policymaking. After 1944, and particularly after Roosevelt's death in 1945, other narratives of Germany and World War II became dominant. Focusing on the issue of reparations, new president Harry Truman laid the blame for the Second World War in large part on the Treaty of Versailles. Truman declared that he was dedicated to avoiding "the same mistake of exacting reparations and then lending the money to pay for them." More important, Truman and others in his new administration increasingly framed the Soviet Union as the ideological heir to Nazi Germany. Truman often described Soviet intrigue in Eastern Europe in light of Munich, suggesting that appeasement of the Soviet Union would have the same result as appeasement of Nazi Germany—disaster. At an address in Kansas City in 1947, to take but one example, he informed his audience that "Hitler's dream of controlling the world was spurred by his belief that the Western nations were weak and lacked the will to resist. Hitler's eagerness for war increased as his estimate of the strength of the democracies decreased." Casting Stalin as the heir to Hitler, Truman endorsed a notion of totalitarianism that went a long way toward absolving the German people themselves of guilt.[13]

Truman, and later Eisenhower, made great use of totalitarianism both to blame the Soviet Union for the breakdown in Allied policy and to mobilize public opinion behind a wide-ranging foreign policy designed to contain the spread of Soviet communism. The interpretive thrust of the

Truman Doctrine (1947) and the Marshall Plan (1948) was that, like German Nazism, Soviet communism threatened world peace and required a firm response by the West. In discussing the American decision to aid Greece and Turkey, for example, Truman told a meeting of the American Society of Newspaper Editors that "we tried going along with [the Soviets] as far as we possibly could, trying to please them. There is no way to please them." Such rhetoric, ridiculing and marginalizing appeasement as an option, extended and deepened the growing comparisons between the prewar experience with Nazi Germany and the postwar experience with the Soviet Union.[14]

Still, despite their growing support for an independent West German state, American policymakers did not back the German people without reservation. In particular, many policymakers could not forget their collective experience with the Weimar Republic. After the birth of the Federal Republic in 1949, the United States and the other Allies retained ultimate authority through the creation of the Allied High Commission. When the United States began to contemplate German rearmament after the outbreak of war on the Korean peninsula the following year, it sought to limit German control over its new forces. As Thomas Schwartz has argued, the "interwar experience continued to dominate the thoughts of policymakers as they tried to break out of history's grasp." Truman remembered that the one-hundred-thousand-man force allowed in the 1920s "was used for the basis of training the greatest war machine that ever came forth in European history." According to Frank Ninkovich, a core theme of State Department thinking during the 1950s was "the cautionary memory of Weimar Germany's shocking 1922 treaty of friendship with the Soviet Union at Rapallo."[15]

To resolve these ambivalent and contradictory memories, American policymakers finally settled upon a strategy that some have termed "dual" or "double" containment. As the name implies, this strategy was designed to contain both Soviet communism and German nationalism. The strategy called for the creation of a number of structures during the early 1950s that would serve as bulwarks against Soviet expansion while at the same time harnessing German power for the good of Western Europe. Worried that an unfettered Germany could wreak havoc in the Cold War world, American policymakers sought to chain it economically, militarily, and politically to its West European neighbors.

In carrying out these policies, the United States gradually loosened the constraints on the Federal Republic. When the State Department took over responsibility for the occupation from the army, it granted limited sovereignty to a newly created government, reserving to itself the ultimate right to intervene. After the beginning of the Korean War, American policymakers calculated that they would need German military might in Europe to offset the drain of American resources to Asia. The assumption of Dwight Eisenhower to the presidency in the middle of the conflict did not bring a change in perspective. His secretary of state, John Foster Dulles, had cut his teeth on the reparations issue at the Paris Peace Conference in 1919 and believed that the result had been unfair to the Germans and helped contribute to the outbreak of World War II. A series of negotiations and domestic political dramas ensued in the early to mid-1950s that culminated in the complete independence of the Federal Republic and its admission to NATO in 1955.[16]

In the transition of Germany from wartime enemy to postwar ally, memories of Germany played an important role in shaping American policy toward the vanquished nation. During the war, Roosevelt's apparent endorsement of a harsh occupation policy was based on his understanding of German history, an understanding that in turn rested on his suspicion that the German people were fundamentally flawed. After taking the Oval Office, Truman, on the other hand, surrounded himself with advisors who blamed Versailles, not the German people or German culture, for Germany's aggression. More important, members of the Truman administration relied on the notion of totalitarianism to link Germany's past with the Soviet, not the German, present. Still, Truman and his advisors remembered Germany's rise during the interwar period and sought to maintain control and limit its growth. Eisenhower, Truman's successor, and his secretary of state shared Truman's historical understanding of Germany and facilitated Germany's eventual emancipation from institutional controls laid down by previous administrations.

"The Boundary Line between Freedom and Suppression Runs through Germany"

As American policymakers wrestled with their memories of Germany, they were aware that many of their citizens questioned their policies in light of their own understandings of Germany's past. In the developing rapprochement between the United States and Germany, American policymakers realized that they needed to mount an aggressive campaign to persuade Americans that their foreign policy was both moral and prudent. This publicity push on behalf of the Cold War narrative of the German people was evident in all phases and administrations of the German occupation and reorientation. To convince Americans that the new Federal Republic was emerging as a dependable ally of the United States, American officials encouraged their people to adopt prosthetic memories of the German people. Policymakers minimized the influence of Nazis on the German population before, during, and after World War II, preferring instead to emphasize the long-standing similarities between Americans and Germans and the readiness with which Germans adopted or supported American-style democracy, capitalism, and culture. To carry out its strategy, the government of the United States used a variety of means to communicate its message, ranging from informal censorship to outright propaganda. State Department officials in particular used established networks to try to shape American impressions of the German people.

Exchange programs represented a consistently popular vehicle for emphasizing the similarities between Germans and Americans. Although the primary purpose of the exchange programs from the American perspective was to use ordinary Americans as agents of Americanization, these exchanges also served to familiarize Americans with "good" Germans. During the 1950s, the State Department and its counterpart, the German Foreign Office, helped arrange exchanges that ranged from housewives to police, prison, and parole officers. They also encouraged cultural exchanges. The State Department funded tours of *Porgy and Bess* and the Howard Singers in Germany. On the other side, the German Foreign Office supported the goodwill tour of Fritz Kortner, a noted German actor and refugee of the Nazis, and his troupe of actors. In 1951, the United States sought to formalize these exchanges with the German government in a cultural treaty, believing that, as a State Department aide put it, such a treaty would help maintain the needed "reorientation" purpose of the Public Affairs Program without appearing to "perpetuate the attitudes of an occupying power." An oft-unstated consequence was that it would also continue American contact with, in the words of Henry

Byroade, director of the Bureau of German Affairs, "carefully selected Germans" who epitomized the Cold War narrative.[17]

While exchange programs were useful, American officials understood that they could not be relied upon exclusively. American government officials pursued aggressive informational policies to convince Americans of the righteousness and efficacy of their approach. In the early years of the occupation, they viewed manipulating information at the source as a necessary first step in creating a desirable image of Germany. To this end, the American military during the occupation sharply defined who would be allowed access to postwar Germany, barring writers who wanted to create "speculative" pieces. They believed such writers would "produce sensational type articles in order to insure market value" and that a "distorted picture would easily result." Such guidelines illustrated the army's desire to exclude journalists and other writers who came to Germany in search of evidence supporting the continued existence of Nazism in German society and politics; in other words, they sought to deny ammunition to those who promoted the world war narrative.[18]

As part of this policy of censorship, the army also denied entry to journalists on the left, precisely because liberals and radicals were often viewed as the strongest supporters of the world war narrative. For example, the army denied accreditation to Mrs. Landrum Bolling of the Overseas News Service because it possessed information that her husband was "a correspondent who has displayed Leftist tendencies and has frequently followed the 'fellow traveler' line." Moreover, Mrs. Bolling's own background was suspect. A report observed that her "education was in the radical school, Antioch College, Yellow Springs, Ohio," and her father, who "was the head of the College," had "received unfavorable publicity for having sponsored the radical teachings of that school." Officials denied entry to another reporter because his magazine, the *Jewish Daily Forward,* was "pro communist and extreme leftist in views." They also refused accreditation to Maurice Goldbloom of the Jewish periodical *Commentary* because he was an employee of the American Jewish Committee and a member of the American Association for a Democratic Germany.[19]

Although the army often invoked the chaotic and impoverished conditions in the American zone to justify the exclusion of undesirables, the military made room and provisions for those whom they wished to accommodate. Officials accredited Joel Carmichael of the *Nation* because of his "moderate articles in [a] leftist magazine." They rolled out the red carpet for Arthur Sulzberger, publisher and president of the *New York Times,* and his son, offering them the "VIP treatment," which included a special mission aircraft for transport from Paris to Berlin. They also violated their ban on the wives of correspondents for those journalists whom they deemed useful and important. By employing this selective approach, the military hoped to exercise informal control over representations of the American occupation and the Germans in the American media.[20]

Sometimes the government's efforts at censorship on behalf of the Cold War narrative were more heavy-handed. In 1946, when policy toward Germany was still in flux, General Lucius Clay, head of the U.S. Office of Military Government, commissioned a film to document the proceedings of the Nuremberg trials. The film's primary purpose was to show the German people the monstrous deeds of their leaders and therefore justify the trials. This task fell to Pare Lorentz, famed documentarist of Depression-era films, who was then working for the army. Lorentz and his team looked at millions of rolls of footage from the trials as well as captured film taken from prominent Nazis. From this mountain of material, they fashioned an eighty-minute film that documented the history of the Third Reich from 1920 to 1946. Emphasizing Nazi war crimes committed in Germany's name in order to discourage support for the old regime, the film understandably stressed collective guilt and suggested the world war narrative. After a rough cut was finished, the film was sent to the Pentagon for approval after which the American army released it in 1948 for circulation in German movie houses.[21]

Once the American press reported the existence of the film, many private filmmakers clamored for release of the film in the United States. After a private viewing, twenty-four journalists, ranging from outspoken critics such as William Shirer to apologists like Dorothy Thompson, demanded its release from the army. The anti-German Society for the Prevention of World War III and prominent Jewish groups also joined the fray. Citing the rough nature of the film and the overabundance of atrocity scenes, the army argued that the film was unworthy of display in the United States. Despite repeated public assertions that their decision was not based on foreign policy considerations, officials argued in private that the film should not be released in the United States in its present form because the "atrocity" footage would "again stir up indignation and hatred precisely at a time when every effort is being made to allay it." The government did not release the film commercially, but kept it available through the Army Signal Corps to avoid charges of suppression. As Jewish groups noted, the effect was the same: censorship. In 1949, Jewish organizations reported that there were only ten prints of the film in circulation throughout the country. With a backlog of seven hundred requests by private and military organizations, the waiting period could last years. What's more, Pare Lorentz claimed in a later interview that the State Department under John Foster Dulles buried the film in the National Archives at the request of West German chancellor Konrad Adenauer.[22]

In these ways, *Nuremberg* highlighted the fascinating tension inherent in much of the American government's public diplomacy programs. In an attempt to discourage support for the old regime and encourage the adoption of American ideals and culture, the American government promoted the world war narrative of the German people to the Germans themselves. But in an effort to sell Americans on the desirability of close ties to their former enemy, the government suppressed these same products at home and sought to promote the Cold War narrative.

At the same time that the U.S. government attempted to suppress negative representations of Germany, it sought to portray positive ones through propaganda. After the birth of the Federal Republic, the American government trumpeted the success of its policies in lecture circuits, State Department publications (such as the *Department of State Bulletin*), and interviews. In these public pronouncements, American leaders carefully crafted a rhetorical strategy that used the Nazi past selectively to bolster American support for the Cold War. Conflating Nazi Germany and the Soviet Union in an invocation of the concept of totalitarianism marshaled powerful emotional forces from World War II to justify the present confrontational course with the Soviet Union while at the same time excusing present-day Germans from responsibility for Nazi horrors. In 1946, Winston Churchill used the term *totalitarianism* twice in his famous speech at Westminster College in Fulton, Missouri, where his references to the Soviet Union suggested obvious connections to Nazi Germany. One year later, in what would become America's overarching strategy during the Cold War, the Truman Doctrine used the adjective "totalitarian" instead of "communist" to describe regimes forced upon innocent peoples. And when selling the Marshall Plan, the other major foreign policy initiative of the period, Dean Acheson said that the purpose was to assist "free peoples who are seeking to preserve their independence and democratic institutions and human freedoms against totalitarian pressures." As Les Adler and Thomas Paterson put it, with the use of the totalitarian concept, "once Russia was designated the 'enemy' by American leaders, Americans transferred their hatred for Hitler's Germany to Stalin's Russia with considerable ease."[23]

American officials also realized that acknowledging existing fears about Germany was crucial to the government's efforts to "inoculate" against criticisms of its policies. In a response to a recent VFW broadcast that had voiced concern about the current direction of Germany, Henry Byroade best outlined this approach in a CBS broadcast:

> I know that you have all heard a great deal about Germany since the war's end some five years ago. American emotions run high on this aspect of our foreign policy in Germany, and there is no lack of opinion as to what we should or should not be doing in Germany. For instance, you have heard that we are rebuilding Germany into an industrial Frankenstein that will again menace the interests and security of its neighbors. At the same time you have heard criticism that we have dismantled Germany's war plants and have thus held her back. You have heard that we have condoned the return of nazism in Germany and that political reform in general is not keeping step with economic recovery; in short, that we are rebuilding Germany again in her own image. Yet others express the opinion that the time has come for Germany to assume control of her own armed forces.

Noting these extremes, Byroade sought to convince the viewing public that the U.S. government was pursuing a prudent yet far-reaching program in Germany. Arguing that "nazism as such is dead" and that Germany constituted the "heart and focal point" of the Cold War in Europe, Byroade promoted the Cold War narrative of the German people to justify the formation of the Federal Republic, the rehabilitation of Germany's economy, and the country's possible rearmament. Although Byroade and others, such as John McCloy, U.S. high commissioner of Germany, were careful not to dismiss fears of a revived Germany, the thrust of their comments, and the comments of others in subsequent publications, was that "the boundary line between freedom and suppression runs through Germany."[24]

As Byroade's remarks indicated, the State Department understood that a substantial number of Americans still adhered to the world war narrative, and thus that a significant facet of this campaign was containing and countering stories that supported that narrative. Under the leadership of Francis Russell, the Public Affairs branch of the State Department began an intensive public relations campaign to familiarize Americans with the issues involved. These activities involved public speeches, pamphlets, articles for publication in the *Department of State Bulletin* and *Fortune,* and appearances on radio and television. In the early years of the occupation, Public Affairs concentrated on educating Americans on the Nuremberg war trials, the question of reparations, and local German elections.[25]

To reach a larger audience, the State Department targeted several private clubs and organizations as conduits for the dissemination of propaganda, organizing question-and-answer sessions with leading American experts. In May and October 1946, for example, the State Department hosted experts who outlined the progress of reeducation in Germany. Public Affairs officials hoped that these types of meetings would convince American organizations that the United States was succeeding in its aims to rehabilitate the Germans. To generate support for a cultural treaty with West Germany, State Department officials sent a copy of the proposed cultural convention to, among others, the American Jewish Committee, the Council on Foreign Relations, the American Federation of Labor, the American Council of Learned Societies, and the Young Men's Christian Association, hoping to persuade these groups of the desirability of closer relations with the Germans.[26]

The response of the State Department to those who criticized High Commissioner John McCloy's handling of the Landsberg decision nicely illustrates this approach. On 31 January 1951, McCloy either paroled seventy-nine of the eighty-nine war criminals still held at Landsberg prison in Germany or reduced or commuted their sentences. Among the most notorious released as a result of this decision was the arms manufacturer Alfried Krupp. To battle angry reactions to the decision, officials from the State Department organized a meeting between the judges involved in the clemency board and a number of groups that were skeptical about the motives behind the pardons. By the end of the meeting, Henry Kellermann of the State Department observed that most of the organizations, especially the Jewish ones, were satisfied with the purity of the motives behind the decisions, if not with the decisions themselves. Based on these reactions, Kellermann suggested that the State Department refrain from further activity and allow these groups to carry the reasoning for McCloy's leniency to their constituencies.[27]

In addition to disseminating their propaganda through such informal channels, State Department officials also sought to shape impressions of Germany through television and film. The State Department enjoyed close relationships with television news producers; relations were so close, in fact, that State Department officials often wrote the scripts of many of these ostensibly independent programs. With its emphasis on interviewing high-ranking policymakers, NBC's *Battle Report—Washington* was particularly dependent on the State Department. In 1951, the State Department used the program to shape American understanding of an East German youth rally in Berlin. The program's script echoed the government's emphasis on totalitarianism, describing the rally as "one of the saddest and most frightening spectacles of the postwar world. Youth, innocent and impressionable, youth caught in the web of power politics and shaped to serve the all-too-familiar strings of Soviet Communists. This is one of the most appalling, disgraceful, and potentially dangerous things the Reds have ever undertaken." Making frequent comparisons between Hitler and Stalin, the State Department used this ostensibly independent program to portray the Soviet Union as the heir to Nazi Germany.[28]

The State Department also maintained an informal relationship with Hollywood, a legacy of the close ties the government and film studios had forged during the war. In late 1949, for example, Joseph Breen with the Motion Pictures Association of America passed to Henry Byroade a script proposal called "The Seven Needles." The broad outline of the story, according to Sylvan Simon of Columbia Pictures, concerns an American who comes across "certain evidence which indicates to him that Adolf Hitler may still be alive." The American then pursues the story, "motivated by his belief in our American democracy," and learns that "the legend that Hitler lives is being used by his followers to provide inspiration to underground Nazis for the time when the allied occupation troops are withdrawn from Germany." The hero succeeds in foiling these plans, proving to the world "the need for vigilance." But Breen assured the State Department that "if there is a disposition in the State Department not to look with favor upon this particular matter, the whole idea will be scrapped."[29]

In reply, Byroade informed Breen that the State Department believed that "The Seven Needles" could have serious negative political effects. For one, he found that it would contribute to "the belief which persists in some circles, in Germany as well as elsewhere, that Hitler is still alive." For another, he felt that "the proposed film would perhaps give an exaggeration of the size and importance of a 'Nazi underground movement' in Germany today." Finally, he believed that such a film would "unwarrantably" contribute to the "existing distrust or hatred for the German people." Such a development, he argued, would not be "particularly helpful to our Government's present policy and purpose of affecting the acceptance and assimilation of the German people in the community of democratic peoples." Byroade concluded by cautioning Breen that decisions about whether to produce "any film about Germany or Hitler or the Nazi movement" warranted "more than usual care." Breen's reply revealed the informal power the State Department wielded. "Your letter is quite clear, and complete," he wrote. "I am reasonably certain that this idea will not be pursued further." And it was not.[30]

As these episodes demonstrated, the U.S. government in the early Cold War period exercised an impressive amount of formal and informal power in support of the Cold War narrative. The government carried out a consistent campaign designed to generate support for its rehabilitation of the German people. In so doing, it laid the groundwork for other likeminded activists to enjoy considerable success on behalf of the Cold War narrative.

"No Permanent Value in a Friendship Created by a Common Enemy"

Despite their effectiveness in promoting the Cold War narrative, American officials were reluctant to rely too much on the government's prestige and authority, primarily because of public fears about government propaganda, especially in the wake of the Smith-Mundt Act of 1948, which prohibited propagandizing the American people in foreign relations matters. To this end, the United States in the 1950s advised and encouraged the West German government to take the lead in promoting Cold War narratives of the German people to the American populace. When the German government sought the advice of American officials on the creation of its public affairs program, the State Department provided substantial documentation outlining its own activities. Thus the U.S. government remained involved, but the new Federal Republic assumed primary responsibility in championing positive portrayals of the German people. This collaboration was a remarkable turn of events: in the early 1950s, the U.S. government helped a state whose previous regime had been so feared that it had prompted the passage of the Foreign Agents Registration Act less than fifteen years ago to propagandize within the United States.[31]

American aid for West German propaganda was entirely necessary. After Germany's defeat in World War II, the changed nature of the power relationship between the United States and the German people as well as the moral ruin associated with the Nazi period brought great changes to German public diplomacy in the United States. From 1945 to 1949, the German people had no sovereign federal government, much less official German representation in the United States. During this period, the main source of influence for Germans was personal contact with American military forces, journalists, and charitable organizations in the American zone of occupied Germany. Although there was no centrally planned strategy for portraying the German people to the American occupiers, a general impression emerged that depicted the Germans as a victimized people, first by the Nazis and now by the communists.[32]

The new Federal Republic in 1949 was far more dependent on the United States than any previous regime had been, and this dependence demanded a transformation in the approach of the German government once it resumed public diplomacy activities in the United States. In contrast to previous imperial strategies of introducing Kultur to the United States and awakening Deutschtum among German Americans, the Federal Republic pursued a much more modest course, one reminiscent of the shrewd policy of Weimar officials. Reflecting its vulnerable position, the West German government sought to ingratiate itself with the American people, to convince Americans that West Germany was different from

Nazi Germany, and to demonstrate that it was a dependable ally of the West. As for America's allies, the Federal Republic's goal was, according to historian Manuela Aguilar, "to establish a positive image in those countries and to convince them that Germany was oriented toward peace and international cooperation and thus worthy to become a member of the community of western democratic nations." In these efforts, the West Germans attempted to carefully navigate around the debris left by their predecessors. These efforts were hamstrung by American fears of fifth column activity, the activities of anti-German groups such as the Society for the Prevention of World War III, and the concerns of alarmed Jewish organizations.[33]

Through his early institutional initiatives, Chancellor Konrad Adenauer demonstrated his understanding of the importance of public diplomacy. Beginning with the hiring of Rudolf Salat to work in the Chancellor's Office Liaison Department to the Allied High Commission, Adenauer emphasized the necessity of reestablishing cultural relations with the Federal Republic's Western allies. One of his most important early actions was the creation of a new institution, the Federal Press and Information Office, designed to handle such affairs. In 1951, the Foreign Office and the Federal Press and Information Office together established Inter Nationes, a semiprivate institution entrusted with the responsibility of creating information for distribution abroad. The Federal Republic also vigorously pursued exchange programs with the State Department, viewing them as an excellent vehicle through which to shape American impressions of Germany.[34]

Much of the informational work of the Federal Republic in the United States during the 1950s was conducted by an American public relations firm. Several West German officials argued that public opinion played an important role in the formulation of American foreign policy, and thus reasoned that the manipulation of representations of Germans in the United States should constitute a major element of their broader plan to win American friendship. Therefore, in addition to the resumption of *Kulturpolitik,* officials realized that they needed to coordinate the dissemination of information in the United States. Public relations firms, several officials argued, were needed to coordinate all of the "multifaceted" propaganda activities of an organization. Dr. Heinz Krekeler, then consul general of New York, found that an "especially important" arm of activity was the "placement" of information and pictures in periodicals.

The employment of a public relations firm would also help sidestep American fears about renewed German propaganda in the United States. As a result, employing an American public relations firm became a priority of the new Federal Republic.[35]

Although several high-profile firms offered their services, West German officials ultimately settled on the Roy Bernard Company. Named after its founders, Roy Blumenthal and Bernard Gittelson, Roy Bernard was a medium-sized firm that handled the accounts of Dresdner Bank, the U.S. Air Force, and the U.S. Public Health Service, among others. Blumenthal and Gittelson submitted their proposal to Chancellor Adenauer in the summer of 1950, and their memorandum became the benchmark against which all other offers was measured. The basis of their strategy was the assertion that "Germany belongs in the Western world" and their proposal served as an admirable blueprint for the promotion of the Cold War narrative.

Blumenthal and Gittelson argued that a number of contemporary developments had had a favorable impact on the relationship between the two nations. First, the division of Europe made Germany the "eastern frontier of the Western world." Second, the State Department understood that only a strong German economy would "prevent the infiltration of Soviet ideology into West Germany." And third, a "miraculous transference of American hostility from Germany to the Soviet Union had occurred." Yet, Roy Bernard contended that there was "no permanent value in a friendship created by a common enemy." It believed that positive connections between the United States and West Germany had to be forged for long-lasting friendship. Fortunately, it argued, the basis for such a relationship still existed, albeit buried under thirty-six years of negative publicity. The company proposed the revival of "traditional" concepts of Germany from the nineteenth century that stressed the quality of German production and the cultural attainments of Germany's literary and artistic communities. In highlighting these, Roy Bernard hoped to emphasize Germany's long history of culture and humanistic values, thereby underscoring the provisional nature of the Nazi regime. It offered to carry out these aims through the establishment of a German Information Service, which would function as a clearinghouse for information on Germany, and a publications bureau, which would publish newsletters, brochures, and the like on positive aspects of Germany.[36]

That the principal partners, Roy Blumenthal and Bernard Gittelson, were Jews with German backgrounds unquestionably helped them
prevail over more seasoned public relations firms. The contract stipu-
lated that Roy Bernard should be "public relations counsel within the
general area of public-relations that shall be considered by the Government of the Federal Republic of Germany conducive to the promotion of harmony, understanding and industrial and cultural intercourse
between the nations of West Germany and the United States." Part of
this responsibility included the preparation of literature, pamphlets, and
brochures as well as the general charge to do whatever it could and
whatever the German government thought was necessary to promote
German interests. The use of an American public relations firm, and one
operated by American Jews, proved to be a savvy move by West German
officials. It lessened concerns about German propaganda in the United
States and neutralized those who sought to raise the specter of Goebbels. More practically, it provided Germans with a knowledgeable staff
that knew how to navigate the difficult American, and especially Jewish American, landscape. Finally, it provided the Federal Republic with
a powerful cultural instrument for marshaling support for Germany in
the United States.[37]

Roy Bernard kept the West German account during the 1950s
because it effectively employed the media to create the impression of
spontaneous approval for the Cold War narrative of the German people. In so doing, it pursued the aims of its initial campaign strategy,
"Germany belongs in the Western world," but proved flexible enough
to take advantage of opportunities as they presented themselves. In particular, it made extensive use of one of its greatest assets—the leader
of West Germany, Chancellor Konrad Adenauer himself. Roy Bernard
helped *Time* write its story on Adenauer before the 1953 election; this
story helped his selection as *Time*'s Man of the Year. By the mid-1950s,
German officials observed that Adenauer was widely known as "Mr.
Germany." They wrote that the identification between Adenauer and
German democracy had become so strong that American policy- and
opinion makers worried about the future of the Federal Republic after
Adenauer stepped down.[38]

Roy Bernard also proved useful in forestalling clumsy and heavy-
handed attempts by the West German government to encourage Ameri-

cans to identify with the German people. In July 1952, for example, Roy Bernard reviewed an Inter Nationes brochure entitled "United States Quartered—Democracy in Peril," which attempted to translate the division of Germany into a fictional American context. The brochure featured a map of the United States divided into four occupation zones administered by the Soviet Union, Mexico, Latin America, and South Africa. Revealing a lack of understanding and sensitivity, the accompanying narrative reported that this division had occurred as a result of a "mere trifle." Without elaboration, the story line suggested that invading armies had suddenly appeared and destroyed all in their path. In the "Washington Agreement," the four allies agreed to the following: the United States was to be quartered; Washington, D.C., and New York each were to be divided into four sectors; the Soviet Union would annex Washington State, with Seattle becoming Pacificgrad; and Boston was to be rechristened Atlanticgrad.[39]

The pamphlet sought to translate the German dilemma in terms familiar to Americans, but officials at Roy Bernard realized that such a brochure might backfire; instead of generating sympathy, its simplistic comparison might raise alarm bells about German propaganda and provoke indignation, suspicion, and the revival of the World War II narrative. Joseph Thomas of the New York consulate concurred. He agreed that it would spark bitterness in the United States and dredge up bad memories of the Germans. Officially, Charles Campbell of Roy Bernard informed Inter Nationes: "We have given the matter much thought and it is our considered opinion that it is unusable in the United States." While it is not clear what effect such a brochure would have had on American public opinion, it is reasonable to speculate that it would not have advanced West Germany's cause.[40]

Roy Bernard promoted the Cold War narrative in other ways. One of its main functions was to serve as the conduit between the press and visiting dignitaries. When Roy Bernard found out, for example, that Dr. Hans Riesser had been named U.N. observer for the Federal Republic, it arranged a press conference at U.N. Headquarters, took photographs, and wrote a newspaper release. But Roy Bernard did not limit itself to official representatives. It made great use of the visit of Miss Germany, Susanne Erichsen, in 1952, scheduling several press conferences and radio and television interviews. Press attaché Walter Gong stated that the value of these appearances should not be underestimated, observing that "pretty girls and pretty dresses always make an impression here." As we shall see, such efforts helped feminize and thus facilitate America's acceptance of the German people. Through these encounters, the Roy Bernard Company sought to familiarize Americans with select Germans who embodied the attributes of the new Germany.[41]

In 1956, Roy Bernard began coordinating the visits of American journalists to Germany. It sent a total of twelve for the year. These reporters were given special tours of facilities, installations, ports, and factories. Roy Bernard also set up appointments for them to interview prominent West German officials and other newsworthy Germans. These guided tours enabled the American public relations firm to indirectly shape American reports of Germany by focusing media attention along favorable lines. The resulting articles, the firm reported, reflected positively on West Germany, especially emphasizing the desirability of reunification and the necessity of rearmament.[42]

Most important, Roy Bernard fulfilled admirably its reputation for success in placing articles in major newspapers and periodicals. As Blumenthal pointed out, placing, or "planting," articles was a delicate business, and not all planned pieces bore fruit. But Blumenthal and Gittelson proved successful at the subtle suggestions, the backslapping, and the general wining and dining necessary to cultivate an atmosphere of cooperation with important editors. In the first few years, it placed articles on children in Germany in *Woman's Day,* on divided Berlin in *Look,* on the breakup of neo-Nazis in *Quick,* on restitution in *Time,* and was instrumental in the publication of a special issue on Germany in *Life,* to name only a few. In the travel sections of newspapers around the country, it placed articles on German food and people. Roy Bernard was responsible for articles on tourism in *Cosmopolitan* and on other subjects related to Germany in *National Geographic* and *Seventeen.* Occasionally it took time for these pieces to materialize, but the firm's skill in placing articles in major American periodicals became well recognized. Through these articles, Roy Bernard skillfully created the impression of spontaneous agreement with the Cold War narrative of the German people.[43]

One of the company's greatest triumphs was the publication of a supplement on Germany in *Atlantic Monthly* in 1957. Roy Bernard began work on this piece in February 1956, visiting editors in Boston to discuss the content. Company officials advised at every step of the way, setting up meetings with German officials, scheduling conferences, and suggesting authors and subjects. It also took a hand in authoring or editing the pieces submitted in the name of Germany's leaders, such as Theodore Heuss and Konrad Adenauer. The resulting supplement trumpeted the virtues of the new Federal Republic. The introduction by the editor congratulated the West Germans on their amazing economic recovery and obvious superiority to their misguided and oppressed brethren in East Germany, while at the same time minimizing their culpability for the unenviable position Germans found themselves in at the end of the war. He painted West Germans as victims of the "bloody and brutal nightmare of the Hitler era" who somewhat undeservedly harbored a "repressed sense of guilt" that "has left many Germans shy of displaying emotions or of showing interest in their fellow man." He noted approvingly that a new generation of Germans was "skeptical, irreverent, and fiercely independent" and that "fascism as a political fact or force is as dead as its leader." The articles included in the supplement, some of them by Germany's top statesmen and artists, attempted to demonstrate the truth of these claims. Overall, it was a major coup for those who supported the Cold War narrative.[44]

Roy Bernard proved equally adept at suppressing or neutralizing alternative narratives. In 1952, for example, the firm discovered that a reporter of *Look* magazine was charged with the task of writing a cautionary essay about the revival of Nazism in Germany. Officials with Roy Bernard approached the reporter with alternative information and effectively purged the essay of much of its aggressive and negative tone. The essay, entitled "Germany: The World's Fate Lies in Its Rubble," was mostly pictorial, with some suggestive captions like "They love a parade—but will they march for the West?" and "Germans see their heritage of guilt—but many openly covet the past." But the last line of text reflected Roy Bernard's strong intervention: "For the Germans, however, unity would let them lift their eyes from the ground and look ahead to their destiny, a destiny which the great majority of that voiceless mass is now convinced lies with democracy." By implying that Germany's silent majority believed in democracy, the article reduced any vocal supporters of fascism to the margins.[45]

Another significant episode involved the coverage of the German-Israeli compact in 1952 whereby the German government agreed to begin paying reparations to Israel in restitution for the Holocaust. Krekeler requested that Roy Bernard find a way to publicize the "moral background of the German decision which was reached despite the strong and threatening protests of the member nations of the Arab League." Roy Bernard organized a conference with journalist Drew Pearson, "whose anti-German history is well-known," and the next Sunday 240 newspapers carried the first pro-German column written by Pearson, in which he "extolled the Adenauer Government for persisting in its attitude towards payments in Israel." At the same time, Roy Bernard worked with America's "largest Jewish organization" to dissuade Walter Winchell, Pearson's "rival commentator," from criticizing the German government in his radio broadcast and columns.[46]

By the end of the decade, Roy Bernard had established itself as the preeminent source for information on Germany, and an increasing number of writers came to the firm in search of story lines on Germany. In 1957 alone, for example, Roy Bernard reported the placement of forty-seven articles in major periodicals. The breadth of the company's influence can be seen in the expressions of gratitude sent to Roy Bernard by editors of major periodicals such as *Time,* the *Christian Science Monitor,* and the *Saturday Evening Post* as well major television studios such as NBC.[47]

Despite these successes, the firm's expertise did not extend to film and television, a failing that would later hamper its relationship with the West German government. Although it successfully influenced a 1952 *March of Time,* a film Walter Gong called "the best propaganda film for Germany which ever ran [in the United States]," Roy Bernard proved of little value in the Federal Republic's efforts to counter *Hetzfilme,* or "smear" or "hate" films, a concern that was often cited in West German reports. In 1952, for example, Heinz Krekeler reported that a "disproportional" amount of entertainment films with negative German stereotypes still appeared on American television in the evening. Cautiously estimating the nightly viewing population at 50–60 million Americans, he wrote that the "taste-less" content of these films was "extraordinarily distressing" from a German standpoint. Krekeler noted that one night he saw a film that featured a "brutal shooting" of French freedom fighters by the SS and another that centered on German spies and saboteurs. Roy Bernard's lone contribution was the enlistment of Martin Ebon of the *Saturday Evening Post* to write an article against the showing of old anti-German movies on TV entitled "Yesterday's Villains."[48]

Observing that many of these programs originated in wartime Britain, German officials believed that over time they would disappear as new programming was produced. To counter these negative images in the interim, German officials considered various ways to place positive images of Germans on television, including the synchronization of German films as well as the production of new films by American companies. By the end of the 1950s, however, the West German government had still refrained from action, believing that new programming would eventually replace these anti-German products.[49]

But West German officials were not so patient with Hollywood. Despite the fact that several pro-German films were produced (among the most egregious was Nunnally Johnson's pro-Rommel film *The Desert Fox*), Germans worried that Hollywood continued to churn out products that defamed the German people. As the consul general from Chicago put it, although actual Hetzfilme were rare, far more common were otherwise "harmless" films that left a subconscious impression portrayed through individual characters that Germans were "back-stabbing, brutal, criminal, in short: villains." This official pointed out such tendencies in *The African Queen, The Greatest Show on Earth,* and *Rope of Sand.* The first contained scenes of brutal German soldiers from World War I, while the latter two featured villainous players with German characteristics. Officials in the Federal Republic identified Paramount, United Artists, and Metro-Goldwyn-Mayer as the three most consistent producers of films with anti-German undertones.[50]

In general, however, West German officials at the end of the 1950s were cautiously optimistic about the success of their campaign. With the help of Roy Bernard, they had effectively promoted the Cold War narrative of the German people while minimizing or marginalizing products that offered less flattering portrayals. But they remained hypervigilant about anti-German products and worried that American media firms would capitalize on their unfortunate history for sensationalistic gain.

"A Purely One-Man Organization"

Both governments were joined by a transatlantic association of private volunteers who willingly devoted their time and talent to the promotion of the Cold War narrative. Although filmmakers, journalists, and writers during this time of consensus voluntarily created cultural products that echoed the propaganda of the American and West German governments, not all cooperation was spontaneous. American government officials and the Roy Bernard Company scripted many of these ostensibly independent products. Nevertheless, many private citizens organized and coordinated activities on behalf of the Cold War narrative. Friends of Germany gravitated toward the American Council on Germany which, along with its sister organization in Germany, the Atlantik Brücke, sought to create a network of like-minded writers and journalists to facilitate understanding and exchange between the two nations. The American Council on Germany was perpetually underfunded, but the organization's chronic lack of funding for its activities only underscored the ideological commitment of many of its participants.[51]

Both of these features of the ACG were evident from the beginning. Estimating an operational budget of $500–$600 a month, the organization initially met in the apartment of one member and planned to establish itself permanently in the backyard office of another. Such a paucity of resources was more than offset, however, by the commitment of its leaders, in particular that of Christopher Emmet, whose apartment witnessed the founding of the ACG in 1952. Born in 1900 and a graduate of Harvard and the University of Heidelberg, Emmet had a long and impressive record of international activism and demonstrated a long-smoldering antagonism to totalitarianism in any form. In the 1930s he participated in the Christian Committee to Boycott Nazi Germany; with William Allen White, he helped organize the Committee to Defend America by Aiding the Allies. In 1941 he helped found France Forever, and after the war, he helped establish, along with Sidney Hook and Norman Thomas, the Committee against Mass Expulsions. In the early Cold War period, he participated in American Friends of Captive Nations, American Friends of Vietnam, and Aid to Refugee Chinese Intellectuals. He railed against the Soviets on his New York radio program dedicated to foreign affairs. By 1952, Emmet had become one of the nation's foremost Cold Warriors. For Emmet, participation in the American Council on Germany was part of his larger mission to smash totalitarianism.[52]

Emmet proved to be a tireless advocate of Germany, so much so that his critics charged that he reduced the ACG to a "purely one-man operation." Emmet's boundless energy was matched only by his impressive network of allies—prominent journalists, members of Congress, and participants in the U.S. foreign policy–making apparatus. He carried on extensive and substantive correspondence with the most powerful molders of American foreign policy and public opinion. During the decade he collected important information for Senator Jacob Javits of New York, consulted Vice President Richard Nixon, politely badgered Arthur Sulzberger about the anti-German tone of Drew Middleton's reports, discussed the finer points of dismantling German industry with journalist Edgar Ansel Mowrer, and provided advice to public intellectual Reinhold Niebhuhr and assistance to the humanitarian International Rescue Committee. Once he fixated on a subject, he could quickly marshal an astonishing amount of attention and publicity on its behalf.[53]

Despite a lack of funding, the ACG, helped by Emmet's energy and connections, generated some early successes on behalf of the Cold War narrative. It helped sponsor Adenauer's successful tour in 1953; it arranged interviews with key German officials; and it mounted countercampaigns against books that sought to promote the world war narrative such as T. H. Tetens's *Germany Plots with the Kremlin,* Hans Habe's *Our Love Affair with Germany,* and Ernst von Salomon's *Fragebogen.* ACG secretary Marcia Kahn helped research and publicize Rainier Hildebrandt's work on the 17 June uprisings in Berlin. These successes, Emmet repeatedly noted, were all carried out by volunteers. In 1956, he complained, "Our basic problem all along has been financial. Our Treasurer, Eric Warburg, is our only businessman. Practically all the rest of the Council are writers, professors or intellectuals of sorts."[54]

Without question, the council's greatest success of the 1950s was mobilizing a response to George Kennan's famous Reith Lectures in December 1957, in which the architect of America's containment doctrine called for the "disengagement" of American troops in Western Europe and the "neutralization" of Germany. Kennan's whole stance was based on recognition of the world war narrative and a validation of Soviet fidelity to it. Because of his stature, Kennan's lectures were widely circulated in Britain and Germany, and several liberals agreed with his conclusions. But Kennan also became the object of spirited and vociferous attacks, as intellectuals from Walter Lippmann to John Dulles declared that his suggestions would threaten Western Europe. Kennan himself later recounted that "the torrents of publicity, the hundreds of comments, the unjust attacks, the telling criticisms" represented for him, "in the most literal sense of the term, a traumatic experience."[55]

Emmet and other officers of the council were among those most alarmed at the popularity of Kennan's views, particularly because of their ramifications for American-German relations and the Cold War narrative. They immediately went to work crafting a public answer and had little trouble drumming up support. Renowned journalists and intellectuals such as Louis Lochner, James B. Conant, H. V. Kaltenborn, Fritz Oppenheimer, and Robert Strausz-Hupe, to name a few, appended their names to the eventual document. In searching for signatories, the ACG targeted prominent Democrats such as Adlai Stevenson and Dean Acheson. As Emmet stated in a letter to Acheson, "In view of the publicity in Germany and elsewhere in Europe, describing Kennan as a kind of semi-official spokesman and super brain-truster for the Democratic Party, it is especially important for Democrats to do something about this."[56]

Acheson decided to do Emmet one step better. With Emmet's support, Acheson crafted his own public response to Kennan. Acheson assured readers that "Kennan's opinion is not shared by any responsible leader in the Democratic party in the United States." Moreover, Acheson argued that "Kennan has never, in my judgment, grasped the realities of power relationships" and suggested that his solution called "for a degree of wholesome purity which does not exist within any state I can think of." A delighted Emmet told Acheson that, after consultation with Shepard Stone, Louis Lochner, Norbert Muhlen, and Jack Jessup, the council had decided to blitz domestic and foreign news agencies with his statement in early January 1958. The council would also solicit opinion from other important American Democrats after its release. For his part, Acheson informed Emmet that he would try and get "[the U.S. Information Agency] to pick it up and give it a whirl."[57]

All major newspapers and periodicals in the United States and Europe published either the entire text of Acheson's reply or excerpts from it. The *New York Times* printed the reply in its entirety. It was, in Emmet's estimation, a great success. Most important, Emmet wrote to C. D. Jackson at *Time,* was the significant European publicity garnered by the release of Acheson's statement. Emmet exulted that "the effect of the counter-publicity with the brilliance of Mr. Acheson's arguments . . . has brought the Kennan momentum to a dead stop." Emmet privately hoped that project "Answer to Kennan" could serve as a future model of collaboration between American politicians and journalists in fighting the Cold War on the information front.[58]

As Emmet constantly pointed out, however, the orchestrated reply to Kennan, like almost all the other ventures of the American Council on Germany, relied on volunteer effort. The members of the ACG were not mercenary publicists available to the highest bidder but ideological warriors committed to promoting the Cold War narrative of the German people. Emmet's extensive network of contacts provided an army of media professionals dedicated to presenting positive representations of Germany to the American people.

"Berlin Has a Special Appeal in the U.S."

Because of its "continued dramatic association with the anti-Communist struggle," Christopher Emmet wrote to Erik Blumenfeld in 1954, "Berlin has a special appeal in the U.S." Berlin, he went on to say, is "disassociated from other past or present American controversies about Germany. There has been much talk in the U.S. about the danger of German nationalism, neo-Nazism, etc., *but that criticism is never applied to Berlin.*" As the emerging symbol of the Cold War for Americans, Berlin was different. Aware that Berlin was their greatest asset for promoting the Cold War narrative of the German people, Americans, Germans, and Berliners sought to keep the city at the forefront of America's consciousness.[59]

From the beginning, America's relationship with Berlin differed markedly from its relationship with the rest of West Germany. Located deep in the heart of the Soviet occupation zone, Berlin, like Germany, was divided into four different sections; but the boundaries separating East Berlin and West Berlin, unlike those separating East and West Germany, were permeable. For many Americans, Berlin became the place where they could see the Soviet method in action. The Soviets had sole occupation of Berlin for almost two months before the other Allies arrived, and by all accounts they made the most of their early entrance by firmly entrenching communist rule.

American diplomatic reports reflected the different ways in which Americans conceived of Berlin. Whereas ambiguity and uncertainty dominated reports from Frankfurt and other areas in the American zone,

reports from Berlin often centered on episodes of Soviet coercion or misconduct. Almost immediately after American entrance into the city, U.S.
political advisor for Germany Robert Murphy began praising certain
segments of the Berlin population for their heroic stances against Soviet
intimidation. Although the Soviet Union had made great inroads into the
Berlin political scene, Murphy reported in August 1945, the "leaders of
the Social Democratic Party and Christian Democratic Union . . . have
impressed American contacts so far as relatively independent and democratic individuals." Murphy also reinforced this separation between Berliners and Nazis by constantly paralleling the methods of the Soviets with
those of the Nazis. The Soviets, he grimly reported, were using former
Nazis in the "same way that Nazi SA won support in 1932 from former
Communists." On another occasion he remarked that the "Russian-
created municipal administration had replaced former Nazi Blockleiter system with similar organization consisting of so-called Haus and Blockob-
maenner." This system of "considerable tyranny," he discovered, received
many complaints alleging that it "was just as objectionable from viewpoint of individual rights and liberties as under the Nazis."[60]

The Soviet blockade of Berlin in 1948 made these feelings more
apparent. As ground traffic to West Berlin came to a halt, the American
government was faced with a difficult decision. Robert Murphy, echoing the beliefs of many policymakers in Washington, argued that since
the conclusion of World War II the "presence in Berlin of Western occu-
pants became a symbol of resistance to Eastern expansionism." For them,
withdrawal from Berlin would signify eventual withdrawal from West
Germany and Western Europe. In addition to these matters of prestige,
Murphy cited another reason for staying in Berlin: "the protection of those
Berlin elements who oppose and indeed manifest courage in preventing
Soviet domination of the largest municipal area in Germany." Through
their bravery in standing up to Soviet intimidation, the Berliners proved
themselves dependable democrats deserving of American protection.[61]

General Lucius Clay echoed Murphy's sentiments. In July 1948, he
wrote, "I cannot but feel that the world today is facing the most critical issue that has arisen since Hitler placed his policy of aggression in
motion." He continued, "The Soviet Government has more force immediately at its disposal than did Hitler to accomplish his purpose. Only
America can exert the world leadership, and only America can provide the

strength to stop this policy of aggression here and now." American policymakers' constant comparisons of the Soviet Union with Nazi Germany
illustrated the importance of Berlin in recasting both Germany's past and
present.[62]

Over the course of the following decade, American policymakers
trumpeted West Berlin and its citizens. They used official organs like the
Department of State Bulletin as well as popular forums such as magazines,
newspapers, and television to disseminate their opinions. Their discourse
constructed Berlin as a bipolar world in which light and darkness, goodness and evil, capitalism and communism battled for the souls of the German people. And they found that the results of that struggle had major
ramifications for people outside Berlin. Looking east, John J. McCloy
claimed that "Berlin is a constant reminder to the satellite people [of Eastern Europe] of the possibility of a different way of life—a reminder which
no amount of propaganda can erase, a reminder which the Soviets recognize as a standing threat to their coercive system." General Maxwell Taylor argued that Berlin also served as a model to those in the West. Upon
his departure from Berlin, he stated that "here is the spirit of the front
line, which brings a solidarity found nowhere else in Germany, perhaps
nowhere else in Europe." Of his successor he said, "He will be another
American who came to occupy Berlin, stayed to defend it, and left a
Berliner."[63]

In addition to this rhetorical support, several American policymakers personally pledged their continued devotion and aid to Berlin. Former
Office of Military Government, Berlin Sector (OMGBS) director General
Frank Howley sent a complimentary copy of his positive autobiographi-
cal account, *Berlin Command,* to the City of West Berlin in thanks for
his time there. Elmer Cox, chief of the information branch of the State
Department, wrote West Berlin mayor Ernst Reuter that he would work
tirelessly to promote the cause of Berlin in the United States. Head of
the German public affairs branch of the State Department Henry Kellermann gave Reuter the opportunity to speak at the Voice of America radio
network to personally describe the issues and problems facing the city.[64]

The various conflicts in Berlin during the 1950s reaffirmed the city's
symbolic role for American policymakers. For example, when an East German communist organization, the Free German Youth of East Germany,
announced in early 1950 that it would stage a massive march in West Ber-

lin, the State Department perceived the action as an attempt to "weaken our position in Berlin." After much debate, American officials countered by planning a major rally on 1 May, May Day, the traditional holiday of labor, and scheduling a series of cultural events throughout the month, including an automobile show by American and European manufacturers, a UNESCO Rights of Man exhibit, and theater and motion picture weeks. The director of the Berlin Element of the Allied High Commission believed that these activities would ensure that the year's May Day celebrations would transcend "exclusively labor manifestations" and be "viewed as [a] collective demonstration [of the people in West Berlin] in support [of] freedom and democracy." Joining the State Department in its concern over Berlin, Christopher Emmet organized Common Cause, a forerunner to the American Council on Germany, to raise support and awareness in the United States over the challenge.[65]

Similarly, when workers in East Berlin protested new work quotas and were violently put down in June 1953, American policymakers interpreted this uprising in symbolic terms. At a news conference, President Eisenhower remarked that the uprising illustrated "the general feeling just behind the Iron Curtain" that ran counter to the communist "propaganda of the happiness and concern for people's governments that we have heard." In a letter to the presidents of the AFL and CIO, he wrote that the government shared their "feelings about the workers of East Berlin who by their heroism have demonstrated that totalitarianism has not extinguished the desire for freedom in the enslaved countries of Eastern Europe." In their attempt to send food to East Germany, American policymakers sought to drive home the point that conditions in the communist country warranted such a revolt.[66]

Finally, when Nikita Khrushchev issued his ultimatum in November 1958, the Eisenhower administration resolved to maintain its position in Berlin largely because of the city's symbolic value. Khrushchev informed the Western powers that they had six months to work out a settlement with the Soviet Union regarding Germany. If they proved unable to do so, Khrushchev warned that the Soviet Union would unilaterally sign a peace treaty with the German Democratic Republic and turn over all institutional and political controls to it. The East German assumption of administrative control of East Berlin would threaten American wartime occupation rights in the city because it would imply that a peace treaty had been reached between the Allies and Germany. A peace treaty between the Soviet Union and the German Democratic Republic also would endanger Adenauer's political position in the West because it would make more permanent the division of Germany. For these reasons, Khrushchev's ultimatum alarmed the West and initiated a heated round of negotiations among the Allied powers.

In private, members of the U.S. government never considered leaving Berlin or entertaining Khrushchev's proposal that Berlin become a free city. They did, however, differ over the extent to which Khrushchev's control of East Berlin constituted a real danger to Allied control of Berlin. On the one hand, Eisenhower did not endorse using force to break through the stoppage of American convoys into the city, believing that such an action would increase the likelihood of war. But on the other hand, the administration did not support the "agency theory" of some that the Allies could deal with the East Germans as "agents" of the Soviet Union and thus not endanger the Western position in Berlin. Although Secretary of State John Foster Dulles flirted with the concept briefly, he ultimately concluded, as did the other major members of the administration, that such a policy would constitute a "slippery slope" toward recognition.[67]

In public, the Eisenhower administration reconfirmed American support for Berlin. On 21 November, Eisenhower's press secretary Jim Hagerty informed Americans that "our firm intentions in West Berlin remain unchanged." Such resolve was echoed in subsequent statements and publications. In discussing the issue, American officials refused to validate Soviet fears about a German revival, thus rejecting any appeals to the past. Eisenhower, for example, found spurious the reason given by the Soviets for wanting to settle on Germany, namely, that they were afraid of German revanchism. He announced in a news conference that the Soviet accusation that the United States had rushed "right in after the war to rearm West Germany" ignored the fact that "there was no rearmament of West Germany . . . until after West Germany had become a member of NATO in 1954." By contrast, "East Germany had 50,000 troops under arms in 1950, and by 1953, had some 225–240,000 militarily active personnel." Americans believed that the tensions in Berlin were fundamentally about the present struggle in the Cold War, not the previous misconduct of the Germans.[68]

West German officials were no more passive in the face of such threats than their American counterparts. Indeed, West Germans were active in publicizing Berlin. The Federal Republic, for example, responded decisively to Khrushchev's ultimatum. West German officials initiated a *Berlin-Aktion,* or Berlin campaign, on 5 January 1959. This campaign was conducted by Inter Nationes, the Federal Press Office, and the Berlin Senate. Together, these organizations invited prominent Americans to Berlin, sent several speakers to the United States to discuss the problem, published pamphlets, and created films and advertisements regarding the crisis. One example from the Berlin campaign was an Inter Nationes pamphlet entitled *Berlin—Cross-roads of World Politics,* which sought to convince Americans that "although Berlin is far from your home," its safety and protection were very important because it symbolized the struggle for peace and freedom. It sought to reduce the complex issues surrounding the Berlin Crisis to a simple metaphor: "Four people sign an agreement that they are going to live together in the same house. Then, all of a sudden, one of them tells the other three to get out." By suggesting that a complicated situation riddled with cross-purposes and encrusted with layers of contradictory memories and misunderstandings could be understood in personal terms familiar to every American, Inter Nationes attempted to galvanize American support for one of the most difficult crises of the Cold War. Although the Berlin campaign ended in August 1959, West German officials believed that public relations work on behalf of Berlin should continue.[69]

Indeed, West Berlin had looked into hiring a public relations firm to promote the city economically and politically earlier in the decade. In 1953, Wolf Citron, an associate of Roy Blumenthal, informed the press office of the City of West Berlin that the reception given to Governing Mayor Ernst Reuter during his recent visit to the United States illustrated that now was the time for a "systematic" public relations campaign on behalf of Berlin. His plea apparently convinced the Berlin Senate to grant the press office a test run of three months, based largely on increasing American interest in the 1954 Berlin International Fair. Roy Bernard went to work in May 1954, setting up a mailing list for the Berlin catalogue, placing material on television and radio and in newspapers and magazines, and convincing Victor Riesel, noted syndicated newspaper columnist, to visit Berlin during the fair and write six columns on his experiences. Roy Bernard also worked Berlin more prominently into its efforts for the Federal Republic. One of its major successes, it bragged in a subsequent report, was the English synchronization and distribution of the documentary *Revolt in Berlin* on the East Berlin uprising of 1953. Based on these triumphs, Roy Bernard made a pitch for the extension and annual renewal of its current contract. Yet a lack of funding coupled with a reluctance on the part of some Berlin officials to support the campaign prevented the employment of any public relations efforts in these early years.[70]

The Berlin Senate tried to take advantage of Khrushchev's ultimatum to press the Federal Republic again for assistance on hiring a public relations firm. Wolf Citron of Roy Bernard used the appearance of a *Time* magazine poll in December to press home the need for a continual and systematic campaign on behalf of West Berlin. The poll noted that 23 percent of Americans did not understand the Berlin Crisis. Armed with this information, the Berlin Senate renewed its efforts to fund a public relations campaign in the United States. But the unwillingness of the Federal Republic to assist in this endeavor delayed the employment of a public relations firm until 1961.[71]

Despite the lack of a coherent strategy to influence the American public, Berlin officials still had some sway. One obvious method of influence was high-profile visits by city officials. The governing mayor was the most visible visitor, but a host of other prominent Berlin personalities also made the rounds in the United States. Whenever they came, heavy demands were placed on their time. When Reuter visited the United States in 1949, for example, he was asked to appear on radio and television programs such as NBC's *Meet the Press,* speak at or attend various meetings, and hold personal audiences with prominent journalists such as Freda Utley. When Dr. Hans Hirschfeld, the director of the Berlin Senate press office, visited in 1955, he was similarly swamped. Hirschfeld's list of sponsors alone was intimidating; it included the Berlin Senate, the State Department's Bureau of German Affairs, the Foreign Policy Association, the American Jewish Committee, and the American Association of Teachers of German.[72]

Easily the most publicized trip, however, was Governing Mayor Willy Brandt's sojourn to the United States in early 1959 after Khrushchev's ultimatum. Prior to his departure, Brandt was inundated with requests for meetings and offers of public relations assistance. In addition to the standard invitations for discussion with labor leaders, Jewish leaders, and congressional leaders, Brandt was asked to appear on *What's My Line?* and invited to give an address to the Lincoln Sesquicentennial Dinner in Springfield, Illinois. In these appearances, Brandt, like his predecessors, emphasized the centrality of Berlin to the West and the similarity of its struggle with despotism with that of the United States. The itineraries of important visitors from Berlin always reflected the high level of American interest in the former German capital.[73]

In the absence of a public relations firm for the city, West Berlin officials themselves worked behind the scenes to influence American reports on Berlin. They cultivated relationships with major journalists such as Freda Utley and William Chamberlain. Their onetime public relations firm for tourism, Stephen Goerl and Associates, helped orient Harry Gilroy, the new *New York Times* correspondent in Berlin, by explaining the needs and goals of Berlin. The firm informed Mayor Otto Suhr in 1956 that Gilroy was "cooperative in the interpretation of Berlin news for U.S. consumption." Hans Hirschfeld introduced popular academic Henry Kissinger to several Berlin editors to acquaint him with the Berlin Crisis in 1958. A Berlin official even attempted to alter an article in the December 1959 issue of *Life* on Adenauer's foreign policy. In these ways, Berlin Senate officials tried to fulfill many of the functions that Roy Bernard performed for the Federal Republic.[74]

Realizing that much of Berlin's dramatic appeal lay in its perilous position in the East-West struggle, officials of the American, German, and Berlin governments promoted Berlin both to protect it and to exploit its symbolic capital. Intra-German squabbles about funding aside, all remained committed to preserving West Berlin as part of West Germany and the Western world. All also realized that the story of Cold War Berlin naturally epitomized the narrative that they sought to apply to the German people as a whole. For those supporting the Cold War narrative, the dramatic events in Berlin, while tense and nerve-racking, provided welcome support for their propaganda campaigns.

In general, officials from the United States and West Germany joined forces with private citizens in both countries to create a formidable coalition in support of the emerging Cold War narrative of Germany. A common purpose justified this coalition and dictated a unified strategy designed to promote prosthetic memories of Germany that encouraged Americans to identify with the nation. The participation of the U.S. government helped to gather allies for the cause, and these different groups collaborated with and supported each other in their orchestrated efforts to sell the Cold War narrative. With the backing of the U.S. government, allies and influence in America's major media outlets, and a pliant population supportive of America's struggle in the Cold War, promoters of the Cold War narrative rightly understood that they enjoyed a dominant position in shaping American opinions of Germany.

"The Fight for Germany"

Such was not the case for those who sought to portray German history differently. The same factors that favored those who sought to disseminate prosthetic narratives of Germany hampered those who attempted to promote narratives that encouraged Americans to maintain differences with Germans. The most significant obstacle for those members of the memory coalition that supported the world war narrative was the political climate sponsored by the American government. Challenging state-sanctioned narratives in a period of consensus became almost impossible for organizations hoping to maintain any effectiveness in American political discourse. Those who did not accommodate to the new reality, such as progressive liberals and the Society for the Prevention of World War III, found themselves on the margins of the American mainstream.

The shifting political winds at the end of the war significantly reduced the influence of progressive liberals, who were among the most ardent supporters of the world war narrative at the war's conclusion. In particular, their clashes with the new Truman administration marginalized their positions within the Democratic Party and within American society at large. While liberals differed with Truman over his conservative appointments and failures to adequately promote or protect significant legislation on labor and civil rights issues, they disagreed with him most over his sharp change in foreign policy. Believing that lasting peace must be found in concert with the Soviet Union, many liberals found Truman's get-tough approach with that nation distasteful and dangerous. Committed to continuing the popular front into the postwar period, they also criticized Truman's aggressive actions against domestic communism.

Even though the war against Germany was over, they clung to the world war narrative, arguing that the greatest threat lay in resurgent fascism. As a result, progressive liberals prioritized the common struggle against fascism that forged the Grand Alliance over the specific territorial issues that threatened to tear it apart. Most liberals believed that the territorial demands made by the Soviet Union grew out of a historically conditioned insecurity, primarily in its relationship to Germany. As Max Lerner, a prominent progressive, put it, "An American foreign policy that is guided by the fear of Russian power must in the end—whatever its other pretensions—be guided by nothing else." Given their fidelity to the world war narrative of the German people, progressives sympathized with fears of German revanchism expressed by Soviet leaders.[75]

Their champion was Henry Wallace, Truman's commerce secretary, who shared their views of the president's policies. Critical of Truman's shift in foreign policy from the beginning, Wallace wrote a memorandum to the president in July 1946, denouncing Truman's aggressive stance toward the Soviet Union. Suggesting that America's recent actions placed the Soviet Union in a defensive posture, Wallace advised Truman to concede on reasonable demands to increase the level of trust between the two powers. Two months later, Secretary of State Jimmy Byrnes's speech at Stuttgart, which heralded the U.S. government's newfound conviction to rebuild Germany, prompted Wallace to go public with his criticisms of the administration's foreign policy. At a rally jointly held in September 1946 by two prominent progressive organizations, Wallace criticized the political climate of the United States. Although he upbraided the Soviet Union for its suppression of civil liberties in the Eastern Bloc, he denounced the anticommunist hysteria mounting in the United States, ending with a plea for the United States and the Soviet Union to rediscover areas of common ground. Faced with a public squabble between two prominent subordinates, Truman supported Byrnes's position, which coincided with his own, and asked for Wallace's resignation. After his dismissal, Wallace continued to blast Truman, arguing that the facile comparisons made by the administration between Stalin and Hitler masked the real areas of agreement between the United States and the Soviet Union.[76]

Although many progressive liberals were dismayed as Wallace's dismissal, interpreting it as the final indicator that Truman had irreparably broken with Roosevelt's legacy, another group of liberals viewed Wallace and his conflict with the administration differently. Writing to Wallace on behalf of the Union for Democratic Action (UDA), James Loeb expressed his regret at the brusque manner in which Wallace had been treated but pointed out that he disagreed with Wallace's position vis-à-vis the Soviet Union and communism in general. As the only liberal group that expressly excluded communists from membership, the Union for Democratic Action throughout the war had challenged progressive assumptions that communism did not threaten American democracy. Although the UDA under the leadership of Murray Gross, Alfred Bingham, George Soule, Freda Kirchwey, and especially Reinhold Niebuhr had emphasized the fight against fascism, its leaders recognized communism as equally dangerous to American democratic institutions. The UDA was already marginalized politically and dwarfed economically by other liberal groups at the end of the war; its leaders widened the distance through their public disagreement with Wallace.[77]

Germany figured prominently in the UDA's reorientation, primarily with regard to the group's greatest and most persuasive speaker, Reinhold Niebuhr. The son of a German immigrant, Niebuhr held ambivalent attitudes toward his father's homeland, ranging from apologia to outrage, from fear to fatalism. Although intensely interested in the German Question, Niebuhr had yet to make up his mind about the German people before he traveled to Germany in a fact-finding mission in September 1946. Touring Germany at the same time that Byrnes prepared to make his famous Stuttgart declaration, Niebuhr came away convinced that the Soviets were determined to establish a communist regime in Germany. Persuaded by German socialists and democrats that they needed substantial American support if they were to avoid subjugation by the Soviets, Niebuhr authored what was perhaps his most widely read piece of writing at the time—"The Fight for Germany"—to drum up support for their cause.[78]

In "The Fight for Germany," Niebuhr criticized Wallace and others for their conciliatory stance toward the Soviet Union. Evincing sympathy for the stated Soviet desire of a buffer zone, Niebuhr nevertheless averred that the Soviets would not stop in Eastern Europe. Viewing with disgust the tactics of the Soviets in Germany, which included the support and encouragement of violence by German communists to achieve their goals, Niebuhr championed the courage of German socialists and democrats in resisting Soviet pressure. Reading this resistance back in German history, Niebuhr contended that a significant opposition against the Nazis had been active since the 1930s, thereby making, in the process, a sharp distinction between Nazis and Germans. Surveying the political landscape, Niebuhr became convinced that the Western policy of impoverishing Germany was ill conceived and could serve only to dissipate the goodwill toward America that Soviet violence and intimidation were fostering. The Union for Democratic Action, agreeing with Niebuhr that a failure to revive Germany might lead to a communist takeover in Europe, called for German revival in an integrated Europe. Henry Luce liked the essay, and ran it in *Time* and *Life*. Later, *Reader's Digest* reprinted the piece for millions to read.[79]

By the beginning of 1947, the split in liberalism had become an organizational reality. The members of the Union for Democratic Action founded the Americans for Democratic Action, while Wallace's supporters established the Progressive Citizens for America (PCA). The fortunes of each reflected the trajectories of the different ideologies. The Americans for Democratic Action became a major player in domestic politics over the next few decades, as liberal anticommunism formed the "vital center" of the Cold War consensus. The Progressive Citizens for America, on the other hand, became the foundation for promoting Wallace as a third-party candidate in the election of 1948. Wallace's crushing defeat signaled the marginalization of the PCA and the progressives whom it represented.[80]

In the early Cold War period, then, liberalism in the United States fractured over American foreign policy. Hoping to maintain both the Grand Alliance and the popular front, progressive liberals emphasized cooperation with communists in the ongoing struggle against fascism. As a result, they encouraged Americans to sympathize with the Soviet Union and view Germans as "others." Conservative liberals, on the other hand, viewed communism as equally dangerous to American democracy as fascism. They argued, as Reinhold Niebuhr did, that Germany lay at the heart of this emerging struggle between East and West. The United States needed to rebuild Germany, they claimed, not only because it made economic and political sense but also because it was morally appropriate, given their newfound appreciation for German resistance against the Nazis.

"The History about the Nazis Is Becoming a Sweet Reminiscence"

Given the developments in liberalism in the postwar period and the centrality of the German Question to the emerging Cold War, American Jewish organizations, the memory activists most likely to remain faithful to the world war narrative, found themselves in a quandary. During the 1940s and 1950s, all Jewish organizations worried about developments in Germany and viewed the Federal Republic against the backdrop of the Third Reich and the Holocaust. In particular, Jews were concerned about the lingering influence of anti-Semitism, renewed nationalism, and the general unwillingness of Germans to acknowledge the immorality of the Nazi regime. But while an overwhelming majority of Jews favored a hard peace for the German people in the postwar period, one that insisted on a thorough punishment of German criminals, the eradication of Nazism, a vigorous reeducation, and a complete demilitarization, Jewish organizations did not agree on the extent to which this should be supported. Some Jewish leaders worried that a seemingly vengeful approach would place them outside the developing Cold War consensus. As the early Cold War period took shape, and the American government's position toward Germany softened, Jewish groups like the American Jewish Committee and the Anti-Defamation League shrank from confrontation with the government, afraid that opposition to American policy would leave them open to charges of communist sympathy. In contrast to the attitude and activities of these two groups, the World Jewish Congress, its affiliate the American Jewish Congress, and the Jewish War Veterans spoke against this shift in American foreign policy, arguing that Germany remained a threat to Jews and world peace.[81]

Although these debates centered on Germany, they were more about Jews than Germans. In their clashes over the proper responses to Germany and German representations, Jewish groups carried out their campaigns in their roles as Jewish defense organizations. In this sense, the struggle over German representations must be understood within the larger struggle among American Jewish organizations to define the interests of American Jewry and to identify which Jewish groups best represented these. Also, within this context it is important to point out that all American Jewish organizations, if forced to choose, prioritized the pursuit of positive Jewish representations over the realization of their respective approaches to Germany. All Jewish groups maintained that positive representations of Jews were in the interests of American Jewry; they differed, however, over which approach to Germany and German images best protected and defended the interests of American Jews. In every way, then, Jewish approaches to German representations were based on what was perceived to be best for American Jewry.[82]

These differences over how to approach Germany—and, more important, how to approach American foreign policy toward Germany—stemmed neither from differences over original goals nor from different perceptions of events on the ground in Germany. In the early years of the occupation, Jewish leaders agreed on the need for implementing the four Ds (denazification, demilitarization, decartelization, and democratization), the desirability of Jewish help in the Nuremberg trials, the importance of restitution for Jews, and the danger of renewed anti-Semitism in Germany (especially among American soldiers). Jewish leaders were also concerned about the fate of displaced persons and the evident failures of denazification in the early postwar period. All Jewish groups complained to the government about the inadequacy of denazification procedures, and all continued to push for conviction of Nazi criminals, even when faced with evidence that the American government and people no longer supported the trials.

Moreover, through the 1940s and well in the 1950s, reports from Jewish representatives stationed in Germany continued to concern the leaders of America's national organizations. In general, Jewish leaders were united in their disappointment with the behavior of Germans. Disturbed by the silence of both the masses and Germany's leaders, Jewish leaders worried about a lack of self-reflection and guilt over the monstrous crimes that had been committed in Germany's name. Reports from Jewish organizations and journalists highlighted that Germans not only refused to admit responsibility for the Holocaust, they refused to condemn it as well. In the early years, no major German leader called on the German people to repent for the genocide, most likely because, as Moses Moskowitz of the AJC concluded, most Germans had convinced themselves that they were victims too. Moreover, because of their contacts within the government, Jewish leaders were aware of the data on anti-Semitism in Germany, and it was not promising. The Information Control Division (ICD) reported that anti-Semitism was on the rise in 1947, with 41 percent of Germans labeled as anti-Semites or intense anti-Semites. This anti-Semitism manifested itself in the desecration of Jewish cemeteries, threats of violence, and nasty letters to newspapers. William Haber, an American Jew who worked with the Office of Military Government for a year during the occupation, concluded that it would take generations to purge anti-Semitism from the German people, advising the American Jewish Committee that money spent on combating anti-Semitism would be wasted. Joachim Prinz, a future leader of the World Jewish Congress, reported that there was a "subtle anti-Semitism" in Germany that had affected even the most "well meaning people."[83]

Although all Jewish groups worried about Germany, the organizations dealt with these concerns differently. On one hand, the American Jewish Committee led a faction that believed it was in the interest of American Jews to prioritize inclusion within the Cold War consensus. Defining Jewish interests in a narrower fashion, the leaders of the American Jewish Committee sought to preserve the gains made by American Jews in the postwar period. Reluctant to mount publicity campaigns that criticized American foreign policy, challenged state-sponsored narratives, and made their Jewishness, and hence their difference, visible, they emphasized working with state power, preferably behind the scenes, to achieve their aims. Even though many within these organizations harbored private fears about developments in Germany, their concerns about opposing the state led them to emphasize Germany's long-term democratic project over mobilizing American public opinion against American foreign policy through the mass media.[84]

By contrast, the American Jewish Congress led a group of Jewish organizations that defined Jewish interests more globally. Believing that threats to Jews elsewhere (as well as threats to other minorities at home) represented a danger to American Jews, they argued for stronger opposition to American foreign policy in Germany. Although they were also worried about how Jews might be perceived in the broader society, they believed that the danger of a renewed Germany warranted a strong public relations campaign to warn Americans about the pitfalls of American policy—even if it threatened to position Jews outside of the mainstream.[85]

This division dominated how Jews approached German representations in the American media in the crucial years during the formation of the West German government. For example, in the debates of March 1949 over how to handle a proposed German industrial fair, in which former Nazis had been allowed to participate, the American Jewish Committee argued that Lucius Clay's stern warning against opposition ensured that resistance would, at best, accomplish nothing, and, at worst, cast suspicion on the whole of American Jewry. The American Jewish Congress strongly dissented, arguing that it was a moral necessity for American Jews to register their disapproval of former Nazis. As a compromise, NCRAC issued a weak note of protest that recognized the importance of rebuilding Germany's economy but stressed the need to do so within a democratic framework. With Jewish communists alone left to demonstrate outside of the fair, a Jewish observer marveled at the apparent cowardice of Jewish organizations in their failure to stand up publicly for their interests when faced with government pressure.[86]

This division was also apparent in how American Jewish organizations approached the issue of a government review of American foreign policy. Although they had failed to make a strong stand against the German industrial fair, all of America's major Jewish groups were sufficiently alarmed by general trends in 1949 to agree on the need for a review of American occupation policy. Professing the need for such a review but unwilling to challenge in open court the wisdom of the state, the American Jewish Committee preferred a less public confrontation through the establishment of a presidential commission. Distrustful of the executive branch and desirous of wide exposure, the American Jewish Congress pushed for an open congressional investigation that would invite extensive press coverage. Unable to reach a consensus on the nature of the investigation, all member agencies except for the American Jewish Congress agreed to defer action until a unified policy had been reached.[87]

Despite this agreement and strictures against independent action on a pending matter before NCRAC, both the American Jewish Committee and the American Jewish Congress carried out their own agendas. The American Jewish Committee held a "private and exploratory" meeting with top government officials in Washington about the German issue. The American Jewish Congress, on the other hand, encouraged several senators to introduce and sponsor Senate Resolution 125, which called for a senatorial investigation of American foreign policy. To encourage passage of the resolution, the American Jewish Congress sent a mass delegation to Washington when the resolution was introduced in the Senate. That fall, the American Jewish Congress mounted an aggressive public information campaign to win support. Its centerpiece focused on the emerging medium of television. The American Jewish Congress purchased airtime on the CBS network for a roundtable entitled *Has the De-nazification of Germany Failed?* Participants included Senator Robert Hendrickson and prominent Republican Charles La Follette. In anticipation of the 25 October airdate, the American Jewish Congress mobilized its local offices to bring as wide an audience as possible to the program. David Petergorsky of the AJ Congress urged local affiliates to find and requisition all available television sets in their areas for listening parties. A model agenda encouraged conveners to lure guests to the host house for *The Milton Berle Show* (the most popular show on television) at 8:00 p.m. and then familiarize them with the issues before the AJ Congress program began at 9:30.[88]

These publicity efforts often explicitly employed the world war narrative. The American Jewish Congress Philadelphia Council published a pamphlet that made a clear connection between the past and present:

> If you have forgotten Buchenwald don't worry about Renazification
> If you have forgotten Adolph Hitler and his cronies don't worry
>   about Renazification
> If you don't care about a third world war don't worry about
>   Renazification
> But
> If you want to honor the memory of six million
> DEAD JEWS
> MURDERED BY THE FASCISTS
> If you care about the peace and security of the peoples of the world
> Then
> What do you think of this record??? [Here the pamphlet
>   enumerated facts about the failure of denazification.] . . . —Is
>   this why we fought the fascists???—Have the Nazis paid for their
>   crimes against humanity?

The pamphlet ended with a plea to contact local representatives of Congress to support Senate Resolution 125.[89]

By the end of the year, mounting reports of renazification in Germany encouraged Jewish groups to overlook their differences, pool their resources, and agree to support either a congressional or a presidential review. In December 1949, Jules Cohen of NCRAC issued a directive to all member agencies "for the beginning of a campaign to mobilize public opinion" on behalf of some kind of review of government policy. He called for Jewish affiliates to link with labor, liberal, religious, and veterans' groups in order to blanket their local print, radio, and television outlets with provided material on the failure of denazification policy in Germany. He concluded that "it is the view of the NCRAC committee that the subject of German democracy should be given a top priority by NCRAC member agencies." In April 1950, the same senators who introduced Senate Resolution 125 sponsored Senate Resolution 260, which called for the establishment of a presidential commission into the failures of Germany's denazification campaign.[90]

The apparent unity in the Jewish community almost immediately weakened, however. A little over a week after the resolution's introduction, the American Jewish Committee informed NCRAC that it was reconsidering its position on the issue. The AJC, constantly concerned about Jews appearing to act alone, made a faltering effort to bring together Jewish and nonsectarian groups interested in Germany through the establishment of the Coordinating Council on German Democracy. At the urging of the AJC, NCRAC had hosted an informal, exploratory meeting of Jewish, liberal, and labor leaders on the German Question in the summer of 1949, a month after Senate Resolution 125 was introduced in Congress. Attended by representatives from all of the major Jewish groups, the Federal Council of Churches of Christ of America, the American Federation of Labor, the UAW, Americans for Democratic Action, the National Association for the Advancement of Colored People, and the American Association for a Democratic Germany, this initial meeting had evinced a great deal of agreement. All representatives, including Reinhold Niebuhr, the prominent Cold War liberal, had expressed concern about the apparent failures of democratization and decartelization. There was also general agreement that liberal and democratic forces needed to be strengthened within Germany. Despite a general agreement on principles, however, several members had worried that criticizing American foreign policy in light of the East-West conflict might "benefit the communists." Ultimately, these differences had been papered over in a general resolve to strengthen democracy in Germany and lobby for stricter American supervision of the occupation.[91]

These vague agreements could not weather concrete policy initiatives, and the fear of opposing the state eventually ripped the Coordinating Council apart. After reading a draft statement of the council, Jay Lovestone of the International Ladies' Garment Workers Union opted out of the organization, explicitly disaffiliating with the American Jewish Congress, arguing that "for us to appear in the public eye as partners of or colleagues with this organization is merely to confuse our members and to hurt our position not only in relation to the democratic forces in Germany but in relation to the American labor movement and the American people as a whole." Perhaps put off by the militancy of the draft statement, Reinhold Niebuhr didn't attend the follow-up meeting, citing a prior commitment, and never returned. Alfred Bingham, who decided to remain in the organization, criticized statements that made no distinction between Germans and Nazis. By the end of 1949, the confrontational stance of the AJ Congress and later NCRAC endangered the nonsectarian nature of the council. Thus, when Senate Resolution 260 was introduced in April 1950, the AJC worried that only Jews would support it.[92]

The outbreak of the Korean War in June 1950 destroyed whatever momentum the council had left and crippled Jewish efforts to encourage a review of American foreign policy. Although many members of the committee recognized the dangers of German rearmament, most realized that it was a fait accompli in the new international environment. Despite the fact that he would later coauthor a press release urging the American government to carefully carry out rearmament (in fact, this would be the only significant act carried to completion by the council), Bingham urged members to recognize that the start of the Korean War meant that Germany would play an increasingly important role in the Western world. The American Jewish Committee found American public support for German rearmament growing. Later, in their respective internal histories of their involvement in the issue of Germany, the American Jewish Congress and the American Jewish Committee emphasized the decisive effect that the Korean War had on opposition to the Cold War narrative.[93]

As the council entered its death throes over the next several months, memory diplomacy on behalf of the world war narrative weakened. With nonsectarian support wavering, the American Jewish Committee argued that non-Jewish participation was essential to avoid "the impression that this is a Jewish issue." If nonsectarian support were not forthcoming, the AJC maintained that the council should be terminated. Moreover, members of the AJC argued that "if we persisted in holding negative attitudes, we would not be heard, but rather would be charged with vindictiveness and pleading." The American Jewish Committee became so concerned about possible charges of Bolshevik sympathy that it eventually issued a memorandum entitled "Communist Propaganda on Germany" in which it distanced itself and American Jewry from criticisms of American foreign policy, warning that "communists and their sympathizers have recently been exploiting Jewish feeling on questions relating to Germany." The memorandum, seeking as it did to undercut the public efforts of Jewish groups such as the American Jewish Congress, incensed AJ Congress representatives who, in turn, demanded a more confrontational course for the council. When told that non-Jewish members of the council would not support such a radical shift in tactics, representatives of the American Jewish Congress concluded that their organization could not support any efforts that did not immediately work to publicize the problems of renazification. Given these intractable differences, the council—and with it the last chance for a unified stance among American Jewish organizations—withered away.[94]

Other factors weakened official Jewish support for the world war narrative. At the same time that Jews were debating the proper course of action regarding Germany, policymakers in the Federal Republic were hiring Roy Bernard, whose principal partners Roy Blumenthal and Bernard Gittelson were former members of the American Jewish Congress, to conduct propaganda in the United States. The following year, Adenauer negotiated the Luxembourg Agreements with Israel, which mollified the hostility of many American Jewish organizations, especially that of the Anti-Defamation League. In hindsight, the years 1949–1951 represented the greatest opportunity for Jewish groups to publicly challenge the American state and its Cold War narrative of the German people. But fears of opposing the state initially undercut these efforts, and then the public diplomacy of the new West German government worked effectively to minimize Jewish hostility and hence marginalize the world war narrative of Germany.

The cumulative effect of these different pressures is evident in the most powerful force representing Jewish interests in American mass media—John Stone's motion picture project in Hollywood. Conceived in 1948 by NCRAC, Stone's office was charged by the Motion Picture Committee with the responsibility of ensuring that "attractive Jewish characters [are] portrayed on the screen even in secondary and tertiary roles." Films that did not directly concern Jewish characters could also "be dealt with on a case to case basis as they may arise." In the beginning, John Stone interpreted his charge with wide latitude, keeping tabs on films dealing with representations of Germans such as *The Desert Fox* and *The Steeper Cliff,* a proposed film about the American occupation. In the case of *The Desert Fox,* as we have seen, Stone deemed it important enough to spend some of his political capital to try to change the direction of the film.[95]

But as the American and West German governments effectively marginalized Jewish criticism of Germany, John Stone stopped reporting on films dealing with Germany. Throughout the rest of the 1950s, he reported on only two films that contained German representations—*The Diary of Anne Frank* and *The Young Lions*—because they contained potentially sensitive representations of Jews. Of the two, *The Young Lions* is especially noteworthy. When it was released in 1958, observers and critics concentrated almost exclusively on its German representations, often mirroring arguments that Jewish organizations and other critics had levied against the "sensitive" or "heroic" Nazi in *The Desert Fox* seven years earlier. That Jewish organizations failed to concern themselves with German representations in this film suggests how far Jewish leaders had traveled in absenting themselves from responsibility for promoting the world war narrative.[96]

The film version of *The Young Lions* departs in two significant ways from Irwin Shaw's 1948 novel. The first concerns the character Noah Ackerman, an American Jew who serves in the American military. In the novel, Ackerman faces a great deal of discrimination from the other men in his military unit. In the film, however, the anti-Semitism in the company is expressed by a single character, a sadistic superior who manipulates the others into despising Ackerman. The other major change concerns Christian Diestl, a Nazi officer. In the book, Diestl degenerates during the war from a sensitive individual into a savage brute, thoroughly corrupted by his Nazi ideology. But in the film, Diestl maintains a moral and ideological detachment from the depravity swirling about him. In the film, he retains his sense of honor and duty, driven to the brink of insanity at the end by the recognition of his participation in monstrous crimes against humanity and decency.[97]

Sources conflict as to the reason for the transformation of Diestl's character from novel to film, but pecuniary factors certainly played a role. In May 1957, executive producer Buddy Adler informed the producer, director, and screenwriter, "We need one good strong German character to speak for the German people as a whole, and to cast the guilt on the Nazis as opposed to the entire German population. A good picture today can take a million dollars out of Germany, and I am sure that unless we do something as suggested in the foregoing, this picture will not be sympathetically received in Germany." Marlon Brando, who played Diestl, on the other hand, was reported in an article in *Life* to have harangued the director and writer for fifteen hours about the need for his character to become an honorable Nazi. In a later interview, the director claimed that he and the screenwriter were responsible for the departure of the film from the novel. However it came about, this change occasioned debate when the film was released. Many regarded it as an improvement. Some reviewers, however, blanched at the suggestion that Nazi officers could be victims, too. One complained that Diestl "has been idealized." He is a Diestl who "thinks of peace a thousand times a day, who risks court-marital to protest the mistreating of French prisoner, who refuses in combat a direct order to shoot a prisoner." The real question for Americans, according to the *New York Times,* was "How much empathy can one feel for a Nazi soldier?"[98]

The organized Jewish community apparently did not regard this as a paramount question, however. Through the vehicle of John Stone's office, the power of organized Jewry instead concentrated on Noah Ackerman, the Jewish character played by Montgomery Clift. Stone's office welcomed the changes in the film adaptation. In Shaw's novel, according to Stone, "anti-Semitism seemed to pervade the entire company—and . . . the other G.I.'s were a lot of brutes." To retain that perspective in the film, Stone argued, might "militate against the sympathy that the script-writers would be trying to build for the Jewish boy" because it would represent a "slur on the character of the non-Jewish GIs." The Hollywood version, if true to the novel, would portray Jews as standing outside the established consensus. Thus, as the screenplay developed, he championed the narrowing of anti-Semitic expression to the sadistic captain alone. Buddy Adler's suggestions to the director and screenwriter reflected Stone's involvement: "I . . . recommend that in the scene in the barracks in which Noah is called 'Jew-boy,' the connotation here should not be that the bullies and the captain dislike Noah because he is a Jew, but because he is sensitive etc. . . . The bullies are angry with Noah not because he is Jewish, but because the whole company is being punished because Noah failed in his duty to keep the windows clean." When the film was finished, Stone made no comment about Diestl's transformation, but he bragged about his influence in minimizing the incidence of anti-Semitism in Ackerman's company.[99]

By 1958, Robert Disraeli of the American Jewish Committee wondered if the Jewish strategy of accommodating the Cold War narrative had backfired. He observed that a number of films, like *A Time to Love and a Time to Die,* a German love story set during World War II, echoed the theme "that the dear little German boys and girls were just sweetly ignorant and did not know about the dictatorship of the Nazi party." He went on to say that "it seems to me that the United States is deliberately forgetting that the Nazis fulminated daily in every newspaper and periodical about their hatreds and what they were doing about them." In these films, he argued, history was being rewritten to appear that "the citizens of this new Reich just did not know or did not understand what was going on. In these motion pictures, the history about the Nazis is becoming a sweet reminiscence. In this type of picture, the German hero or heroine lifts up the background of Nazism to a heroic level and makes recent German history, if not acceptable, at least tolerable to the American audience." As a member of the powerful Motion Picture Committee of NCRAC, Disraeli bore some responsibility for the very situation he deplored. By prioritizing inclusion in the Cold War consensus, his organization, the American Jewish Committee, along with both official American pressure and German courting, had helped discourage national opposition to the Cold War narrative.[100]

"What Hideous Cause They Are Unwittingly Serving"

The Society for the Prevention of World War III remained the most faithful member of the memory coalition in support of the world war narrative. Founded during World War II for the express purpose of propagandizing on behalf of that narrative, the society initially enjoyed a great deal of power and prestige. The organization's trajectory, however, mirrored the diminishing influence of the memory coalition in support of the world war narrative. Unlike Jewish groups, however, the society refused to change course, and by the end of the 1950s was thoroughly marginalized in American society.[101]

The origins of the society lay in the experiences of Rex Stout, the famous author of the Nero Wolfe detective stories. After the disastrous Munich Conference in 1938, Stout became an active propagandist on behalf of an interventionist foreign policy. Working on behalf of the Friends of Democracy, an organization dedicated to combating extremists on the left and on the right, Stout appeared often on the radio show *Information Please* in support of Roosevelt's policies such as Lend-Lease, the lifting of the arms embargo, and military preparedness. He later became a founding member of William Allen White's Committee to Defend America by Aiding the Allies and participated in its subsequent rebirth as the Fight for Freedom Committee. In the early fall of 1941, on the eve of American entry into World War II, Stout served as trustee, along with Dorothy Thompson and others, of Freedom House, an umbrella organization of all interventionist groups.[102]

Stout's skills as a propagandist were eventually realized by the U.S. government, and in April 1942 he became chairman of the Writers' War Board (WWB). During the next four years, Stout mobilized over five thousand authors to drum up support for the war. In its first year alone, the WWB conceived of and placed over eight thousand pieces of propaganda. Stout toured the country, making speeches and participating in roundtables. Along with Freedom House, the WWB made especially effective use of CBS's *Our Secret Weapon,* a radio program dedicated to debunking Nazi propaganda.[103]

Under the direction of Stout, this propaganda took on a decidedly anti-German flavor. Stout sought to convince Americans, many of whom were predisposed to blame the war on a few politicians and industrialists, that the German people themselves were responsible. "The chief difficulty to any peace in this world is not the momentary, spasmodic vices of the Nazis but the inherent anti-democratic traits in the German character," Stout argued. "I am willing to grant any grown German one right and one only—the right to a decent burial."[104]

Several criticized the direction of the WWB under Stout's leadership. Henry Seidel and Arthur Garfield Hayes voiced concern about damning a whole people. Carl Friedrich criticized the emotional appeal of hate, and *Common Sense* charged Stout with trying to "subhumanize" the Germans. Criticism became even more intense once Stout, along with Isidore Lipschutz, a Belgian refugee, helped found the Society for the Prevention of World War III (SPWWIII). *Common Sense* called the SPWWIII "a monstrous assault on human rights." In June, the journal published letters by John Marquand, Frederick Lewis Allen, Alfrid Kazin, Quincy Howe, and Max Easterman criticizing Stout's stand. Dorothy Thompson argued that Stout had reduced the WWB to a propaganda arm of the SPWWIII; at a town hall meeting in which Stout and Thompson debated the issue, a near riot broke out and the police had to intervene.[105]

The world war narrative of the German people explicitly lay at the heart of the new organization. The very name of the organization suggested the importance of this narrative to the society's conception of itself. Through its title, the organization tried to project its understanding of the German past into the future. In the SPWWIII's Statement of Policy, it contended that it would be impossible to "take the necessary steps to prevent a third world war" unless Americans understood the "German master-race obsession." It argued that "the widespread habit of setting the Nazis apart from the German people results from an inadequate knowledge of German history." Such knowledge would prove that "the forces in Germany that raised Hitler to power and have maintained him, are the identical forces that stood behind Bismarck, and Kaiser Wilhelm." The organization identified these forces as "Pan-Germans," members of the German race dedicated to an aggressive, expansionist foreign policy.[106]

Throughout the life of the organization, the causes offered to explain Pan-German aggression varied. Many authors focused on the enduring rule of economic elites, whether those were described as cartels or Junkers. According to many, German economic elites spurred war for national reasons as well as personal profit. Others argued that there was something defective in the German race itself. Alvin Barach maintained that "a recognition of their unique and unmistakable disturbance in mental functioning, including their traditional longings for dominance and cruelty, can be expected to be more helpful" than assuming, as many did, that Germans were just like Americans. Regardless of the cause of the obses-

sion, the point was driven home: the Germans were fundamentally different from Americans.[107]

As the war wound down, the society constantly warned that the apparent defeat of the Nazis masked a greater German conspiracy to use the
peace for their advantage. In late 1944, Louis Nizer wrote that apparent
defeat was disguising "Plan II," which called for the same militarists who
had supported Bismarck, Kaiser William, and Hitler, and who had squir-
reled away hundreds of millions of dollars in neutral countries and American financial institutions during the war, to disavow the Nazis and claim
the mantle of democrats. "To make the picture of the German Republic
convincing, Hitler and the other leading Nazis will be murdered by the
militarists themselves," Nizer contended. "It will be wonderful how few
Nazis there will be after defeat."[108]

Nizer and others maintained that the key to the Pan-German plan
would be the work of German apologists, men and women in Allied
nations like the United States who would trot out the following litany
of arguments in support of a lenient peace: democracy needs a chance;
all Germans are not responsible for the actions of a few; harsh reparations will only encourage a new Hitler; and good Germans suffered, too.
Believing that those who pushed for a soft peace were Nazi tools or dupes
laying the groundwork for the next war, SPWWIII officials hammered
away at perceived apologists. Another contributor denounced "professional sentimentalists" as "pupils and dupes of Goebbels," while Nizer
claimed that "unwitting" apologists, ignorant "who their bed-fellows are,
and what hideous cause they are unwittingly serving," were more dangerous than Germans. To counter the work of German apologists, society
officials maintained a steady media barrage. They condemned apologist
organizations such as the Council for a Democratic Germany, the American Association for a Democratic Germany, and "Free German" groups.
They took issue with films such as *The Hitler Gang* and *The Seventh Cross*
for their depiction of heroic Germans. And the society promoted works
such as T. H. Tetens's *Know Your Enemy.*[109]

The heyday of the society was undoubtedly in 1944 and 1945. Its message was sympathetically received while the United States was still at war
with Germany. With the support of the Roosevelt administration, the
society enjoyed a great deal of power and prestige. As head of both the
society and the WWB, Stout channeled the efforts of the Writers' War

Board to produce propaganda against the Germans. Roosevelt invited Stout to the White House often, Elmer Davis, director of the Office of War Information, defended the work of Stout and the WWB, and Henry Morgenthau publicly praised his work. Army orientation officers from around the country exhorted Stout to continue his struggle against the German people.[110]

After Roosevelt's death, however, the society found itself in frequent disagreement with the new Truman administration and its policy of German rehabilitation. Its willingness to confront the state and publicly criticize the failings of the American occupation in its official publication, *Prevent World War III,* affected its relations with other memory activists. Jewish groups were reluctant to appear publicly with the society, and Cold War liberals kept it at arm's length. The disintegration of the Writers' War Board in the immediate postwar period also deprived Stout and his colleagues of their easy access to the media. By the early 1950s, *Prevent World War III* switched tactics; aware that a stridently anticommunist position was necessary in the new Cold War environment, the society revived the specter of German-Soviet rapprochement, linking Germany with the Soviet Union through several articles and its heavy promotion of T. H. Tetens's new controversial book, *Germany Plots with the Kremlin.* None of its maneuvering was effective. Its sense of betrayal was evident in the society's new targets; rather than attacking Germans or German apologists, it increasingly criticized American officials such as Theodore Draper, Lucius Clay, and John Foster Dulles, whom the society held responsible for betraying the punitive peace the United States should have imposed on the Germans.[111]

Members of the world war narrative coalition found it difficult to maintain their public support. Political pressure prevented open organizational dissent against the position of the American government. Above all, liberals and Jews feared opposing the state in an era of consensus that sought to contain ideological difference. With the notable exception of the Society for the Prevention of World War III, members were not willing to risk other goals and interests in pursuit of a punitive peace with Germany.

The postwar period witnessed the formation of competing memory coalitions dedicated to supporting and promoting different narratives of the Germans. On one side, the American and West German governments, along with their agents and allied pressure groups, promoted a Cold War narrative that depicted the Germans as the first victims of Hitler, a people who now vigorously stood with the United States in support of democracy in Europe. Stories of Cold War Berlin were among the most valuable and effective in their campaign. On the other side, progressive liberals, Jewish organizations, and related pressure groups struggled over how best to keep alive the world war narrative, an interpretation of the German people that emphasized the crimes of Germany's past and encouraged Americans to remain vigilant against German revanchism. The power of the American government, especially in the context of the emerging Cold War, played a decisive role in shaping the extent to which organizations felt comfortable registering dissent from established policy. As the next chapter demonstrates, the power of the Cold War narrative was evident in how Americans responded to cultural products—in large part because of the work these products performed in constructing American identity in the postwar period.

3

"Your Post on the Frontier"

Germany in an Age of Consensus, 1945–1959

On 30 March 1949, an irritated executive at Metro-Goldwyn-Mayer wrote a letter to Secretary of State Dean Acheson regarding MGM's recent film *The Search*. One of the first films shot on location in occupied Germany, *The Search* told the story of the fond relationship that developed between a young refugee boy and the handsome American soldier who rescued him from starvation, took him into his home, made plans to bring him back to the United States, and finally, when he discovered that the boy's mother still lived, helped reunite mother and son. Starring one of the bright young talents in Hollywood, Montgomery Clift, the film earned significant accolades in the United States, garnering Academy Award nominations for best actor, director, and screenplay. Noting its virtues and accomplishments, the executive wrote to Acheson that his fine film had suffered severe "mutilation" at the hands of censors in Spain. He complained that "all suggestions of cruelty visited upon the boy and others by Nazi Germany" had been purged, leaving the "appealing frightened waif, the central character of the film . . . a depressingly backward youngster." In a similar vein, he observed that "no mention of Germany remains [and] thus the picture is weakened by having its action take place in an apparently mythical kingdom." To top it all off, he bitterly wrote, all scenes depicting the "nobility of the American military government," such as the one showing "the American officer's intention to abandon his much desired permission to return home to the United States, in an attempt to aid the waif," had also been excised. He surmised that Spanish regulations against "grieving" nations friendly to Spain, and especially those who had assisted Spain in its civil war, must have led to the changes, "which have mutilated the story and seriously destroyed its entertainment, cultural, and pro-American value."[1]

Had Peter Viertel, the original screenwriter of *The Search,* read this letter, he would have found it high comedy indeed. Viertel's original story was a scathing indictment of both the Germans, whom it portrayed as secretly working to hamper and sabotage the aims of the American occupying forces, and the American occupying soldiers themselves, whom it depicted as too callow, too corrupt, or too involved in sexual adventures to recognize this duplicity and to discharge their responsibilities competently and honorably. At first, Fred Zinnemann, the director of the film, shared Viertel's concept of the film. But in the end, Zinnemann, along with Swiss producer Lazar Wechsler, decided to drop both Viertel and his vision. In contrast to Viertel's designs for a critical inquiry into the nature of American occupation, the final film portrayed the Americans as heroic and compassionate occupiers and minimized the responsibility of the Germans for the chaotic situation in Europe, a depiction more in line with the developing Cold War consensus.[2]

Through the ideological conflict present in its production and the resolution of that conflict in the film's final form, *The Search* represented in microcosm the larger cultural milieu in which it was created. Although the end of the war brought a conclusion to the fighting and killing, it did not resolve one of the most contested issues of the war—the uncertain relationship between Nazism and the German people. By the end of the 1940s, however, a consensus emerged as the Cold War narrative of the German people became the dominant interpretation. Based on the view that a militant minority had taken advantage of desperate times to waylay German democracy and hijack an entire nation, the narrative suggested that the destruction of the Nazi leadership translated into the destruction of Nazism and the emancipation of the German nation. Accordingly, the Cold War narrative focused on the growing role of West Germany as the eastern frontier of freedom and on the brave and courageous actions of West Berliners in standing up to Soviet intimidation. For adherents of this narrative, World War II was an aberration in the history of Germany, one that did not warrant excessive attention or discussion. Germans were like Americans, according to this interpretation; the only difference was that Americans had traversed further along the path of democracy and capitalism.

The Cold War narrative of the German people gained ascendancy in the early postwar period because it both reflected and contributed to the emerging Cold War consensus, a mainstream interpretive community that championed the status quo of American society in a period of rapid change and upheaval. In addition to trumpeting the virtues of U.S. capitalism, consumerism, Christianity, and limited social democracy, the Cold War consensus sought to "contain" ideologies such as socialism and communism that offered alternative political and social systems as well as radical dissent from the racial and sexual status quo. As an interpretive community, the Cold War consensus fundamentally represented both the celebration of American national greatness and a paranoid repression of dissenting perspectives in the 1940s and 1950s.[3]

The Cold War narrative nicely affirmed this ideological framework. The emerging Cold War, the clash between the United States and the Soviet Union in Germany, and particularly the struggle in Berlin, helped Americans conceive of Germany as a battleground between capitalism and communism, a place where these different systems could be contrasted for the rest of the world to see. In this growing identification between Germany and the Cold War, Germany helped shape American attitudes toward the Cold War. The concept of totalitarianism, and Nazi Germany's pivotal role in that concept, encouraged many Americans to view the Cold War as a conflict of ideologies, a struggle between democracy and totalitarianism. In the process, by blaming an ideology and not a people for the sins of Nazism, Americans absolved the Germans. Postwar images of a German landscape dominated by rubble and fräuleins encouraged American men to conceive of Germany as a nation rid of its Nazi oppressors and in need of masculine protection. Feminizing Germany in this way reaffirmed traditional gender roles in America in an era of "sexual containment." The progress that Germans made during the 1950s in terms of democratization and capitalism emphasized both the general innocence of the German people and, when compared to the fate of East Germany, the superiority of American civilization. Finally, as the emerging symbol of the Cold War, Berlin itself brought many of these issues together as well as highlighting the bravery of Germans in standing up to the Soviet menace.[4]

"Nothing Is Gained by Appeasing Hungry Power"

The developing Cold War provided a necessary backdrop for the transformation of American attitudes toward Germany, primarily through the proliferation of anticommunist sentiment in American society. As the international drama unfolded in Europe and Asia and as American attitudes toward the Soviet Union hardened, American opinion concerning the Germans changed. Although a number of factors played a role in this growing rapprochement, public commentary, public opinion polls, and the records of the Office of Public Opinion Studies in the U.S. State Department suggest the extent to which the emergence of the Cold War was intimately intertwined with American perceptions of Germany.

At the end of the war, American attitudes toward the German people were decidedly negative. Americans were especially hostile to members of the Nazi Party. When queried about the fate of Nazi officials who claimed that they were "just following orders," Americans supported in equal percentages immediate execution or trial and punishment if found guilty (19 percent each). The largest group, 42 percent, favored just throwing them in jail. In the spring of 1945, when Gallup asked Americans what the fate of Hermann Göring should be, 67 percent supported execution, with many of them arguing that the "manner of death should be made as unpleasant as possible." Asked about the proper fate of Gestapo agents and storm troopers in the summer of 1945, 50 percent of Americans said that they should be "quickly destroyed." Gallup found that one in ten respondents thought in terms of more than death: "They want SS troops and Gestapo men to die, but they want them to die slowly, they want to torture them, some suggesting 'hard work and starvation' as the means. Imprison them . . . jail them . . . cage them . . . exile them . . . isolate them . . . treat them as they treated others . . . no punishment is bad enough. These are just a few of the suggestions." Reaction to the Nuremberg trials confirmed American antagonism to the Nazi Party. Of the 90 percent who had heard of the trials, only 4 percent said that the sentences were too severe, and almost 40 percent said that they were "too lenient."[5]

American anger toward the Nazis spilled over into attitudes toward the German people. Results from surveys by the Office of Public Opinion Research at Princeton indicate that American attitudes toward rank-and-file Germans hardened appreciably over the course of late 1944–early 1945. In particular, although a majority of Americans held the Nazi government primarily responsible for the "cruelties of war," increasingly, Americans saw the German people themselves as to blame. By the summer of 1945, over half of Americans believed that the Germans bore some, if not full, responsibility for the concentration camps. Their anger over this translated into a waning willingness to continue rationing to feed starving Germans and a marked interest in exacting reparations from Germany after the war.[6]

Still, even during this nadir in U.S.-German relations, there was never strong support for a brutal and devastating peace. In the last months of 1944, only a third of Americans supported destroying Germany as a "political entity" and in the spring of 1945 less than half approved of "splitting Germany into a number of smaller countries." Public commentary on the Morgenthau Plan suggested that American opinion makers were also against "pastoralizing" Germany. Clergy, in particular, opposed terms that would be harsh for the "masses of the people of defeated countries." H. Schuyler Foster of the State Department observed that "church leadership opinion on treatment of enemy people is considerably more humane than the expressed opinion of the general public." Major Christian publications campaigned against the Morgenthau Plan, and many even criticized the Allied insistence on unconditional surrender. The Catholic publication *America* claimed that the Morgenthau Plan would "sentence sixty million Germans to a future of misery and despair." In the spring of 1945, a majority of Americans rejected the Morgenthau Plan, arguing that the United States should help get German peacetime industries going again.[7]

Prior to the outbreak of the Cold War, then, Americans despised Nazis and distrusted Germans but did not seek to permanently cripple or destroy the German nation. As a result, mainstream Americans backed a policy geared toward controlling, transforming, but ultimately reconstructing German society in the months after V-E Day. Polls during 1945 and 1946 suggest a healthy support for the maintenance of occupation forces, a nagging skepticism that Germany could be trusted to govern itself, and a general level of satisfaction with the occupation. But as the rivalry between the United States and the Soviet Union emerged over the course of the next few years, Germany, with its centralized geopolitical location, important historical legacy, and physical division between East and West, became enmeshed in the developing Cold War. Increasingly, Americans found it impossible to discuss Germany apart from its central role in the conflict with the Soviet Union. As commentator Joseph Phillips wrote in 1948, "We have stopped thinking about Germany as the German problem and have taken to thinking of it only as a part of the Russian problem."[8]

Discourse on German participation in the Marshall Plan illustrates how involved Germany was in the Cold War story. In general, German participation was discussed in the context of the overall struggle with the Soviet Union. The rehabilitation of Germany through the Marshall Plan was tied to both the humanitarian reconstruction of Europe and the anticommunist effort to "contain" Soviet expansion. *U.S. News and World Report* observed that the Marshall Plan in Europe and Germany was "intended to rebuild the co-operating nations and to save Western Europe from Russian domination." Referring to Germany as the "worst slum in Europe," the *New York Times* called on the American government to raise German production levels and enable it to resume trade with the outside world. For these reasons, State Department officials recorded that most public commentators welcomed German "inclusion in the [European Reconstruction Plan]."[9]

Opposition to Soviet communism also dominated discussions of unifying the western zones. Most American commentators welcomed plans for the combination of western zones in the London program. *Time,* for example, claimed that the scheme was a "keystone in the dike against communism which the U.S. is trying to build." Ignoring the war memories of the French, the *Wall Street Journal* and others criticized French leaders for dragging their feet. Overall, the six-power plan met with "broad approval in the nation's press and radio comment," according to the State Department. Public comment was also "virtually unanimous" in recognizing currency reform in the western zones as "long overdue" and a "necessary step" for the economic rehabilitation of Germany and its role in the Marshall Plan. Many opinion makers supported the move even if it meant problems in Berlin.[10]

With its physical division between East and West on a smaller and more personal scale, Berlin proved to be even more caught up in the ideological struggle. Although much more will be said about the role of Berlin later, it is important to emphasize here that the Cold War unquestionably shaped and defined American attitudes toward Berlin and Berliners from the beginning. For example, the results of the municipal elections in late 1946, in which Berliners voted overwhelmingly against the newly formed Communist Party, proved a welcome surprise to many commentators. The State Department found nearly unanimous the view that the results signaled a vote against Russia and demonstrated that "when people have a chance to vote in free elections, they reject Communism." Commentators for the *Christian Science Monitor,* the *Des Moines Register,* the *Nation,* and the *St. Louis Dispatch* argued that Berliner bravery represented a "challenge" to the West to prove that democracy would pay off for the German city.[11]

For American commentators and policymakers alike, the U.S. decision to stay in Berlin after the Soviet cut off ground transportation to the western part of the city in 1948 was based purely on factors relating to the Cold War. Militarily it was untenable. Economically it made no sense. Only in the context of Cold War politics could the decision to airlift tons of food into Berlin daily be greeted with such overwhelming support in the United States. Even from the beginning of Soviet harassment, American commentators urged policymakers to stand firm. As policymakers contemplated Soviet action in the face of currency reform, U.S. observers counseled determination. And once the Soviets announced the blockade, American support for staying in Berlin was overwhelming. Elmer Davis said that Berlin represented the "struggle for Europe." The *Wall Street Journal* argued that "we ought to have learned from Hitler that nothing is gained by appeasing hungry power." The *Milwaukee Journal* announced that "General Clay will have the backing of every real American when he says that the only way to push our troops out is by battle." Over the next year, support for West Berlin stayed high. The National Opinion Research Center found that 79 percent of Americans preferred to stay rather than "avoid trouble." What's more, 75 percent of respondents favored force if necessary to supply food and coal to "people in our part of Berlin."[12]

Although the plan for West Germany was conceived before the Berlin Blockade, the blockade and subsequent airlift proved important in their roles as midwives. During the blockade, an unpublished survey reported that 80 percent of Americans who had developed an opinion on the matter supported the plan to create a West German state. The blockade also helped convince Americans that Germany would not start another war within the next twenty years. By September 1949, a few months after the end of the blockade, the State Department reported a "strong majority for the various measures taken during the past eighteen months in the western zones" that would culminate "in the establishment of a Federal Republic."[13]

The Cold War context helped gather American support for the West German state, but doubts lingered about the readiness of Germans for complete independence. In the summer of 1949, for example, Gallup found that less than a third of Americans believed that the people of Germany could be trusted to govern themselves in a democratic way. This sentiment was shared by American opinion makers. A majority backed the creation of the Federal Republic, but a majority also supported limiting its sovereignty. The State Department reported that most "spokesmen favor returning to Germans a considerable degree of self-government, but support the retention of Allied controls over such vital matters as security, disarmament and foreign affairs." Such restraint seemed appropriate, especially given the alarm in some quarters over renewed German nationalism.[14]

The question of German rearmament highlights this caution but also underscores the power of the Cold War context to affect American perceptions. In May 1950, a majority of American respondents to a Gallup poll were against German rearmament. When told that the Soviet Union was building an army in East Germany later that year, however, over 70 percent of Americans favored the creation of a West German army. Germany's willingness to participate in the European Defense Community (EDC) and France's hand-wringing regarding the proposed organization furthered American support for the Germans. American commentators lamented France's "progressive decline in European leadership." They saw French "weakness" and "instability" constituting "a grave problem for the Atlantic Alliance." Public reaction against the French refusal to ratify the EDC was swift and decidedly in favor of the Germans, as American commentators blamed the "shortsightedness" of France and worried about the effect of its rejection on Adenauer. In the fall of 1954, Americans indicated a strong preference for Germany over France. According to a Gallup poll, a majority of Americans had a favorable attitude toward Germany, while almost two-thirds had a negative opinion of France.[15]

German willingness to help shoulder the burden in the struggle against the Soviet Union helped cement the Cold war narrative, so much so that by the time of France's rejection of the EDC serious noise was already being made about full German independence. A Senate resolution on German sovereignty was favorably received that year, and it was in this context that the movement in Congress to return German assets was accelerated. The French rejection of the EDC only spurred this movement along. "Now the blow has been delivered," the *Baltimore Sun* declared, "a search must be made for a second-best plan. A way must be found toward sovereignty for a Bonn republic still tied, in some way, into security arrangements with [the] rest of [the] West." In October 1954, a Gallup poll indicated that Americans felt that West Germans should be granted their sovereignty, and when it came in 1955, many Americans hailed it with gratitude and joy. Congressional leaders on both sides of the aisle welcomed West Germany into the "family of free nations." The *Chicago Sun-Times* opined, "There is every reason to believe we can place full reliance in our new West German allies in the struggle against communism—militarily and ideologically." In November 1955, ten years after the conclusion of the bloodiest war in history, an overwhelming majority of Americans stated that they would like to see Germany, the country that had started the war in Europe, reunified.[16]

As indicated by evidence of public opinion from the early Cold War period, the emerging Cold War played a decisive role in shaping how Americans viewed the Federal Republic of Germany. The anticommunism of the hardening Cold War consensus offered a powerful context for framing the German people as allies against the Soviet menace, a framework that other elements of representations of Germans would build on.

"The Center of Totalitarianism Is in Russia"

At the same time that the Cold War was shaping American attitudes toward Germany, Germany was shaping American attitudes toward the Cold War. As we have seen, Germany helped influence U.S. perceptions of the Soviet Union during the 1930s, a time in which many Americans equated Nazi fascism and Soviet communism under the general term "red fascism" and drew parallels between the two in their leaders and their economic, domestic, and foreign policies. After a brief hiatus during the Second World War, in which Americans were encouraged to divorce the Soviet Union from Nazi Germany for the sake of the Grand Alliance, Americans revived the concept during the Cold War. Over the next several years, totalitarianism became a major category for interpreting the communist menace in light of the Nazi experience.[17]

To a large extent, it should come as no surprise that the concept of totalitarianism reasserted itself so rapidly. After all, totalitarianism fit in neatly with long-standing traditions in American culture. In the broader narrative of the American nation, Nazism and Soviet communism represented only the latest chapters in the United States' epic struggle with authoritarianism. Beginning in the seventeenth century with Puritan John Winthrop's telling characterization of America as the "city upon a hill," Americans urged European governments to overthrow their despotic governments and institute American-style democracy and freedom. With the onset of the Cold War, America's more proactive stance of working in the world to advance the causes of freedom, first articulated in the American entry into World War I and later revived in World War II, became a permanent condition of both American foreign policy and American identity. In this broader narrative, oppositional Nazi Germany became a part of Western history, not just German history. As totalitarianism emerged as one of the central pillars of the Cold War consensus, representations of Germany played an important function in affirming and supporting the overall edifice.[18]

And so as Americans grew increasingly concerned about Soviet behavior in the last few months of war, Germany proved crucial to the revival of totalitarianism as a category of analysis. In the spring of 1945, Eugene Lyons, the former editor of *American Mercury,* wrote, "Now that Fascism in Italy and Germany is being destroyed, the center of totalitarianism is in Russia." Acting Secretary of State Joseph Grew told President Truman in the summer of 1945, "Communists have the same attitude as Goebbels did—that the civil liberties of the democracies are convenient instruments for Communists to facilitate their tearing down the structure of the state and thereafter abolishing civil rights." Congressmen criticized the Soviet Union by comparing it to Nazi Germany. James Eastland of Mississippi spoke for many when he said, "Tales of totalitarianism, cruelty and oppression are leaking out of Europe. The very things we fought to exterminate, the very things we abhor, the very things the American people loathe, and things we were assured would be crushed are now in control."[19]

Over the course of the next few years, the concept increasingly dominated American discourse about the emerging Cold War. From 1945 to 1950, as Abbott Gleason has argued, "the idea that the United States had to meet the totalitarian challenge came to hold undisputed sway as the key to America's future and had its most direct influence on American political thought and foreign policy." In the most important intellectual works on totalitarianism, Nazi Germany played a significant role. Although George Orwell's famous dystopian novel *1984* never referred explicitly to Nazi Germany or Soviet Russia, *Life*'s editors, like others, understood Big Brother, the central totalitarian figure, as the "mating" of Joseph Stalin and Adolf Hitler. Germany's centrality to the concept was evident in one of the most important political and philosophical tracts of the postwar period, Hannah Arendt's *The Origins of Totalitarianism*. Moved by the horrors of the concentration camps, Arendt began work on the book in 1945. Her avowed aim was to "find out the main elements of Nazism, to trace them back and to discover the underlying real political problems." It was not until 1947, after the Cold War had begun in earnest, that she concluded that Soviet totalitarianism would constitute a major portion of the work. For her, the primary link between Nazi Germany and the Soviet Union was the systematic use of terror by the state, as epitomized by the concentration camp. When the book was published in 1951, the earlier purpose of her work was obvious to many reviewers, who contrasted her sure grasp of events in Germany with her shaky handling of the Soviet Union. Arendt's *The Origins of Totalitarianism* was perhaps the defining work on the subject, and the book's emphasis on Nazi Germany confirmed the importance of the German experience to the overall concept.[20]

Much of the literature on the concept of totalitarianism has stressed how it enabled Americans to transfer their anger from Nazi Germany to the Soviet Union. As Peter Novick put it, "Whatever the theory's analytical merits, in the 1940s and 1950s it performed admirable ideological service in denying what to the untutored eye was a dramatic reversal of alliances. It only *seemed* that way, the theory asserted; in fact the cold

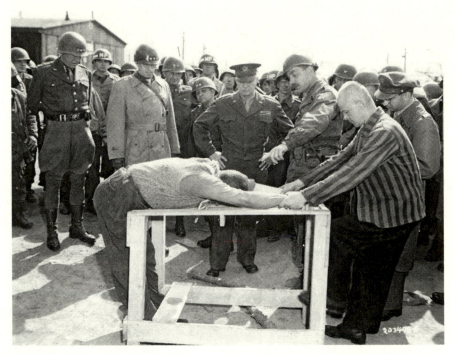

General Dwight D. Eisenhower observes survivors of a concentration camp demonstrate methods of torture (1945). (National Archives)

war was, from the standpoint of the West, a continuation of World War II; against the transcendent enemy, totalitarianism, first in its Nazi, then its Soviet version." But at the same time that Germany's past was shaping present-day understandings of the Soviet Union through totalitarianism, the Soviet Union's present was shaping understandings of Germany's past. In other words, as Americans used totalitarianism to indict the Soviet Union, they also used it to absolve the German people. As Novick notes, totalitarianism "pointed toward a plenary indulgence" for the German people because the concept argued that "opposition within the totalitarian state was impossible" and thus "even active support of the Nazi program could not be considered criminal."[21]

In particular, totalitarianism stressed the guilt of ruling cliques and the relative innocence of general populations. In the case of Germany, this led naturally to the conclusion that the German people should be absolved for the sins of the Nazi regime. For example, a month after the liberation of the concentration camps, *Time* magazine warned against viewing them as "a German crime," encouraging its readers instead to understand them as the product of totalitarianism. In 1948 President Lewis H. Brown of the Johns-Manville Corporation claimed that the "Russian people, like the German people do not want to rule the world, but they are helpless slaves of the ruling clique that dominates the people through fear and terror, through concentration camps, and secret police and through the whole mechanism of totalitarianism."[22]

Indeed, as if to drive this point home, conservatives in the United States constantly worried about the possibility of totalitarianism in America through "creeping socialism." Friedrich Hayek's *Road to Serfdom* emphasized, according to Gleason, the "slippery slope that allegedly led from almost all forms and degrees of economic planning to totalitarianism." When Truman offered his national health care plan to Americans, Dr. Morris Fishbein of the *American Medical Association Journal* wrote that the measure was "the first step toward a regimentation of utilities, of industries, of finance, and eventually of labor itself. This is the kind of regimentation that led to totalitarianism in Germany and the downfall of that nation." The plans of Henry Wallace were subject to similar criticisms. Ayn Rand's *Atlas Shrugged* at the end of the 1950s depicted an America in the grip of "looters" who sought to deprive able people of their livelihoods, possessions, and souls—all in the name of the "people."[23]

"Rubble Women"

While the concept of totalitarianism provided an intellectual justification for supporting the Cold War narrative, images of rubble and women offered an emotional rationale for sympathizing with the plight of Germans. Both the land and its people inspired pity in many Americans. For Americans who had visited Germany before the war, the postwar landscape was hard to fathom. Germany had been populated by thriving metropolises that both displayed the Old World charm of other major European cities and projected the frenetic sense of purpose and industry that characterized many of America's great urban centers. Now there was only rubble. Images of a destroyed, emasculated Germany encouraged Americans abroad and at home to feminize Germany and conceive of it as a land in need of masculine protection, thus affirming gender roles crucial to the Cold War consensus.

U.S. political visitors to Germany were appalled by the destruction. President Truman, arriving in Berlin for the Potsdam Conference in 1945, noted "the depressing sight" of "ruined buildings" and the "long, never-ending procession of old men, women, and children, wandering aimlessly along the autobahn and the country roads." After visiting the former capital, Arthur Millis said, "This is more like the face of the moon than any city I had ever imagined." In 1947, an unsympathetic delegation arrived in Germany to assess the needs of the people. After a tour, its members returned to support the military's reconstruction program, in General Lucius Clay's words, "to the last penny." Clay remembered that "they were touched by the conditions that they saw."[24]

The absolute devastation also had a major impact on many of the journalists who came to Germany. In an article for *Ladies' Home Journal,* Dorothy Thompson concluded, "Germany is finished." Saddened by the overwhelming destruction that he saw, a reporter for the *American Mercury* exclaimed, "This is the goddamndest place now that has probably ever existed since civilization began." "For the Germans the war is definitely over," he concluded. "They all want to be your friend and simply jump to oblige you if you want anything." "You can tell the Germans by their manner," a *Life* columnist remarked. "They are stunned and tired and beaten and frightened; they start when spoken to; they smile timidly, ingratiatingly and beg information most humbly." Many visitors were convinced that the Germans had suffered enough.[25]

Without question, the group most affected by the German plight was the American military. Not only were American troops immersed in this environment longer, many of them experienced it more sensually through fraternization with German women. Indeed, fraternization quickly emerged as one of the most vexing problems for the American military and concerned citizens back in the United States. Worried about the moral purity of the occupying mission, the U.S. military issued a ban on fraternization. It also tried to discourage inappropriate contact in other ways, such as through the creation of a new cartoon character to portray German women. Designed to discourage fraternization and promote abstinence, Veronica Dankeschon (or V.D. for short) was an unattractive, filthy, and disease-ridden figure looking for naïve American soldiers. Despite these measures, however, the military was forced, according to a journalist for the *American Mercury,* to "set up prophylactic depots all over the place."[26]

Back home, many Americans worried that contact with Germans threatened to impair the occupying mission. As J. P. O'Donnell of *Newsweek* observed, the GI's "judgment seems particularly blurred when referring to his own Gretchen." In an influential report, Richard Joseph, an interpreter during the war, and Waverley Root, author of *Secret History of War,* observed that American GIs preferred serving in Germany more than any other place because, among other things, they viewed the "Germans as the friendliest people in Europe." In particular, the two found that the young GIs had trouble reconciling the stories of atrocities that they heard with the civilians whom they met. Germans told the GIs that they were the "good Germans" who had been ruthlessly suppressed by Hitler. Now that the Americans had eliminated the Nazis, these helpful Germans concluded, the Germans and the Americans could be allies again. The results of this deception, Joseph and Root argued, could be disaster: "And now he [the American GI] is coming home, full of this feeling that his enemies are closer to him than his allies. He is returning by the millions, to take his opinion into every corner of the United States. . . . These impressions can have a tragic effect on our nation's destiny. . . . They could help a defeated, humiliated, desperate, vengeful Germany rise from its ashes for a third try at world domination." Despite such fears, constant violations forced the military to abandon the ban on fraternization and eventually relax restrictions against marriage.[27]

These encounters, recent scholarship has shown, did affect military perspectives of Germans. In their relationship with women, American soldiers were sensitized not only to the personal hardships of their companions but also to the suffering of their families. With this emphasis on material deprivation, Germany was domesticated and feminized in the eyes of American occupying forces. Replicating the turn to domesticity in the United States, American soldiers in Germany perceived themselves as responsible for providing for their fräuleins and surrogate families. In the words of Petra Goedde, "American GIs became providers and protectors, first literally for the women they dated, and later figuratively for what they perceived to be an emasculated, starving population."[28]

One of the best examples of the impact of Germans and Germany on visitors is the story behind the production of the Hollywood film *The Search,* which gives an insight into how dramatic and extensive the effect of this experience was. It also illustrates how the American military—

now, for the most part, in support of rehabilitating the German people—could further shape these impressions. Most important, the genesis of *The Search* illustrates how a visit to Germany could transform an individual's perception of the German people.

The film's origins can be traced to the summer of 1946, when Swiss producer Lazar Wechsler traveled to Hollywood and approached director Fred Zinnemann and writer Peter Viertel about producing a film about displaced persons in Germany. Impressed by both the "enormous generosity of Americans" and their "total lack of comprehension of the depth of human suffering in Europe," according to Zinnemann, Wechsler wanted to make a film that educated Americans on the plight of the most desperate of Europe's population. Zinnemann and Viertel, both promising talents in Hollywood, realized that the proposed film offered a vehicle for addressing many of the problems of American policy in Europe. Self-styled European leftists, they saw the film as an opportunity to express their position on a number of interlocking debates. In particular, they wanted to address the need to aid displaced persons in Europe, the ineptitude and corruption of the American occupying forces, and the unreconstructed nature of the German people.[29]

The first treatments that Zinnemann and Viertel developed reflected these desires. Both the initial plot, created jointly by the two in California, and the subsequent screenplay, written by Viertel in Switzerland, that fleshed out this design, sought to inform Americans at home about the tragedies occasioned by the American occupation in Germany. Viertel's screenplay told the story of Carl and Susan, two Czechoslovakian children, not related, who break out of a displaced persons (DP) camp somewhere in the Bavarian Alps. Wandering with no destination in mind, they fall in with a gang of homeless German children living wild. The leader, Ernst, keeps Carl and other potential troublemakers in line through displays of cruelty. On the outskirts of a German town, Ernst makes contact with an older man, "a cynical Nazi diehard, whose function in life has become the corrupt hindrance of the local military government." The man uses the children to wreak havoc on the occupation authorities. During a sabotage operation, Carl, blackmailed into his role by threats against Susan, is captured by the American military. The officer in charge, Patterson, takes pity on the boy. Moved by this unexpected act of kindness, Carl discloses the location of the group. The troublemakers are captured, and Susan is saved. Patterson takes Carl and Susan into his home.[30]

Patterson's encounter with Carl substantially complicates his life. Previously, Patterson had simply done his duty, thinking only of returning home. But, impressed by the courage and fortitude of the young boy, Patterson finds his priorities beginning to change. As Viertel wrote to Zinnemann while in Switzerland, "Carl begins to infuse the young officer with a completely new sense of what his work in Germany should be." At the same time, Carl and Susan's eruption into Patterson's life ruins his relationship with his live-in German "occupation wife," who declares that she does not want to keep the children. Shocked, Patterson tries to explain that he "feels it is his duty to look after these two human beings, who have endured so many hardships already." In Viertel's description:

> Their discussion becomes more heated, and the girl tells him bluntly that she has greater pity for German children now struggling against the odds of life. Patterson tells her he feels pity for them too, and then more discerningly he asks her why she makes this differentiation. . . . Is it perhaps a feeling of guilt that makes life with Carl and Susan intolerable for her? Guilt? The girl flings back at him . . . I don't believe in guilt. There are only those lucky enough to have won, and those that have been beaten. . . . Patterson is shocked again by this revelation. He never suspected that this woman was anything but an anti-Nazi. Now he sees the same signs of nationalism in her that he has seen in others.

Patterson leaves the German woman and takes the children to Czechoslovakia to look for their families. Unable to find them, Patterson leaves them with the proper authorities. Susan is adopted, but Carl, in a sensational scene, is revealed as a Jew. Told that he will be shipped to Palestine, Carl escapes and starts wandering again.[31]

Many of the themes that Viertel and Zinnemann had originally discussed in California were substantially developed by Viertel in Switzerland in this initial treatment. For one thing, it painted the Germans as incorrigible. Ernst, the leader of the German band of youths, keeps order through terror and cruelty. His contact in the city is a "Nazi diehard" dedicated to the disruption of the occupying army. Most of all, the character of the

Ivan Jandl on location in Germany shooting *The Search* (1948). (MGM Photofest ©MGM)

"occupation wife" strengthened the indictment against the depravity of the German people. Patterson's German lover had effectively fooled him into believing that she was different until she railed against the prospect of caring for children whom she did not believe worthy of attention.

Additionally, Viertel's screenplay depicts the American forces as corrupt. Patterson is an exception to the rule: Viertel made him an officer precisely because he believed that at the top of the military hierarchy "the love of the Germans [and] the cynicism toward Russia and the whole world" was most apparent. In contrast to his colleagues, Patterson "has to be sensitive, keenly aware of things that an intelligent human has to be sensitive [about], keenly aware of things that an intelligent human being feels." In sum, he wrote to Zinnemann, "He must be you and me without our left European background." By making Patterson unique in his motivation, insight, and intelligence, Viertel simultaneously condemned the present situation in Germany while offering his vision for its possible redemption.[32]

From California and New York, Zinnemann encouraged both the author and his script. As the date for his departure to Europe grew nearer, he became even more enthusiastic. At one point, he wrote Viertel that they had "a hell of a chance to make an honest and strong movie about Europe today," and that if they muffed it "both of us deserve to get our balls cut off." Zinnemann approved wholeheartedly of the story's thrust, even proposing the inclusion of more damning episodes. He suggested that Viertel include other GIs in the story—"some of whom could no doubt advance the popular theory about the Germans being the nicest, cleanest people in Europe and the most similar to Americans." He believed that the gang of kids should become "involved in some more sinister Nazi underground activity." He suggested that an "old guy" somewhere should "point out the growing parallel between 1919–1920 and today—when the first peace was sold out from under the nose of a fat, dumb and happy America, that wanted [nothing] but to go to sleep again, just like today." In all of this, however, he cautioned, the film must "be built up" with "great skill," otherwise "you'll get nothing but bitter resentment of the goddam foreigners and dirty Jews." Naturally, Viertel welcomed such comments and support. He wrote Zinnemann that he eagerly awaited his arrival.[33]

But Zinnemann changed his mind after coming to Europe. In a letter to his agent, Abe Lastfogel, he explained why he now agreed with the producer that Viertel must be replaced as screenwriter. France "had suffered tremendously from the war," he wrote, declaring that such destruction and suffering "cannot be explained unless you have seen the landscape and have looked into the eyes of the people you talk to." His visits to the displaced children's institutes were particularly heartbreaking. Thus, while he found Viertel's script a "good job of writing" and the "basis of a fair movie," Zinnemann believed that it "did not seem to encompass the tragedy of European children today." He told Lastfogel that he would have more of an idea of what kinds of themes to address in the film when he had traveled to Germany.[34]

After his experience there, Zinnemann's criticism of Viertel's work expanded. In a letter to William Wells, the film chief of the United Nations Recovery and Rehabilitation Administration (UNRRA), Zinnemann wrote that in his two weeks in the U.S. zone he "saw and heard things that constitute the most powerful kind of raw material for a motion picture." Along these lines, he informed Wells that Viertel's original story was rejected because "it seemed too remote from reality and . . . lacked inner truth and strength." He believed that "no one has the right to make a mediocre film about a subject of such tremendous importance." For Zinnemann, a director who prided himself on realistic films, Viertel's decision not to visit Germany again before writing the script consigned his story to inevitable failure.[35]

This issue was fleshed out even more clearly when an injured Viertel angrily wrote Zinnemann after parts of Zinnemann's letter appeared in *Variety.* In a serious lapse of judgment, Wells had forwarded Zinnemann's letter to the magazine, apparently in hopes of garnering free publicity. In addition to the expected concerns about friendship and privacy, Viertel's letter addressed Zinnemann's criticisms of his script. Viertel noted that in their meeting in Zurich, Zinnemann had said that the script was a "good job" yet "insufficient" but never that it "was removed from reality and lacking in inner strength and truth." "If you were suddenly outraged at my script, following your trip through Germany," Viertel suggested, "please remember that again you are dealing in concepts that are not fixed by anything more than opinion and sensitivity, and that what I put into my script was not a Hollywood pipedream, but the unforgettable pictures that my mind's eye collected while I was in Germany [two years earlier]." In essence, Viertel challenged Zinnemann's claim to realism, arguing that reality depended on perspective and experience, and that Zinnemann's perspective was no more "real" than his.[36]

Zinnemann's reply to Viertel suggests the extent to which his trip to Germany had influenced his opinion of Viertel's script and of Germany itself. Although he apologized for the public way in which his opinions had been aired, he defended the views themselves. He agreed that his comments in Zurich were "*exactly*" what he thought "*at the time.*" "It was not until late January," he wrote Viertel, "when I went to Germany for the first time and was literally hit over the head by things of enormous, you might say monstrous, emotional impact, that my feelings in regard to your script began to change." Zinnemann's experience in Germany validated his earlier belief that Viertel should have proceeded to Germany without delay, because there he saw and heard things "that defy the imagination of any essentially normal person, [no] matter how talented." The fact that Viertel had visited Germany two years earlier struck Zinnemann as irrelevant: "Germany as a whole is like an express train moving at full speed without an engineer." He believed that "the whole landscape has changed in those two years, the whole fabric, the whole psychological basis of existence, the whole climate." No one could understand the "insane, unnatural, non-human pattern of reactions, the psychological wreckage left lying around in the wake of recent history" or the "situations, incidents, characters that make up the witches cauldron called Germany" without "direct physical contact." One could not conflate the Germany of two years previously with the current Germany, he believed, without "losing the inner truth."[37]

Yet Zinnemann's own visit to Germany was heavily supervised, designed to provide a narrative of Germany that the army was interested in fostering. Prior to his dismissal, in fact, Viertel had warned Zinnemann about the ways in which Wechsler, the Swiss producer, and Theresa Bonney, an American war journalist, would color his experience in Germany. He believed that Wechsler, whose "approach" was "always from the top," "would get us entangled with more colonels and Generals." He wrote Zinnemann, "Believe me, if I've learned anything at all in the past four years, those are the boys that don't know nothing." He felt Bonney was even worse, calling her a "bullshit artist from way back," a "sort of an official army gal, decorated from a—— to elbow," and an "apologist for the US army." In his opinion, he and Zinnemann had to strike out on their own: "Alone we could mooch around the right places, and hear the truth instead of what they want us to hear." But in the end, Zinnemann dismissed Viertel's advice along with Viertel, and accompanied Bonney on his initial tour of Germany.[38]

Thus, when Zinnemann traveled to Germany in 1947, many of the men and women he encountered had already become convinced of the importance of rehabilitating the German people. Judging by Zinnemann's subsequent correspondence, he became well acquainted with these contacts, relying on them for information and even remaining in communication with a few after the film was completed. One army officer, for example, continued to write to Zinnemann after the director returned to Hollywood. This individual, known to posterity only as Dick, spoke frequently of personal and occupation issues. Most telling, perhaps, of the extent to which Zinnemann had become enmeshed within this system that he and Viertel had initially intended to denounce were the names of his good friend's wife and nanny. Dick often mentioned that his wife Gretchen and newborn Linda were doing well, the latter especially so under the "fanatically good care" of nanny Frau Niletz. Of Frau Niletz, Dick observed, "there are damn few like her either in Germany or back home."[39]

In the end, the restricted context in which Zinnemann visited Germany played a decisive role in shaping the film he created. *The Search* ultimately focused on the experiences of two displaced persons, a mother and her lost child. The American military, portrayed largely through the winning persona of actor Montgomery Clift, is angelic. As for the Germans, Zinnemann virtually removed them from the script altogether. There are only two direct references to the Germans, one when an UNRRA administrator excuses German boys who adopt other identities because they are "hungry, too." The final product, contrasted with Zinnemann's original ideas in collaboration with Viertel, makes clear that the director's stay in Europe fundamentally changed his mind regarding the nature of the German people.[40]

Reception of the film in official military quarters was reportedly quite positive. Dick wrote to Zinnemann that "all who have seen [the film] are happy," and that "our man in Frankfurt gave it a '4-handkerchief rating.'" He also claimed that "the ICD [International Control Division] people were greatly pleased with it as were the people at Eucom [European Command]." Lieutenant Colonel William Rogers of ICD verified this positive appraisal, adding that "there were no cuts necessary from a political standpoint." He concluded, "Everyone liked the spirit and the feel of the picture very, very much."[41]

As the production of *The Search* illustrates, visions of the landscape and people of Germany had a far-reaching impact. Faced with the devastation and impoverishment of a once advanced nation, many American visitors came to feminize the Germans and conceive of them as a people in need of protection. Images of Germany that made their way back to the United States had a similar effect, with Hollywood films such as *The Search* often serving as the vehicles.[42]

Indeed, a few Hollywood films were shot in Germany in the early years after the war. As with *The Search,* many of them tried to take advantage of their location to comment on the situation in Europe. *Berlin Express,* for example, was a plea for continued cooperation among the Allies. *The Big Lift* was a laudatory tale of the Berlin airlift that also sought to tackle issues of the German occupation. Billy Wilder's *A Foreign Affair* was a bitterly satirical indictment of American behavior in Germany. And *The Devil Makes Three,* the only avowed anti-German film of the era, tried to alert Americans to German revanchism. All found their messages subverted to an extent by images of rubble, women, or both.

Filmgoers found the German landscape in these films overpowering. As a movie reviewer for *Time* wrote about *Berlin Express,* the film is really two movies: "one in the background, the other in the foreground. The background is an album of postwar Germany: a series of malignantly beautiful photographs of rubbled cities, taken with a depth of focus that clarifies the year in every handful of dust. Unfortunately, the view of this film is frequently obstructed by the one in front of it." Another reviewer wrote that "shots of bombed out Berlin and Frankfurt alone make 'Berlin Express' worth the price of admission." A third observed that "the devastation left by Allied bombers is caught with striking fidelity by the camera: the sheer destruction is indeed appalling." Similarly, a reviewer of *The Search* reported that "the shocking background of ruined Germany is well—but not too well—photographed." A different reviewer of the film had difficulty in deciding which aspect of the film was most "stirring": the film's plot or the "shots of devastated Germany."[43]

But many critics found that the symbolic, moralizing plots of these films threatened to obscure the value of such scenes. One reviewer wrote that the message of *Berlin Express,* that world brotherhood is the antidote to world conflict, communicates a "truism that has not been widely disputed since the years of the Trojan War." Another found that the "film was elementary and confused when it came to the issues of national sover-

John Lund in *A Foreign Affair* (1948). (Paramount Pictures/Photofest © Paramount Pictures)

eignty, resurgent Naziism and world peace." The reviewer who lauded *The Search*'s camera work condemned the film as no more than a "fairy tale for old ladies to weep over." He concluded, "'The Search' manages only to be sentimental about a subject that demands anger and shame."[44]

Many reviewers assessed George Seaton's *The Big Lift* in a similar way.

Director Billy Wilder shooting *A Foreign Affair*. (Paramount Pictures/Photofest © Paramount Pictures)

Marlene Dietrich and Jean Arthur in *A Foreign Affair*. (Paramount Pictures/Photofest © Paramount Pictures)

Montgomery Clift and Cornell Borchers on location in Germany shooting *The Big Lift* (1950). (Photofest)

The Big Lift tells the story of two American GIs, Danny (Montgomery Clift) and Hank (Paul Douglas), stationed in Berlin during the Berlin Blockade and airlift. In the semirealist style popular at the time, the film depicts the measures undertaken by the occupation forces to feed and protect the citizens of Berlin. It also portrays the heroic actions of the Berliners in facing the staggering sacrifices involved. Reviewers praised the depiction of the airlift. Robert Hatch wrote in his write-up for the *New Republic* that the actors in those scenes "are naturally, wonderfully dexterous and casually ingratiating." As a reviewer for *Time* noted, the film is "at its best" as "an absorbing documentary of the airborne supply of Soviet-blockaded Berlin." As was the case with *The Berlin Express* and *The Search,* viewers praised the camera work, which "does full justice to the brooding ruins of Berlin."[45]

But all of this serves merely as backdrop for a morality play focusing on the relationships that Danny and Hank form with German women, and how these relationships reveal the problems in democratizing Germany. As Hatch remarked, the confused film made one point very clear: "Fliers should confine their activities to airplanes and leave politics and ethics to people equipped to deal with them." Many reviewers believed that the film's too-obvious symbolism threatened to wreck what value it possessed. One critic groaned at George Seaton's simplistic attempt "to reduce the meaning of it all to elementary terms, in an a-b-c kind of dialogue between the 'Kraut'-hating [Paul] Douglas and a pert fräulein." Another groused that Seaton "endeavored to give the illusion that these four [characters], as soldiers and their girls, are in truth generally symbolic of relations as they prevail." Another wrote that the film went really wrong "in having Douglas spout repeated primer-level sales talk for democracy at his girl friend," with the result being "clumsy propaganda in a movie that would be excellent propaganda without it."[46]

For some, images of the landscape in *A Foreign Affair* were more offensive than the risqué subject matter. The *Los Angeles Times* observed that "the film becomes one of violent contrasts—the ghastly destruction on the one hand, the feverish tormented life in a black market world where all values are distorted." Another reviewer wrote: "This comedy of American occupation is played out against the ruins of Berlin, which—as every filmgoer knows—are as photogenic as they are horrifying. . . . Any person of normal sensibilities who had never gone into a cinema before would be profoundly shocked, I believe, by *A Foreign Affair;* as indeed might the enthusiastic filmgoer if he were to find here, not Berlin, but Hiroshima as the vista for sparkling romance."[47]

Oddly enough, given Billy Wilder's reputation for pushing boundaries, his original aim was not to make an offensive film. Wilder ostensibly began *A Foreign Affair* with the intent of producing an acceptable piece on the reeducation of Germans. In the summer of 1945, while Wilder was in Berlin helping the U.S. government assess and denazify the German film industry, he imagined a film about an American GI who is "not too sure what the hell this war was all about" and the fräulein he enlightens and gives "something new to live for." He assured his superior that this would not be a sentimental film with "pompous messages" and a happy ending. Through witty dialogue and sophisticated writing, Wilder boasted, "you will find this 'entertainment' film the best propaganda yet."[48]

But over the course of the next several months, as Wilder continued his research in Germany, the film became something different—a biting indictment of the American occupation. The final film released in 1948 showed randy American soldiers running wild in the streets of Berlin. The primary character, Captain Pringle, carries on an affair with Erika von Schlütow, a seductive ex-Nazi, while trying to convince a prying congresswoman named Phoebe Frost, that fraternization is not a problem. By the end, Pringle (after learning the error of his ways) and Frost (after she is suitably feminized, or "defrosted") fall in love and leave von Schlütow behind. Because of the film's focus on these starkly different women—the virginal, innocent, and naïve Frost and the seductive, corrupt, and amoral von Schlütow—many scholars have, understandably, viewed this as an isolationist tale.[49]

Although contemporary viewers also focused on the female characters, they did not see them in terms of an isolationist/interventionist dichotomy. Instead, they viewed Jean Arthur's Frost as the comic center of the film and Marlene Dietrich's von Schlütow as the straight person symbolizing postwar Germany. The only German main character, von Schlütow was in many ways also the most sympathetic. Her cabaret songs, such as the famous "Black Market," describe a Germany hounded by hunger and desperation and taken advantage of by occupying forces. For many reviewers, her strong will to survive, not an inherent moral perfidy, explains her shifting alliances. In his review of the film, Bosley Crowther recalled Dietrich's previous role as a cabaret singer in *The Blue Angel* and found her current character to be "the same indestructible female who presumably rode the Nazi wave, slipped out the side door when it came crashing down and is now back in business again." The *Los Angeles Times* observed, "Miss Dietrich in her songs expresses the cynicism of the war's results," and Seymour Peck of the *New York Star* wrote that "there are moments in Miss Dietrich's performance when she gets across, possibly even more than . . . Wilder intended, the rottenness and desperation of people who live without scruples." And of course, Dietrich's sexual allure did not hurt reception of the film. After summarizing several reviews of the film, a writer for the *Hollywood Reporter* perhaps said it best when he wrote: "We haven't space to print all the reviewers' raves on the GREAT, GREAT grandma. But all inferred that any wise wolf would pass up Little Red Riding Hood for a grandma like the legsquisite Dietrich."[50]

Dietrich's von Schlütow represented a generation of women who were old enough during the war to be aware of and perhaps implicated in the

Nazi regime. But many images of fräuleins depicted a more innocent generation. Such was the case with Pier Angeli's character in MGM's 1952 *The Devil Makes Three,* in which the fräulein character played an even more subversive role. *The Devil Makes Three* was easily one of the most fervently anti-Nazi films produced during the 1950s, and the only one to deal with the American fear of revived nationalism in the Federal Republic.

Produced by Richard Goldstone and directed by Andrew Marton, *The Devil Makes Three* was based on an actual case history taken from the files of the Air Force Criminal Investigation Division (USAFCID). Lawrence Bachman, then stationed with the High Commission for Occupied Germany (HICOG), wrote the original story of a U.S. Air Force officer who was approached by a smuggling ring in Germany. As the case file revealed, the officer alerted his superiors, who told him to pretend to collude with the plot. The smugglers outfitted the officer's car with several small compartments in which they placed ball bearings and other contraband items. Over time, these items disappeared, but the officer was still paid to drive his car and leave it at a certain place for a certain period of time. One day he had an accident and discovered that his original bumper had been replaced with one fashioned from gold. The CID figured out that the smugglers had been smuggling gold out of Germany for some time and arrested the criminals.[51]

From May to June 1951, Jerry Davis of MGM conducted research in Berlin, Frankfurt, Wiesbaden, and Munich. What he found validated the general contours of Bachman's story. Verifying the aims and methods of the Criminal Investigation Division, he discovered that it had been particularly involved in cleaning up the black market in Germany. In the case of this particular story, Davis was satisfied that the GIs involved were effectively duped by the smugglers, not criminals themselves. The smugglers consisted mainly of DPs out of Poland. Davis noted that "they were completely apolitical. Their only object was to make money."[52]

In translating this story to the screen, Davis and director Andrew Marton dramatized the film in a way that promoted the world war narrative. They transformed the smugglers from apolitical Polish displaced persons to fanatic neo-Nazis. They changed the purpose of the smuggling ring from a moneymaking operation to a means of funding a neo-Nazi rebirth in Germany. And in a particularly nasty twist, the story line connected the smuggled gold to its original owners—Jews murdered in the concentration camps. They cast Gene Kelly to play the air force officer, and created a character played by Pier Angeli, a misguided German girl who ensnares Kelly in the smuggling ring.[53]

According to Richard Goldstone, the filmmakers had to agree to portray the American reconstruction effort in Germany in a positive light in order to secure the State Department's approval and assistance in making the film. But the State Department, worried that the producer and director might make changes to the script during filming, instructed HICOG to keep a close eye on them.[54]

In an oral history interview, Goldstone related that he and his crew felt a great deal of anger toward the Germans while making the film: "A number of us, of course, were Jews, and there was Hans Habe . . . , there was Bundy Marton, myself, Henry Henigson, the production manager, and I think our own feelings were very ambivalent. We were cynical of the good will that we were being shown [by the Germans]. I think we were angry and I think all of these feelings are reflected in the film itself." Later, Goldstone agreed that he, the screenwriter, and the director "viewed the Germans as gangsters who are really in need of serious supervision." In the making of many scenes, especially the last one, in which American military police guards chase Nazis over a frozen lake, Goldstone felt that the watching crowds were "definitely hostile to us."[55]

Yet the filmmakers' anger was not apparent to viewers of *The Devil Makes Three*. Although all of the reviewers recognized the presence of neo-Nazis in the film, none judged the movie to be particularly anti-German. Instead, most focused on the protective relationship that develops between the American flier and the beautiful fräulein. One reviewer of this "sympathetic" tale wrote that Kelly, after his shock at finding Angeli's character employed as a B-girl, played "the protective friend turned lover with restraint and complete persuasion." The review went on to say that the plot about the neo-Nazis, the major issue as far as its producers were concerned, "detracts from the serious and poignant aspects of the story." The reviewer in *Commonweal* even suggested that Kelly is motivated by "guilt feelings." A major reason for this common interpretation was Angeli, who played her role with "appealing, girlish charm" and "with emotional shadings that assure its believability." In large part because of the romantic relationship at the center of the movie, reviewers did not understand the theme of the film as Richard Goldstone had intended: that Germans are "gangsters" in "need of serious supervision." Rather, critics came to the conclusion that "Germans are people," as the *Saturday Evening Post* argued. "During the war," it continued, "it may have been necessary to bomb and destroy indiscriminately, but now, the war over, one must discover them as individuals." The reviewer argued that some Germans were die-hard Nazis, but most were coerced into supporting the system. The report by the West German consul general in Chicago found this interpretation to be common among Americans. This reception of *The Devil Makes Three* illustrates the power of German fräuleins to shape American perceptions at home.[56]

The American enchantment with and protective feelings toward German women could take on a darker hue, however. One of the most notorious effects of the *Truemmerfrauen* (rubble women) images was to suggest to Americans that the streets of Germany were choked with beautiful, desperate women. Confronted with pictures of gorgeous fräuleins in American movies, magazines, and other major media outlets, some American men sought out women in Germany. Several men envisioned a Germany populated by so many beautiful women that they could have their pick. One audacious individual wrote to Ernst Reuter, the governing mayor of West Berlin, and asked him to place a personal ad in the newspaper for him. He told Reuter that he was thirty-two years old, possessed of a good income, and looking for a girl about five feet two with a "reasonably good figure and looks." Another suitor, approximately sixty years old, sought a "young good looking girl or widow in the age bracket of 22 to 30." The widower insisted that "she must be well built and good looking" and informed Reuter that he would appreciate it "if you would have several write to me and send their photos so that I can have my pick."[57]

Thankfully, evidence of such disturbing attitudes is relatively rare. Most Americans moved by images of rubble and women did not attempt to procure a love fräulein. Instead, many who wanted to help Germans sent aid. CRALOG (Council of Relief Agencies Licensed to Operate in Germany) began operations in April 1946 and was followed in June by CARE (Co-operative of American Remittances in Europe). By the next year over 60 percent of CARE packages went to Germany. Moved by the images of rubble and women they saw in the United States, many Americans sought to help through sending material support.[58]

"Model T of the Jet Age"

Anticommunism, totalitarianism, and images of rubble and women helped establish Germany's central role in America's Cold War consensus. Historians have described this widespread consensus during the 1950s as one that revered American-style democracy and capitalism while loathing Soviet communism. Scholars such as Arthur Schlesinger Jr. wrote triumphalist tracts that extolled the virtues of the American system of political and economic governance, while historians like Louis Hartz minimized conflict in American history and highlighted continuity in the nation's leaders from George Washington to Franklin Roosevelt. According to this prevailing view, American civilization was the greatest the world had ever known.[59]

A central facet of the Cold War was the U.S. desire to spread this superior form of civilization around the world. John Fousek persuasively argues that this impulse sprang from an ideology of "American nationalist globalism." Indeed, in terms of ideological conflict, this was the central issue: which system—American capitalism or Soviet communism—was the superior form of organizing political and economic activity. In this regard, Germany was an important element of America's Cold war consensus. Because the United States had unprecedented power and authority to remake West German society, and because the Soviets were in a similar position with regard to their sphere of occupation, the Federal Republic became a litmus test for how effectively American policies, ideas, and dreams could be translated to other nations and regions. Put another way, a widespread belief that Germany represented a successful example of Americanization would further the faith of many in the United States in the American way of life.[60]

Americans took particular pride in Germany's postwar "economic miracle." One American observer noted that while *miracle* was the only word to describe the amazing reversal in economic fortune, the phenomenon was "readily explainable"; it was thanks to American intervention. Several praised the currency reform that the United States spearheaded in the western zone. Many also claimed that the Marshall Plan deserved recognition for providing the necessary stimulus, which *Newsweek* claimed had "sparked the industrial revival." *U.S. News and World Report* asserted that aid from the European Recovery Plan "laid the foundation for recovery."[61]

Mainstream publications were quick to claim U.S. influence on the policies of the Federal Republic. *Newsweek* argued that the "chief factor in the opinion of many observers has been the application of the old-fashioned, liberal economic principles of free enterprise to Germany's economy." *U.S. News and World Report* concurred, noting that "a policy of free enterprise unleashed the constructive forces of private initiative and self-interest in the smashed country." *Time* made explicit what was implicit in the other reports: "Germany's rebirth is the kind of economic miracle Americans can understand. At a time when other European nations were leaning toward socialism, Germany plumped for free enterprise." By appropriating "free enterprise" as an American value, major American observers trumpeted Germany's economic miracle as an American success.[62]

Americans also did this by appropriating the value of "hard work." Harkening back to positive appraisals of German industry from the eighteenth and nineteenth centuries, Americans repeatedly praised the physical efforts of Germans in discussions of Germany's economic situation. *Time* said the chief ingredient in Germany's success was "hard work." *U.S. News and World Report* hailed the "determined drive and hard work" of Germans in rebuilding their country. In describing the personality of Heinz Nordhoff, the head of Volkswagen, as "an engineer salesman who combines the drive (and fluent English) of an American with the perseverance of a German," *Time* again made explicit what was implicit elsewhere: hard work was a laudable value that Americans champion around the world.[63]

American observers also approvingly noted the growing consumer culture in Germany. One reporter noted that economic minister Ludwig Erhard, a champion of free enterprise and the father of the economic miracle, "prodded manufacturers to stimulate a demand for goods which the Germans persist in regarding as luxuries but which the Economic Minister thinks they should view as necessities—particularly long-term household goods such as electric refrigerators and gas stoves." In his pitch, this reporter remarked, he was "fond of pointing to the U.S. as an example." *Time* approvingly recorded that German "shops are loaded with consumer goods and crowded with substantial looking buyers." The *Saturday Evening Post* ridiculed the rhetoric of Otto John, the Western secret service head who defected to East Germany in the mid-1950s and criticized West

Germans for, among other things, "plunging into debt by buying luxuries on the installment plan." The *Post* had a field day mocking John's statement that in East Germany "pensioners . . . are at least spared having to walk by shop windows filled with tempting goods."[64]

One German product in particular caught the eye of Americans. The success of the Volkswagen Beetle, many felt, was an American success story. The narrative presented the kind of rags-to-riches story that Americans loved. Hitler had founded Volkswagen to produce "people's cars"; in crushing Hitler's dream for a thousand-year reich, the Allies also destroyed his ambition for Volkswagen. But enter the aforementioned Heinz Nordhoff, a German trained in the United States and head of a subsidiary of General Motors. British authorities induced Nordhoff to take over Volkswagen production in their zone, and by 1953, Nordhoff's twenty thousand employees were finishing a Beetle every eighty seconds. That same year, Volkswagen sold almost two hundred thousand cars in eighty-three countries. *Time* credited Nordhoff's American experience for Volkswagen's success: "Because of his years of American training in G.M. Opel, Nordhoff did not wear the pompous, punctilious air of German industry's traditional Herr Generaldirektor. He spent hours on the production line, talking to workers and explaining what he was trying to do." *U.S. News and World Report* went one step further in appropriating the success story; it helped popularize that notion that the VW beetle was the "model T of the Jet Age."[65]

Of all the stories of success and heroism that Americans found in Germany, however, none were appropriated more frequently and with such enthusiasm as those that involved the former capital of the Third Reich.

"My Fight Too"

For the American people, Berlin became the defining symbol of the Cold War. It simplified an increasingly complex and global struggle by casting the United States as the heroic defender on the frontier of freedom and the Soviet Union as a despotic murderer that imposed a bankrupt and ineffective ideology on an unwilling populace. It also brought together many of the elements previously discussed in this chapter and portrayed them in a dramatic and highly visceral fashion. In this narrative that Berlin spun, West Berliners emerged as a strong, powerful people bravely fighting the totalitarianism of the Soviet Union just as many of its citizens had previously fought against the totalitarianism of Nazi Germany. In West Berliners' strength of purpose and willingness to stand up to the Soviet Union, many Americans fancied that they saw a reflection of themselves.

Major mainstream magazines spontaneously echoed the official emphasis on and interpretation of Berlin. The city revealed the superiority of Americanization and the West in a number of ways. First, the physical appearance of "gay bright" West Berlin, in contrast to the "drab dinginess" of East Berlin, demonstrated the better standard of living offered by capitalism. Second, the apparent similarity between East Germany's form of government and that of Nazi Germany illustrated the barbaric nature of communist governments. That people from East Germany and Berlin were leaving in droves for the West seemed to confirm both of these points. The fact that so many people chose to "vote with their feet" illustrated that the Cold War fundamentally was a choice between two systems and ways of life—and that the West was winning this contest for the hearts and minds of the people. All of this was communicated in simple, personal stories: kidnapped family members, divided streets, and military marches.

During the occupation, it was evident that American observers and journalists in Berlin focused more on present Soviet misconduct than past German sins. As *Newsweek* journalist James O' Donnell reported in 1946, "The four-power administration of the German capital inadvertently has given the Western Powers a city-sized glimpse of the tactics the Russians have applied to half a continent." In addressing the frequently cited factors for the apparent change in American GI attitudes toward Germans, O'Donnell in another article argued that Soviet activity in Berlin played more of a role than American fraternization with German women.[66]

Reinhold Niebuhr, one America's most important theologians and philosophers, became a staunch supporter of the policy of containment after his visit to Germany and Berlin during the occupation. In one article, he drew explicit links between Nazi totalitarianism and Soviet communism. "Russian truculence cannot be mitigated by further concessions," Niebuhr flatly stated. "Russia hopes to conquer the whole of Europe strategically and ideologically." Anyone who saw things differently suffered from "illusions similar to those held by the conservatives of another decade in regard to Nazism." The Russians, Niebuhr contended, sought to exploit the same weakness the Nazis had: the "reluctance of democracies to risk war." Thus the American policy should be one of firmness. And such firmness was especially needed in Germany, where the Soviets had already realized the importance of the German Question. In Berlin, the "heroic" refusal of socialists to merge with the Communist Party revealed that Germans could be counted on in America's struggle against Soviet totalitarianism. Niebuhr reported that one such "heroic anti-Nazi" had told him, "The rigor of our fight against Communism must be our penance for having allowed the Nazi tyranny to arise." To continue the fight, Niebuhr concluded, these good Germans needed sweeping economic reforms that could revitalize their industries.[67]

The behavior of Germans in West Berlin received extremely favorable press in the United States during the Berlin Blockade. Several articles on the crisis in Berlin were accompanied by stock images of men, women, and children with upturned, expectant faces, watching American and British planes come and go. Soon after the crisis began in June 1948, *Life* magazine, for example, included a special report on the situation in Berlin. One reporter in the city became reacquainted with a teenager, Siegfried, who had helped him conduct research when the Americans arrived in 1945. His encounter with the German teenager triggered memories of the Soviet occupying forces at that time: "These were the wild days when the men from Mongolia came to almost every house for a woman or a piece of pretty cloth and might be distracted by an electric light switch or a doorlock or a toilet in which they could stand barefooted and exultantly cheer the gurgling water and splash it on their dark and wondering eyes." This negative portrayal was juxtaposed with an extended discussion of the "Good Germans" (as the article's subheading read) now living in Germany. Heinrich Droms, sixty-year-old leader of a transport union, was a good example. "Between democracy and dictatorship, compromise is impossible," Droms informed *Life*. "We had 12 years of one. Now we're going to fight for the other. The Russians and the communists have no weapon, however terrible, that we have not learned about from the Nazis." Additionally, the article, drawing on the language of separation and division, contained a graphic depicting West Berlin surrounded by an imaginary wall.[68]

In these ways, the Berlin Blockade hardened the linkage between the Nazi past and the communist present. Even after the blockade was lifted,

American observers from the mass media continued to make the connections. The caption for photographs of East German police in the *New York Times Magazine* drew attention to their "Nazi-style uniforms." A *Time* correspondent interviewed a man named Depper shortly after the blockade was lifted. "Vote '*Ja*,' indeed," exclaimed Depper. "They pick a slate of their stooges and then ask you to vote yes so they can claim the stooges are democratically elected. The last time we had the choice between '*Ja*' and '*Nein*,' it was forced upon us by another great democracy named Adolf Hitler."[69]

Without question, the greatest booster of Berlin and Berliners in the American media was *Life* magazine. Throughout the early postwar period, the most popular news magazine in the United States carried a number of significant pieces that trumpeted the virtues of West Berliners and deplored the state of affairs in the East. In 1950, for example, *Life* published a substantial photo exposé of West Berlin. The cover was graced with the picture of a beautiful Berlin girl stroking a German shepherd, and emblazoned with the title "West Berlin: A Gay and Courageous City." Inside the article detailed the everyday exploits of average Berliners, beginning with Herr and Frau Fritz Kehl. Illustrated with a dramatic photo of the Kehls enjoying a quiet dinner in their bombed-out villa, the article stated that they were bravely optimistic even though "overshadowing their lives was grim knowledge that Russia surrounded them on every side." How, wondered *Life*, is it possible for the inhabitants of this "beleaguered island of freedom" to show such confidence "right on the doorstep of the power most feared by the free world?" The answer, it found, was threefold: the "Berliner's cocky, stubborn attitude," the fact that "he has already touched bottom," and the "confidence which the Allies built up by the Berlin airlift and the recent reinforcements." *Life* went on to document the ways in which these brave people strove to be like Americans. Additional photographs illustrated hardworking Germans, the Berliners' love for their pets, and the little vanities of women as they sought to make themselves look better through consumerism.[70]

At the same time, *Life* heavily underscored the negative aspects of East Berlin. In 1952, the magazine's reporters were allowed to photograph the tremendous building project taking place at Stalinalle in East Berlin. Rather than deliver the positive appraisal that the GDR's leadership was surely hoping for, *Life* used the opportunity as a springboard to criticize the methods and products of communism. Despite efforts to the contrary, communism "could not hide the fact that neither propaganda nor commissars' threats could keep people on the job." Even though it diverted massive amounts of capital from other areas in an effort to create a showcase of socialism, Stalinalle was founded on "slip-shod building methods" that exemplified the bankruptcy of communism.[71]

Thus it was unsurprising to *Life* that such a contrast between East and West would encourage citizens of the GDR to flee westward, and the magazine wasted no time in relating these adventures. In 1953, for example, it included an article on the harassment measures of the GDR and the Soviet Union. The article described common methods of traffic disruption such as tearing up tramlines, blocking streets with trees, and sabotaging S-Bahn lines. The effect of these measures, according to *Life,* was twofold: one, it induced a growing exodus from the East to the West, forty-one thousand in the last month alone; and two, it effectively constrained traffic between East and West, so much so that, in the evocative words of a *Life* correspondent, "the streets that mark the frontier between East and West become an eerie no man's land." Two years later, *Life* related the personal tale of the Schmidtkes, "an ordinary family" that "suffered most poignantly" when East German police abducted the mother and son after the family had fled to the West.[72]

By no means was *Life* the only publication to portray Berlin as the salvation of Germany and the West. After an extended tour of Western Europe, German expatriate Martin Gumpert wrote an article for the *American Scholar* on the conditions he found. Gumpert observed a "latent" crisis that gets "louder as one moves east; it cries in your ears in Germany; it screams in Berlin." He found that the Germans suffered from neurosis; they downplayed the terrible nature of their actions during the war by pointing to examples of American misconduct, such as the bombing of Hiroshima, as worse. He claimed that the average German was "full of contempt for the Western occupying powers," but wanted their presence because he was "full of fear of the Russians." The situation in Berlin, however, was different. "Berlin," he argued, was "the most reassuring place in Germany." Here he sensed a change, "the kind of change one ardently had hoped to discover in Germany elsewhere." The "lesson" he believed Berliners had learned would keep them "from the old German vice of self-treason." Gumpert found this hopeful because "Europe's fate is decided here, by the people of Berlin." West Berlin was vibrant, while East Berlin had the "old Hitler look of terror." He argued that the maintenance of this "show window of resistance within the Eastern area of distress" was "of the utmost vital importance for the life of all Europe." He ended his article with a plea of support for the good Germans.[73]

During the 1950s, Joseph Wechsberg began writing a series called "Letters from Berlin" for the *New Yorker* that provided an in-depth look at the lives of average Berliners. Wechsberg repeatedly drew contrasts between West Berlin and East Berlin and between West Berlin and other West German cities. West Berlin was much livelier than East Berlin, he found. In a visit to a theater in East Berlin in 1953, for example, he discovered that the "novelty" of visiting a communist country "wears off fast." The West Berliners were also beating the East in the competition to clean and rebuild. In considering differences between West Berlin and other West German cities, he observed that denazification was "less of a comedy here." In Wechsberg's rendition, West Berlin exemplified the best the Germans had to offer.[74]

Coverage of the major Berlin conflicts demonstrated the truths that Berlin ostensibly revealed. The forced march of East German youth during the religious week celebrating Pentecost (Whitsuntide) in 1950 (discussed in the previous chapter), for example, illustrated in a very real way the imposition of a totalitarian system on poor and defenseless children. For major American media outlets, the march itself confirmed two interrelated truths: one, little difference existed between communism and fascism; and two, communism, like its totalitarianism forebear, was bound to fail. Given the perceived militaristic nature of both regimes, few events could have evoked more comparisons than a military march. The major media outlets wasted little time in drawing similarities between the two, and the 29 May 1950 cover of *Newsweek* featured a severe-looking band of youths marching in lockstep above the caption "Red Nazism on the March." Keeping the focus on the parade itself, *Life* found that the Free German Youth "cheered Stalin and marched in a manner frighteningly reminiscent of Hitler's *Jugend*." *Time* reported that all Americans who witnessed the spectacle experienced a sickening sense of déjà vu. The youth march confirmed American beliefs about the relationship between fascism and communism.[75]

And still, though this sight was frightening to the West, it was quite apparent that the communist system was unsustainable. The march, although exuding order and power, appeared forced and unwanted. In a poignant and illustrative passage, *Life* reported that the "pinched suspicious" faces of the Free German Youth "revealed far more the gray and hopeless pressures that had driven them into uniforms again." Indeed, even more indicative of the shortcomings of the communist system were the extracurricular activities of the Free German Youth in the West. All of the major media outlets reported that East German youths stole across to the West, where they could enjoy the simple pleasures of capitalism. Terming Whitsuntide a "sodden flop," *Time* described AWOL East German youths gorging themselves on Western-style food and entertainment. Based on the actions of these defectors, *Time* concluded that the "Reds had trapped themselves into a severe propaganda defeat."[76]

The march on Whitsuntide also offered another opportunity for Americans to reaffirm the importance of standing firm in the face of totalitarianism. In a piece on the crisis, David Perlman and Seymour Freidin argued that the march on Whitsuntide was nothing less than a Soviet initiative designed to drive the West out of Berlin. An American failure in Berlin, they feared, would signal a weakening American resolve. It would also help convince the Germans that they should jump on the Soviet bandwagon. For Americans on the ground, Whitsuntide reaffirmed the practical importance of Berlin. Edward Page, chargé at Berlin, stated that the "vital importance of Berlin for both West and East [was] again emphasized," arguing that, for the West, Berlin "constitutes the most potent weapon against communism," while for the East, it "represents [a] continuing menace which must be neutralized [as] soon as possible."[77]

Nor was the significance of the East Berlin uprising of 1953 lost on the American press. The rebellion, in which East Berliners carried out a general strike only to be put down by Soviet tanks, appeared to illustrate the human spirit's desire to throw off the yoke of Soviet communism. The cover of *Newsweek* showed protesters marching under the Brandenberg Gate with the caption "Berlin Revolt: The Kremlin Is Shaken." The most significant passage concluded: "But the final victory belonged to these Germans. The men and boys hurling stones at tanks, burning Red flags, and attacking the Red Police demonstrated that force alone was not enough to break the human spirit. And they were able to fight the good fight in a showcase along the dividing line between West and East Berlin, where their heroism could stimulate the entire free world. For two days they showed the West how weak its enemy was and how strong it was—if it had the courage to use that strength."[78]

Life covered a funeral for eight men killed during the riot; 125,000 mourners attended. According to *Life,* the East Germans finally admitted that they made an "error" after "foolishly blaming the riots on western saboteurs," promising more housing, consumer goods, food, and freedom. *Newsweek* and the *New Republic* also carried significant pieces on the importance of the East Berlin uprisings.[79]

In response to these events and others, the media sought to clarify the importance and significance of Berlin for American citizens. An examination of the hundreds of letters that Americans sent to officials in West Berlin reveals that Americans responded favorably to these efforts. These letters demonstrate that Americans identified strongly with Berlin. Although a few writers mentioned Berlin's checkered past, these citizens took pains to place those events in the past. Now, they wrote, the Soviet Union is our common enemy. And the way that they described Soviet communism illustrates that they understood communism as an evil force that must be stopped. One writer believed that "communism will be 1000 times worse than Hitler and his gang and the terrible Gestapo." He went on to say that "documents and treaties didn't mean a thing to them any more than [they] did to Hitler." Another, believing that the Cold War was fundamentally the struggle between good and evil, wrote that brute force was the only way to deal with the Soviet Union: "The way to steer a dumb ox is to hit him right on the nose with a club."[80]

A uniquely illustrative depiction of the Soviet Union came from an American citizen who wrote to Reuter in 1950. In his letter of praise, this individual included a florid passage on what a picture of Stalin said to him:

Gaze upon me, observe my features closely. Look into my eyes; behind them. What do you see? An apparition perhaps; too real! The specter comes to life and his Nibs, upon being summoned from his quiet repose, gleefully stretches his netherworld body. And emitting putrid breath, he bombastically introduces himself. "How'dy Comrads." (A greeting to lost souls who wander into his domain; the fools!) I'm Lucifer, I live in Purgatory; I'm master of your destiny. I hate everything and everybody. My savage voice makes them tremble in terror. My baleful eyes cower and pierce their dazed brain. My barbed tail stings them with excruciating pain. My sharp horns gore and rip their tender bowels. Their agonizing shrieks are music to my grotesque ears. To gulp their gushing blood is ecstasy. I delight in tearing their mangled bodies with my cloven hoofs. It thrills me to crunch their broken bones with my venemous fangs. The nauseating odor of carrion facinates my carnal nostrils. The saliva drools from my hideous mouth, in anticipation. . . . What more can be said of the Communists' World Revolution. . . . Shall we worship the devil and his works?

The author mentioned that he had included this passage in a letter to the editor of *Reader's Digest.* It was, perhaps unsurprisingly, rejected. And yet his sentiments, while overwrought and overzealous, represented the feelings of many of his fellow citizens regarding the Soviet Union and its leaders.[81]

With this Cold War backdrop, West Berlin became the front line in the battle against evil for many Americans. A housewife expressed her personal gratitude to Berlin "because I am protected by your post on the frontier." A Pennsylvanian wrote Governing Mayor Willy Brandt that Germany is the "keystone country" just like Pennsylvania is the "keystone state," and that "the battle which you wage is one upon which the eyes of the world have been focused, with issues at stake that concern us all." An aspiring songwriter felt compelled to send along the sheet music for an original song entitled "Keep Freedom Everywhere!" Another correspondent viewed Berlin as the appropriate place to launch a "free world" symbol he had created, imploring Brandt to encourage those behind the iron curtain to chalk it on the walls and "embarrass and frustrate the communists."[82]

Often this love and respect for West Berlin extended to its governing mayors. A banker from Sioux City, Iowa, praised Ernst Reuter in 1951 for everything he had done for "Berlin and for the German people" and expressed thanks that "there are men of your calibre in Europe" during a time when democracy and freedom would be tested. The same sorts of sentiments were far more prevalent for Willy Brandt. A schoolteacher thanked Brandt for all he was doing for the world: "As long as I have the ability to teach I shall endeavor to impress upon my students the importance of the life and work of Willy Brandt." Another American congratulated Brandt on his reelection in 1958, offering his belief that "God himself inspired once more the overthrow of the Communist party." On a more personal note, an American wrote Brandt that "I have seldom had the pleasure of meeting anyone who at first acquaintance seemed more like the kind of man I should be proud to have for a son or younger brother." A former soldier wrote: "For the first time, in my entire thirty-six years on this most beloved earth, I am, for reasons which I cannot fathom, impelled to write this communication to a courageous, humane, and most patriotic personage."[83]

Indeed, a number of former soldiers wrote the governing mayor of West Berlin to let him know that the past was behind them. This ex-soldier said that he bore "no hatred" and that all U.S. soldiers of the past felt as he did. "For the first time in my life," he went on to say, "I want to tell someone, be he king or slave, tycoon or worker, rich or poor, that I am grateful for his devotion to duty in carrying on a fight WHICH IS IN REALITY MY FIGHT TOO." Another soldier wrote that while he was part of the occupation force in Germany he had worried about the "after-effects of the Nazi regime." Now his fears were allayed. "Perhaps Berlin cannot speak for Germany," he stated, "but I think and hope that Berlin answered that question for me in the days of the Luftbruecke [airlift]." For him, that was why Berlin was "so close to my heart." These soldiers suggested the power of Berlin to represent the nature of America's self-appointed struggle against evil.[84]

Heartfelt letters were not the only things that Americans sent to demonstrate support for Berlin. Moved by the depictions of Berlin in the mass media, many sent tangible items of support. Several sent CARE packages. One group of young men from California included a message saying that they had "the greatest respect and admiration for you and the people of Great Berlin and the way you have stood up to the Russian bully boys." The Fraternal Order of Eagles offered to send one hundred tons of food to West Berlin. Others earmarked their packages for the influx of refugees. One couple mailed fifteen boxes of used clothes and two specifically for Berlin/Steglitz High School. The Moorestown Rotary Club also collected and sent clothing in response to Ernst Reuter's "urgent plea."[85]

Others simply sent cash. Gus Petrit send two donations of $58.15 to Reuter, noting, "We're seeing quite some of Berlin on television these days besides reading our newspapers." Another was moved by a talk given by Reuter in Minneapolis and sent $5 to help in "this great fight for freedom." After reading an article on children in Berlin in the *Los Angeles Times,* a couple sent $5 "to help send some poor child on a much needed vacation." Many Americans clearly felt moved to give more than just encouraging words.[86]

Some were willing to give more than money, food, or used clothing. A number of Americans offered themselves to Berlin to help with the struggle for freedom. A former soldier who had lived in Germany during the years of occupation offered his services to the city a month after Khrushchev's ultimatum in 1958. He sought no financial compensation; he simply wished to aid Berlin in this battle with tyranny. Two boys at Malvern Prep School in Malvern, Pennsylvania, wrote Brandt asking if they could help. They said that they had planned to go straight to college, but after reading the 15 December issue of *Life* they wanted to do something more with their lives. "We are average American boys and therefore hate communism," they wrote. "To us, you are the paragon of a living, fighting resistance to the greatest danger in the world today." Some Americans envisioning Berlin as the front line of the fight against communism sought to defend liberty at its farthest outpost.[87]

Events in Berlin had a positive impact on the self-esteem of German Americans, which had been in tatters since the Great War. One American bragged to Reuter during the airlift that she was a genuine Berliner, baptized in the water of the Spree River. A student of German heritage wrote that people now looked on Germany with respect and admiration. "Today, unlike the past," he commented, "our German heritage produces feelings of proudness." During the Berlin Crisis, several Americans with the last name Brandt wrote to Brandt wondering if (and hoping that) they were related. Even dogs of German ancestry got in on the act. One woman, at the urging of her friends, sent a snapshot of her five-month-old dachshund to Brandt. She informed the governing mayor of West Berlin that in her "search for a fine German name" for her puppy she had taken the suggestion of a professor at the University of Tennessee that she call him after one of the most beloved figures in the United States—she named the pooch Willy Brandt.[88]

But for all of the power of Berlin to evoke a democratic ideal, a few still associated it with Nazi Germany. A sixteen-year-old boy of German descent wrote Reuter for information on "the former Nazi form of government under Adolf Hitler," noting that the material he had access to "was limited" and possessed "too much American influence" to enable him to "get the real meaning." He asked for more unbiased information. Others wrote to Berlin officials requesting memorabilia from the Nazi era. Although the link between Berlin and the Third Reich had been severely weakened, a few Americans still thought of Berlin in a world war context.[89]

In a similar vein, some Americans railed at the media's efforts to whitewash Berlin. Following *Life*'s feature on Berlin in 1950, for example, many subscribers responded negatively, invoking instead memories of World War II. John Maass of Los Angeles angrily wrote: "Millions of people are still homeless, hungry or crippled because of what the Berliners and their friends did to them." Rather than recall this unsavory past, *Life* thought it "ducky that the perfume and nightclub businesses in the unrepentant capital of the Third Reich are booming once again." Joseph Krinsky pointed out that "Berliners were also gay and brave when London was blitzed, when France was invaded and plundered, when innocent Lidice was destroyed without a trace and when thousands of peaceful, helpless people were killed in gas chambers and concentration camps." In an interesting commentary on the seeming flexibility of American sentiment, Eda Tevlin furiously argued that "one of these days *Life* will feature the 'gay Muscovites.'"[90]

But for the most part, Berlin offered a simple, powerful narrative. The German people resisted communism, and the Soviet Union was driven to extreme measures to protect its puppet regime. The American government, the German and Berlin governments, and the American media all interpreted and promoted events in Berlin the same way. The evidence suggests that mainstream Americans shared this interpretation of Germany. Although most Americans supported Berlin, however, a distinct community of memory devoted to the world war narrative endured.

"I Hate Germans"

Indeed, while the majority of Americans during the early years of the Cold War supported Germany, and an overwhelming number supported Berlin, a significant hard-core minority remained unconvinced. This memory community drew widely on different groups in the United States, including socialists, veterans, African Americans, and Jews in its ranks. No discernible pattern ties these disparate individuals together other than a shared memory of and unremitting antagonism toward Germans. As one American wrote to the German periodical *Der Speigel,* "I am delighted to inform you that I hate Germans, Germany and everything which your culture, as represented by your many aggressions through out your recorded history, represents." He continued that he taught his children to hate Germany, and sought to influence his friends and associates to act to destroy Germans, claiming that the Germans "have excluded themselves from the human race."[91]

Of all groups, however, American Jews were most successful in resisting the hegemonic power of the U.S. government, its allies, and Jewish groups' own leaders in forging a memory coalition in support of Germany's rehabilitation. Evidence suggests that many rank-and-file Jews refused to fall into lockstep with their organizations' efforts to whitewash Germany's past. At a meeting of the Detroit Jewish Community Council in 1951, to take one example, members balked at the desire of their leadership to sponsor the visit of West Berlin mayor Ernst Reuter to Detroit. "The discussion in favor of this motion reached an extremely high pitch," wrote one observer. "There was bitter criticism from the delegates who spoke, predicated in general on the following arguments: (1) It is too soon after Hitler for Jewish organizations to extend official friendship to a German official; (2) the fact that Reuter survived the Hitler regime must mean that he was not sufficiently anti-Nazi; (3) the personal sufferings of some of the delegates and their kind were set forth." Based on such reasoning (or such unreasoning, at least in the second argument), a motion to withdraw support was "passed overwhelmingly." In another example, this from 1955, students at Hebrew Union College publicly protested a concert in Cincinnati by the Berlin Philharmonic; they did this despite the fact that the Anti-Defamation League strongly discouraged them from taking such a stand.[92]

Cincinnati was in fact the site of one of the most disruptive and embarrassing blows to the efforts of memory activists on behalf of the Cold War narrative. In early 1951, Jewish leaders there became aware that their city fathers had proceeded with a plan to make Munich a "sister city" of Cincinnati. Incensed that their city would be so closely identified with the birthplace of Nazism, many swung behind a movement to stop the process. Fearful that such protests could endanger relations with the German people, the State Department sent Geoffrey Lewis of the Bureau of German Affairs to Cincinnati to argue its case. Lewis discouraged Cincinnati leaders from taking a course of action that appears "to the Germans to be a slap in the face, which could be used by Communists and other enemies of the United States as a propaganda weapon with the aim of convincing the Germans that the people of the United States have no interest in promoting democracy in Germany." Despite such a plea, the Jewish leadership insisted successfully that the city withdraw official recognition of any relations that independent groups might develop between the two communities.[93]

A few years later, when the U.S. government was beginning the ramp-up to the launch of Eisenhower's ambitious People-to-People Program, an American official telephoned a colleague in private industry to find out about the status of the Cincinnati-Munich negotiations. His source informed him that "certain elements in Cincinnati did not want this idea to progress," and that the "few gestures made by the Mayor's office have been done as a 'courtesy'—as a cover-up for a very embarrassing situation which the city got itself into." A follow-up visit to the city a month after Eisenhower kicked off the initiative confirmed the opposition. According to the visiting official, the mayor of Cincinnati, Charles P. Taft, was "very much opposed to an organized publicity campaign aimed at setting up Munich as a sister city of Cincinnati" because of "the consensus of opinion in Cincinnati regarding Munich." A similar dynamic played out ten years later, when Milwaukee, under the leadership of its mayor, considered affiliation with Munich. Loudly calling Munich the "greatest cesspool of crime the world has ever seen," local Jewish and Polish leaders effectively blocked the mayor's fledgling efforts to reach out to the German city. Cincinnati and Munich finally became sister cities in 1990.[94]

In more ways than one, the Cold War proved decisive in shaping American perceptions of Germany in the United States during this period. The unfolding drama of the developing struggle between the United States and the Soviet Union moved Americans to support the rehabilitation of Germany. The widespread popularity of the concept of totalitarianism in defining the Cold War encouraged Americans to excuse the German people for past crimes committed in their name. Images of rubble and women suggested that the German people were in need of defense against the Soviet menace. The popular belief that Germans were successfully Americanizing fueled American certitude in the ideological contest with the Soviet Union. And Berlin's growing power to symbolize the issues at stake in the Cold War convinced many Americans to stay and defend their part of the former capital of Germany, no matter the cost.

The success of the Cold War narrative was based on the notion of consensus. As we have seen, dissent from the mainstream position remained, and at times this dissent was effectively mobilized. But the overall point should not be lost: the new atmosphere of the Cold War shaped American attitudes in ways that encouraged the embrace and forgiveness of the German people. As long as mainstream Americans supported the Cold War posture, strategies, and foreign policies of their government, they also supported the Cold War narrative of the German people. In this way, the nature of American support for Germany was directly tied to Germany's role in the Cold War. As we shall see, this close relationship between American support for the Cold War and American support for Germany became particularly evident when the Cold War consensus itself begins to fracture during the 1960s.

4

"The Anti-German Wave"

Maintaining and Challenging Consensus in an Age of Chaos, 1959–1969

On 14 December 1961, in the Congress Hall of West Berlin, governing mayor of West Berlin Willy Brandt addressed an international assemblage of military figures, diplomats, and journalists in attendance for the world premiere of Stanley Kramer's controversial film *Judgment at Nuremberg*. Hoping to capitalize on the recent international tension surrounding the construction of the Berlin Wall a few months earlier, Kramer and United Artists spared no expense for the premiere, flying reporters in from around the world and inviting representatives from a hundred different nations stationed in the divided city. Among the attendees were General Lucius Clay, President Kennedy's personal representative in Berlin, Major General Albert Watson, the American commandant, twenty ambassadors from various countries, and officials of the Bonn government. As one American reporter put it, "Mr. Kramer and his associates found themselves in the ideal position of having an attraction and a locale of unparalleled interest." Warning this august audience that "it will be difficult for some of us to watch and hear this film," Brandt nevertheless agreed that Berlin, "as the center of spiritual conflict," was the best place to begin wrestling with Germany's past.[1]

Representatives from the American and West German governments had been aware of Kramer's plans for the premiere for months, and both sides had harbored concerns. In the short term, they feared that the film could have serious repercussions in a delicate international environment. The Berlin Wall had been constructed just five months earlier, and the city still seethed with hurt, anger, and discontent. At the same time, the trial of Adolf Eichmann, a former Nazi captured in Argentina for his role in the destruction of European Jewry, was rapidly reaching its conclusion in Israel, and the West German government was worried about its image in the world. For these reasons, Kramer's film was especially timely—and especially dangerous. As a film that addressed the guilt of the German people for their crimes against the Jews while at the same time suggesting that the Cold War, specifically the conflict over Berlin in the late 1940s, had helped whitewash that guilt, *Judgment at Nuremberg* could potentially threaten years of careful work.[2]

Moreover, German officials worried that the release of *Judgment at Nuremberg* was part of what they increasingly referred to as an *antideutsche Welle*, or anti-German wave, in the American mass media. During the late 1950s and early 1960s, many German observers detected a recognizable pattern of anti-German material coming from film, television, and the print media in the United States. In addition to *Judgment at Nuremberg*, officials cited the televised trial of Adolf Eichmann and the publication of William Shirer's *The Rise and Fall of the Third Reich* as major elements in this phenomenon. They feared that such programs and images would poison American attitudes toward the Federal Republic, with particular worry directed at the impact of these programs on America's youth.[3]

In this way, the world premiere of *Judgment at Nuremberg* in the Congress Hall of West Berlin dramatized the two conflicting narratives of the German people in a shifting context. On the one hand, the film about the Nuremberg trials threatened to resurrect world war narratives of the German people that painted them as arrogant, servile, cruel, and ultimately unrepentant for their crimes in World War II. On the other hand, the spectacle associated with the location and host of the premiere—West Berlin and its governing mayor, Willy Brandt—presented a Cold War narrative that portrayed the Germans as heroic people standing firm on the front line of the Cold War. This event served as an important marker in the ongoing conflict in American collective memory over the nature and meaning of the German people.

More specifically, the production and circulation of *Judgment at Nuremberg* foreshadowed a more difficult decade for those who supported

Children play amid the ruins of East Berlin (1961). (National Archives)

Cold War understandings of Germany's history. Triggered by events in West Germany that echoed Germany's unfavorable past, aided by apathy in the American government, and monitored (and occasionally abetted) by American Jewish organizations, an anti-German wave of cultural products spread across the American media landscape during the 1960s, according to observers in the West German government and the American Council on Germany. Inspired and framed by current events that reminded the world of Germany's past—swastika daubings and other anti-Semitic desecrations and manifestations in 1959, the Eichmann trial in 1960–1961, the debates over the extension of statutes for war crimes in West Germany in 1965, the surprising electoral success of the right-wing West German National Democratic Party (NPD) in 1966, and the appointment of Kurt Georg Kiesinger, a former member of the Nazi Party, to the highest office in West Germany that same year—a new discourse about Germany emerged in the 1960s that threatened the hard work of the West German government and its allies in rehabilitating Germany's image. With these reminders and a new attitude in Washington that questioned Cold War orthodoxy, major actors interested in representations of Germany saw space for new narratives of Germany. Still, although discursive space opened up to promote narratives more critical of Germany, major memory activists stopped short of an open break with the dominant narrative.

Memory activists also recognized and responded to the dominance of television. By 1965, 93 percent of American homes had a television set, and 22 percent had two or more. According to A. C. Nielsen, daily set use rose from 5.85 hours in 1963 to 6.5 hours in 1970. Now firmly entrenched as the dominant medium, television sought to offend as few as possible, offering bland and escapist programming during one of the most challenging decades in postwar American history. To the delight of the memory coalition in support of the Cold War narrative, television shied away from confrontation and criticism of American foreign policy, making its tasks easier. Still, at the same time, fictional portrayals of the Second World War witnessed a resurgence in American media, and particularly on American television, a phenomenon that Germans felt powerless to counteract.[4]

"Frontiers of Freedom from Viet-Nam to West Berlin"

As was the case during the previous decade, the U.S. government remained the most important actor in shaping images of Germany in the 1960s. But unlike the favorable American stance during 1950s, the U.S. attitude toward Germany cooled in the Kennedy and Johnson years. Several issues emerged during the decade that plagued German-American relations. The most important was the desire of both the Kennedy and Johnson administrations to push for détente with the Soviet Union. West German officials rightly feared that this meant a weakening American commitment to German reunification. Another issue was the American desire to see a revived West Germany share more of the burden for its own defense and the defense of Western Europe. Flowing from these two issues, the United States and the Federal Republic wrangled over policy concerns such as the Multilateral Force, the construction of the Berlin Wall, the limited test ban treaty, Vietnam, the U.S. balance of payment deficit, and the ascension of Kurt Kiesinger, a former Nazi, to the office of chancellor.[5]

In addition to these concrete issues, a more critical understanding of Germany's history within both administrations also contributed to the strained relationship. In their private debates, American officials, even

Kennedy and Johnson themselves, recalled Germany's past aggression in framing current foreign policy subjects. Despite this more critical private stance, however, these Democratic administrations did not depart significantly from their predecessors. In a country descending into chaos, Lyndon Johnson deployed the Cold War narrative to legitimize his foreign and domestic policies. Thus while Johnson was critical of the Germans in private, he often invoked Cold War victories in Germany and described current American foreign policy as spanning from "West Berlin to Vietnam." Indeed, despite these problems, as Thomas Schwartz has pointed out, the German-American relationship remained strong, and by the end of Johnson's tenure it was in better shape than at the beginning of the decade.[6]

A change in approach was apparent even before the Kennedy administration took power. By the end of the 1950s, a new cohort of Democratic politicians was questioning the state of German-American relations, specifically America's long-standing pledge to German reunification. Some Democrats who won congressional elections in 1958, such as William Fulbright, Mike Mansfield, and John F. Kennedy, criticized the Eisenhower administration for its Cold War inflexibility. JFK was particularly critical. In 1957, he censured American reliance on Adenauer, arguing that "the age of Adenauer is over." JFK also denounced the American pledge to German unification as an obstacle to improved U.S.-Soviet relations. In his 1960 campaign for the presidency, JFK claimed that German reunification was "certainly not in the cards for many years" and that Adenauer was "too rigid and unyielding to changing currents in European politics." A new course for a new administration was almost assured when a German Defense Ministry study about the consequences of a Kennedy victory was fed to the *Baltimore Sun*. Its headline was "Nixon More Acceptable to Germans."[7]

After Kennedy won the presidency, he and his administration maintained a cautious and suspicious attitude toward Germany's economic and political renewal. Kennedy did not mention Berlin or Germany in his inaugural address, an omission roundly criticized in both the German and American media. Kennedy tried to allay fears by saying that he did not want to "provoke either action or comment in the matter." Nevertheless, Averell Harriman announced in Berlin that the Kennedy administration would not bind itself to previous negotiations with Moscow, and Charles Bohlen acknowledged that everything was negotiable. More sympathetic to Willy Brandt and the Social Democratic Party, they feared that German conservatives might embark on an independent and dangerous course. In an interview with Nikita Khrushchev's son-in-law, Kennedy said that "as long as German forces are integrated into NATO . . . there is security for all. . . . Now if the situation changed, if Germany developed an atomic capability of its own, if it developed missiles or a strong national army that threatened war, then I would understand your concern and I would share it. After all, we have had two wars in Europe, as well as you." Reflecting this new tone in Washington, Kennedy's first meeting with Adenauer went very poorly.[8]

Kennedy's successor held similar attitudes toward the Federal Republic. Lyndon Johnson informed the Germans that he sympathized, to a degree, with Russian fears about Germany. In April 1964, he told a German magazine that Germans needed to consider the Soviet "point of view." In discussions about the Multilateral Force, an effort to create integrated nuclear forces to defend Europe, Johnson revealed that his ideas about nuclear sharing were motivated in large part by an intention to keep Germans in line. He told his advisors: "The Germans have gone off the reservation twice in our lifetimes, and we've got to make sure that doesn't happen again, that they don't go berserk." He told the British that "the object [in the Multilateral Force] was to keep Germans with us and keep their hand off the trigger." The British prime minister later told his cabinet that he was "surprised at the intensity of the President's anti-German feelings." In dealing with the balance of payments problem with the Germans, Johnson informed his speechwriter that "there's only one way to deal with the Germans. You keep patting them on the head and then every once in a while you kick them in the balls." He later informed John McCloy: "I know my Germans . . . I lived in Fredricksburg [Texas], grew up in Fredricksburg; they are a great people, but by God they are stingy as Hell."[9]

Kennedy and Johnson brought up Hitler and Nazis in public far more than did Truman and Eisenhower; but, despite their private misgivings, they did not invoke them to discuss present German-American relations. Rather, both used Cold War narratives of Hitler and Nazi Germany to reinforce their foreign and domestic policies. In foreign policy, Nazi Germany was used to defend the Cold War in general and the war in Vietnam in particular. In an interview with William Lawrence of ABC in December 1962, Kennedy invoked the specter of totalitarianism and championed the United States as "the great means of defending first the world against the Nazi threat, and since then against the Communist threat." Johnson explicitly deployed Hitler and Nazism to justify intervention in Vietnam in his famous "Peace without Conquest" speech of 1965. "The central lesson of our time is that the appetite of aggression is never satisfied," Johnson declared. "We must say in southeast Asia—as we did in Europe—in the words of the Bible: 'Hitherto shalt thou come, but no further.'" At a press conference in 1967, Johnson compared Hitler's invasion in Poland to "some big bully" who saw "a little child in this room who was trying to waddle across the floor" and "grabbed it by the hair and started stomping it." Maintaining that it was a mistake to allow this kind of violence to occur prior to American involvement in World War II, he averred that he would not allow it to happen in Vietnam.[10]

At the same time, Johnson tried to use Nazi imagery to defend his policies against critics on the right and the left. In his presidential election campaign of 1964, he equated Republican critics of American military readiness with Roosevelt's opponents during the war, claiming that they encouraged Hitler to bring on World War II "because he [Hitler] didn't think we could get ready or we were ready or we would do anything about it." He clumsily compared Barry Goldwater, his opponent in the election, with Hitler when he argued that twentieth-century leaders are so powerful that they must be responsible. "When Hitler found out that he could mash a button and make a decision" it turned out to be disastrous; "whose thumb will be close to that button" Johnson asked the American people, when "Moscow is calling?"[11]

Johnson also used images of Nazis to challenge opponents of the Vietnam War on the left. When asked in a press conference in May 1967 if "the general level of dissent throughout the Nation on Vietnam has reached a particularly critical point," Johnson pointed out that "eloquent voices" had argued against the draft "a few days before Pearl Harbor, after France had fallen, after Hitler had successfully performed the conquest of France." In comparing critics of the Vietnam War in 1967 to critics of military preparedness in 1941, Johnson suggested that pulling out of Vietnam could have disastrous consequences. In general, however, Johnson minimized the breadth of youth-driven antiwar dissent by remarking that similar concerns during World War II had proven to be groundless. "I remember the doubters who thought all of our youth were going to the dogs because of the sit-down movements."[12]

In reaffirming Cold War narratives of the German people in public, both the Kennedy and Johnson administrations put much greater emphasis on post–World War II events in Germany, and particularly on events in Berlin. Along these lines, the Democratic administrations of the 1960s made a sharper distinction between West Berlin and West Germany than had previous administrations. In his second presidential debate in 1960, Kennedy called Berlin "a test of our nerve and will" and "a test of our strength"; in the third, he stated that Berlin was a "commitment that we have to meet if we're going to protect the security of Western Europe." A State Department planning document on Germany and Berlin revealed the priorities of the Kennedy administration. The first three bullet points outlined the need to maintain the "presence and security of Western forces in," "the security and viability of," and "physical access to" West Berlin. It was not until the fourth point that maintaining the security of the Federal Republic was mentioned. According to a media report to the American people, Kennedy told Khrushchev as much in Vienna: "The security of Western Europe and therefore our own security are deeply involved in our presence and our access rights to West Berlin." In his famous July 1961 speech, in which he exhorted Americans to greater civil defense, Berlin lay at the center. Here he gave one of the best descriptions of the importance of Berlin to Americans: "It is more than a showcase of liberty, a symbol, an island of freedom in a Communist sea. It is even more than a link with the Free World, a beacon of hope behind the Iron Curtain, an escape hatch for refugees. West Berlin is all of that. But above all it has now become—as never before—the great place of Western courage and will, a focal point where our solemn commitments stretching back over the years since 1945, and Soviet ambitions now meet in basic confrontation."[13]

Berlin's value as a symbol of the Cold War only increased after the construction of the wall in August 1961. For policymakers in the Kennedy and Johnson administrations, the Berlin Wall represented a stark commentary on the nature of the Cold War: it hindered personal movement, that most basic of all freedoms, and the wall's very construction was an admission of failure on the part of the East German communist system to provide the basic necessities of life. The constant stream of stories about East German efforts to circumvent the wall and escape to the West provided a consistent source of pride and faith in the superiority of American capitalism. Then Vice President Johnson, after returning from his trip to Berlin in the wake of the construction of the wall, observed, "No person can see what we saw without deeply feeling the great responsibilities that America has to the people of West Berlin, and to humanity . . . and together we are going to march shoulder to shoulder to the end that freedom is preserved in the world." The next year Kennedy wrote to Senate and House Republicans: "There can be no disagreement among Americans, nor among free men anywhere else about the meaning of that wall. . . . It is important to peace and to the freedom of the brave people of West Berlin that it be understood in every capital that on this matter we, as a Nation, are united in our determination." Kennedy's steadfast insistence to remain in Berlin signaled his desire to protect the city—but his tacit acceptance of the wall reinforced the impression that he did not support German reunification (because the division of Berlin implied the division of Germany). Perhaps most telling, in his famous 1963 speech, Kennedy claimed to be a Berliner, not a German.[14]

Abroad, policymakers invoked Berlin in discussions with other leaders to highlight the righteous nature of America's mission in the world. For example, in an effort to court neutral India a few days before the erection of the Berlin Wall, Undersecretary Chester Bowles "underscored the vital importance" that the United States attached "to the right of the people of Berlin to self-determination" to Prime Minister Jawaharlal Nehru. Bowles claimed that the "difficulties" that the Soviet Union faced in central Europe "stemmed in large measure from the utter failure of the East German government under Ulbricht." Kennedy drew heavily on the Berlin Wall in a tour of Latin America promoting the Alliance for Progress and American-style economic reforms. In Caracas, he observed that the "wall in Berlin" along with other failures of the communist system elsewhere demonstrated that "liberty and economic progress go hand in hand." In Bogotá, Kennedy claimed, "The fact is that the [Berlin] wall and rifle squads of the last twelve months have shown us again—if we did not need to be shown—that when such doctrines face the united will of free men, they have been defeated."[15]

Most important, from internal debate it is evident that Berlin played a major role in how policymakers conceptualized and framed the war in

Friendship at the East-West Berlin border (1961). (National Archives)

Vietnam. In 1965, Maxwell Taylor, Johnson's special consultant on Viet-nam, observed that the Vietnamese communists "have thus far given no indication of an intention to mend their ways. But neither did the lead-ers in Moscow give any indication of calling off the Berlin airlift or the

North Korean-Chicom leaders of abandoning their effort to take over South Korea until the game had been played down to the last card. Up to that point, their attitude was one of defiant, aggressive confidence. We should expect nothing different from Hanoi now." Another official agreed, stating, "We can either get out of their way and let them have it or we can meet them. . . . When I spoke of 'securing Viet-Nam without major bloodshed' I was referring to the contingency that the other side may look down the road ahead and decide that it is too costly or too dangerous for them to persist. This has happened with the Greek guerillas, the Berlin blockade, Korea, and the Cuban missile crisis." The intractability of all communists was pointed out by Ambassador Henry Cabot Lodge in Hanoi, who criticized those who assume that communists "are in effect like misguided Americans who will reciprocate our kindness and our toleration and our sense of fair play when every experience we have had with Communists, whether at the United Nations, or Panmunjom, or in Berlin, shows that the reverse is the case and that they can only be induced to follow certain course by the application of pressure."[16]

Equally evident was the way in which Kennedy and Johnson sought to use images of Berlin to justify America's growing involvement in Vietnam. Kennedy, for example, in several speeches defined the "frontiers of freedom from Viet-Nam to West Berlin." In March 1962, Kennedy told members of the American Legion, "We assist countries stretching all the way from Berlin around to Saigon to maintain their independence under great pressure." By circumscribing the free world at Vietnam and Berlin, he effectively related American involvement in Southeast Asia to that in Berlin. Thus the meaning that Kennedy inscribed on Berlin, a defensive struggle to maintain the independence of a free people, became the meaning that he gave for the growing American presence in Vietnam. Again, at an address at Independence Hall in July, he invoked Berlin and independence: "If there is a single issue that divides the world today, it is independence—the independence of Berlin or Laos or Viet-Nam, the longing for independence behind the Iron Curtain." In his 1963 State of the Union address, Kennedy claimed that the Third World was coming to understand independence as the central issue, that it was beginning to recognize that "the longing for independence is the same the world over, whether it is the independence of West Berlin or Viet-Nam." As the world had witnessed in Berlin and elsewhere, Kennedy lectured, "such independence runs athwart all Communist ambitions but is in keeping with our own."[17]

As the war in Vietnam dragged on, Kennedy's successor became even more forceful in framing Vietnam using Berlin. In his first speech to Congress after Kennedy's death, Johnson invoked the linkage: "This Nation will keep its commitments from South Viet-Nam to West Berlin." More than Kennedy, Johnson employed both Nazis and Berliners within the established totalitarian narrative to justify American involvement in Vietnam. On the day after he appeared on television regarding the Gulf of Tonkin incident in 1964, Johnson informed Congress, "The challenge that we face in Southeast Asia today is the same challenge that we have faced with courage and that we have met with strength in Greece and Turkey, in Berlin and Korea, in Lebanon and in Cuba." In asking for more aid for Vietnam in May 1965, Johnson stressed that "if our word and our treaty in southeast Asia is no good, it is no good in Berlin." In 1968, the twentieth anniversary of the Berlin airlift, Johnson tried to draw on that memory to blunt the impact of the Tet Offensive on American public opinion. Before delegates to the National Farmers Union Convention in March, he compared the "struggle in Southeast Asia to stop the onrushing tide of Communist aggression" to Greece, Korea, and the Berlin airlift, in which "we had to fly [in] zero weather into Berlin to feed the people when that city was beleaguered and cut off." "We have had our will tested before," he told the delegates to the Conference of the Building and Construction Trades Department of the AFL-CIO that same month. "We have seen it tested over the skies of Berlin when the people of that desolate city were hungry and we had to feed them with our courage, with our planes, and with our cargoes landing, many times, in zero-zero weather." Emphasizing the hardships faced by Americans in the Berlin airlift reinforced Johnson's message of American involvement in the world based on the principles of human dignity and rights.[18]

Kennedy and Johnson invoked America's struggle against totalitarianism not only to defend their foreign policy but also to justify their domestic visions of America against their political opponents. Kennedy repeatedly stressed that the United States needed to be strong at home if it wanted to meet its obligations in places like Berlin. In discussing the nation's health, Kennedy pointed out that the number of men rejected for military service for preventable health reasons "represents more soldiers than we now have stationed in Berlin and West Germany ready to defend freedom." In promoting his domestic agenda in 1962, Kennedy argued, "Unless we are strong here in this country, unless we are moving ahead, unless our people can find work, unless we're educating our children, unless we're providing the kind of society where every person has an opportunity, regardless of his race or his creed or his color, to develop their resources," the United States would fail to maintain its strength "from Berlin in a great half circle to Viet-Nam."[19]

America's commitment to Berlin was especially invoked in the area of civil rights. In June 1963, Kennedy noted on television that "when Americans are sent to Viet-Nam or West Berlin, we do not ask for whites only. It ought to be possible, therefore, for American students of any color to attend any public institution they select without having to be backed by troops." Johnson was even more insistent in using Berlin to smash segregation. "Today, Americans of all races stand side by side in Berlin and Viet Nam," he observed in his 1964 State of the Union address. "Surely they can work and eat and travel side by side in their own country." Later that month, he argued, "If men can stand side by side in Korea, and Viet-Nam, and along the Berlin Wall, and die together regardless of their race or their religion, or the country of their ancestry, if they can do that in the uniform of this country, protecting our flag, then they ought to be able to walk down the assembly line together or cafeteria line together, or go to the same water fountain."[20]

In these ways, the Kennedy and Johnson administrations recognized the rhetorical power of Berlin for shaping views of American foreign policy. Yet, they realized that the very elements of Berlin that invested it with such persuasive power also kept the city in perpetual peril. Berlin's power derived from being on the front line of the Cold War; almost by definition, the situation on the front line in any conflict is dangerous and unpredictable. After the construction of the wall, two major events illustrated the tenuous nature of the situation. First, in late October 1961, American and Soviet tanks faced one another across Checkpoint Charlie over the issue of untrammeled access for Western diplomatic and military personnel to East Berlin. With Lucius Clay eager to destroy the newly erected wall and Kennedy and other Western allies concerned that this was a difficult issue on which to challenge the Soviets, Western newspapers ran headlines like "Gun Turret to Gun Turret, Eyeball to Eyeball" to demonstrate the charged atmosphere. Although the situation resolved itself without catastrophe, it reminded policymakers of the unpredictable and dangerous situation in Berlin.[21]

The second happened the following year. In August 1962, Peter Fechter, a German teenager, was shot while trying to escape to West Berlin near Checkpoint Charlie. Fechter did not die immediately; he was left to suffer for an hour in East Berlin territory as horrified West Berliners looked on. American reports out of Berlin indicated that angry West Berliners were taking matters into their own hands through mob activity, particularly against Soviet buses near Friedrichstrasse. From Paris, General Lauris Norstad expressed concern: "We cannot let mobs dictate actions in a time of such sensitivity and on a matter of such importance." In Washington, Clay worried that this "recent development has hurt us with the people primarily because of [a] lack of reaction on our part." Unlike the previous incident, in which the West provocatively challenged the Soviet Union, the shooting of Peter Fechter highlighted that Western weakness in Berlin could also destabilize the situation.[22]

These incidents and others made it clear to American policymakers that they needed to provide firm assistance to West Berlin. The United States established a number of Berlin viability projects, measures designed to stimulate the city's economy and reassure Berliners that Americans would never abandon them. These measures were intended to supplement projects that the Federal Republic had already established to strengthen ties with West Berlin. Together, the United States and the Federal Republic sought to intensify the cultural connections between West Berlin and the outside world through increased opportunities for exchange in education, art, and music. They both supported the Berlin Information Center, an office designed to share knowledge about Berlin's plight with the Federal Republic and the rest of the world. The two nations worked together to establish a center for less developed countries in West Berlin in an effort to centralize West Berlin in the West's initiative to promote reform in the Third World. The United States also sought to encourage American interest and investment in the beleaguered city. Through these efforts, the United States and the Federal Republic attempted to stabilize one of their most important assets in the struggle for Cold War legitimacy.[23]

"No Other Land in the World Is Similarly Propagandized in the US as the Germans"

The more critical private views of the Kennedy and Johnson administrations reflected a broader trend in American public discourse about the German people during the 1960s, a trend that did not go unnoticed by West German officials. Beginning in the early 1960s, German officials expressed concern that an increased flow of anti-German films, documentaries, and books were poisoning American opinion against the Germans and therefore ruining much of their hard work in favor of the German people. West German officials referred to this outburst of anti-German products as the antideutsche Welle. Concern over this anti-German wave of products was so great that Chancellor Adenauer brought it up with American officials in 1961, and German Foreign Office (AA) officials vigorously debated if Chancellor Erhard should discuss it with Johnson in 1965.[24]

Throughout the 1960s, West German officials reported a large number of stories on unfavorable events in West Germany appearing in America's mainstream media, events that often drew unwelcome and damaging connections between unsavory elements of Germany's past and its present. For example, the prominence of the Eichmann trial led to a renewed worry over a revival of the Right in Germany. With Israel's "forthcoming trial of Adolf Eichmann . . . forcing attention again on the enormity of what the Nazis were," Sydney and Flora Gruson wrote in a typical piece, "who speaks for the new Germany?" Was it Konrad Adenauer and others, "conscious as they write that their readership includes watchful foreigners," or was it "swastika daubers and the furtive souls who creep anonymously into cemeteries to smash tombstones and wreak still more vengeance on the dead?" In the *New York Times Magazine* Richard Lowenthal echoed a common fear that the "Germans are beginning to feel like Germans again." Lowenthal pointed out that after the war, Germans had subordinated everything to economic reconstruction. But the "spiritual void" left by the collapse of the "Nazi myth" remained unfilled. Lowenthal feared that if the United States did not take a firm stand in settling European problems, the Germans might strike out on their own.[25]

From the perspective of German officials, one of the most troubling news reports was CBS's *The Germans,* which premiered in 1967. *The Ger-*

mans focused on life in Nuremberg and drew a number of controversial conclusions from its examination of the city. Among them, it charged that the danger of neo-Nazism was much greater than the Foreign Office and the Press Office believed. German officials found much of the "factual" reporting tendentious. Even Joseph Thomas, a German official at the German Information Center, who generally did not express the same level of concern that other Germans did over the anti-German wave, was incensed by it. Thomas wrote a detailed letter to CBS outlining their grievances against the program. German officials were joined in their outrage by the citizens of Nuremberg, who did not take kindly to the implications of the program.[26]

While much of the mainstream reportage of Germany focused on current events (often framing these events in light of Germany's unflattering history), German officials also worried that the anti-German wave was rewriting Germany's past. German officials believed that William Shirer's 1960 *The Rise and Fall of the Third Reich*, which had become the standard American work on the Nazi period, continued to have an extremely negative impact on public opinion. The most damaging aspect of the book, from the point of view of the German Foreign Office, was not the historical description of the Nazi regime but Shirer's introduction, in which he argued that Nazism was the logical outgrowth of the German national character. A correspondent in Berlin during the Third Reich, Shirer enjoyed a great deal of legitimacy on the subjects of Germans and the Third Reich, and his book and opinions were disseminated widely.[27]

West German observers also worried about the work of their own historians, in particular Fritz Fischer's *Griff Nach Der Weltmacht* (*Germany's Aims in the First World War*), which made an instant splash in the Federal Republic and the United States. Based on a significant amount of archival research, Fischer's book contained a relatively simple argument: the Central Powers were responsible for the outbreak of World War I. Thus Fischer's thesis rehabilitated the war guilt clause of the Treaty of Versailles, angering many Germans who preferred to think of their involvement in World War I as morally equivalent at worst and morally superior at best to the Allied Powers. It also offered a powerful revision to the American understanding of World War I, which also tended to blame the Allies for the Great War. Unsurprisingly, Fischer encountered a great deal of criticism in both Germany and America, but the strength of his research led many to reevaluate their understanding of World War I.[28]

Of greatest concern to West German officials, however, were representations of Germans in American popular entertainment, and in visual products in particular. Among the most egregious films to West German officials were Hollywood war films such as *The Battle of the Bulge, The Blue Max, Is Paris Burning? The Ship of Fools* and, worst of all, Stanley Kramer's 1961 *Judgment at Nuremberg.* German officials objected to the ways in which Germans were stereotyped in these films, railing against their seeming imputation that Nazism formed a constitutive part of German culture.[29]

The German Foreign Office and the Federal Press Office proved most concerned about anti-German programming on American television. According to them, programs like *Combat! Rat Patrol,* and *Hogan's Heroes* portrayed the Germans as a dumb, vicious, and cruel people. They were especially disturbed about the effect these television programs were having on children. Having banked on the hope that wartime portrayals of the Germans would fade away with time, they were alarmed to see the defamation continuing. They also worried about the effect these programs were having in the Third World; on a number of occasions, German officials reported that they were breeding hate for Germans in Latin America.[30]

German officials offered a variety of reasons for the anti-German wave. Most believed that Americans still nurtured a lingering hatred of Germans who, despite their steadfast alliance with the United States, could not escape their past. One official blamed powerful Jewish liberals in the United States, who exercised a "great influence in the modern communication industry." This official expressed his belief that Jews targeted Nazism in Germany while privately harboring sympathy for the communists. But officials in the German embassy offered the most reasonable explanation: the recent revival of interest in Nazism was part of a greater rediscovery of the dramatic potential of World War II. Stories of the war would naturally portray the enemy in a very unfavorable light. The Eichmann trial and the success of the NPD in 1966, these officials pointed out, only spurred this revival along.[31]

German officials tried a number of tactics to stem the tide of the anti-German wave. They discovered that they were alone in these endeavors, for the American government, led by an indifferent Kennedy and Johnson, refused to assist them. Worried that lodging an official protest against a particular film or program would only serve to provide it with free publicity, West German officials preferred private initiatives. In a return to prewar practices, the German Foreign Office encouraged German American groups to protest the defamation of Germans in the American media. Along these lines, they supported the idea of a German Anti-Defamation League. They wrote private letters of protest to executives of media outlets, asking for their cooperation in improving the images of Germans on television. And in at least one instance, Joseph Thomas wrote a major columnist to suggest an idea for an anticommunist movie (as opposed to an anti-Nazi film) that she could perhaps pass along to someone in power in Hollywood.[32]

But the Federal Republic's primary response to the anti-German wave was to step up German cultural and social representation in the United States through the creation of the German Information Center (GIC). Many officials in the Federal Republic did not believe that Roy Bernard was doing enough to counteract the anti-German wave, and so the GIC took on many of the public relations company's duties and responsibilities. Jointly administered by the Foreign Office and the Federal Press Office, the GIC's primary function was to serve as a source of information on the Federal Republic, but it was also expected to *place* information in major American periodicals. German officials chose as its director Dr. Joseph Thomas, a German who had served as press officer as well as deputy chief director of the American Desk in Bonn. The GIC began operations in late 1960; in this new configuration, Roy Bernard's role was reduced to advisor to the Federal Republic.[33]

In addition to this more positive approach to the anti-German wave, the Foreign Office occasionally moved more forcefully. Sometimes such actions had disastrous results, as when the Foreign Office cut funding for a lecture circuit planned by Fritz Fischer. As one American official put it, "The controversy over Fischer has unquestionably undone years of effort by the representatives of the Federal Republic in the United States to encourage a favorable image of the new Germany." Fischer had received funding from the Goethe Institute to present a series of lectures at U.S. universities on his recent work *Germany's Aims in the First World War*. In the fall of 1963, the German government informed the universities that Fischer had refused the invitation. Since Fischer was personally in contact with some members of the faculties, the lie was readily discovered. The Goethe Institute then informed Fischer and the universities that a mistake had been made, and that funds were unavailable. American professors reacted angrily, embarrassing even Fischer with the strident tone of their missives to the German Foreign Office. In due course, these professors convinced the American Council of Learned Societies to fund Fischer's trip. Once it became aware of the new funding, the Foreign Office dispatched a high official to Hamburg to plead with Fischer not to go. According the American report, the official "made a strong appeal to Fischer's German patriotism and tried to show Fischer that his trip to America would harm the favorable image the Germans had been trying to create in the United States." Fischer countered that at this point it would be more damaging not to go. Eventually Fischer came to the United States and gave his lectures. The American consulate in Hamburg was left to conclude that "one can only agree with the general evaluation of the American professors on the stupidity and lack of comprehension of the German Foreign Office demonstrated by its activities in the Fischer affair. . . . Now, too many Americans will agree with William Shirer, that 'the Germans never change.'"[34]

And yet despite their damaging experience in the Fischer controversy, Foreign Office officials considered even more drastic measures to bring American film and television producers to heel. They strongly considered an embargo on the firms or sponsors affiliated with anti-German products. They noted that this strategy had worked well for Japan in the early days of its new government; as a result of this Japanese action, the Motion Pictures Association of America (MPAA) practically forbade the production of films with anti-Japanese themes or representations. Yet before they took this radical step, they needed proof that these films were having a negative effect on the American people.[35]

Government officials had already received anecdotal evidence suggesting that these products were having a deleterious effect on American public opinion. One piece came from a concerned German who passed along a letter from his son, who was studying in the United States. His son's classmates often asked him if he were a Nazi or a communist, even though he had been born after the war. His son blamed American television programs on the World War II era that portrayed the Germans as "hard,

unscrupulous, vicious, and always ready to say 'Heil Hitler' or 'Jawohl.'"
In a later letter, the son expressed frustration at having to carry this heavy
burden, when he himself had "done nothing bad." A German American
living in California warned Chancellor Kiesinger that American children
were being educated by the television, which was teaching them that the
German was a "stupid, brutal animal. No other land in the world is similarly propagandized in the US as the Germans." Another German wrote
the Federal Press Office about a conversation he'd had with an American
on a plane in which the American had echoed such negative portrayals.[36]

The German Foreign Office decided that anecdotal evidence was not
enough to move forward with serious countermeasures, however. It needed
to know when anti-German programs were shown on television, where on
television they could be found, and who was sponsoring them. And most
important, it wanted to know if American attitudes had changed as a
result of these cultural works. Officials in the embassy wanted concrete
data before they decided to recommend economic sanctions or suggest
high-level discussions on the matter. As a result, the Germans commissioned a survey to find out the attitudes of Americans.[37]

The results of this survey were a great relief to German officials. The
poll found that the Germans were second only to the British of "best-
liked" people. Most encouraging to the Federal Press Office was the finding that the anti-German wave had virtually no effect on public opinion.
A mere 7 percent of respondents said that the anti-German programs
reflected their true feelings. In answer to a separate question, 24 percent
said that there was no relationship between the depictions of the programs
and present-day Germany, and the other 76 percent apparently had not
even recognized a possible connection. Graf Schweinitz of the Federal
Press Office wrote exultantly to a member of the Free Office that this
poll, and not the apparent anti-German wave, revealed the true feelings
of the American people. Given the state of affairs at the end of the war,
Schweinitz claimed that this poll indicated the outstanding success of
the BPA in affecting American public opinion. By the end of the decade,
Joseph Thomas reported that *Rat Patrol* and *Combat!* had been cancelled,
and that humorous depictions of Germans in *Hogan's Heroes* and *Laugh-
in* did not have an adverse effect on the image of Germany. Although they
remained concerned, West German officials concluded that the anti-German wave had not affected the American understanding of Germany.[38]

"The Swastika Is Vanishing from West Germany"

The concern of West German officials over the new tone in 1960s America was shared by their greatest boosters in the United States, the American Council on Germany, led by Christopher Emmet. Dedicated to furthering close relations between the Federal Republic and the United States, the ACG worried that the new political and cultural climate in the United States would threaten this relationship. Emphasizing the importance of the anticommunist agenda, the ACG sought to use its political connections to blunt the push for détente in the Kennedy and Johnson administrations. Painting anti-German products as sponsored by communist or communist-friendly agents, the ACG pulled out all the stops to counteract the perceived effects of the anti-German wave. Overall, the ACG prioritized the maintenance of the German-American relationship to the point that it annoyed erstwhile Jewish allies who sympathized with some of the anti-German views expressed.

A new initiative in promoting German-American understanding was the establishment of a series of American-German conferences. Jointly sponsored with the ACG's sister organization, the Atlantik-Brücke, the first of these conferences occurred in 1959 in Bad Godesberg, with subsequent conferences taking place every two years in locations alternating between the United States and Germany. High-powered affairs, these conferences brought together prominent policymakers from both sides of the Atlantic. Over the course of the 1960s, the list of participants on the American side included such luminaries as Hubert Humphrey, Lucius Clay, John McCloy, George Ball, Henry Kissinger, Jacob Javits, Dean Acheson, and Christian Herter. They were joined by an equally impressive list of Germans, including among others, Chancellors Adenauer, Erhard, Kiesinger, and Brandt, and Franz Josef Strauss, Karl Schiller, Walter Scheel, and Helmut Schmidt. Grants from the Ford Foundation covered the expenses of the American representatives, while the Atlantik-Brücke was responsible for organizing and funding the activities of the German participants. According to the reports of the ACG, these conferences were harmonious affairs, even given the difficulties the German-American relationship faced during the decade.[39]

Typical was the second American-German conference, held in February 1961 in Washington. Scheduled the month after the new Kennedy administration took power, the conference was both affected by the new regime's attitude and provided with an opportunity to mitigate it. Chancellor Adenauer had made plans to attend the conference, but the new president indicated that he was not ready to meet the German leader yet. Respecting Kennedy's wishes, Adenauer instead sent Foreign Minister Heinrich von Brentano, who was joined by his counterpart Secretary of State Dean Rusk as the headliners of the opening session of the conference. Both men used the occasion to reaffirm the commitment of their respective countries to the relationship and to the resolution of the outstanding differences between them. Their conciliatory tone set the tenor for the rest of the meeting, as the conference broke into three panel groups focusing on different aspects of the relationship. These panels, especially the one on economics, engaged in vigorous yet civil off-the-record debate on the issues, with the balance of payments and dollar deficit problems drawing a large amount of attention. The four-day conference also included several opportunities for socialization, with events sponsored by the American Council on Germany, the State Department, and the German embassy. Emmet hailed this conference, as he did others, as an opportunity to keep up cordial dialogue and positive momentum in the face of difficult diplomatic problems and hostile media representations.[40]

For Christopher Emmet and his colleagues, these conferences were a crucial part of the struggle to maintain a strong German-American relationship during a trying period of U.S. diplomacy. Throughout the decade, they worried about the direction of American foreign policy, especially under the leadership of the Democratic Party. As committed Cold Warriors, members of the American Council on Germany feared the growing movement for détente among younger Democrats. During the election of 1960, Emmet privately expressed to his friend the journalist J. P. O'Donnell that he had serious misgivings about Kennedy's views regarding Eastern Europe. Although describing himself as a "liberal anti-communist" who "nearly always voted Democratic in presidential elections," Emmet confided that he was "compelled" to vote for Richard Nixon because his views "will be nearer to my own views on certain vital foreign policy issues." After Kennedy's death in 1963, Emmet confessed to Democratic senator Thomas Dodd that he had underestimated both the depth of Kennedy's commitment to détente and the progress it had made in his administration. Worried that Johnson would continue along the same course, Emmet vowed that he would continue to fight against this policy in the new administration.[41]

Emmet's most visible fight against the growing movement for détente occurred in 1963. That year, freshman senator Claiborne Pell became the lightning rod for Emmet and his associates who were concerned about the new thinking on foreign relations in the Democratic Party. On 11 April, Pell gave a speech in the Senate on the Berlin problem that was warmly received by some of his Democratic colleagues and the American media. Arguing that "there is no situation in the world today where our forces and our flag occupy a more vulnerable position" than in Berlin, Pell proposed a solution to the tense situation that involved conceding several points that had been previously off the table. To gain what he saw as the essential Western demands for a peaceful resolution to the Berlin Crisis— land access to West Berlin, "iron-clad" guarantees of security for West Berlin, and unfettered rights to garrison the city—he proposed recognizing the division of Germany, the existence of East Germany, and the border of East Germany at the Oder-Neisse line. As if these suggestions were not threatening enough, Pell devoted much of his speech to validating the fears of Russians and Eastern Europeans about German revanchism—in other words, he spun a classic world war narrative of the German people.[42]

Emmet's network went into high gear. Emmet himself wrote a lengthy rebuttal to the well-known columnist Arthur Krock, who had agreed with Pell's conclusions publicly, and sent a copy of it to Pell himself, initiating a cordial yet pointed correspondence with him. Emmet also sent a copy of the Krock letter to New York senator and longtime ally Jacob Javits, pointing out that both the warm reception of Pell's speech among prominent Democrats such as Mike Mansfield and Hubert Humphrey and the close personal relationship Pell enjoyed with the president necessitated an effective counterresponse. Emmet requested Javits to address the issue on the Senate floor when he had a chance. Finally, Emmet's organization coordinated its efforts with West German officials. Through Egon Bahr, head of the Press and Information Office in West Berlin, Emmet offered Governing Mayor Willy Brandt copies of his correspondence with Pell. He also extended an invitation to put Brandt in touch with Leo Cherne, an individual whom Emmet said had a good relationship with Pell and might be able to advise in the matter. Emmet observed that Senator Pell had inherited "a deep prejudice against Ger-

U.S. soldiers stare across the border at the Friedrichstrasse crossing (1961). (National Archives)

mans" from his father, who was a prominent official with the Society for the Prevention of World War III.[43]

Under Emmet's leadership, the American Council on Germany understood and shared West Germany's concern about the effects of détente upon Berlin. During the 1950s, Emmett had been vocal in under-scoring the special significance of Berlin for American-German relations, and the heightened drama in Berlin during the early 1960s only strength-ened his belief in the importance of maintaining Berlin's freedom. In 1960, the council began sponsoring annual meetings both to memorial-ize those killed during the East Berlin uprising in 1953 and to empha-size "the unanimous anti-Communism of the [German] people, the total unreliability of the satellite armies and police, and the fact that commu-nist rule in all of Eastern Europe depends on Russian tanks and troops alone." After the construction of the wall in the late summer of 1961, the ACG moved quickly to assuage German fears of American abandonment. Council officers lobbied Vice President Johnson to visit Berlin to demon-strate American resolve, and distributed memoranda and reports to signif-icant and influential Germans to highlight negative American reactions to the Berlin Wall. In 1964, Emmet hosted Norbert Muhlen and J. P. O'Donnell on his radio program to talk about the new phase of terror initiated by the building of the wall. Along with the West German and American governments, the American Council on Germany offered its resources to preserve the importance of Berlin to the relationship between the two countries.[44]

Emmett and his organization, perhaps even more than West German officials, worried about the impact of the anti-German wave in the Ameri-can media. Echoing the observations of West German officials, Emmet argued that the swastika daubings in Germany, the publication and distri-bution of William Shirer's popular *The Rise and Fall of the Third Reich,* the broadcast of the Adolf Eichmann trial in Israel, and the release of Stanley Kramer's *Judgment at Nuremberg,* all within the span of two years, had generated a climate that encouraged and sustained anti-German senti-ment. Unwilling or unable to see a connection between the changed tone in Washington and the emergence of a discourse more critical of Ger-many, Emmet and his colleagues complained that the anti-German wave could not have come at a worse time. "Just at the time when the pro-longed crisis over the freedom of West Berlin precipitated by the Soviet Union has made a close American-German understanding more neces-sary," conservative William Chamberlain argued in an article on the sub-ject, "American public opinion has been the target of the most intensive 'Hate Germany' campaign since the war and immediate postwar years."

In the opinion of Chamberlain and many of his colleagues, the campaign sought to persuade Americans that "Nazism was not a horrible aberration, but a characteristic manifestation of German character." For Emmet and his crew, the wave represented the gravest threat to their activities, and they organized and coordinated a well-executed assault against it.[45]

In their counterattacks, which appeared in electronic and print media, members of the ACG attributed the anti-German wave to a number of reasons, none of which took the anti-German arguments at face value. In general their arguments cohered around three themes. The first, and most obvious given the climate of the Cold War, was the assertion that the primary actors were communists or communist sympathizers. In a fund-raising pitch, Emmet credited the key elements of the anti-German wave with furthering "the principal Soviet objective—to weaken NATO by dividing Germany from the West." The second theme suggested that the anti-German wave stemmed from and was nurtured by a group of "hard core irreconcilables," Americans who were "convinced that nothing good can come from Germany." The third was a "crude commercialism" that sought to capitalize on Germany's current misfortunes by creating cultural products that echoed events in West Germany. Unwilling to consider the possibility that the proponents of the anti-German wave may have revealed a dangerous streak in German society, members of the ACG sought to delegitimize any expression of concern or alarm about West Germans.[46]

The American Council on Germany focused on exposing what it saw as the constitutive parts of the anti-German wave. To combat concerns about West Germany that stemmed from an outbreak of swastika daubings, Emmet and fellow council member Norbert Muhlen coauthored *The Vanishing Swastika* in 1960. In this pamphlet, published by the conservative Henry Regnery Company, Emmet and Muhlen carried out a comprehensive investigation of contemporary attitudes in Germany, and concluded, as the title suggested, that "the Swastika is vanishing from West Germany." To publicize their findings, they purchased a full-page ad for the book in *Foreign Affairs*. Based on the book's widespread publicity, Emmet and Muhlen made several television and radio appearances in which they shared their views. The American Council on Germany followed up this success by publishing a pamphlet, *Germany's Democracy in Perspective,* which was a published television interview with distinguished German academics Max Horkheimer and Ferdinand Hermens.[47]

Berliners welcome American troops (1961). (National Archives)

To blunt the message of those concerned about the swastika epidemic, Emmet hosted alarmists such as Irving Engel on his radio show. Although Engel appreciated the efforts of the West German government, he expressed great concern about the swastika incidents, suggesting there was still a "hard core" of Germans who were "still infected" with Nazism. Dismissing such fears as "exaggerated," Emmett pinned the responsibility for the swastika epidemic on East German communists and pointed to "encouraging" signs of change in Germany. Norbert Muhlen policed the letters to the editor of the *New York Times,* personally challenging those who questioned the resolve of the Federal Republic in the situation, while George Shuster, president of the ACG, published two letters in the *Times* on the subject.[48]

Like West German officials, members of the ACG reserved special vitriol for William Shirer's *The Rise and Fall of the Third Reich.* ACG officer Joseph Kaskell wrote to George Shuster calling for a muscular and coordinated campaign to battle what he believed to be the falsehoods of the book. In his article on the anti-German wave, Chamberlain called

Shirer a "war pamphleteer" who promoted a "crude" conception of German history that lacked balance and an understanding of totalitarianism. Norbert Muhlen claimed that Shirer, to make his case that the Third Reich was "the true expression of the German character," "continuously" argues "without proof and sometimes against available evidence."[49]

The American Council on Germany also went after *Judgment at Nuremberg.* Norbert Muhlen contended that screenwriter Abby Mann distorted history to make American anticommunism the major reason for accommodation with the Germans. William Chamberlain also took issue with the representation of American-German friendship, pointing out that the collaboration between Americans and Germans against communism was likened to Nazi aggression. He also did not care for the general implication of the German people in the Holocaust. He argued, "There is no recognition of the fact that the average German could no more have prevented what a small group of fanatics and sadists did in concentration camps than the average Russian could have stopped the maltreatment and starvation of millions of victims of Stalin's slave labor camps."[50]

In addition to challenging specific incidents and products that were seen as major reasons for the onset of the anti-German wave, the ACG battled against fears of renewed and dangerous German nationalism, including those expressed in *The New Germany and the Old Nazis* (1961), a book published by their familiar nemesis T. H. Tetens. These arguments in defense of West Germany intensified in the latter half of the decade, when Emmet and his colleagues dealt with the NPD vote and the election of Kurt Kiesinger to the chancellor's office.[51]

Emmet's often over-the-top defense of Germany and his unwillingness to consider the possible validity of views expressed by his opponents clearly rankled some of his associates, especially on the Jewish side. When he asked for support from the conservative American Jewish Committee in his crusade against the anti-German wave, AJC officials questioned his objectivity and commitment to justice in West Germany. When Emmet asked Irving Engel to review *The Vanishing Swastika* before publication, Engel sent him a detailed response, carefully encouraging Emmet to eliminate any material, of which there was plenty, that might give the impression that Emmet (and by extension the ACG) was an "apologist" for Germany's past. In addressing the work's central argument after its publication, Simon Segal complained to Engel that there was "no proof whatsoever that the Communists instigated the swastika incidents." When Emmet sought support for the organization's follow-up pamphlet, *Germany's Democracy in Perspective,* Eugene Hevesi of the AJC argued against sponsorship, claiming that the new pamphlet "does not reflect adequately the full picture of German reactions of Nazism and anti-Semitism." A year later, Paul Freedman called Emmet a skillful "lobbyist" and "knowledgeable radio commentator" who was nevertheless overreacting to the perception of an anti-German wave. Later, in 1966, the AJC criticized a signed statement circulated by the ACG on the significance (or insignificance) of right-wing political strength in West Germany following the succession of Kiesinger to the chancellorship and the success of the NPD in national polls. Emmet's zealous defense of West Germany, an effort he thought necessary in the context of world and domestic politics in the 1960s, cost him and his cause some support among conservative Jews, who had been, given their position and worldview, among the most useful allies in promoting American-German relations.[52]

"Symbols of Defiance of Authority or . . . Evidence of Nazi Ideological Attachment?"

As the reaction of American Jewish organizations to Emmet's efforts suggests, the course of events during the 1960s encouraged even the most supportive groups to reconsider their position toward representations of Germans in the American media. Beginning with evidence of lingering anti-Semitism in West Germany at the end of the 1950s and continuing through the election of a former Nazi as chancellor of West Germany, American Jewish organizations debated vigorously the appropriate responses to representations of Germans in the American mass media. The relative coolness of the Kennedy and Johnson administrations to West German concerns opened up space for Jewish leaders to promote more critical narratives Germany's past. Still, most Jewish leaders refrained from endorsing the kinds of world war narratives advanced by William Shirer and Abby Mann, preferring instead to highlight the lessons that Germany's past held for Americans in the present.

Anti-Semitic manifestations at the end of the 1950s fostered a lingering sense of unease among even the most supportive Jewish organizations. In April 1958, the American Jewish Committee reported results of a recent poll indicating that 30 percent of Germans were still "definitely anti-Semitic," moving some in the organization to conclude that a substantial number of Germans were "still harboring deep prejudices and animosities against Jews." To address these concerns, the AJC employed a mixture of approaches. Along with representatives from other Jewish organizations, including the American Jewish Congress, the president of the American Jewish Committee met with West German president Theodore Heuss in June to discuss these issues. In line with the accommodationist approach of his organization, he couched his concerns as a threat to the outstanding work already done by the Federal Republic's leadership rather than challenging the leadership structure itself. And the AJC continued to advocate education as a means for furthering the democratic project in Germany, concentrating on the issue at the first German-American conference organized by the American Council on Germany and Atlantik-Brücke in 1959. Still, in a break from its pattern of avoiding sponsorship of controversial narratives, the AJC privately encouraged Rex Stout's appearance on NBC's *Open Mind*.[53]

Reacting more strongly to incidents of anti-Semitism, the American Jewish Congress published a pamphlet entitled *The German Dilemma*, in which it sought to remind Americans of World War II narratives of Germany. Although praising certain segments of the German population that sought to establish a "more humane and free order" and thanking the Bonn government for paying reparations to Israel and indemnifying victims of the Holocaust, the pamphlet argued that indifference or hostility to cleaning out anti-Semitism had led to the restoration of a number of prominent ex-Nazis to power in Germany.[54]

The desecration of a synagogue in Cologne on Christmas Eve in 1959 and the numerous incidents of anti-Semitism that followed exacerbated these already simmering concerns. AJC officials met with the German ambassador soon after the American press reported the desecration, insisting on the arrest of the perpetrators, the removal of former Nazis from official positions, the banning of fascist and Nazi groups, and intensified efforts to educate German youngsters in democratic concepts. Dissatisfied with the ambassador's attempts to blame the incidents on communist subversives, some officials even questioned their own moderate postwar position on the West Germans. Max Horkheimer, an AJC consultant, argued that the incidents proved that "there is no democratic tradition in the consciousness of any age groups and the young generation [has] no feelings about democracy." At a summer meeting of the AJC's National Advisory Council, chairman Fred Greenman pointed out that the organization had repeatedly raised concerns with American and German officials, including as recently as the American Council on Germany's first conference in Bad-Godesberg the previous year. Despite the concerns expressed within the AJC, other accomodationist organizations, like the Anti-Defamation League, remained steadfast supporters of Cold War narratives of the German people.[55]

More militant organizations interpreted the incidents as justification for their long-held suspicions regarding the German state. They argued that the desecrations revealed the "inadequacy of the German government in rooting out former and neo-Nazi groups." In a public statement, NCRAC strongly reminded Americans that "Germany remains the breeding ground of anti-Semitism, the manifest source of an infection that can spread swiftly." News reports of strong reactions to the incidents in Germany, as well as careful West German diplomacy, capped by a historic meeting between Adenauer and David Ben-Gurion in New York in March 1960, mollified these harsh attitudes somewhat.[56]

In any event, within weeks, the incidents in Germany were eclipsed by a far more ominous development: copycat acts in the United States. By October 1960, conservative estimates put the number of U.S. incidents at 750, whereas more liberal estimates counted more than 1,000. At both ends of the spectrum the figures rivaled the number of estimated incidents in the Federal Republic. In some extreme cases, the violence was shocking: the most serious case involved a boy of sixteen in Gadsden, Alabama, who bombed a synagogue and shot two members of the congregation. Of greatest concern, however, was what the investigations into these acts discovered: a youth underground fascination with Nazi Germany, as evidenced by neo-Nazi youth groups in high schools across the country and a "lively traffic" in Nazi souvenirs.[57]

Jewish organizations wrestled with the implications of these findings. The American Jewish Committee carefully differentiated between the incidents in West Germany and the United States, arguing that the acts in Germany represented resurgent Nazism while those in the United States were a product of latent anti-Semitism. Shad Polier of the AJ Congress, on the other hand, cautioned, "It would be well . . . for all of us to avoid falling into the error of thinking that anti-Semitism in Germany—different as it may be in its implications and to an extent, to its causes—is something to which we in the United States are immune." Regardless of the nature of the anti-Semitism, however, most Jewish leaders at the national and local levels appreciated the universal condemnation of the acts, from President Eisenhower to local religious leaders and law enforcement. In one extreme example, a New York City magistrate held three alleged offenders for treason.[58]

Of most concern to Jewish organizations were the motives of the perpetrators. As a memorandum entitled "Bombs and Swastikas" wondered: "Why did they do it? Were the swastikas they traced merely symbols of defiance of authority or were they evidence of Nazi ideological attachment?" On this there was no agreement. As Shad Polier pointed out, "The outbreak has been variously attributed to juvenile and adult delinquents, crackpots and emotionally disturbed individuals, as well as to neo-Nazis inspired, if not guided by, the remnants of the Hitler apparatus." Although the last explanation, that of an international conspiracy at work, was a popular fear, especially in light of the phenomenon's international reach—copycat incidents happened in Latin America and elsewhere—it was dismissed by most Jewish organizations. At work, most believed, was a "latent anti-Semitism" or an "unexpunged residue of ill feeling against Jews in Western civilization." Polier compared the manifestations to the "fever of the human body"; in this case, the illness was "anti-Semitism, which neither had its beginnings in Hitler nor was destined to an automatic end with the destruction of Hitler, even though in the struggle against Hitler, the western world witnessed the ultimate horrible consequences implicit in anti-Semitism."[59]

National Jewish groups based these conclusions on a number of studies of the phenomenon, which found that most of the perpetrators were children or adolescents. Based on in-depth interviews with these offenders (discussed in much greater detail in chapter 5), researchers found that many of the youth maintained an "image of Hitler as a strong, masculine type" and that neo-Nazi groups fed on racial tension (particularly in the South), unemployment, and local problems in communities. All of the reports recommended that Jewish groups move to "immunize the general population" against the contagion of anti-Semitism.[60]

The greatest effect of the swastika epidemic was to force a thorough reappraisal of the response of Jewish groups to the Holocaust. At the national level, the overall strategy had been based on an assimilationist ethos—that Jewish groups should avoid emphasizing Jewish identity. In this context, it meant that national Jewish groups had been reluctant to talk about the Holocaust publicly out of fear of encouraging mainstream Americans to think of Jews as a victimized group. They also were afraid that bringing up German atrocities against Jews threatened American foreign policy aims, taboo in the age of McCarthyism. But the swastika epidemic suggested to national Jewish organizations that not talking about crimes committed against Jews had been counterproductive: silence had in fact encouraged more of the same in the United States.

Thus Jewish organizations emphasized the need to promote a greater awareness of the destruction of European Jewry in American public memory. However, Jewish groups sought to avoid publicity "just for the sake of publicity" because it could simply encourage more copycat incidents. They welcomed media reports of non-Jewish leaders condemning the acts because "such expressions . . . establish a climate of community opinion which puts the swastika smearers completely beyond the realm of respectability"—that is, such reports placed the perpetrators, not Jews, outside of the American consensus. But Jewish leaders did not like news accounts that painted Jews as victims. For these reasons, Jewish organizations argued that "a return to normalcy and the maintenance of public order require a cessation of news which creates the impression that the Jews are an easily attacked group, readily injured by anti-Semites."[61]

Given the demographics—most of the offenders were young—Jews prioritized a long-term plan of Holocaust education. Disturbed at "the apparent receptivity of people across the nation to anti-Semitism in light of the horrible experiences of the world during the Hitler period," the American Jewish Committee laid most of the blame for the epidemic with American schools, which had failed "to give proper emphasis to the Nazi period in contemporary history." In a stinging and highly suggestive comparison, the American Jewish Committee pointed out that failures in American education were equally deserving of attention as the "German education problem." Shad Polier of the AJC argued that the most "significant aspect of the plague" is that "most of the persons have been children and young people. They are of a generation that was born or grew up after the end of the second world war. Obviously, something has been wrong with their education and, I would add, with their religious teaching. We are witnessing the results of the failure of our schools, both public and private, and the failure of their homes as well as our churches." Emphasizing the need for greater education, Polier cautioned that there were no "quick cures."[62]

The 1960s proved to be an important decade in the transformation of Jewish and mainstream American consciousness regarding the Holocaust, and many have pointed out various events that may have sparked it—including the Six-Day War and the Adolf Eichmann trial. But evidence suggests that the commitment national organizations made during the swastika epidemic to promote knowledge of German crimes against Jews came to fruition later in the decade. Philip Klutznick of B'nai B'rith afterward highlighted the importance of swastika daubings on Jewish consciousness: "The swastika incidents in late '59 and '60 which involved several countries, but included Germany, pointed up the sharp distinction in the public mind and especially the Jewish mind where Germany is concerned."[63]

Almost immediately after the swastika epidemic died down, Jewish groups were faced with a decision regarding how Germans and the Holocaust should be presented to the American people. On the heels of the epidemic, Adolf Eichmann was captured in Argentina. His trial over the following year offered American Jewish organizations an opportunity to clarify how they wanted—and, perhaps more important, did not want—the Holocaust to be portrayed. As historian Shlomo Shafir has observed, the public debate of American Jewish organizations highlighted that the trial was more about the domestic Jewish scene than "the community's attitudes toward Germany." As the leaders of American Jewish defense organizations, they understood that how Americans interpreted the Holocaust would have a great effect on how Jews both in the United States and in Israel were viewed.[64]

First, and this should not be taken for granted because Jews were very wary of talking about the Holocaust publicly in the 1950s, American Jewish organizations supported Israel's abduction and trial of Eichmann, seeking to convince American official and public figures that Israel's actions were justified. They were joined by other Jewish individuals. Major organs of the Jewish press supported Israel, including the influential periodical *Commentary*. Rabbis from all major denominations lobbied government and major newspapers as part of a public push to make people aware of and supportive of Israel's actions.[65]

The organizations' stance on Eichmann was opposed by several prominent Jews, however. Nahum Goldman hoped that Eichmann would be turned over to an international tribunal. Unfazed by the swastika-daubing incidents, Joseph Proskauer worried that the trial would increase anti-Semitism in the United States. Instead he wanted to foster an environment that would "permit America to furnish Israel with defensive weapons to meet the Russian threat." The American Council on Judaism was the most important critical organization, and Oscar Handlin its most persuasive spokesman. Claiming that Israel did not represent all Jews and that Jews were not the only victims, he argued that Israelis were using the trial to validate the Jewish state.[66]

As Eichmann's wartime actions were revealed during the trial, controversy also ensued over how to interpret them. In public, the Anti-Defamation League and the American Jewish Committee sought to frame the Eichmann trial along the lines of the Cold War consensus. In what would later become known as the universalist interpretation, they tried to present, in the words of John Slawson, "Eichmann as having perpetrated crimes against humanity, not merely Jews." In the view of the ADL, the Israelis sought to "alert the conscience of the world to the fearful consequences of totalitarianism." "What happened to the Jews of Europe," the organization contended, "can very well happen to other people oppressed by totalitarianism." In universalizing Eichmann's evil, American Jewish groups sought to avoid charges of Jewish vengefulness while building bridges to other groups.[67]

The very public debate among Jewish groups over how to present the Holocaust shifted from the Eichmann trial itself to the most influential critique of the trial—Hannah Arendt's 1963 *Eichmann in Jerusalem*. In 1961, the *New Yorker* asked the political theorist to cover the trial of Eichmann, and her report was originally published in a series of articles for the magazine. Significantly, she did not question Israel's right to try Eichmann (she even defended Israel's actions against one of her advisors), nor did she challenge the sentence of death. Rather, she was critical of the nature of the trial itself—she claimed that it was a show trial—and, perhaps more important, she offered a different interpretation of Eichmann and the Holocaust that challenged comfortable notions of Jews and

Germans. The Jewish response to *Eichmann in Jerusalem* represented the greatest effort by Jewish groups to affix the meaning of Eichmann and the Holocaust in the early 1960s.[68]

America's major Jewish organizations took issue with two major lines of Arendt's interpretation, both of which were central to her book and both of which were threatening to Jewish interests in the United States. The first major contention, and probably the most significant, was that Jews were complicit in their own destruction. As she argued, the "role of the Jewish leaders in the destruction of their own people is undoubtedly the darkest chapter of the whole dark story." Using Raul Hilberg's work, she pointed out that, for different motives, Jewish leaders from Central to Eastern Europe cooperated with German authorities in the ghettoization and deportation of the Jewish people. She found fault with the Eichmann prosecution for not shedding enough light on this part of the story, alleging that it was ignored because it would have damaged "the prosecution's general picture of a clear-cut division between prosecutors and victims."[69]

The second issue, and the more relevant for our study on German representations, concerned Arendt's interpretation of the nature of Eichmann's evil. She argued that he was neither the "perverted sadist" nor "abnormal monster" that the prosecution made him out to be. Rather, she argued that his evil sprang from more "banal" sources—career ambition, moral apathy, and blind authority. In that sense, Eichmann, and the many like him, were "terribly and terrifyingly normal;" for her, he represented a "new type of criminal" who "commits his crimes under circumstances that make it well-nigh impossible for him to know or to feel that he is doing wrong." In describing Eichmann in this manner, she sought to tie the meaning of Eichmann and his trial to her larger work on the effects of totalitarian systems on individuals.[70]

Given their understanding that anti-Semitism motivated violence against Jews (as evidenced in the swastika epidemic), their efforts to portray the Holocaust as a crime against humanity, and their ongoing attempt to include Jews within the American consensus, Jewish leaders harshly attacked Arendt's interpretations. Joachim Prinz of the American Jewish Congress charged her with painting Eichmann as a "sweet, misguided man." A reviewer whose work was circulated by the ADL claimed that Arendt was upset that Eichmann failed to "beat what the author clearly regards as a 'bum rap.'" The ADL itself said, "It is common knowledge that Eichmann himself deliberately planned the cold-blooded senseless liquidation of an entire people." They were joined by other prominent voices. Norman Podhoretz claimed that Arendt's interpretation "violates everything we know about the Nature of Man." "No person could have joined the Nazi party, let alone the S.S.," he went on, "who was not at the very least a vicious anti-Semite. No banality of man could have done so hugely evil a job so well; to believe otherwise is to learn nothing about the nature of evil." Banding together, America's major Jewish organizations put on an all-out media blitz against Arendt.[71]

These two events—the first the swastika epidemic, which suggested that a Jewish failure to educate about the Holocaust had left children to draw erroneous conclusions about the nature of the Nazi regime, and the second the Eichmann trial, which inspired a work that threatened to overturn much of their public relations work so far—encouraged Jewish organizations to adopt a more aggressive posture against anti-Semitism at home and abroad. The need for a more forceful public campaign against anti-Semitism became even more evident after it became clear, in the words of the AJC, that these events were "providing a macabre springboard for anti-Semitic propagandists and has apparently triggered threats and malicious acts against Jews in a number of countries."[72]

Many major racist and anti-Semitic organizations sought to deny the facts presented in the Eichmann case. The National States Rights Party conducted a "counterattack against the Jew propaganda Eichmann trial." As Merwin K. Hart's *Economic Council Letter* put it, "Is it not likely that many of these six million, claimed to have been killed by Hitler and Eichmann, are right here in the United States and are joining in the agitation for more and more support for the State of Israel—even if the American public goes down?" Observing such activity, the fact-finding division of the American Jewish Committee noted a year later that the neo-Nazi movement was ushering in its most "brazen" phase since the end of World War II, primarily because of the swastika epidemic and the Adolf Eichmann trial. "During the past five years, a series of acts of terror has, apparently, enlarged the public 'tolerance' or 'expectation' of such acts. In the United States for instance, we have become 'familiar' with a chain of bombing and attempted bombings of synagogues that began in 1957, continuing into this year. Our shock at Rockwell's demands of gas-chambers for Jews has likewise become blunted by sheer repetition." (Rockwell is discussed in the next chapter.)[73]

America's Jewish organizations kept close tabs on the actions of anti-Semites in the United States and abroad, paying especially close attention to meetings between Nazis of different nationalities. The chief method for dealing with rabble-rousers was advanced by Sol Fineberg of the American Jewish Committee. Reasoning that Rockwell and his ilk gained power or influence only through publicity, Fineberg called for a strategy of "quarantining" rabid anti-Semites by limiting, as much as possible, their access to the media. Many Jews were initially uncertain about his policy, but eventually all, with the exception of the more militant Jewish War Veterans (which had a difficult time remaining silent when confronted with Rockwell's inflammatory rhetoric), lined up behind it.[74]

Spurred by the perceived neo-Nazi specter and the awakening of Holocaust consciousness at home and abroad, and encouraged by the space created by strained German-American relations and the relaxation of East-West tension, American Jewish organizations took a more assertive stance against signs of neo-Nazi or anti-Semitic activity in Germany. For example, American Jewish groups became involved in a campaign to extend the statute of limitations for prosecuting Nazis from the World War II era which, according to the German penal code under which Nazis had been tried and punished, would expire in mid-1965. Adenauer believed that the trials of Nazi war criminals needed to stop because, as he informed Israeli ambassador Eliezer Shinnar in 1963, they represented a painful reminder of the German past that damaged the Federal Republic's present international standing. The Federal Republic announced in late 1964 that it would not extend the statute of limitations for war crimes. In response, American Jewish organizations lobbied legislators on Capitol Hill, and Senators Jacob Javitz and Abraham Ribicoff introduced a sense-of-Congress resolution calling on the president to formally request an extension of the statute of limitations from the Federal Republic.[75]

Although all Jewish groups believed that the trials should continue, they disagreed on how hard and in what way to push for it. Again, the familiar cleavages became apparent. The AJC argued against using media protests, preferring indirect means. The president of the AJC, for example, met with the West German minister of justice in Bonn to persuade him to extend the statute. Although Jewish groups shied away from promoting negative representations of Germans in the media, they nevertheless were willing to threaten to do so. Back in the United States, the AJC's Jacob Blaustein warned the German ambassador to the United States, Karl Heinrich Knappstein, "Germany would make a grievous mistake if it acted under the erroneous impression that U.S. public opinion—either non-Jewish or Jewish—was no longer sensitive as to what Germany does or does not do from here on."[76]

Others, however, preferred a more public approach. The Conference of Presidents of Major Jewish Organizations and NCRAC approved of public relations campaigns that fostered picketing of West German consulates and the recruitment of nonsectarian groups to publicly call for extension of the statute. The Jewish War Veterans (JWV) carried out the most aggressive campaign. During a heated exchange with West German representatives in which the JWV protested the position of the West German government on the issue, a JWV participant observed that Knappstein became emotional and exploded, "You are threatening us!" A few months later, the JWV sponsored one of the most challenging public relations initiatives of the decade.[77]

On 18 February 1965, the *New York Times* carried a page-long advertisement entitled "A Message for the Conscience of the World." Sponsored by the JWV, the advertisement sought to alert world opinion to evidence, like the statute of limitations issue, that Germany was turning "its back on its moral obligations to the world," threatening world peace, and betraying "the very people to whom it owes the greatest moral debt." Specifically invoking world war narratives of the German people, the JWV cited these issues as evidence that "the weaknesses and defects of German character once again have begun to show signs of dominating German life." In linking Germany's invidious past to these contemporary concerns, it sought to delegitimize Cold War aspects of Germany, arguing, for example, that viewing Germany as "an ally in the struggle against community tyranny" was not enough because Germans have "accepted such alliances before for their own terrible ends." Although such pressure was eventually successful in convincing the West German government to extend the statute, this assault on Germany revealed the limits accepted by mainstream Jewish opinion. Julius Klein disaffiliated himself from the JWV, an organization he used to represent, and Philip Klutznick tried to use his personal friendship with the president of the JWV, Monroe Shein-berg, to de-escalate tensions.[78]

Finally, Jewish groups made known their displeasure at the perceived rise of German nationalism, as reflected by the gains made by the NPD and the election of Kurt Georg Kiesinger as chancellor in 1966. In a news-letter to Jewish groups after returning from a trip to Germany, Joachim Prinz argued that it was "stupid on the part of the German people to have elected Kiesinger at a time when the NPD, a neo-Nazi party, gar-nered 250,000 votes in the state of Hesse and 750,000 votes in Bavaria." For Prinz, Kiesinger's election meant "that membership in the Nazi party is no longer a political stigma in Germany." Although alarmed, Prinz asked that his report remain "off the record." In typical belligerent fash-ion, the JWV eschewed such deference and publicly rejected Adenauer's plea to accept Kiesinger, stating in a press release that his election was "unacceptable."[79]

Still, despite these concerns—and their newfound willingness to voice them—Jewish organizations continued to refrain from a more aggressive course of action. The space opened up by the easing of the Cold War and the strains in the American-German relationship afforded Jewish groups greater opportunities to promote, endorse, or, at the very least, acknowl-edge narratives that invoked Germany's Nazi past. But most Jewish groups believed that enough progress had been made in advancing their interests that it was more useful to cooperate with West German officials than to openly antagonize them. Moreover, mainstream Jewish organizations did not seek to take public stances that would place them in opposition to the American government, even though its legitimacy was coming under increasing scrutiny during the Vietnam period.

The 1960s ushered in a different political atmosphere for actors interested in memory narratives of Germany. The cooling of Cold War ardor and the willingness of Kennedy and Johnson to consider détente with the Soviet Union opened up permissible space for narratives more critical of Ger-many and its past. Sensitive to shifts in attitudes related to the German-American relationship, officials from the Federal Republic of Germany and the American Council on Germany understood the dangers inherent in this new political environment. But they overreacted and disappointed their allies in the American government and in American Jewish circles with their overheated rhetoric, costing them political support for some of their initiatives. Still, even though events of the 1960s frayed the coalition in favor of Cold War narratives of the German people, it remained intact because of the continued Cold War framework and the effective public diplomacy initiatives by the West German government.

What all parties interested in German representations failed to understand, however, was the impact of these depictions on American attitudes. The following chapter seeks to understand the effect of these narratives, and particularly the anti-German wave, on American beliefs.

5

"We Refuse to Be 'Good Germans'"

Germany in a Divided Decade, 1959–1969

When Stanley Kramer's controversial *Judgment at Nuremberg* was released in late 1961, American and West German officials who worried about the film's impact on U.S.-German relations could not have foreseen the profound but ambivalent reception it would have over the course of the decade. Rather than stimulating a wave of anti-German sentiment, the film elicited a variety of responses over the next several years that underscored the erosion of the Cold War consensus, as reactions to three separate screenings of the film indicate.

Before the upheavals began in earnest, spectators at a preview of the film held in San Francisco on 12 August 1961 focused most of their substantive comments on the degree of guilt that average Germans bore for Nazi Germany and the Holocaust. For those who interpreted the film as a righteous effort to tackle the issues of the Nazi genocide, the film "outlined and detailed the German character perfectly in their denial of knowledge and or responsibility." Others argued that focusing on the Germans was a distraction: "Why not save resentment for the communist[s], instead of a party that is no longer in power? Let us live in the present not in the past." Moviegoers who saw the film at this exhibition early in the decade interpreted it in a classic Cold War context, one in which the main terms of the debate revolved around traditional issues of German culpability for the horrors of World War II.[1]

This now-classic Cold War interpretation of Germans was affirmed at the world premiere of the film hosted by Willy Brandt in Berlin four months later. But this time, given the locale of the screening, the new capital of freedom, journalists in attendance focused less on the negative representations of past Germans and more on how present-day Germans were reacting to the film. Interpreting the movie in the context of their German surroundings, many were impressed with the willingness of most Germans to face up to the damning work. Reporters noted that the Germans were "grim" or sat through the film in "stoic silence." Others described German viewers as "pleasantly surprised" or "dazed" by the film. Although a few Berliners denounced the film, according to the reviewers, most hailed it for its "piercing honesty." Discussed in the context of Brandt's opening comments and the circumstances of the city of Berlin itself, these reports of the German reaction suggested that Berliners would lead the rest of the country into an honest appraisal of the German past. In this framework, then, the emphasis on the bravery of present-day Germans in facing the communists and their own horrific past suggested that Germany had made substantial progress in its effort to become like the United States. When compared to the test screening that took place in the United States, the Berlin premiere shifted the focus of moviegoers from the guilt of past Germans to the attitude of present ones in dealing with their history.[2]

But by the middle of the decade, the interpretation of the film had shifted dramatically. When *Judgment at Nuremberg* appeared on television on the same day in 1965 that Alabama state troopers attacked peaceful marchers at a bridge in Selma, Alabama, many viewers used the film as a basis to judge Americans rather than to evaluate Germans (past or present). Millions of Americans received their first images of "Bloody Sunday" when the film was interrupted by *ABC News* that night to display footage of the carnage. Several viewers believed that the footage of Selma was actually a part of the film. Andrew Young, member of the Southern Christian Leadership Conference, wrote, "The violence in Selma was so similar to the violence in Nazi Germany that viewers could hardly miss the connection." The meaning that many Americans drew disturbed them greatly. "The pictures from Selma were unpleasant," wrote Warren Hinckle and David Welsh of the publication *Ramparts*. "The juxtaposition of the Nazi Storm Troopers and the Alabama State Troopers made them unbearable." As a result, many Americans framed their outrage with officials in Alabama through the prism of Nazi Germany. As one concerned citizen from Wisconsin wrote to his senator, "Are we seeing the days of Hitler lived in our own country? Disregard politics—fight for human rights, stop all Federal money going to Mississippi and Alabama." In Congress, angry representatives compared George Wallace to Hitler and Alabama state troopers to Nazi storm troopers. Walter Mondale, senator from Minnesota, declared, "This is totalitarian oppression at its worst—it is what we fought against in World War II and it is what we are fighting against in the cold war today." In the increasingly difficult decade of the 1960s, many Americans stopped worrying about Germany becoming like America and started worrying about America becoming like Nazi Germany. Faced with scenes of brutality such as had occurred in Selma in their own country, Americans increasingly felt uncomfortable sitting in judgment on the Germans.[3]

These radically different meanings drawn from the same film over the course of the 1960s suggest that the easy official American and West German assessments of the origins, course, and ultimate resolution of the "anti-German wave" often missed the complex cultural milieu in which these representations were taking place. When faced with evidence that anti-German attitudes did not attend the proliferation of anti-German products in the 1960s in the United States, some West German officials declared victory, concluding that their public diplomacy work had staved off mass adoption of anti-German sentiments. But as the reception of *Judgment at Nuremberg* suggests, a close reading of these texts and their reception in American society indicate that the story of German representations in American society during the 1960s is both more complex and more interesting. Beginning with an examination of some of these programs and products and then shifting to how these representations functioned in American society, this chapter argues that the anti-German wave had a limited impact, not necessarily because of the superior public diplomacy work of the Federal Republic but because the Cold War consensus, of which German representations were a constitutive part, fragmented during the decade.

Pinpointing an exact time for the breakdown of this consensus in an almost impossible task; instead, it is more useful to think of it as a process spurred on by great changes in society. The outbreak of an effective African American civil rights movement represented the first real crack in the Cold War consensus. It was not that the methods and strategies of organizations like the Southern Christian Leadership Conference (SCLC) were radically anti-American (in fact, many historians have argued that leaders of the civil rights movement were inheritors of the democratic traditions of Jefferson and Lincoln). Rather, it was the fact that, with the help of the new medium of television, Americans in the North came face-to-face with a cruelty and savagery that many would never have imagined possible in their fellow citizens. Martin Luther King's strategy of nonviolent resistance exposed the rabid and irrational fear that many southerners held of African American equality. And yet as the decade wore on, the focus and mood of the civil rights movement turned angrily toward de facto segregation in northern and western states. In the process, northern whites went from disapproving moralizers to desperate defenders of the status quo. The struggle over racial equality in the United States revealed a nation not nearly as perfect as it had believed itself to be. As African Americans pushed for full participation in American society, a growing number of young affluent whites became intent upon refashioning that society. Drawing from the malcontent beat generation of the 1950s, the New Left, under the direction of Tom Hayden and others, criticized contemporary American society for its impersonal, bureaucratic nature. They assailed all of the cherished beliefs of the liberal Cold War consensus, charging that contemporary America denied Americans the power to shape their own lives. Included in this broadside against American society was a scathing indictment of American foreign policy in the Cold War. While he did not condone the repressive conduct of the Soviet Union, Hayden, author of the Port Huron Statement, the manifesto of the Students for a Democratic Society, accused the United States of morally bankrupt policies in the Third World, in the process mocking the notion that the United States headed a "free world." Hayden and others lambasted the bruising conformity of Cold War anticommunism, arguing that it blinded Americans to racial and ideological injustices in the domestic sphere and to postcolonial pain and inequality in the Third World.[4]

As the decade wore on, the war in Vietnam became the lightning rod for such sentiments. Indeed, as the futility of the war in Southeast Asia became apparent and the conflict appeared increasingly immoral, Vietnam became the symbol of another, far different historical narrative.

Rather than casting the United States as the defender of the free world, this new narrative portrayed it as an imperialistic nation bent on world domination. Historians of the New Left highlighted the ways in which the United States sought to paralyze underdeveloped Third World nations as permanent vassals of American capital, citing U.S. involvement in the Western Hemisphere and Asia and the quest for global markets as proof of the capitalist system's insatiable appetite. By far, the most influential of these works was William Appleman Williams's *The Tragedy of American Diplomacy,* which used the literary trope of tragedy to underscore the betrayal of American ideals in American foreign policy toward the Third World. Williams and his emerging Wisconsin school forged a new narrative, heavily dependent on the notion of expansionist tendencies in American-style capitalism, to explain the conduct of American foreign policy. In this narrative, Berlin became irrelevant and the issue of West German revival became a stain on the American conscience. By the end of the decade, a growing number of Americans viewed their country in an unfavorable light.[5]

As the Cold War consensus that had supported and defined America's role in the world publicly splintered during the 1960s, Cold War narratives of the German people did also. The Cold War understanding of Germany remained hegemonic, but other memory communities drew different lessons from that interpretation. Cold War narratives of Germany had been formed in an age of consensus and agreement about the superiority of American civilization, and this meaning remained among mainstream products, which continued to use Cold War narratives of the German people to celebrate the United States by drawing distinctions between American society and totalitarianism. But that interpretation was now joined by a host of others that sought to understand these stories in light of the different circumstances of the 1960s. Liberals used these comparisons to urge reform of American society by making people aware of its shortcomings and encouraging them to agitate for legislative change. Radicals used them to advocate the overthrow of capitalist society by convincing people that the system was exploitative abroad and repressive at home. Conservatives sought to reform society by persuading people that liberal domestic policies were dedicated to concentrating power in the hands of the state. Finally, the burgeoning white supremacist community rejected the premise of the Cold War narrative, arguing that Germany's history had been misrepresented by Zionist forces. Rather than believing in the redemptive power of the United States, they subscribed to the saving power of Nazi Germany and sought to incite a race war by persuading people that the system was run by Zionist Jews dedicated to destroying the white race. Oddly enough, as the ideological platforms of these communities demonstrate, events of the 1960s, along with the revival of interest in Germany, reinforced the Cold War narrative interpretation rather than reviving world war narratives of Germany, precisely because the close identification between the United States and Germany was the basis for much of these narratives. Berlin and, more important, the Berlin Wall did not remain immune, although they provided useful and ultimately decisive support for traditional interpretations of the Cold War narrative.

It is important to bear in mind that the revival of interest in Germany's past, in particular its World War II past, was spurred in large part by events taking place in the 1960s. In late 1959, juvenile delinquents in Cologne desecrated Jewish synagogues with swastikas, sparking an international wave of anti-Semitic violence. In May the following year, Israeli agents captured Adolf Eichmann and transported him back to Jerusalem, leading to a yearlong trial that was broadcast around the world. In the middle of the decade, the Federal Republic experienced a wrenching debate over extending the statute of limitations for war crimes. Later in the decade, the electoral successes of a neo-Nazi party, the National Democratic Party (NPD), highlighted the continuing appeal of anti-Semitism in Germany. Finally, in 1966, Kurt Kiesinger, a former Nazi functionary, became the chancellor, inciting an international debate on his past. The evolving applications of Cold War narratives of Germany's past were influenced by these events in Germany's present.[6]

"The Grocery Clerk Killed the Superman"

The visibility of Germany in the 1960s, particularly during the first half of the decade, prompted an upsurge in American entertainment of portrayals of Germany's role in World War II. During the 1960s, big-budget films and television shows dealing with the subject more than doubled over the previous decade. In many ways, the renewed focus in the 1960s on the European theater of war established a trend in representing the war that continued for the rest of the century. Representatives from the

West German government worried about the prevalence of films such as *The Battle of the Bulge* and *Is Paris Burning?* but they failed to realize these depictions were more concerned with maintaining the Cold War consensus than reviving the world war narrative.[7]

The Battle of the Bulge, a film about the last German offensive in the West, is a perfect example. With a big budget and star-studded cast, the film forsook strict historical accuracy in an effort to maximize profit through reaffirming the Cold War consensus. Its representations of Americans were entirely consistent with established stereotypes. The key American figure is Kiley, played by Henry Fonda, a former police officer now in the army. With his hunches shaped by police training and American common sense, Kiley epitomizes the capability of America's average fighting man. Surrounding Kiley are dedicated superiors and heroic colleagues; taken together, the characters constitute a paean to the determination and essential goodness of the U.S. Army and American society.[8]

The film's representations of Germans are also reminiscent of the 1950s. Portrayals of German leaders cover the spectrum. Living in an opulent bunker with attractive courtesans while waiting for German scientists to perfect jet planes, the V-2 rocket, and the atomic bomb, the character Kohler is lazy and corrupt. On the other hand, Hessler, the great panzer commander, is austere, dedicated, and completely fanatical. Rebuking Kohler's easy lifestyle and rebuffing one of his courtesans, Hessler initially appears to be a sober, responsible, and moral officer. But as the war continues and his bloodlust overtakes him, it becomes clear that his militaristic leanings stem from more than professional pride. After a military victory, Hessler exults to his subordinate Conrad: "The best possible thing has happened—the war will go on. Indefinitely, on and on."

Conrad serves as the "good German," the voice of concern and conscience, which by the 1960s, in the words of *New York Times* film critic Bosley Crowther, had become "inevitable now in war films." After learning of Hessler's militaristic fervor, Conrad denounces him: "All you believe in is a war. You have a war—you *like* war. . . . You are a murderer. You would murder my sons, you would murder my country, you would murder the whole world to stay in that uniform." Demoted to fuel-truck duty after his criticism of his superior, Conrad survives the titular attack on Allied forces, drops his gun, and walks back to Germany with the other defeated troops, ostensibly to begin the process of rebuilding a country destroyed by reckless superiors. In a further effort to soften representations of Germans, the controversial massacre of American prisoners of war at Malmédy is treated in a perfunctory, almost obligatory manner.[9]

While blockbuster films like *The Battle of the Bulge* offer a good place to understand mainstream representations of Germany, an even better place is television, which in the 1960s had become the country's most conservative medium—and the one that German officials seemed most worried about, given its extensive influence in American society. German officials expressed repeated concerns about two shows in particular: *Combat!* and *Hogan's Heroes*. Although both dealt extensively with Nazis, a close reading demonstrates that they were more interested in using World War II as a setting to reaffirm the truths of the Cold War narrative than in reviving hatred of the German people.[10]

Broadcast for five seasons, *Combat!* remains the longest-running World War II drama in television history, with 152 hour-long episodes. It was popular, often among the top-ten shows on ABC. Despite its success (or perhaps because of it), *TV Guide* reported in 1963 that "the filmmaking team responsible for the show has held such diverse opinion of how the war should be treated that the battle has often appeared to be taking place not so much in Normandy as in the front office." Premiering on 2 October 1962 and ending its run in 1967, the show spanned the middle part of the 1960s, when the American people were undertaking crucial debates about the nature of U.S. society. The brainchild of Robert Pirosh, a World War II veteran who was also involved in cinematic depictions of the war such as *Battleground, Go for Broke,* and *Hell Is for Heroes, Combat!* became widely known for its cutting-edge, gritty, and realistic style. It also became well known for its violence. To enhance its sense of realism, the series often integrated actual footage from World War II. The participation of the army in *Combat!*'s production also aided the show's realism. Despite these innovations in production values and concerns about realism, the themes of the series were quite conventional and in line with the Cold War consensus, a comfort to American viewers in a period of societal upheaval and chaos. In particular, the portrayal of Germans reinforced the Cold War consensus in every way.[11]

The series emphasized three interconnected themes. First and foremost, it was a celebration of American values and those who fought against totalitarianism in World War II. Second, the series often commented on the horrors of war. And third, the show reinforced the notion of totalitarianism by pointing out the consensus distinction between SS men and officers on one side, and regular, everyday German soldiers on the other. In all three themes, German representations played a crucial role.

Combat! presented American soldiers as a brave and virtuous lot, bent but not broken by a vicious war. Representations of Germans served as a necessary backdrop for the celebration of these virtues, the reasons for which heroism was necessary or compassion desperately needed. These qualities were highlighted in several episodes, most often through the soldiers' dedication to one another. The American GIs frequently risked themselves or the squad in an effort to save a colleague. The greatest and most persuasive personification of these ideals was Sergeant Saunders, played by Vic Morrow. Saunders epitomized values revered in American society: strength, intelligence, bravery, determination, loyalty, compassion, and leadership. Saunders was usually the moral compass of the show. If he temporarily lost his center through the brutality of war, he was sure to find it by the end of the episode. The producers of the show often used German characters as foils to highlight both what Americans stood for and what they stood against.

The soldiers often remind each other (and the viewer) of the greater purpose of their efforts. In "The Duel" (1964), when a German tank approaches a broken-down American fuel truck, Saunders helps the panicking driver, a young man who wants to abandon his repair efforts and flee (remarking that heroism "ain't in my blood"), to discover his inner courage through the realization of the importance of his delivery to American soldiers. In "A Rare Vintage" (1964), the loyalty of Saunders and his company to commanding officer Lieutenant Gil Hanley convinces a self-interested private to sacrifice himself for the rest of the men. In "The Masquers" (1967), soldier William Kirby's selflessness impresses a wisecracking American deserter, who shakes his head in wonder that "you tried to talk him [a German] out of killing me, even though you knew you would get it."

The soldiers often have a transformative effect on allies and adversaries alike. In "Gadjo" (1967), Saunders convinces Barbu, a Gypsy resistance leader who has pledged himself to exact revenge on a German prisoner of Saunders who might have valuable, timely information, that ending the war is more important than retribution. "I made that promise to avenge my tribe," Barbu tells Saunders. "I care nothing for your information. It is not my war." Saunders retorts: "This is your war. . . . Now don't tell me before the war that your camps were attacked and your women and children were murdered." He goes on: "All that's important to me is to get this war over. And if I can get him back alive and save a day or an hour then it's worth it." By the end, Barbu is convinced by both Saunders's words and his selfless actions that "this is our war."

In "The Cassock" (1965), a German soldier disguises himself as a priest in order to blow up a key bridge. Constantly thwarted by good-natured American troops seeking to help or spend time with him, he is visibly moved when, to maintain his cover, he is forced to hear a U.S. private's confession:

> Bless me, Father, for I have sinned. It's been six weeks since my last confession. Since then, I've taken the name of our Lord in vain and I've been selfish, Father. I prayed for an end to the war for personal reasons so that I might go home and see my family and a girl that I want to marry. I have forgotten about the oppression that we are fighting and that the defeat of the enemy would mean the end of oppression for millions of people. And I have thought only of myself. I'm sorry, Father. I'm sorry for these and all the sins of my past life. Help me, Father.

The private's confession in this episode baldly illustrates how the series sought to portray Americans in general. Shaken and torn about where his true duty lies, the German consoles the American GI in a halting manner: "In war it is not easy for a soldier to see where his duty lies. . . . Perhaps you have done all you could. Go now in the knowledge that you have been forgiven."

The goodness and innate virtue of Americans is often brought out in interactions like these between American and German characters, sometimes with potentially good Germans, as in "The Cassock," and other times with bad Germans. In "Masquerade" (1963), Saunders faces off against Kanger, a clever, cold, ruthless, and thoroughly "inhuman" SS killer masquerading as an American GI. When Kanger believes that he has bested Saunders, he crows before the prostrate American: "All Americans believe. The great American sucker. Make 'em cry and you can sell 'em anything you got for sale. [When I lived there for ten years] they tried to get me to go for their sentimental emotionalism. I wouldn't buy it, I never forgot who I was." In "The Long Walk" (1964), another episode about Nazi infiltration, SS captain Friedrich Kleppner revels in the apparent success of his deception at the end: "If you were in my unit I would have you shot. You are stupid and you are gullible. I couldn't walk and you carried me where I wanted to go." In "The Long Way Home" (1963), Saunders and his men are detained at a POW camp run by evil SS captain Steiner. Hoping to get information out of Saunders but reckoning that he would not break under torture, Steiner beats Private Gates, a meek grocer turned soldier, reasoning that Saunders will talk because the great weakness in the "powerful" American army is "compassion."

Such was the nature of America's fighting men, according to the show. When Hanley squares off against a formidable bomb maker in "The Enemy" (1965), the German marvels at his adversary: "You're not a professional soldier, are you, Lieutenant? I find it amazing that you people have lasted this long. Inferior material, amateur soldiers. Take you and I, for example. What did you have? Six months' training? I was schooled for eight years on how to meet the enemy." In "The Cassock," a German officer asks Saunders, "How long have you been in combat, Sergeant?" In a war-weary voice, Saunders quips, "It seems like my whole life." The officer presses the issue: "You don't like being a soldier?" Saunders's reply typifies the attitude of most GIs in the show: "It's not whether I like it or not. It's just a job that needs to be done."

It is important to point out that, despite German superiority in training and experience, the Americans always come out on top, often *because* of their American values. A distrustful German patrol kills the "inhuman" Kanger in "The Masquerade" because it believes him to be a GI, while an American patrol rescues the wounded Saunders even though he cannot provide all the necessary identifying information. As he is carried off, Saunders, ironically echoing Kanger's insult about Americans, mutters, "Suckers," thereby underscoring that American trust and compassion save lives. In "The Long Walk," it turns out that Saunders is smarter than Kleppner, having convinced the German that he was taking him to a Nazi rendezvous point when in truth he was carrying him to American lines. Saunders drives the point home by inquiring, "Who's gullible now, Captain?" Although on the surface, Americans might seem soft and out of their league, *Combat!* reinforced that they could fight smarter and harder than their adversaries without losing their compassion and humanity. As Saunders notes after Gates kills the sadistic Steiner in "The Long Way Home," "The grocery clerk killed the superman."

The second major function of German representations in the show was to highlight the horror of war. And here again, German representations brought home this message in both the background and foreground of the various narratives in the episodes. In the former, Germans represented the force against which Americans were fighting, in the face of which they found themselves in danger of losing what made them uniquely American. In the latter, Germans (often good Germans) made Americans aware of how war drives people apart.

Germany's role as the oppositional force for Americans is starkly portrayed in "Doughboy" (1963), an episode in which Saunders encounters Philip, a shattered World War I veteran who believes that he is still fighting in the Great War. Mistaking Saunders for a German, Philip fires on him, yelling that the Americans are going to "take your von Hindenburg and wrap him up and ship him back to President Wilson for Christmas." After Saunders subdues him, he informs Philip, "It's not von Hindenburg and President Wilson. It's Hitler and President Roosevelt, and this is World War II." Saunders is eventually able to enlist Philip's aid in knocking out a big gun, prompting a happy Philip to declare, "After we win this war it will be peace forever." Through Philip's destroyed mental condition and his naïve fidelity to Wilson's World War I rhetoric, "Doughboy" uses the struggle against Germany to underscore the destructive nature of war.

The senselessness of war is best drawn out in "Hills Are for Heroes" (1966), regarded by many critics as the show's best episode. Hanley's men are repeatedly ordered to take a hill with very little support. As wave after wave fail and American casualties mount, Hanley and his men uncharacteristically question American leadership, Kirby foremost among them. Hanley is emotionally torn as he is forced to send men on what he knows is a suicide mission while he stays behind. Eventually, Hanley's men take the German bunker, but shortly thereafter are ordered to withdraw from their position because of German advances elsewhere on the front. War here is shown as lethal and pointless.

With Saunders the focal point of the show, the effects of war on him were often most highlighted. In "Survival" (1963), a relentlessly grim and bleak episode, a wounded Saunders, delirious and in pain, tries to find his way back to Allied lines. In "Odyssey" (1965), Saunders, again wounded, is trapped behind enemy lines. Assisted by a French gravedigger who finds him and provides him with a German uniform, Saunders impersonates a German soldier suffering from shell shock in an attempt to elude capture and make it back to American lines. Along the way, he has this exchange with an American POW, who learns his true identity and questions him about the soldier's uniform he is wearing:

American POW: What was his name?

Saunders: Keller, Ernst Keller.

American POW: I knew a Keller once, back in Newark. Hey, look at this [looking through Keller's wallet], five kids. How can they put guys at the front with five kids like this, huh?

Saunders: They figure that they can kill you just like anyone else.

American POW: Right now just another dead kraut, huh?

Saunders: How long were you up on the lines?

American POW: Five days, why? What's that got to do with it?

Saunders: Let me tell you something: don't go through that stuff.

American POW: I don't suppose there's much chance this guy made it through alive, huh?

Saunders: No, not much.

American POW: I mean that old man wouldn't have taken a uniform off of a live one. Did you ever think that you might have killed him yourself? I mean, when you first moved in on that town?

Saunders: Yeah, I thought about it.

American POW: And?

Saunders: I stopped thinking about it.

American POW: It's kind of like opening a grave.

Saunders: Keep it closed.

American POW: No, I don't want to. There's a guy's whole life wrapped up here. Somebody ought to look who cares, more than just a joker from the burial detail. Maybe some day one fat kraut will be going through your things.

Saunders: Maybe.

American POW: Did you ever think about that?

Saunders: Try not to.
American POW: You don't let yourself think about much, do you?
Saunders: Not if I can help it.
American POW: You're kind of the iron man, aren't you? The old
    pro. They ought to let you guys take over and send us recruits
    home.

The effect of the war on Saunders is also evident in "The Wounded Don't
Cry" (1963). When Saunders and his men take over a German field hospi-
tal as a base, Saunders proves unwilling to provide needed medicine to the
German patients. When one of his men urges mercy, Saunders says that
he does not trust any German because he has seen too many examples of
"kraut humanitarianism." He tells a subordinate that the man he replaced
was killed by a "wounded SS man waving a white flag" who killed "six
trusting Americans."

Of course, in these types of episodes Saunders eventually regains his
sense of humanity, often through interaction with "good Germans." It is
through such interactions that the show tries to illustrate how war can
drive good people apart. In "Cry in the Ruins" (1965), a woman franti-
cally searching for her baby in a town's ruins convinces American and
German units alike to put down their weapons and help her. Hanley's
men and their opposite numbers work together to rescue an innocent life
in the middle of a horrible war. But the war intrudes in the form of a
German captain who makes his way to the digging site and attempts to
resume the fight. He is killed by an American soldier, prompting the German commander to question their course of action in the middle of a
vicious war: "I am a soldier. I should have remained a soldier," the German Markes laments. "There's no room for anything else." "Isn't there?"
Hanley counters. "Then why were we digging?" "Perhaps we are digging
to find something that we have lost," Markes acknowledges, ordering his
men to continue the search for the missing baby.

A similar dynamic emerges in "Entombed" (1967), an episode that
finds Hanley and his men trapped in a caved-in mine tunnel with German soldiers and French resistance fighters. Away from the war, these
enemies recover their common humanity, especially after they encounter
a French woman and her lover, a wounded German soldier, hiding deep
in the recesses of the mine. Although the resistance fighters initially see

her as a collaborator and the German soldiers view him as a coward and deserter, all parties are eventually moved by the couple's sincere affection and love for one another. Moreover, two young soldiers, one American and one German, find that they hit it off very well. When Bishop the American marvels at the absurdity of laboring alongside a German "working my fool head off to save us both," Wexler the German drives home the point of the episode: "My father once told me, 'There's no such thing as born enemies.'" If it were not for the war, people such as these would be free to care for each other.

These types of encounters emphasize the third way in which German representations affirmed the Cold War consensus. Representations of Germans in the series reinforced the consensus distinction between SS men and officers on one side, and ordinary German soldiers on the other. Most episodes that featured interaction with Germans included both a bad and a good German, the former highlighting what Americans were fighting against and the latter showing the redemptive promise of the German people after the war. As we have already noted, the "bad German" was often represented by the SS. Private Newman makes this explicit in "The Wounded Don't Cry" when he advises Saunders, "Look, Sarge, there is a difference between the Wehrmacht and the SS." SS men like Kanger, Kleppner, and Steiner were responsible for the war, the fanatics who believed in it as a conflict of racial supremacy.

Representations of German officers offered a transitional category. In all instances, German officers were represented as formidable, urbane, and, on the surface at least, gentlemanly. Some turn out to be honorable; some do not. In "The Chateau" (1963), the best episode of this type, the squad encounters Major Richter while hiding out in a French chateau. Although he initially appears kind and urbane—the chateau's master goes so far as to tell his daughter that he is "obviously a gentleman, well-educated, proper" because "breeding always tells"—Richter reveals himself to be a cold-blooded killer who has come to raid the chateau of its treasures, including its most precious possession, the family's daughter. This theme is replicated in "No Time for Pity" (1963), which features a German officer seeking to use his power to win the favors of an innocent woman while holding a group hostage. Observing the German officer bullying a young man, the woman successfully distracts him, buying time for the others to escape, by flattering him in the terms he wants to hear: he is "strong" and a "conqueror."

Not all officers were diabolical. Some were simply coldly capable enemies. In "The Hunter" (1964), Saunders squares off against Captain Heisman, a Junker who employs a special hunting rifle in their episode-long
duel. To Heisman, Saunders is no better than an animal; when he appears
to have bested Saunders at the end of the episode, he calls his opponent
"the most interesting animal I've ever killed." After the walls cave in on
Heisman during a well-timed American air raid, the episode ends with
the prostrate German caressing his rifle as his surroundings blow up.

In "The Enemy," Hanley captures Karl, a bomb expert, just as the
German finishes rigging a town that the Germans are evacuating. Hanley manages to enlist Karl's help in defusing the bombs through both
the threat of force (the point of a gun) and the revelation that the towns-
people are about to return. Averring that innocent civilians should be off
limits, Karl agrees to deactivate bombs intended for American troops.
Karl proves himself to be a highly capable, even talented soldier—he has
set out the bombs very cleverly, based on his knowledge of American GIs'
habits. He is also a principled soldier, evinced in both his desire to save
innocent lives and his repeated attempts to escape Hanley's clutches—the
first duty of any captured soldier. Karl's humane qualities are driven home
at the end of the episode: he has maneuvered the unwitting Hanley into
the vicinity of a hidden bomb, but the American's life is spared by the
fortuitous appearance of a nun—unwilling to kill her as well, Karl makes
the bomb's location known. After he defuses the bomb, he declares to the
nun, "You may always remember, Sister, that on this day and in this place
you have deprived my fatherland of one of its most resourceful soldiers."

And sometimes officers were just good guys. In "Just for the Record"
(1963), a French woman, Annette, hides Saunders in her apartment, where
he witnesses the loving relationship between her and her German lover, a
gentle, generous officer named Kurt. "There is no war" in her apartment,
Kurt tells her, and he is angry that "Berlin lies to us." Even when Saunders
is forced to wound him mortally after discovering him, Kurt prioritizes
Annette's life, imploring her to flee with Saunders to safety. His nobility
is eclipsed by that of a German general in "Escape to Nowhere" (1962);
involved in an assassination attempt against the Führer, he is a man genu-
inely torn over the honor and patriotism of his actions, especially after his
daughter finds out and denounces him to the SS.

More often, however, "good Germans" were represented as enlisted soldiers or men unaffiliated with the military. As the kindly German Carl Dorffman put it in "Forgotten Front" (1962), "I am no one's enemy. I never had any fight in me. . . . I say to my father, 'It's easier to smile than to fight.'" The predatory German lieutenant in "No Time for Pity" is balanced out by a kind, harmless German who fumbles with a French-German dictionary and refuses to fire on fleeing children. The ruthless Kanger in "Masquerade" is countered by Lieutenant Comstock, another infiltrator among the American soldiers, who blanches at shooting at his own troops to maintain his disguise and seeks to revise the mission to save them instead.

In some cases, extremely good Germans have a transforming effect on Americans, especially Saunders, who is constantly threatened by the prospect of losing his humanity. In "The Wounded Don't Cry," Saunders is reminded of their common humanity by German medic Carl Bauer, who is dedicated to the wounded, kind to animals (he even helps a fallen bird return to its nest) and, most important, opposed to the SS. He denounces its members as "fanatics" and "butchers" and, incredibly, joins Saunders in a firefight against them in the climactic finale. The German chaplain in "The Chapel at Able-Five" (1966) criticizes both Saunders and his German adversary for "being so dedicated to destruction that you can't see that it is all a waste"; the chaplain makes the ultimate sacrifice at the end by throwing himself on a grenade to save both men. In "Odyssey," Saunders is visibly affected by a German soldier who believes Saunders is a comrade of his from the Afrika Korps and protects him against those who question Saunders's cover story of shell shock. After his protector dies in a skirmish with American troops, Saunders insists on going through his things personally—the very thing he had warned the green American POW against in the beginning. A simple enlisted man shows Saunders how to regain his humanity.

A close reading of the series shows that West German officials who worried about *Combat!* were off the mark. Regardless of its setting and although *Combat!* included some German representations that were less than ideal, the series as a whole was more concerned with shoring up American confidence than defaming Germans as part of an anti-German wave. And its general interpretive thrust was not to revive the world war narrative but to affirm the notion of totalitarianism and point out the horrors of war.

Although *Hogan's Heroes* took place in World War II Europe also, it departed from *Combat!* in significant ways. Unlike *Combat!* which took itself and the war seriously, *Hogan's Heroes* was a situation comedy that sought to play up war for laughs. In one ill-conceived radio promotion for the show, star Bob Crane quipped, "If you liked World War II, you'll love *Hogan's Heroes.*" Consisting of 168 episodes spanning six years from 1965 to 1971, the show focused on an Allied team of heroes stationed at a prisoner-of-war camp in German territory to gather information and wreak havoc. Unlike *Combat!* there was no conflict of vision regarding the show. The production team was stable and committed to portraying the war as farce. Also, a much smaller cast of characters meant that characterization could be more precise and thoroughly rendered. Finally, the location of the action, behind German lines in a German prisoner of war camp, allowed the series to detail the absurdities and failings of the totalitarian regime from the inside. These differences aside, however, the general thrust of *Hogan's Heroes* mirrored that of *Combat!* almost exactly.[12]

Like *Combat! Hogan's Heroes* was first and foremost a celebration of American values. And like Saunders, Hogan as the lead character embodied all that was good about America. Hogan is resourceful, clever, brave, dedicated, and compassionate. Almost every woman he encounters (most of them beautiful) falls for him. He has his men's complete trust, and he is committed to the war effort. In "Hogan Gives a Birthday Party" (1966), Allied pilots encourage Hogan to return to England with them. Hogan replies bravely, "Don't tempt me. Unfortunately, there's a war going on." And although there is a clear pecking order within the camp among the POWs, Hogan rarely has to pull rank. His men follow his lead without question, even when he barks apparently absurd orders without divulging his true plan (which is often). It is a functioning, effective bureaucracy based on trust and honor.

The men Hogan leads represent a mini-re-creation of the Allies, almost in the style of *The Berlin Express.* As LeBeau, Robert Clary plays to all the positive stereotypes of the French: he is the resident chef who is fond of fine food, drink, and women. Richard Dawson plays Newkirk, a British confidence man and tailor, adept at cards, magic, and other forms of deception. They are joined by two American soldiers, Kinchloe and Carter, the former a communication expert, the latter a munitions specialist. The character of Kinchloe (or Kinch for short) was remarkable for the time because he was played by Ivan Dixon, an African American; and as Hogan's putative second in command, he enjoyed respect and authority among the men and was almost always the straight man (as opposed to a buffoon, a common depiction of many African American characters before him). In commanding such a diverse group so effectively, Hogan demonstrated the virtues of American leadership.

Present in the pilot but notably absent in the rest of the series was Ivan Minsk, a Russian soldier. Accounts differ as to why Minsk was dropped from the cast of characters. Leonid Kinsky, who played Minsk, claimed that it was his decision to leave the series because of moral concerns: "The moment we had a dress rehearsal and I saw German SS uniforms, something very ugly rose in me." That Minsk was not replaced with a similar Russian character (as Kinchloe was replaced with an almost identical black character in 1970) suggests that, regardless of what Kinsky's personal reaction may have been, Minsk did not "work" for the purposes of the show. This was the explanation given by the show's creators. Including a Russian character as part of a team led by an American would have harkened back to a World War II view, not a Cold War one. Instead, the Russians were represented by Marya, an occasional character who worked with Hogan but still was not entirely trusted by him.[13]

The major theme of the show was the superiority of American civilization, as exemplified by Hogan, over the German one in which he and the others were held captive, a theme symbolized by the title card, which featured Hogan's hat casually tossed over a spiked German helmet. As such, the primary thrust of the show was to highlight the dysfunctional nature of the Third Reich. As writer Richard Powell explained, "I tried to show that the whole Nazi regime was based on fear. In a lot of my scripts I would have the Gestapo come in and throw the fear of God into everybody." Hogan would not have been nearly as successful with his limited resources if he could not exploit that fear to achieve his purposes. In that sense, the show was a classic indictment of totalitarianism, a description that Hannah Arendt would have easily recognized and endorsed.[14]

We see this fear at work most in the show's primary German representations, Colonel Wilhelm Klink, commander of Stalag 13, the POW camp, and his subordinate Sergeant Schultz. Both men try to navigate the system to survive. The greatest German fear, and the source of Hogan's greatest leverage, was relocation to the Russian front, a concern best explored in "Don't Forget to Write" (1966), an episode in which a Luft-waffe official comes to Stalag 13 to recruit Klink to fight in the East. In characteristic fashion, Hogan tries to save Klink, concerned that he will be replaced by someone more competent. He convinces a desperate Klink to avoid food and sleep in an effort to fail his impending physical exam. As a result, Klink is gratified to hear the German medic declare that he is "in terrible physical condition" but crestfallen to learn that he has "passed the one important test for combat assignment to the Russian front—you are breathing." The arrival of Klink's replacement, Gruber, realizes the fears of both men: Gruber proves to be a tough disciplinarian with the POWs, his harshness prompting Klink's superior General Burkhalter to admonish Klink: "I hope that you just learned something, Klink, in case you ever come back from the Russian front—which is doubtful." The resourceful Hogan, of course, figures out a way to save Klink.

As "Don't Forget to Write" and countless other episodes empha-size, Hogan's men and the leaders of Stalag 13 are often thrown into an unlikely alliance. Their common enemy is totalitarianism, as manifested by the SS and the Gestapo, which were often conflated in the show. In fact, the show strongly plays up *Combat!*'s distinction between the SS and the Wehrmacht. In "The Battle of Stalag 13" (1966), the SS and the Wehrmacht literally threaten war with one another in a conflict manufac-tured by Hogan to exploit the tension. In the pilot, Klink confesses that he does not sympathize with the "New Order." In "Praise the Führer and Pass the Ammunition" (1967), Schultz denounces the "crazy SS." Klink finds himself almost involuntarily blaming Hitler for inflated expecta-tions in another episode, and then catches himself, muttering, "What am I saying?"

Still, the show highlights important differences between officers, as represented by Klink and others, and soldiers, as represented by Schultz. As we learn in the pilot, Klink is a member of the Prussian aristocracy. In "The Great Impersonation" (1966), Hogan instructs Schultz in how to impersonate a German officer: "To be a German officer, you have to be mean and nasty and arrogant. Arrogance is what makes a German offi-cer." In "Operation Briefcase" (1966), an episode about the 20 July 1944 attempt to assassinate Hitler, Hogan is instructed by operatives in London to provide a bomb briefcase to a general. In their verbal exchange Hogan damns the German military for its role in Hitler's rise:

Stauffen: We are determined to destroy this fool at any cost.
Hogan: I know who the fool is. Who is we?
Stauffen: The greatest military minds that Germany has ever
    produced. He dares call himself supreme commander. But we'll
    put him out of business, I promise you.
Hogan: It's the least you could do, considering—
Stauffen: Considering what?
Hogan: You're the same bunch of guys that put him in business.

The entire show was predicated on comparing the American and
Nazi systems, and the show's writers often hammered their points home,
using Hogan to comment on the superiority of the American order. After
listening to Klink agonize over how to navigate the deadly labyrinth of
Nazi politics in "Heil Klink" (1967), Hogan trumpets the superiority of
the American political system by asking, "Wouldn't it be easier if you
people just had an election every four years?" After maneuvering Klink
into doing what he wants in "Hogan Gives a Birthday Party," Hogan
tells Klink, tongue-in-cheek, "Every time I come face-to-face with this
cruel German cunning, I wonder why *my* side is winning." Hogan rarely
missed an opportunity to tout the superiority of American civilization to
the viewing audience.

While many of the most popular films and television shows of the
1960s contained representations of Germans that were construed as negative by the German government, a close reading of these cultural products
reveals that they were more concerned with affirming Cold War truths
than mounting an anti-German wave. Because of the heightened visibility
of World War II issues following the Eichmann trial and the publication
of William Shirer's book, many of these cultural products used wartime
Germany to emphasize mainstream values.

"Could We Be Nazi Followers?"

Not all visual products about Germany during the 1960s were so conservative, however. There was a small coterie of films that participated
in a general trend among American liberals to use the Cold War narrative to highlight the shortcomings of American society, using Germany
as a metaphor. Although the German government expressed great alarm

at these films because they seemed on the surface to indict Germany, a close reading illustrates the true target of their attacks. Unlike the more conservative "anti-German" products, which were primarily interested in bolstering American morale, these products sought to challenge comfortable notions of American superiority and righteousness in the Cold War.

These films were part of a larger movement among liberals to employ German representations to criticize American society. Many influential liberals sought to use the dominant lessons of Nazi Germany to highlight the faults of U.S. society and thereby galvanize Americans into corrective action. In some of the most important works dealing with issues of American society in the 1960s, representations of Nazi Germany played a crucial role in framing the problems. For example, the Holocaust was marshaled to challenge the racial status quo. Stanley Elkins used Nazi imagery, and specifically the Holocaust, in *Slavery: A Problem in American Institutional and Intellectual Life* (1959) to argue that "closed systems" like concentration camps and slavery, in which a few held near-absolute power over many, were so degrading that they infantilized human beings unfortunate enough to dwell in them. He pointed out that prisoners who had been in concentration camps for an extended period of time sought to emulate their SS guards. In a similar way, slavery created Sambo, a slave "docile but irresponsible, loyal but lazy, humble but chronically given to lying and stealing." By explicitly linking the Holocaust and slavery, Elkins marshaled German representations to champion the cause of "damage liberalism," which argued for federal assistance to African Americans by highlighting the damaging effect that discrimination had and continued to have on them.[15]

The initial reception of Elkins's work was lukewarm, but when the civil rights movement went mainstream, so did his book. After 1962, sales averaged twenty-five thousand copies a year. Many professors began to assign it in their courses. Jewish intellectuals like Nathan Glazer, Norman Podhoretz, and Howard Zinn praised it. Non-Jewish intellectuals such as William Styron, Charles Silberman, and Michael Larrington used his ideas without critical evaluation. The height of its influence may have been when Glazer passed the book on to Daniel Moynihan, the assistant secretary of labor, who in turn distributed copies of it to his staffers. Believing that the nation needed to move beyond civil rights to embrace issues regarding employment and economic resources, Moynihan authored a memorandum entitled "The Negro Family: The Case for National Action." Moynihan used Elkins's comparison to dramatize the linkages between Nazism and black segregation and discrimination and to marshal emotions on behalf of African Americans. He clearly believed that the power of representations of concentration camps might influence Americans to support affirmative action.[16]

Feminists also used Cold War understandings of Germany to further their sociopolitical agendas. Betty Friedan employed the Holocaust to frame her arguments in her famous tract, *The Feminine Mystique* (1963). Friedan argued that American culture (she specifically accused women's magazines, colleges, and the advertising industry) had elevated the ideal of female domesticity. But she asserted that this "feminine mystique" was a lie that made many women feel degraded and debased. To make her point, she compared suburban homes to German concentration camps in one of the book's last chapters, "Progressive Dehumanization: The Comfortable Concentration Camp." She concluded, "The women who 'adjust' as housewives, who grow up wanting to be 'just a housewife,' are in as much danger as the millions who walked to their own death in the concentration camps."[17]

Her own experience and those of her colleagues informed her understanding of women's constricted role in the suburban home. To flesh out the concentration camp side of her argument, she drew from Bruno Bettleheim's 1960 *The Informed Heart*. Bettleheim, emphasizing that the SS had sought to destroy prisoners mentally and psychologically, saw troubling parallels in America's mass society. As he put it: "My interest is not in the importance of this process within a now defunct system, but that similar tendencies are present in any mass society and can be detected to some degree in our own time."[18]

Friedan used this insight to criticize America's Cold War consensus. America's leaders had trumpeted the American home, with a woman at its center, as a refuge and a defense against communism and totalitarianism. She made fun of Adlai Stevenson's claims that a housewife "inspired in her home a vision of the meaning of life and freedom." She argued that these sanctuaries, these bastions of Americanism, were themselves sites of totalitarian terror. Women had not volunteered for this role; they were pressured into it by the feminine mystique. Even more alarming were the number of women who, like their captive counterparts in the concentration camps, voluntarily contributed to their own subjugation. Despite the harsh tone of her criticism, she held out hope for reform, calling for a massive government program to uplift women, "a national education program, similar to the GI Bill."[19]

The greatest expression of this liberal desire to use the Nazi period to highlight the weaknesses of American civilization appeared in Stanley Milgram's work. Milgram began his famous experiment on obedience to authority in 1961, a few months after the Eichmann trial began. He wanted to explore why Germans had participated in the Holocaust. He was greatly influenced by Shirer's book, writing, "What I wanted to study was those characteristics in the Germans that permitted the history of the Third Reich to unfold." Subscribing to a world war narrative of the German people, he initially conceived of them as a unique case. Seeking to examine Germans and Americans in a cross-national comparison, he deliberately designed his experiment at Yale University to see how far subjects were willing to follow an authority figure's orders to punish another human being. He wrote at the time, "Let us stop trying to kid ourselves—what we are trying to understand is obedience of the Nazi guards in the prison camps, and that any other thing we may understand about obedience is pretty much a windfall, an accidental bonus."[20]

In the first paragraph of his first paper on his obedience experiment in 1963, he wrote: "It has been reliably established that from 1933–1945 millions of innocent persons were systematically slaughtered on command. Gas chambers were built, death camps were guarded, daily quotas of corpses were produced with the same efficiency as the manufacture of appliances. These inhuman policies may have originated in the mind of a single person, but they could only be carried out on a massive scale if a very large number of persons obeyed orders." After he carried out his initial experiment, he reported to the National Science Foundation that he had "once wondered whether in all of the United States a vicious government could find enough moral imbeciles to meet the personnel requirements of a national system of death camps, of the sort maintained in Germany. I am now beginning to think that the full complement could be recruited in New Haven." His results convinced him that Americans were no different than Germans—they, too, had the capacity for unthinkable inhumanity. As a result, he was very sympathetic to Hannah Arendt's conclusions in *Eichmann in Jerusalem,* and praised Vietnam War protestors. After 1969, he drew major comparisons with Lieutenant William Calley, the soldier responsible for the massacre of hundreds of Vietnamese civilians. The epilogue of his monograph on his research centered on My Lai: "The catalogue of inhumane actions performed by ordinary Americans in the Vietnamese conflict is too long to document here in detail. . . . To the psychologist these do not appear as impersonal historical events but rather as actions carried out by men just like ourselves who have been transformed by authority."[21]

American mass media publicized Milgram's experiments far and wide. Over the next several years, before Milgram published his monograph, his results were published in periodicals ranging from *Science Digest* to the *National Enquirer*. Many framed his experiments in the same way he had done, as their headlines indicate—"You Might Do Eichmann's Job," "If Hitler Asked You to Electrocute a Stranger Would You?" "Could We Be Nazi Followers?" *Science Digest* asked: "Does it take a madman or do the seeds of such slavish inhumanity exist in all of us?" Milgram received several letters from Americans who were horrified to discover that they could be Nazis. One high school student who had copied Milgram's experiment and reproduced its results with his classmates wrote that American teens were "comparable to the Nazi youth groups who were completely dominated by Hitler's ideas and followed his orders without hesitation." A school librarian voiced her concern over "the shockingly close parallel in the behavior of Americans in the 1960s and functionaries of the Nazi party in Hitler's Germany."[22]

Liberal filmmakers drew on these kinds of works to shape their approaches to Nazism. Abby Mann's work typified this approach. Collaborating with Stanley Kramer, Mann made three films during the 1960s that used the metaphor of Germany to explore moral issues involving the United States. In an unflattering piece, *Time* magazine called him "the crusader," judging him to be "a young man of great energy, some talent, and no humility" who nevertheless was the "most active screenwriter in Hollywood." In accepting the best screenplay Oscar for his most influential work, *Judgment at Nuremberg,* Mann told the audience that the inspiration for the film came to him as his sat in his "barren room in Manhattan" and "pondered what he could do for mankind."[23]

His crusading zeal is evident in his two most significant films, *Judgment at Nuremberg* and *Ship of Fools. Judgment at Nuremberg* focuses on the experiences of an American judge, Dan Haywood, who comes to Germany to preside over the trial of four German judges indicted for crimes against humanity during the Nazi period. The movie follows Haywood as he listens to the arguments of the lawyers, contemplates the actions of the defendants, keeps company with a beautiful German widow determined to prove to him and all Americans that not all Germans are monsters, and mingles with ordinary Germans in an effort to understand them and why they allowed National Socialism to happen. In the midst of the trial, the Berlin Blockade begins, and the American military starts pressuring the prosecuting attorney and Judge Haywood to go easy on the German judges because the United States needs the Germans as allies in the developing Cold War. Both refuse and the judges are sentenced to life in prison.[24]

Abby Mann and Stanley Kramer said that they wanted the film to challenge prevailing American attitudes toward the Federal Republic of Germany. When Mann first began his screenplay, he remembered, "It was considered a breach of good manners in polite society to bring up the subject of German guilt or the victims of the Third Reich." For Mann, this repression stemmed from an American desire to whitewash the German people in the name of Cold War expediency. As evidenced in his screenplay, Mann believed that there was no "ground zero" in which Germany democracy was reborn. Most of the Germans in his film come across as servile, arrogant, or cruel. For example, in one of the most powerful moments of the film, the German defense attorney approaches Judge Haywood after the conviction of his clients and informs him that, despite his ruling, his clients will go free in five years. Haywood compliments the young lawyer on his pragmatic assessment but sternly lectures him that its likely accuracy does not make it right. In the script, Mann writes that the defense attorney "is a little stunned. HAYWOOD has stopped him for a moment, making him think. But only for a moment. It is not long until the old rationalizations come into his face. He is indeed the symbol of the new Germany." In this way, Mann's screenplay echoed the sentiments of Shirer's work.[25]

And yet Mann maintained later that the film was about more than Germany. In a sense, Mann believed, he failed to portray what he had intended because, as he said in an interview, "I wasn't writing about Germany, I was writing about patriotism, to say that patriotism is evil." This intent can be seen in the way he juxtaposed unsavory episodes in American history with elements of Nazism. Perhaps the most obvious (and the one that several German viewers noticed) was the German defense lawyer's invocation of the widespread American belief in eugenics, as articulated by Supreme Court Justice Oliver Wendell Holmes in the early twentieth century. Other parallels existed also, including the willingness of American military personnel to subvert justice for national advantage in the Cold War. As the script, film, and interviews with Mann show, Mann's prey was the United States as much as Germany.[26]

Mann's *Ship of Fools* (1965) continues the themes found in *Judgment at Nuremberg*. Based on Katherine Porter's sprawling epic, the screenplay and film use Germany as a powerful prism through which to view the failings of Americans. In a far more didactic fashion than *Judgment at Nuremberg*, the film damned Americans who blithely tolerated the systematic abuses of American society as "good Germans," and criticized those on the left who championed revolution but failed to consider equality of the sexes.[27]

The titular vessel is a cruise ship traveling from Veracruz, Mexico, to Bremerhaven, Germany, just before the advent of the Nazi regime. A dwarf named Glocken serves as the audience's tour guide, often breaking the fourth wall and addressing viewers directly. Glocken informs the audience that he is on a "ship of fools" of all different sorts, and he warns them that they might find they themselves are fools or share some of the vanities and failings of the ship's passengers. The film follows several different characters, including the ship's doctor, the captain, a Spanish countess, a bile-spewing nascent Nazi, a Jew who fancies himself more German than Jewish, two idealistic American painters, and a group of Spanish laborers. With this cast of characters, Mann and Kramer spin an allegorical tale that challenges Americans to rise from their complacent slumber.

The dominant theme is that of the fool, and the most important fool in Mann's view is the normal "good citizen" who is nevertheless complicit in the evils of his or her state. Through repeated incidents, Mann hammers home the notion, popular among those in the New Left at the time, that everyday citizens who do nothing about injustice are no better than those who commit the crimes. This is a German boat, and the film takes place in the year 1933, offering Mann an ideal platform from which to make his case. One incident involves Herr Freytag, a German who is removed from the captain's table at the request of the bilious Nazi Rieber because it is discovered that he is married to a Jew. Relegated to a table with a Jew and a dwarf, Freytag seethes with anger at the self-righteousness of those who displaced him. Unable to contain his rage, he confronts the Germans at the captain's table. Addressing them as "good people," he says that his wife "never hurt anyone in her life . . . and you, you good-to-middling people, you are unfit to be in same world as her. I saw some of you in the chapel this morning. You kneel there and pray and pretend that you are good people—you can't even exist without your prejudices. And the worst thing about you is that you don't even recognize what you are." In the film the speech is directed to 1930s Germans, but the real audience is 1960s America, where similar sins were being committed. Later, however, the audience discovers in the most compromising scene of the entire movie that Freytag, who had appeared to be such a strong protector of his wife, had actually capitulated to social norms and peer pressure and left his wife—his impassioned speech, then, stemmed not from righteous anger but from guilt-induced loathing.

Mann uses the German Jew Lowenthal to strongly denounce patriotism and acceptance of the status quo. Throughout the voyage, he endures Rieber's taunts with patience and good humor. At one point, after Lowenthal helps Rieber, who is suffering from seasickness, Rieber privately tells Lowenthal that he should not take his public diatribes against Jews personally. In the next breath, however, Rieber dares Lowenthal to deny that Jews are the cause of Germany's past economic difficulties. At a party, Lowenthal's reasons for being so patient become more manifest. He tells Glocken that hearing German music makes him feel special and proud. When Glocken informs him that he is the most "German" person he knows, Lowenthal proudly displays his war medal—Iron Cross Second Class. Glocken concludes that Lowenthal is the "biggest fool on this boat." Lowenthal denies that the actions of those on the ship accurately represent the sentiments of the German population; Glocken counters with the results of recent German elections. Lowenthal insists that German Jews are special: "We are Germans first and Jews second." He counsels more patience. Besides, he argues in a bit of irony, there are a million Jews in Germany—"What are they going to do? Kill all of us?"

Although Mann's films were the most obvious examples of this use of Germany as metaphor, several other films also did so. Greatest among these was Rod Steiger's *The Pawnbroker* (1965), which used the Holocaust as a powerful means for understanding the shortcomings of the United States through the tale of Sol Nazerman, a Holocaust survivor and pawnshop owner in Harlem. In an attempt to start life over, Nazerman left the Old World many years ago. But he lives in the shadow of his Holocaust experience, in which everything he loved was destroyed. He shuffles through life like a zombie, without a care for anyone or anything; as his lover's father points out, he is a dead man walking, with no passion in his life. He never addresses the human problems of the people who visit his shop. He is heartless to them; in one telling example, a pregnant teenager comes in to pawn her diamond engagement ring. Without a note of compassion, he informs her, "It's glass." He does not believe in God, science, or politics; he believes only in money. He later explains to another character that he has withdrawn from life to protect himself.[28]

However, as the twenty-fifth anniversary of his Holocaust experience approaches, he begins having intense flashbacks to his former life (neatly done by director Sidney Lumet). Some are triggered by mundane things, such as a barking dog or riding in a subway car. But many more of the flashbacks are set off by violence. The sight of a young man attempting to flee a vicious gang beating prompts the memory of his friend's unsuccessful attempt to scale a concentration camp fence and escape. The most powerful memory, however, comes when a prostitute tries to sell Nazerman a gift given to her by a client. When she bares her breasts in a heavy-handed attempt to sweeten the pot, the sight of her flesh triggers paralyzing flashbacks to women in the concentration camp, most notably his own wife, who were raped by German soldiers. In relating the prostitute's situation to that of his deceased wife, Nazerman redefines his relationship to her pimp, Rodriguez, a man for whom he launders money. He now sees that he himself is implicated in the same kind of evil that afflicted him and his family. He is horrified by the realization, but he is unable to successfully sever his ties with Rodriguez. Rather, he tries to maneuver Rodriguez, and later street hoodlums seeking to rob him, into killing him and putting him out of his misery, but his assistant, the prostitute's boyfriend, sacrifices himself and takes a bullet meant for him. The film ends as the grief-stricken Nazerman wanders back out into the streets after witnessing his assistant die in his arms.

In addition to these films, popular songs circulating in the American mass media landscape satirized both Germans and America's easy embrace of comfortable notions of American superiority. Tom Lehrer's "Wernher von Braun" poked fun simultaneously at the famous rocket scientist's morality and at the United States, which had eagerly recruited the former Nazi. "Gather 'round while I sing you of Wernher von Braun," croons Lehrer, "a man whose allegiance / is ruled by expedience." In the middle of the song, Lehrer punctuates von Braun's moral bankruptcy: "'Once the rockets are up, who cares vere dey come down? / Dat's not my department,' says Wernher von Braun." Similarly, the Mitchell Trio savaged the Cold War narrative in songs like "I Was Not a Nazi Polka (Sieg Heil!)" and the "German Twelve Days of Christmas." Both songs ridiculed the notion that Nazism died with the Third Reich. In the first, Germans eager to whitewash the past insist, "Goering was a crazy we wanted to deport," "Dachau was just a resort," and "We tried to throw off Hitler right from the start." In the second, the gifts given on the twelve days of Christmas include Rudolf Hess's blessings, anti-Semites, and swastika scribblers. Artists like these shared in the broader effort to draw attention to American shortcomings by focusing on the failure of Germany to purge its Nazi past.[29]

Pioneering work by social scientists and psychologists, message movies by liberal filmmakers, and satirical songs all sought to repurpose the lessons of World War II and challenge comfortable assumptions about American moral superiority. By highlighting similarities between Nazi Germany and contemporary America, many of these works sought to mobilize action against continued injustice in U.S. society. Their goal was primarily reform—their belief was that the basic structure of American society was sound, and that most Americans, once made aware of the country's faults, would bring about the needed changes.

"The Perils of Silent Obedience"

The ideological (and often biological) children of American liberals, the New Left took this perspective further. Although both generations were saturated by the Cold War narrative through the mass media, their different collective experiences encouraged them to interpret the narrative in different ways. Todd Gitlin remembered, "The Jewish Cold Warriors of the Fifties and early Sixties were dead set on stopping Communism precisely because they had failed to stop the Nazis—whereas to me and people I knew, it was American bombs which were the closest thing to an immoral equivalent of Auschwitz in our lifetimes." To a generation that had no living memory of the Second World War but was confronted on an almost daily basis with the Vietnam War on television, the lessons of the Cold War narrative became inverted. The United States, not the Soviet Union, was the totalitarian menace that had to be stopped. America's young radicals concluded that the greatest lesson to be learned from Nazi Germany was not so much the importance of standing up to aggressors abroad but of standing up to a totalitarian system at home. They were convinced that the imperialism they witnessed in the Third World and the repression of dissent at home were linked, and the best way to combat this totalitarian system was to strike at its heart. Gitlin went on to observe, "There were some, or many for whom the Holocaust meant that nothing—neither private satisfaction nor the nation's greater glory—could ever supplant the need for a public morality. There were many Christians as well as Jews who concluded that they would never end up 'good Germans' if they could help it." Many young Jews gravitated toward this understanding of the relationship between Germany's past and America's present. The 1960s thus witnessed a widening gulf between the generations: the older's urge for reform inherent in the liberal critique and the younger's growing involvement in America's burgeoning radical movement.[30]

For many radicals, Nazi Germany was an entirely appropriate metaphor for the domestic scene of the United States. For Terry Robbins, leader of the midwestern Up against the Wall, Motherfuckers, the model to emulate was "the resistance in Europe during World War II." According to one activist: "Their analysis was that the U.S. was like Nazi Germany and the white working class was bought, and that the only thing a white radical could do was to function as a saboteur." *Fascism* was a term thrown around easily. Many radicals denounced the House Un-American Activities Committee hearings as fascist, and an underground satirical paper at Berkeley was called the *Fascist*. Protestors often invoked Hitler in their rhetoric. Mob resistance to a student demonstration in Bloomington, Indiana, led activist Jim Bingham to conclude, "Hitler would have been proud of such mob hysteria." When confronted with Pennsylvania state troopers attempting to remove students from the driveway of the Penn State president, seventy-five members of the Students for a

Democratic Society (SDS) screamed, "Heil Hitler" and "Gestapo" at the policemen.[31]

Radicals consistently applied such an understanding of the Cold War narrative to American participation in Vietnam. At a debate at Penn State, a supporter of the university's involvement in the Institute for Defense Analysis, a consortium of universities that carried out defense research for the government, invoked the consensus view of totalitarianism, arguing that "university-military research was necessary to prevent the rise of future Hitlers" and that such research "had saved the United States from Nazi domination in the 1940s." A member of the SDS rejected the comparison between Hitler and Ho Chi Minh, arguing that the United States was "the fascist nation," not North Vietnam. At Harvard University, the SDS repeatedly invoked the notion of totalitarianism to frame the war in Vietnam. Members of the organization handed out flyers on campus: "Did you know that General Ky's [an air force general in Vietnam] personal hero is Adolf Hitler?" In November 1966, SDSers at Harvard surrounded Secretary of Defense Robert McNamara and chastised him as "fascist" before he was rescued by police. At SUNY–Buffalo, students argued that "there is no difference between the American government [in this war] and the support the German people gave the Nazi government when it destroyed six million innocent people."[32]

The totalitarian image popped up at the watershed moments of the radical movement. Participants in the Free Speech Movement at Berkeley drew heavily from German representations to frame their understanding of academic repression. One observer recalled that university president Clark Kerr's attempt to prevent student Mario Savio from speaking offered eerie parallels for those in attendance. "We all heard stories of older professors who had escaped Nazi terror," David Goines remembered, "and who, stunned by what the police had done before their very eyes, expressed shame and rage that they had condoned an administration which resorted to Storm Trooper tactics to prevent one student from speaking to a crowd." The students drew heavily on German representations to articulate their need for action. One argued, "People only deserve the civil liberties they utilize and are willing to fight for. Hitler marched into Germany and took away civil liberties and few protested. If we are to criticize the Germans for being afraid to resist we ourselves must not be afraid." Another activist argued that his fellow revolutionaries were nothing like Eichmann; members of the Free Speech Movement understood "the perils of silent obedience" and were standing up for "one of the great moral issues of our century."[33]

Radicals believed that the incident that best encapsulated the wide gulf between liberals and radicals in applying the lessons of the Cold War narrative was the Democratic Convention of 1968. According to Todd Gitlin, the lessons of Germany for this younger generation had completely changed. "If Dean Rusk thought Vietnam was Munich, much of the movement thought Chicago was Mississippi—or the early days of Nazi Germany." Gitlin recalled that Tom Hayden had become "obsessed by a passion not to be like 'the good Germans.'" Gitlin at the time concluded that "the best of the good Germans were probably people who in their time were working on parliamentary reform, trying to keep their jobs, trying to keep their family and not make too many waves . . . but didn't see the big picture, that there was no possibility of peaceful reform." As she readied to march in protest, radical Susan Stern thought about "bullets ripping through flesh," "napalmed babies," "Malcolm X and lynching and American Indians," and "Auschwitz, and mountains of corpses piled high in the deep pits dug by German Nazis." At one violent clash between protestors and police, Elinor Langer remembered that half of the fleeing protesters saluted the police with "Heil Hitler." After the Chicago convention, the New Left continued to view the incident in a totalitarian context. Gitlin wondered, "Were we on our way to The Revolution or to the concentration camps? Was it Revolutionary Year Zero or fascism's Last Days?" Lawrence Lipton of the *Los Angeles Free Press* assailed a documentary created by Mayor Richard J. Daley's staff that portrayed the violence as necessary for "law and order," comparing Daley to Hitler and calling the documentary a model of Nazi-type propaganda.[34]

Inside the convention, however, members of the Democratic Party used some of the same rhetorical strategies. Of the massed police force outside, George McGovern remarked to a reporter from the *New York Times* that he had seen "nothing like it since the films of Nazi Germany." During the convention itself, Abraham Ribicoff stumped for McGovern, arguing, "With George McGovern as president, we would not have to have such Gestapo tactics in the streets of Chicago." Standing just twenty feet away, Daley hit back (and unwittingly furthered the comparison), shouting, "Fuck you you Jew son of a bitch you lousy motherfucker go home."[35]

The rhetoric surrounding the subsequent trial of the Chicago Eight (later the Chicago Seven after Bobby Seale's trial was severed from the rest) was suffused with notions of totalitarianism. The trial itself was interrupted by the profanity-laced diatribes of the defendants. In one of the most famous, Jerry Rubin denounced the judge, Julius Hoffman: "Every kid in the world hates you because of what you represent. You are synonymous with Adolf Hitler. Adolf Hitler means Julius Hitler." Before his severance, Bobby Seale was so adamant and vocal in framing his understanding of the issues in a totalitarian context that he was eventually removed from the trial. Before he was bound and gagged and then hauled away for contempt, Seale repeatedly referred to Hoffman as a "fascist," "fascist dog," and "pig," and called the police officers in the courtroom a "bunch of fascists."[36]

Indeed, as his subsequent memoir, *Seize the Time*, suggests, Bobby Seale and the Black Panther Party, which he cofounded, relied heavily on images and representations of Germans to define their opposition to the state. In briefing children about proper relations with the police, for example, Seale advised them to be quiet. "They're going to try to ask you questions in some kind of way, about yourself, gangs, and people in the community, so they can focus in on you cats," he warned. "That's trying to use you like Germany used little kids." Seale and the Panthers argued that "the power structure uses the fascist police against people moving for freedom and liberation." In their party platform and program of 1966, they called for an "end to the robbery by the white man of our Black community." They demanded the forty acres and two mules promised by the American government over one hundred years ago, framing their petition explicitly in terms of Nazi Germany. Noting that the "Germans murdered six million Jews" and now the German government was "aiding the Jews in Israel for the genocide of the Jewish People," they claimed that their demand was "modest" in light of the fact that "the American racist has taken part in the slaughter of over fifty million black people."[37]

Writing about his incarceration, Seale repeatedly referred to American prisons as concentration camps. "In prison those guys go out and they work like dogs. They are enslaved. These are our initial concentration camps," he said. "The prison system doesn't rehabilitate and doesn't really serve society." Later, Seale compared the jail in Salt Lake City to "a streamlined concentration camp." Seale remembered that the Panthers often referred to the CIA as the American SS. In countless confrontations with the police, they called officers fascist pigs; in one memorable encounter Huey Newton, asked if he was a Marxist, replied with another question: Were cops fascists? Even *pig* the term for police officers that Seale credited the Panthers with introducing to the national lexicon, was explicitly linked with Nazi Germany. Seale argued that one could only understand its full meaning if one looked "at the history of the KKK and Hitler's Gestapo." Seale concluded that the "greatest danger facing young people right now is the coming of a fascist state, like the one described by George Orwell in *1984*."[38]

After the implosion of the SDS in 1969, the Weathermen emerged as the most radical organization in the country. Like the SDS and the Black Panthers, they framed much of their activity in terms of the totalitarian framework. On the importance of Nazi imagery, historian Jeremy Varon notes, "Germany played a role in the minds of American activists, who often invoked Nazism to denounce their own government, whether for its 'genocide' in Indochina or its 'fascist' response to protest." One leader of the Weathermen announced before a violent rebellion began, "We refuse to be 'good Germans'!" In her memoir of her time in the Weathermen, Susan Stern wrote, "We were serious revolutionaries, who felt the necessity of doing something so earth-shattering in America that the American masses would finally take notice. Mr. And Mrs. America would . . . see our bodies being blasted by shotguns, our terrified faces as we marched trembling but proud, to attack the armed might of the Nazi state of ours." In comparing Nixon to Hitler, the Vietnamese to the Jews, and the United States to Nazi Germany, Stew Albert called the Weathermen "perfect" in their moral outrage.[39]

As the various movements—student, civil rights, and feminist—radicalized during the 1960s, they drew heavily from Cold War narratives to frame their revolutionary rhetoric and opposition to the state. Comparing their situation to that of Nazi Germany, they drew lessons from the failed resistance to Hitler and refused to be complicit "good Germans."

"All the Power Adolf Hitler Ever Had"

The Left did not monopolize the Cold War narrative in framing critiques of the United States—far from it. The emerging conservative movement also drew from its shared understanding of the German past to articulate deficiencies in American society. Like their counterparts on the left, American conservatives also struggled among themselves over how properly to apply the lessons of the past to the present. Also like their opposite number, Americans on the right did not shrink from framing their fellow conservatives as Nazis if it suited their purposes. Unlike the Left, however, the conservatives believed the greatest danger to American society came not from a fascist police force or an imperialist foreign policy but from the totalitarian tendencies inherent in the large liberal welfare state created by the New Deal and nurtured by successive administrations.

As we have seen, conservatives during and after the war employed German representations to frame their critique of American society. People like Albert Jay Nock referred to themselves as "the Remnant" that wanted to stay true to conservative ideals. He was joined by Friedrich von Hayek and Milton Friedman, whose core beliefs were founded on the premise that freedom required government to stay out of people's lives. "It is necessary to now state the unpalatable truth that it is Germany whose fate we are in some danger of repeating," Hayek wrote in 1944. Hayek also believed in the need for a strict moral code because otherwise a society tended toward totalitarianism. During the 1950s, William F. Buckley's *National Review* emerged as the vehicle most consistently used to denounce the liberal welfare state as a way station along the road to communist totalitarianism. Right-wing organizations such as the Minutemen and the John Birch Society became convinced that the liberal welfare state was a Trojan horse for communism. The John Birch Society infamously accused President Eisenhower of being a communist stooge. Recalling Nazi tactics, one Bircher wrote, "Our enemy is not only aware of the decay within America, but he takes it into account in all his calculations—and depends upon the supporting role to be played by his openly active fifth column."[40]

But it was not until the 1960s that the conservative movement began to go mainstream. In January 1960, House Republicans sought to bring together a coalition against excessive spending and "statism." Representatives John Rhodes of Arizona and Thomas Curti of Missouri aimed to battle the "octopuslike growth" of statism, believing that the New Deal was the first step toward totalitarianism. Barry Goldwater's presidential campaign in 1964 relied extensively on the Cold War narrative to make points in both foreign and domestic policies. For the Goldwater campaign, the fights against totalitarianism abroad and at home were linked. In *Conscience of a Conservative,* Goldwater warned that leaders in both the Democratic and Republican parties subscribed to the "first principle of totalitarianism," the belief that the government could and should do whatever is needed by society, rather than adhering strictly to the limits laid down by the Constitution. Goldwater voted against the Civil Right Act of 1964 precisely because he thought that it would lead to a "police state" and the "destruction of free society," although he later tried to finesse his reasons for the vote.[41]

Goldwater also used the Cold War narrative to endorse the fight against international communism and rail against attempts to negotiate or reach détente with the Soviet Union. He argued, "The Kremlin's hope is that they will persuade the American people to forget the ugly aspects of Soviet life, and the danger that the Soviet system poses to American freedom" through negotiation, cultural exchanges, and the like. Drawing on the Cold War narrative, he contended that "it would not have made sense, midway through the Second World War, to promote a Nazi-American exchange program or to invite Hitler to make a state visit to the United States," just as it did not make sense to invite Khrushchev to America or to promote Soviet-American exchanges. During the campaign, he compared the Russians to the Nazis, and suggested that the United States blockade Cuba. For Goldwater, the Soviet Union was an implacable enemy, just as Nazi Germany had been.[42]

Goldwater's supporters hammered home these themes. An old political adversary of Johnson appeared on a statewide television advertisement sponsored by "Texas Doctors for Goldwater." He charged that Lyndon Johnson was like "Hitler and his crew of very curious people" and that the Civil Rights Act gave Johnson "all the power Adolf Hitler ever had." In a speech late in the Goldwater campaign entitled "A Time for Choosing," Ronald Reagan told the audience the choice was not between left and right but between up and down: "up to the maximum of individual freedom consistent with law and order, or down to the ant heap of totalitarianism; and regardless of their humanitarian purpose those who would sacrifice freedom for security have, whether they know it or not, chosen this downward path."[43]

Young conservatives flocked to Goldwater's banner. Tony Blankley, former lieutenant for Newt Gingrich, remembered that "I and my colleagues thought of ourselves as right-wing Trotskyites. We were [as] outraged by the government's domestic politics as the left was by its foreign policies." Members of the Young Americans for Freedom (YAF) attacked liberalism and the New Frontier. Stanton Evans charged that Kennedy's policies would lead to a rigid, orthodoxy totalitarianism. In 1969, Harvey Hukari, leader of a prominent YAF chapter at Stanford, coordinated hecklers who chanted, "Pigs off campus" during an SDS march and held signs stating, "SDS is revolting" and "If you like Hitler, you'll love SDS."[44]

But traditional Republicans drew yet another analogy from Nazi Germany in observing the rightward turn of the GOP. After a Young Republicans convention, Nelson Rockefeller criticized YAF and conservatives, arguing that "tactics of totalitarianism" had been used at the convention by "purveyors of hate," "a radical, well-financed and highly disciplined minority." Rockefeller was shouted down by Goldwater supporters after he denounced "anonymous midnight and early morning telephone calls, unsigned threatening letters, smear and hate literature, strong-arm and goon tactics, bomb threats and bombings, infiltration and take-over of established political organizations by Communist and Nazi methods." Watching the reaction of Goldwater supporters frightened Jacob Javits, the moderate senator from New York. "It chilled me with the thought," he observed later, "that I might be seeing the beginnings of an American totalitarianism." After Goldwater took the nomination, traditional Republicans backed away from him. California senator Thomas Kuchel believed that the Republican Party had reached a crossroads, arguing that in his home state "all of the odious totalitarian techniques of subversion and intrigue are now being used by a frenetic and well-disciplined few to capture and control our party, and to make it an antiquated implement of embittered obstruction." Other politicians described Goldwater's supporters in the same manner.[45]

The mainstream media, and especially the Democratic opposition, exploited this division and use of the Cold War narrative. Even before Goldwater captured the nomination at the Republican convention, Daniel Schorr explicitly linked the candidate with radical right-wingers in Germany, announcing that Goldwater, if nominated, would start his presidential campaign in Bavaria, "the center of Germany's right wing." Schorr said that Goldwater had received and accepted an invitation from his friend Lieutenant General William Quinn to visit Berchtesgaden, Hitler's old hangout. Schorr further alleged that Goldwater's recent interview with *Der Spiegel* was an obvious overture to right-wing elements in Germany. *Fact* magazine found in a questionnaire of several psychiatrists that a majority did not think that Goldwater was "psychologically fit" to serve as president of the United States. One wrote that he was a "compensated schizophrenic" like dictators Hitler, Stalin, and Castro.[46]

Democrats likened his supporters to fascists. After Goldwater's acceptance speech, Pat Brown, governor of California, announced, "The stench of fascism is in the air . . . by stating that political extremism is not a vice, Senator Goldwater encourages the bigot, the Ku Klux Klan, the Bircher." He went on, "All we needed to hear was 'Heil Hitler.'" When Lady Bird Johnson was met by a hostile crowd holding signs reading, "Johnson's a Nigger Lover" and "Black Bird Go Home" in Charleston, Louisiana, congressman Hale Boggs called the crowd "a Nazi gathering." Celebrity liberals chimed in. Jackie Robinson stated, "I believe I know how it felt to be a Jew in Hitler's Germany."[47]

Like their counterparts on the left, conservatives used metaphors from Nazi Germany to criticize current policies in the United States. But they differed mightily over what lessons should be drawn from the war period. They formed a community of memory in which the primary lesson learned from the German experience was the tyranny of unchecked federal power. In contrast, however, their opponents, both within their own party and without, viewed the emergence of the New Right as the real analogue to the Nazi regime.

"We Like Eich"

A major part of the problem for conservatives like William F. Buckley was the growing presence of a radical Right dedicated to white power that used Nazi imagery in a completely different manner. Rejecting the Nazi half of the totalitarian image, they sought to emulate elements of Nazism to solve America's perceived racial and social problems. Throughout the 1950s, conservatives understood the danger of being called extremists. Leaders such as Buckley and Elizabeth Churchill Brown discouraged affiliation with those who espoused anti-Semitism. Buckley sought to distance himself from those on the radical right like

George Lincoln Rockwell, but maintained friendly relations with the John Birch Society.[48]

The radical Right dedicated to white supremacy took part of its impetus from southern rebellion against forced integration. South Carolina's William D. Workman, editor of the *Charleston News and Courier*, wrote a book called *The Case for the South*, in which he criticized northern liberals and southern moderates. Building on the work of other conservatives who used Cold War narratives of Germany to criticize the liberal state, Workman brilliantly added racial integration to the witch's brew of large federal bureaucracy, socialism, and fascism. For him, organizations dedicated to desegregation, such as the NAACP, labor unions, and church groups, smacked of "socialist tendencies." He observed that "in the South never has there been any broad support for a strong centralist government, which is the essence of totalitarianism, whether termed fascism or otherwise." He went on, "The fact of the matter is that, had the German people manifested the same determination on the local level to resist the establishment of an all-powerful centralist state [as white southerners have], there might never have been a Nazi Germany." Richard B. Russell described Eisenhower's dispatching of the 101st Airborne to Little Rock to enforce school integration in 1957 as "Hitler-like." When *The Conscience of a Conservative* appeared in 1960, southern conservatives deeply appreciated Goldwater's linking of racial integration with socialism and totalitarianism and his unabashed attack on Democrats and those within his own party who facilitated the growth and maintenance of the large welfare state.[49]

Perhaps more disturbing than the use of Nazi Germany and ideology to maintain racial segregation and discrimination, however, was the mounting evidence that neo-Nazism was gaining strength across the country. By the mid-1950s, intergroup relations organizations began noting the reappearance of swastikas after ten largely dormant years. The symbol began to appear regularly in the literature of "hate" groups and of high school groups that began collecting German war memorabilia. It was found scrawled on tombstones and bathroom walls. Until the late 1950s, however, the appearance of the swastika remained a local and intermittent phenomenon.

The phenomenon caught national attention with the swastika outbreak of 1959–1960, in which as many incidents of desecration of Jewish sites took place in the United States as in West Germany itself. Even after the swastika epidemic, Nazi symbols became highly visible during the 1960s. The growing popularity of these symbols revealed the importance of taking into account how ostensibly anti-Nazi books, films, and television programs could be interpreted and understood in surprising ways. Many participants credited these products with giving them the idea to indulge in Nazi-related activities. Feeling that Americans had gone astray by veering into socialism and race-mixing, and fearful of the atomizing effects of a soulless consumer society, these participants believed that society needed to be purified. Many of the people who participated in these events were not actively ideological, but rather were drawn by the attractions of solidarity and a sense of belonging. Numerous studies were carried out to determine the nature and extent of the participation.[50]

Spurred by the desecration of a synagogue in Cologne on Christmas Eve, 1959, the swastika epidemic in the United States lasted approximately nine weeks during the first part of 1960. By the time it had spent itself in March, 643 incidents had occurred, according to one study. Of these, 64 percent were simply the painting of the swastika symbol; 16 percent involved anti-Semitic slogans. Half were directed against Jewish targets; the other half involved some kind of anti-Semitic message or act on non-Jewish public or private property. An analysis of the evidence suggests that in both large and small communities, anti-Semites committed the first acts against Jewish targets. Bandwagoners joined them in search of publicity after a few weeks. But then the bandwagoners, with no particular animus against Jews, dropped off, leaving the anti-Semites alone to continue the desecrations until they became tired of the activity. By the end of March, 167 people had been apprehended in connection with these incidents, and law enforcement officials discovered that an overwhelming number of those apprehended were youths: 70 percent of the culprits were between thirteen and eighteen years old. Most acted as part of a group; the typical offender was a teenager participating in a gang of two or three.[51]

In an effort to understand why these young people had engaged in such activity, law enforcement officials and researchers conducted interviews with some of those arrested. In the end, forty-one interviews conducted with these young persons were deemed to be of sufficient quality to warrant examination. In general, studies of these interviews found that half of these participants were ideologically committed to the ideas of

National Socialism and/or anti-Semitism. These individuals often held views ranging from mild distrust of Jews to outright hatred. Many of them claimed to be familiar with both the history of Nazi Germany and the principal elements of Nazi ideology. A good example was a nineteen-year-old man who had plastered a Nazi sticker on the car of a Jewish woman who was friendly to him. Calling himself a real Nazi and a "blood Aryan," he claimed that he and his group wanted to make America "racially pure" through a process he called "schwitzing," a term derived from Auschwitz meaning the extermination of non-Aryans. He informed his interlocutors, "I have a passion for hunting. I have a passion for killing." He once marched around the block carrying a Nazi flag and wearing a Nazi armband.[52]

The other half of the culprits seemed to have little knowledge of the meaning of the swastika, anti-Semitic literature, World War II, or concentration camps. Many of those, deemed "non-ideological" participants in incidents of "random hostility," claimed they had acted out of a prankish spirit. One said, "We did it for fun, for thrills." Evidence suggests that these youths were feeling antagonistic toward American society, and that the swastika simply offered a means for expressing that dissatisfaction. As one study concluded, "It is possible that the swastika itself is so intensely charged a symbol for most Americans that, even aside from its particular anti-Semitic connotation, it is an ideal shorthand for hostility and violence."[53]

Many of the neo-Nazi clubs discovered in the United States during the early part of 1960 were comprised of an ideological leader and a number of nonideological followers. Twenty-four such clubs were found, in such diverse locales as California, New Jersey, Florida, and Wisconsin. Some dedicated themselves to collecting symbols of the Third Reich, like uniforms, flags, insignia, and slogans. If authentic items were not available for purchase or theft, they were sometimes created. Until the swastika epidemic, most of these groups confined their activities to meeting and talking about the organizations and history of the Third Reich. The groups often integrated elements of the Third Reich with American culture. Some of the clubs showed a high level of structural organization; the bylaws of one read:

The requirements for the Fuehrer are: (1) He must be of high intelligence; (2) he must be able to speak English; (3) he must sign a document dedicating himself to the party. The fuhrer has direct power over all members and over all peoples in territories occupied by the Nazi party. THERE WILL BE NO OPPOSITION TO THE FUHRER. Der Fuhrer is to be known as Le Magnifique. He is to reside in Berlin. His salary is to be $500,000 American per year. . . . [The minister of war] has absolute power of the Army, Navy, and Air Force, and shall reside in Honolulu. . . . All high ranking members of the party shall be exempt from all taxes and civil laws to insure their freedom of decision. . . . No Jews or Negroes can become members of this club.

This group consisted of three members, and the fourteen-year-old Führer was the only one who really demonstrated any real anti-Semitism, and that primarily through his artwork.[54]

A structured group in Kansas City issued membership cards that read, "By the order of der Fuhrer —— is a member of the 4th Reich." This same group apparently distributed a credendum reading, "Our founder is Adolph Hitler. The war ended in 1945. The ideas of national socialism have not died." One of the boys in this group had a small cache of explosives at his house. Such committed groups often did not restrict themselves merely to meetings. One group of three wrote a vicious letter to a Jewish fraternity house: "REMEMBER BUCHENWALD. This may happen to you. . . . We don't want you JEWS to ruin us, Americans, as you destroyed the GERMAN spirit and dignity. THIS is directed to all JEWS who fall back on THEIR heritage instead of OUR heritage, the American heritage. MAGGOTS don't feed on the corpse of your heritage, think of AMERICA instead of ISRAEL." The missive was signed: "Those against Jewish VANITY."[55]

Other groups were not ideologically committed at all. The leader of one large group that had painted a swastika on two temples and an apartment building said that they did it "for kicks." They collected Nazi memorabilia because "you wouldn't want to start a Japanese club and have everyone calling you oong-soong." Founding a British club would mean that "you'd have to drink tea, and American things were too easy to get and French too hard to find, so there was German."[56]

The media played an important role with all of these groups. Many swastika-painting culprits said that they had read about or seen on TV similar incidents, encouraging them to copy the act. A common response was "It was shown on TV and seemed to be a thrilling thing to do." More important, however, 60 percent of participants interviewed cited the media as a source of information about the Nazi Party—newspapers, radio, television, and film. Even more important, some films intended as anti-Nazi works, such as *The Young Lions* and *The Twisted Cross,* served as a source of inspiration to these youths. Respondents claimed that they fixated on the militaristic parts of these films and were unaware of any larger thematic elements. The members of one club had seen *The Twisted Cross* several times, and "each time the emotional swell created by the homogenous chanting to the leader, the uniforms, the drums, and the unity of the movement overwhelmed the rest of the picture and its message."[57]

With these types of reactions to German representations, many boys and young men fashioned a pro-Nazi, rather than an anti-Semitic, ideology. Many of these individuals came from broken homes, and one study concluded that their world was characterized by "marginality, boredom, rootlessness, and an absence of family or other available figures with whom to identify." For them, Nazism represented strength and unity. One boy believed that painting a swastika, "the emblem of strength and power," on a nearby synagogue was a suitable way to express his increasing feelings "against society the way things are going," in particular the practice of "giving away millions and millions of dollars for foreign aid when [Americans] haven't cleaned up their own back doorstep."[58]

These national findings were echoed in an AJC-sponsored study of New York City and a nearby industrialized area undertaken by the New York School of Social Work. The study examined the motives of forty-three males from different class backgrounds between the ages of nine and twenty-one who had been apprehended for participating in the swastika epidemic. The study made a similar distinction between what it called "vindictive" vandalism, activity with a hateful or threatening message, and "wanton" vandalism, activity of a frivolous or spontaneous nature. The analysis also found that many of these acts were carried out by groups; only one of the seventeen incidents was carried out by a loner. Two of the thirteen groups were considered Nazi-oriented gangs. The others were loose groups of boys who participated in this activity not out of virulent anti-Semitism but out of a desire to do something fun.[59]

Again, representations of Germans in the media were cited as critical, especially to the participation of these loosely affiliated groups of boys. In addition to noting the impact of the coverage of the swastika daubings itself (for example, two boys who "wanted to do something" painted swastikas on a church, garage, and firebox because they had seen "pictures of similar incidents in the newspapers and on television"), the study found that books such as the anti-Nazi *The Scourge of the Swastika,* records such as *Hitler's Inferno* (Nazi marching music), and movies and magazine stories about Nazis served as a source of knowledge and stimulation for these young men. Replicating the observation of other studies, this analysis pointed out that such media products "are usually published and sold for the avowed purposes of exposing the totalitarian nature of Nazism and for revealing the horrors associated with the movement." But the descriptions of Nazi leaders in these products often provided young males with "role models." In a context of "racial tension in the South, increased unemployment nationally, local problems in given communities such as school bond issues or fluoride treatment of water supply," these young people likewise interpreted Hitler favorably as a "strong masculine type." Studies of the swastika epidemic concluded that local and national events played an important role in determining how these young people interpreted the German representations they saw in America's mass media. For these youths, confronted with difficulties at home and abroad, representations of Nazi Germany provided a model of strength and purity.[60]

Despite the fears of Jewish and liberal groups, however, no connection was made between these juvenile groups and the burgeoning adult white supremacist and neo-Nazi movement in the United States. White supremacist groups have a long and varied history in the United States, dating at least as far back as the first Ku Klux Klan, organized just after the Civil War. During World War II, white supremacy in the United States briefly took the guise of Nazism through the Silver Shirts and the German American Bund, but it was not until after the war that Nazi ideology took firm, and public, root in the United States. According to many observers of the phenomenon in post–World War II America, neo-Nazi groups are characterized by their use of the swastika and other symbols of Nazi Germany, their high regard for Hitler, and their reference to themselves as National Socialists. And although the first neo-Nazi group of the postwar era was James Madole's National Renaissance Party, most observers trace the origins of the movement to George Lincoln Rockwell and the American Nazi Party. An examination of Rockwell and the party reveals the importance of both the media and contemporary American society in providing context for their interpretation of Nazism.[61]

Nothing in Rockwell's background suggested that he would become America's most visible Nazi. Indeed, early on in his career at least, Rockwell would have been viewed as a "nonideological" neo-Nazi. Rockwell's leading biographer avers, "Those looking for the key to Rockwell's pathological anti-Semitism in his family or his upbringing will be largely unsatisfied." Although his family passed along racist stereotypes, Rockwell's father, whom he idolized, had a number of Jewish friends. George Lincoln Rockwell was born in 1918 to Claire and Doc Rockwell, the latter a rising vaudeville comic who moved in influential entertainment circles, befriending major figures such as Fred Allen, Groucho Marx, and Benny Goodman. His parents' divorce in 1924 had a scarring effect on the young man. Although Rockwell fought against the Nazis in World War II, he had a conversion experience in 1952, when he "met Adolf Hitler" spiritually and become a rabid anti-Semite.[62]

Rockwell's understanding of the media played an important role in his conversion. Because of conservative and nonconformist views nurtured by his father, Rockwell was drawn to "masculine" leaders such as Joseph McCarthy and Douglas MacArthur early in his life, men whom he believed were treated unfairly by the mainstream press. When he sought to drum up support for MacArthur in San Diego, he was informed by a fellow conservative, to his outrage, that the Jews would never allow him to secure a public space for such a rally. This contact proved to be his entrée into radical politics. An introduction to right-wing publications convinced Rockwell that the Jews were conspiring to take over the world, and he gradually came to see the media as one of the most powerful weapons in the Jewish arsenal. Consequently, he dismissed everything reported in the mainstream media as lies fabricated by Jews. He then took the next logical step: convinced that Adolf Hitler had been right about Jews, Rockwell found and devoured a copy of *Mein Kampf.* By the end of the book, he was thoroughly persuaded of Hitler's genius and fully committed to his cause.

Over the 1950s, Rockwell sought to find a place for his newfound ideology. He tried to convince his family and others close to him of a Jewish conspiracy and the need for an American Nazi Party. His family never warmed up to the idea—his father went so far as to disown him. He tried to get involved in conservative and right-wing politics, but prominent conservatives such William F. Buckley constantly rebuffed his overtures. Rockwell also found fault with many conservatives groups, such as the John Birch Society. Although he believed they sympathized with him and his ideas, he denounced them for failing to name the true source of the communist menace: the Jewish conspiracy. The year 1958 proved an eventful one for Rockwell: at the urging of right-wing extremists DeWest Hooker and Harold Arrowsmith, he openly converted to Nazism and officially established the American Nazi Party; he was also accused, for the first time, of anti-Semitic violence in the bombing of an Atlanta temple, although he denied involvement.[63]

Over the next decade, Rockwell's small party was very active. For Rockwell, publicly embracing Nazism, and the swastika symbol in particular, was crucial to his overall strategy of media management. Believing that the mass media were firmly under Jewish control, Rockwell argued that he had to outwit Jews and use their own instruments against them. Learning an effective strategy from Martin Luther King and the civil rights movement, Rockwell hoped to provoke Jews with his inflammatory rhetoric and actions to the point that they would violently attack his followers in front of a captivated American media. Such violence would, in his thinking, galvanize the white masses, inspire a general race war, and pave the way for his assumption to power. During 1960, he carried out well-covered demonstrations in Washington, D.C., and New York. In 1961, Rockwell aided the National State Rights Party in its "counterattack against the Jew propaganda Eichmann trial" by picketing in Washington. One of his signs read, "We Like Eich." His storm troopers rode "the Hate Bus" in mocking imitation of the Freedom Riders. Two years later, he asked for and received an opportunity to speak to Elijah Muhammad's Nation of Islam. His reference to Muhammad as "the Adolf Hitler of the black man" drew international coverage.[64]

Rockwell became convinced that the chaos of the 1960s would provide him with the opportunity to take over the country. He believed that a growing backlash against the civil rights and radical movements would move the American people to embrace a law-and-order candidate such as himself in the 1972 election. His presidency would achieve ambitious goals: the execution of the vast majority of American Jews; the elimination of "disloyal Jews" from positions of power and influence in the

government, media, education, and the legal system; the public hanging
of all non-Jews found to assist "Jewish treason"; and the exportation of
all African Americans back to Africa. Rockwell planned to move blacks
who would not go voluntarily to "relocation centers" in desolate parts of
the United States, where they would be monitored as wards of the state.
His platform was a clear attempt to use Nazi principles to solve what he
believed to be America's problems.[65]

Embracing the swastika and other trappings of Nazi Germany proved
to be a double-edged sword. On the one hand, it provided him and his
party with a torrent of publicity all out of proportion to the meager number of members in his party. Indeed, part of his strategy for building a
mass movement was to shock the American people out of their complacency. He knew that he could not win over intellectuals; his goal was to
appeal to the emotions of the general population. He thought that the
civil rights issue was a perfect springboard for recruiting, and his protests in Washington and New York during 1960, the same time the swastika daubings took place, gave him incredible exposure. But his open
embrace of Nazism distanced him from other groups on the right. His
attempts to establish an international Nazi movement through the World
Union of National Socialists misfired when he was arrested in Britain and
deported. He failed to court wealthy right-wing extremists in the United
States. When he tried to stage a counter demonstration to "Martin Luther
Coon's" March on Washington in 1963, he was unable to convince arch-
segregationists George Wallace and Ross Barnett to participate.[66]

His failures convinced him to mute the National Socialist elements
of his campaign. While many Americans may have been sympathetic
to Nazi ideals, especially regarding race, he concluded that images of
Nazism were abhorred by most. By the mid-1960s, he limited the visibility of National Socialism in his activities. In his campaign for the gover-
norship of Virginia in 1965, Rockwell replaced references to Adolf Hitler
with paeans to Wallace and Orville Faubus. The swastika was relegated
to a small gold lapel pin, and by the middle of the campaign it was gone
entirely. Although he garnered only sixty-five hundred votes statewide,
this was a much larger display of support than he had previously received.
When Stokely Carmichael inaugurated the Black Power movement the
following year, Rockwell responded with White Power. As outlined in his
book of the same name, Rockwell's strategy was to create a mass following

of pan-white inclusion, in which all non-black Americans, including Slavs and Mediterraneans, would be invited to join. His strategy appeared successful in a 1966 counterdemonstration in Chicago, where ethnic whites rallied against Martin Luther King's call for open housing.[67]

Still, although Rockwell and his rechristened National Socialist White People's Party sought to downplay overt signs of Nazism in their campaigns, the influence of Nazi thought remained important in the party. Rockwell used his understanding of Nazism to lay the groundwork for what would become the central planks of the White Power movement in the future. For example, throughout the 1960s, Rockwell was on the front line of the growing Holocaust denial movement. By 1967, Rockwell was claiming that the Holocaust was a "monstrous and profitable fraud" and employing the work of writers such as Harry Elmer Barnes, Charles Tansill, and Freda Utley to make arguments that framed German aggression to the Jews as comparable to Allied aggression toward German civilians. Rockwell created the popular graphic novel *The Diary of Ann Fink* to ridicule and discredit Anne Frank's moving account. His biggest forum for distributing Holocaust denial propaganda came in an interview with Alex Haley in *Playboy* in 1966.[68]

For ideologically committed leaders of the neo-Nazi movement, representations of Germans offered a solution to the problems of a Jewish-dominated and race-mongrelizing society. Rather than posing a threat to American values, Nazism, in their eyes, provided a means of reinvigorating white America. Rockwell and his neo-Nazis tapped into a vocabulary that resonated with Americans disaffected with the changes of the 1960s.

"A Clothesline Is a Berlin Wall"

As it had earlier, Berlin amplified and sharpened representations of Germans in the 1960s. The construction of the Berlin Wall in the late summer of 1961 created a powerful new metaphor for understanding narratives of both the United States and Germany, bolstering an interpretation of American superiority that was increasingly faltering and under assault. The power of human stories associated with the wall simplified the nature of the Cold War for many. One American, for example, wrote to his congressman with the suggestion that all young leaders of recently decolonized countries should tour Berlin to ensure they properly understood the nature of the Cold War. Many Americans continued to believe that, as President Kennedy said, the Berlin Wall "is the obvious manifestation, which can be demonstrated all over the world, of the superiority of our system."[69]

Although the continual flow of stories about the wall meant that representations involving Berlin did not experience as wide a range of interpretations as those involving Germans more generally, the city's image was still susceptible to some of the same dynamics when the American Cold War consensus fragmented during the 1960s. For critical Americans, Berlin became a potent rhetorical device. They used the powerful emotions associated with the former German capital to suggest that the United States was no better than the Third Reich. They inverted the power that American officials invested in the Berlin Wall to suggest that the United States had become indistinguishable from the oppressor that it battled in the Cold War. Critics of America argued that the United States had become the antithesis of its ideals—that it had in fact become its own "other."

Because so many stories about the Berlin Wall involved the forced separation of peoples, the wall became a particularly powerful symbol for highlighting segregation in the American South. In Selma, Alabama, African American demonstrators composed an impromptu song entitled "Berlin Wall" to describe a clothesline that Selma police had strung across Sylvan Street to keep them from leaving their designated area.

A clothesline is a Berlin Wall,
Berlin Wall, Berlin Wall,
A clothesline is a Berlin Wall,
In Selma, Alabam'.

In Los Angeles, African Americans used the power of the wall to attack de facto segregation. Referring to a street that marked the beginning of an all-white neighborhood, one black resident remembered, "We used to say that Alameda was the Berlin Wall." For African American activists, the use of Berlin or the Berlin Wall to describe their own situation demonstrated the changing understandings of the struggle of the Cold War.[70]

Away from the troubled domestic scene, American leaders had a difficult time manipulating how other leaders understood Berlin. In discussions with Prince Sihanouk of Cambodia, for example, State Department officials learned Sihanouk read the German question quite differently. While paying tribute to Khrushchev for his "sincere desire" to solve the Berlin problem, he had nevertheless publicly called for the "strict and sincere application of the self-determination principle for Berlin as well as all other conflicts." Sihanouk believed that a "solution should also envision German reunification and neutralization, thus creating a neutral buffer between the opposing blocs analogous to the neutral buffer [Khrushchev] has advocated in Southeast Asia." Whereas Sihanouk cast the German problem in light of the situation in Vietnam, Dutch diplomats used Berlin to justify Dutch policy in West New Guinea. In a discussion between the Kennedy administration and Foreign Minister Joseph Luns and Ambassador J. H. van Roijen over the Dutch position, Luns maintained that "there is no difference in principle between maintaining self-determination for the population of West Berlin or West New Guinea." The ambassador remarked, "The Dutch could not sacrifice national honor any more than the United States could run out of West Berlin." As the Cambodia and Dutch examples illustrate, American officials could not always control the reception of Berlin in foreign relations discourse.[71]

The construction of the Berlin Wall seemingly provided visceral proof of American claims in the Cold War. The wall further illustrated the belief that the communist system was a failure, able to keep its citizens loyal only through coercion and terror. And yet the primitive power of Berlin could be co-opted by critics of American policy and society to highlight the hypocrisy of America's own ideals.

The breakdown of the Cold War consensus during the 1960s splintered American understanding of Germany. New memory communities coalesced around shared understandings of what Germany's past meant for the United States in light of new circumstances. Traditional Americans continued to see Nazi Germany as the foil to American values, and their viewpoint was represented in the most conservative (and popular) medium of television, through shows such as *Combat!* and *Hogan's Heroes.* Liberals drew uncomfortable comparisons between present-day America and the Third Reich to spur Americans to support necessary reforms. Believing that the American capitalist system was hopelessly corrupt, radicals made even stronger comparisons in an effort to foment revolution.

Conservatives linked the large American welfare state to totalitarian predecessors in their attacks on big government. And, white supremacists looked to Nazi Germany for solutions to their concerns about a weakening, mongrelizing society. Together these memory communities offered rhetorical strategies that would endure through the rest of the century.

6

"The Hero Is Us"

Representations of Germany since the 1960s

On 9 November 1999, the U.S. Congress took a break from the day-to-day administration of the country to spend a few moments commemorating a "transcendent" moment in America's recent past. House Concurrent Resolution 223 called upon the United States to join with other nations, "specifically including those which liberated themselves to help end the Cold War, to establish a global holiday called Freedom Day." The resolution glided through the House, passing by a vote of 417–0. Later that day, the Senate passed a similar resolution.[1]

The movement for designating 9 November as Freedom Day began with the work of Ben Wattenberg, a syndicated newspaper columnist and senior fellow at the American Enterprise Institute. In December 1991, Wattenberg proposed a new national holiday to commemorate the end of the Cold War. He set up a contest in which he asked readers to give it a name, designate a date, and propose a method of celebration. Several hundred people provided suggestions. Some of the names offered were Ronald Reagan Day, Gorbachev Day, Thaw Day, Peace through Strength Day, E Day (short for Evil Empire Ends Day), E2D2 Day (Evil Empire Death Day) and Freedom Day. One of the dates suggested was 5 June, Adam Smith's birthday, but most gave 9 November, the date in 1989 that the Berlin Wall fell. Based on the overwhelming number of people suggesting Freedom Day as a name and 9 November as the date, Wattenberg proclaimed the proposed holiday as such and called upon legislators to recognize it. As evidenced by the inauguration of Global Freedom Day, by the 1990s the Berlin Wall had emerged as a clear signifier of the Cold War, and as such, played a decisive role in how Americans remembered and discussed the Cold War. Invoking the "fall of the Berlin Wall" became shorthand for the complex, cataclysmic process involved in the dissolution of the Soviet Union and the end of the Cold War.[2]

At the same time, however, other communities chose to focus on different meanings of the date. Indeed, the celebration of the tenth anniversary of the fall of the wall in Berlin itself was complicated. Joined by George H. W. Bush, Mikhail Gorbachev, and Helmut Kohl, all of whom recounted their role in the historic days of 1989, Chancellor Gerhard Schroeder, in addition to lauding the "civil courage" of Germans in bringing down the East German regime, invoked Kristallnacht, reminding celebrants in Berlin that 9 November was not only a day of joy but of "shame" and "reflection" as well. American media covering the event noted the dual recognition of the day; "This being Germany," the *New York Times* observed, "perhaps it was inevitable that light and dark should so mingle a decade after Europe's division was ended and half a continent was set free." For some in the United States, however, simply mentioning Kristallnacht was not enough. Werner Renberg argued that in its coverage of the anniversary the *New York Times* failed to give a sufficient account of the persecution of German Jews on the Night of Broken Glass.[3]

The multiplicity of meanings attached to 9 November demonstrates how the patterns of memory diplomacy established in the first two decades after the Second World War continued to shape American understandings of both Germany and the United States throughout the rest of the century. Although Americans continued to debate the meaning of Germany for American identity, they did so with a vocabulary and set of signifiers already established earlier in the Cold War. Familiar memory actors echoed and circulated time-honored narratives. The Berlin Wall and the Holocaust emerged as the most powerful reference points for invoking German history in understanding American identity—and by the end of the century, both reinforced a triumphalist, mainstream narrative of American influence and power, while marginalized communities clung to different memories.

"Tear Down This Wall"

The enduring nature of these established tropes is particularly evident in the failure of the Nixon administration (and later the Carter administration, to a degree) to reinscribe Berlin with a different meaning. Indeed, both administrations tried to transform the meaning of Berlin in light of their strategy of détente from a symbol of confrontation to a harbinger of cooperation. Carter, as was typical of his entire foreign policy, was caught between a moralistic reading of the wall and his desire to continue with the principles of détente. Along with external factors such as the outbreak of the Soviet war in Afghanistan, the wall proved decisive in ensuring that both Berlin and Germany remained firmly wedded to a narrative of American triumphalism.

Upon assuming the White House, the Nixon administration attempted a new emphasis in American foreign policy, understanding that the consensus that had shaped American foreign policy for more than two decades was badly damaged. In an era of weakened governmental authority and in an increasingly multipolar world, the Nixon administration recalculated the geopolitical landscape and sought to build on some of the efforts of Kennedy and Johnson to relax tensions between the United States and the communist world. A major part of this new strategy was de-emphasizing the moral aspects of America's struggle against the Soviet Union. Because of the tension and unpredictability that had surrounded Berlin during the Cold War, Nixon and Kissinger rightly perceived that an agreement stabilizing Berlin would make an excellent contribution to their larger aim of détente. They found a valuable, although in their minds unreliable, partner in Willy Brandt, formerly West Berlin's mayor and now the Federal Republic's new chancellor. Brandt initiated what became known as *Ostpolitik,* which sought to recognize the status quo in Eastern Europe in the hopes of reducing the likelihood of war while increasing commercial contacts between the Federal Republic of Germany and Eastern European nations. Even though Ostpolitik was consistent with their larger aim of relaxing tension with the communist world, Nixon and Kissinger worried that an independent European initiative could simultaneously threaten American leadership of the transatlantic alliance and strengthen the standing of the GDR and the Soviet Union. The negotiations over the status of Berlin in 1971 enabled Kissinger to influence Ostpolitik. The resulting Quadripartite Agreement promised Western access to Berlin and allowed West Berliners thirty days each year to visit family in the East, while agreeing that Berlin was not a "constituent part" of the Federal Republic and banning the practice of parliamentary meetings held in Berlin to elect the president of the Federal Republic.[4]

With the successful negotiation of the Quadripartite Agreement, the Nixon administration sought to inscribe new meaning on the city of Berlin. Whereas previous administrations had invoked Berlin as one of the most important symbols of America's commitment to stand up to communism, Nixon and Kissinger described the city as an example of the growing détente between the Soviet Union and the United States. Indeed, as the Nixon administration's policy of détente appeared more successful, Nixon increasingly credited the Quadripartite Agreement with making everything else possible. Nixon remarked that this agreement of "historic significance" moved "us to conclude that now was the time for a summit meeting." In a televised conversation with Dan Rather on CBS in January 1972, Nixon again claimed that "what broke the back [of resistance] as far as having the Moscow summit was concerned . . . was the Berlin agreement" because it "indicated that the United States and the Soviet Union, agreeing on that critical area, might find a possibility of agreeing on other problems, where our interests might run in conflict—possibly the Mideast, possibly arms limitation, certainly trade and other areas." Just prior to the summit, Nixon reminded reporters, "Perhaps the single event which brought about the decision on the part of the Soviet leaders and our decision to go to the summit was the success of the understandings on Berlin. We thought that if we had made progress in that very critical area for both of us that we should try with some hope of success of making progress in other areas that were also difficult."[5]

Indeed, once the Quadripartite Agreement was signed, normalizing the status of Berlin, Roy Blumenthal's agency, now in the employ of the City of West Berlin, worked tirelessly to convince Americans of the virtue of the accord. In the process, the agency found itself in competition with the inflexible Axel Springer and his conservative American allies, who viewed détente as a sellout of Western aims in the Cold War. Blumenthal and his associates believed that they needed to place stories and pictures in periodicals that emphasized the "human implications" of the agreement. They also hoped the new agreement could encourage tourism to Berlin.

They thought they could pitch West Berlin "as a unique window on to life in a communist country, but with harassment and tension now erased."[6]

Initially, the mainstream media interpreted the Quadripartite Agreement favorably, lauding the Nixon administration for gaining significant concessions from the Soviets. The guarantee of access to West Berlin, the assurance of Bonn's presence in Berlin, the concession of Bonn's right to represent West Berliners abroad, and permitted visits by West Berliners to family in East Berlin—all these far outweighed the inauguration of Soviet representation in West Berlin and the end of a "full-dress parliamentary session in Berlin" to elect West Germany's president. *Newsweek* reported that the Soviets sought to secure their western flank because they feared a revived China. *Time* stated that "the draft agreement is a plus for the West, neutralizing a pressure point that the Communists have squeezed on and off as their interests required since the Berlin blockade of 1948."[7]

And yet the mainstream media resisted Nixon's efforts to reinvent Berlin as a symbol of cooperation. Despite their support for the Quadripartite Agreement, mainstream media outlets continued to find the visceral power of Berlin compelling. When confronted with a situation that ostensibly contrasted the two systems of government, as was evident by Easter visits across the wall, journalists of all stripes were drawn to the inherent drama and tragedy found in Berlin. *Time* noted that West Berliners trudged past the "tank traps, the death strip, the watchtowers" and most of all the wall, "the concrete monstrosity that divides the city." Visitors from West Berlin found the "large lifeless squares and sterile Marxist-modern, glass-sheathed buildings . . . utterly foreign." *Newsweek* emphasized the political, rather than altruistic, reasons undergirding the East German government's decision briefly to open the wall. By making West Berliners grateful for the opportunity, the East German government hoped to secure West German support for Ostpolitik. The governing mayor of Berlin, Klaus Schütz, thought that it proved the wisdom of a policy designed for the relaxation of tensions.[8]

Just as the larger foreign policy reorientation of détente experienced significant bipartisan criticism for being "immoral," so, too, did this effort to remake Berlin's symbolism. Critics in the U.S. Congress relied heavily on the Cold War narrative, continuing to emphasize the inhumanity of the Berlin Wall. Representative Benjamin Blackburn of Georgia made a concerted effort to remind members of Congress of the frightful statistics associated with the wall. According to his figures, over 451 people had died attempting to escape over the Berlin Wall by 1974. Representative Jack Kemp claimed that this wall—"built to divide not only Germans but the family of man"—represented the truly tyrannical nature of communism.[9]

Nixon's successor fared worse, partly because he attempted to continue détente while emphasizing human rights, but partly because conservatives, who had gained ascendancy in the Republican Party, felt free to take the gloves off with a Democrat back in the White House. Carter had campaigned on restoring morality to American foreign policy, which often took the form of emphasizing human rights, but he also wanted to deepen the relationship with the Soviet Union and reach agreement on substantive issues like nuclear disarmament. Carter wanted to move away from an "inordinate fear of communism" toward the positive impact of American values abroad, including human rights, democracy, and prosperity in the Third World. Carter's attempted synthesis can be seen in his public utterances on Berlin. On the one hand, he clearly subscribed to the Cold War symbolism of the city, because it seemed to epitomize everything that he espoused about America's role in the preservation of human rights. In remarks at a wreath-laying ceremony at the Airlift Memorial in Berlin in July 1978, Carter recognized the airlift as a "time when people everywhere began to understand that the dispute over Berlin was not a local issue, but a great defense of freedom and democracy, with permanent worldwide interest and significance." Later, in a question-and-answer session with Berliners, Carter claimed that nothing "can hide the image of the deprivation of human rights exemplified by the Wall," citing the familiar refrain that this was the first time that a wall had been constructed to keep its people from escaping. At the same time, however, Carter tried to depict the 1971 Quadripartite Agreements on Berlin as an excellent validation of détente. During the same visit, Carter declared that "Berlin and the Quadripartite Agreement are symbols not only of the values that can never be compromised nor negotiated but also of the practical improvements that can be achieved by those who are willing patiently to negotiate."[10]

Carter's attempted synthesis gave conservatives the opportunity they were looking for. Conservatives like Ronald Reagan who had been highly critical of Nixon and Ford's foreign policies were more than happy to point out the inconsistencies and failures of Carter's. Even Democrats raised serious doubts about his efforts at arms control with the Soviet Union. In the end, Carter's inability to reconcile these approaches helped contribute to his reelection defeat. His successor promised a return to the moral certainty of the early Cold War. Reagan's declaration that he would restore America's confidence included harsh rhetoric against the Soviet Union. "They have told us that their goal is the Marxian philosophy of world revolution and a single one-world Communist state," Reagan declared to Walter Cronkite in the early days of his administration, "and they're dedicated to that." In some of his more infamous early speeches, he used millennial rhetoric, denouncing the "evil empire." It was clear to many that Reagan's presidency, at least his first administration, represented a return to the early rhetoric of the Cold War.[11]

Reagan's rhetoric was echoed in a string of commemorations during the 1980s. The fortieth anniversary of World War II in 1985, for example, prompted American musings on the German role in the war, but these thoughts rarely intruded upon American conceptions of the Cold War. In a special report to the *San Diego Union-Tribune*, Robert Zimmerman reported that Berlin was placed in an unusual position for the upcoming celebration of V-E Day. Observing that the celebration only reminded West Berliners that they were still technically under the jurisdiction of the Allies, he quoted one West Berliner: "We are tired of being told to feel guilty." These problems of guilt paled in comparison, Zimmerman reported, to the forced celebration in East Berlin, in which the Soviets attempted to celebrate the imposition of "a Communist system so oppressive and lacking in rewards that only the wall, barbed wire and minefields prevent mass defections to the West." Although the story commented on the reasons for the division of Berlin, the focus clearly was on the different systems in place in East and West Berlin—in effect, on the Cold War itself.[12]

The twenty-fifth anniversary of the construction of the Berlin Wall in 1986 offered another opportunity to reflect on the Cold War implications of the wall. While it was commemorated in different ways by East and West Berlin, observers in the United States continued to focus on the personal drama associated with the wall: separated families, restricted movement, and spectacular escape attempts. The *Los Angeles Times* gave a detailed and dramatic recounting of the more famous efforts to escape—over the wall, through the air, underwater, under the ground, and through the clever use of deception. In the *New York Times,* Krista Weedman detailed life in East Berlin, outlining the various ways in which the wall had wormed itself into the psyche of children, whose artwork and playtime often centered on representations of imprisonment. That same year, the world witnessed numerous escape attempts, as twelve East German reservists tried to reroute a subway train west, three East Germans rammed a dump truck through a checkpoint, and a teenage couple swam to safety in the West.[13]

The commemoration of Berlin's 750th anniversary in 1987 offered perhaps a better opportunity for a more nuanced reflection on Germany's past, but instead, many Americans remained engaged in the Cold War narrative. Some mainstream outlets reflected on the reason for this division in the first place. Richard Reeves, columnist for the Universal Press Syndicate, outlined how Berlin was not a city but a "political message": in that sense, Berlin was a "monument to arrogance and desperation and stupidity that led Germany to provoke World War II," and that "new generations of Germans" were "doomed to pay the price of postwar conflict." West Berlin hoped to broadcast the message of "prosperity" with a "great (and deserved) propaganda victory" during this anniversary.[14]

President Reagan used the occasion of this anniversary as an opportunity to address the inhumanity of the Berlin Wall. In a speech that reminded some of Kennedy's "Ich bin ein Berliner," Reagan stood in the shadow of the wall and demanded, "Mr. Gorbachev, tear down this wall." Although some were impressed by this rhetoric, others found it hollow and self-serving. The Bonn government worried that Reagan was inflaming East-West tensions; the Berlin police force of ten thousand, deployed to provide security, was forced to arrest several bands of anti-Reagan demonstrators; and the crowd that showed up to support the speech was relatively small at twenty thousand. Some Americans even defended the gradual pace of Gorbachev's reforms. While initially unheralded, Reagan's speech would benefit from ensuing events, later coming to join the pantheon of great speeches delivered by American presidents at the Berlin Wall.[15]

Amid these anniversaries centered on Berlin and the Berlin Wall, few mainstream commentators questioned the primacy of the Cold War narrative in the Berlin context. However, some World War II veterans and

American Jews clung to an alternative memory. In a letter to the *Los Angeles Times,* John T. Kelly of Long Beach, for example, "vigorously" disagreed with Reagan's "challenge to the Soviet Union to tear down the Berlin Wall." Believing Germany "guilty of starting two world wars in my lifetime and causing much loss of life and property throughout Europe," he argued that "the wall should stay put well into the 21st Century as a daily reminder to all German people that they are not to try to conquer the nations around them ever again." Moshe Kam of Philadelphia called the Berlin Wall "Cain's Mark," arguing that the wall "is a central part of the punishment cast upon the German nation for its World War II atrocities." Worried that the stories of Germany's victims would become "normalized" when the survivors passed away, he felt that "the only memorial and warning sign will be the continuous partition of Germany, and its ugly symbol—the wall." Speaking from different perspectives, these individuals nonetheless adhered to a similar, albeit marginalized, narrative.[16]

By the 1980s, a seemingly never-ending commentary about the inhumanity of the wall was the writing on the wall itself. Seven months before the wall fell, Mary Beth Stein published an essay analyzing the graffiti on the wall from a folkloric perspective. Pointing out that the wall in many places was set back ten feet from the border, she argued that all graffiti must be considered political to some degree since perpetrators risked trespass onto East German territory to carry out their commentary. Focusing on those writings that sought to make an explicit statement through humor, she found that much of it made fun of the East German regime, such as "SED = Selten Etwas Da" (Socialist Unity Party = seldom anything there), which satirized the frequent shortages in the GDR, and "East German High Jump Training Area," which simultaneously ridiculed the wall as a hurdle for escaping East Germans and touched on the sore spot of professionalized amateur sports in the GDR.[17]

At first blush, the fall of the Berlin Wall in November 1989 did not drastically alter American understanding of the Cold War or Germany. Without a doubt, there was a great deal of enthusiasm and excitement in the United States about the fall of the wall. In a *BusinessWeek*/Harris poll taken a few days after the wall came down, 90 percent of Americans felt that "the tearing down of the Berlin Wall" was "one of the most exciting and encouraging signs for peace in the world in years." In the same poll, 76 percent of the respondents favored German reunification. A 26

November *CBS News* poll echoed these findings. When questioned about reunification, 67 percent of respondents believed that East and West Germany should be reunited, with the most popular reason being that the "German people should be together." Seventy-three percent said that they did not fear German revanchism.[18]

At the same time, polls conducted right after the fall of the wall revealed that Americans did not believe that the end of the Cold War was nigh. The November *CBS News* poll found that only 37 percent of Americans thought that the Cold War was over in light of recent events. Even more telling, only 6 percent of respondents believed that the United States and its allies had won the Cold War. While enthusiastic about the direction of world affairs, Americans polled at the time did not feel that the fall of the Cold War's preeminent symbol translated into the end of the Cold War, and certainly not into a clear-cut American victory.[19]

Amid the general euphoria, a few soberly noted the fate of the wall, a fate that foreshadowed later widespread disillusionment with the promise of 1989. With the destruction of the wall came a whole new industry dedicated to profiting from it. Street vendors rented out hammers to tourists so they could break off chunks as souvenirs. Within a month, companies were selling pieces of the wall to the U.S. market for Christmas. East German citizens were disappointed and the East German government was unhappy—that is, until it decided to get into the game itself. Although several Americans seemed somewhat disturbed by the avarice of these wall entrepreneurs, few acknowledged the poetic justice of the phenomenon: such practices were part and parcel of the capitalist system that they had been promoting for years in the city.[20]

After the Soviet Union dissolved in December 1991, Americans began to remember the fall of the wall differently. Before then, the fall of the Berlin Wall had signified the permissiveness of Gorbachev's regime; after the dissolution of the Soviet Union, it began to signify the end of the Cold War, and in time, American victory in the Cold War. Since the Cold War was posited by many as an ideological struggle between democratic freedom and communist despotism, the dissolution of the Soviet Union could mean nothing less than the righteous victory of American ideals.

The recognition of the tenth anniversary of the fall of the Berlin Wall illustrates this triumphalist mood. As one man from Centerville, Ohio, wrote to the *Dayton Daily News*:

Much more important [than presidents] in ending communist rule were generations of American servicemen and servicewomen who braved numbing coldness and dangers against great odds in Korea, who faithfully fought communist forces in Vietnam, who quietly served aboard our planes and ships risking their lives in anonymity during the Cold War and who never asked for anything in return.

While many people attended college, pursued their careers or debated politics, many others sacrificed to make that way of life possible in a free country. They did such a good job of preserving our free country that today, many Americans cannot even perceive that there were and still are threats to our welfare that constantly must be faced.

And don't forget the generations of nameless bureaucrats, families of veterans and plain old U.S. taxpayers who supported the struggle for freedom, which eventually caused the communist system to recognize its failure.

There always will be politicians who would take credit for all the work and sacrifice of others. Don't let them do it. The hero is us.[21]

In addition to claiming victory in the Cold War, Americans insisted that its conquest had resulted in a better life for those formerly under the yoke of communism. Celebrating the tenth anniversary of the fall of the wall on 9 November 1999, major outlets such as the *Washington Post,* the *New York Times,* and the *Boston Globe* noted the positive changes wrought by the fall of communism, including "improved living standards" and increased "prosperity and freedom." They observed that those states, such as Poland, Hungary, Lithuania, Latvia, and Estonia, that "bit the bullet first" by closing inefficient industries and reducing state subsidies immediately fared the best. According to these publications, those who had not fared as well were to blame for their misfortune because they had not embraced capitalism completely and fully. The *Boston Globe* observed that there was a "misplaced nostalgia growing in former communist countries for the certainties of tyranny," reducing and ridiculing the sentiments of those unhappy with the changes brought about by capitalism. As the *New York Times* pointed out, "Except for unreconstructed Communists, few wish to go back" as "in country after country the tyranny enforced behind the wall seems a rapidly receding memory." In this way, Americans blamed Eastern European nations that remained economically backward for their own plight.[22]

By the end of the century, mainstream America had returned to a familiar place. Recognizing the challenges of the Cold War consensus, Nixon and Kissinger had attempted to transform American political culture on the Cold War. But they found that Americans were more receptive to a moralistic understanding of foreign policy, something that Reagan provided. The manner and timing of the dissolution of the Soviet Union, especially in light of the fall of the Berlin Wall, confirmed this moralistic view of the conflict, so much so that evaluations of former East Bloc countries years later blamed them (and the old communist system) for their economic difficulties without considering the possible flaws in the capitalist system foisted on them. In this respect, mainstream America of the 1990s was not unlike mainstream America of the 1950s.

"A Proper Dose of the Holocaust"

On 11 April 1985, Ronald Reagan's staff announced that, as part of his upcoming visit to West Germany, the president would lay a wreath at a German war cemetery in Bitburg where many Nazi soldiers were buried. Having been criticized by Germans the year before for their exclusion from D-Day celebrations, Reagan sought to make a gesture to the German people emphasizing German-American friendship. When it was discovered that the cemetery also contained the remains of SS troops, Reagan's visit became a hotly contested issue both in the United States and the Federal Republic.

Almost immediately the Reagan administration came under withering fire from Jewish groups, veterans' groups, and both political parties. Reagan's position was further compromised when his decision to visit the German cemetery was juxtaposed with his previous admission that he deliberately left out of his itinerary a visit to a German concentration camp because he thought it would be "out of line." Elie Wiesel, chairman of the United States Holocaust Memorial Council, criticized the president, urging him to cancel his trip. Reactions from the Jewish community varied from the politely dissenting (the national director of the Anti-

Defamation League of B'nai B'rith) to the caustic (the associate executive director of the American Jewish Congress). Even the American Legion, one of Reagan's staunchest supporters, denounced the president's plan to commemorate Nazis.[23]

Despite heavy domestic opposition, the president persevered with his plans, primarily because he felt that canceling the trip would be tantamount to criticizing the Germans. As a halfhearted concession, Reagan included a visit to a former concentration camp in his itinerary. Yet disapproval at home remained incredibly strong. On the defensive, Reagan only fueled the fire when he justified his decision to visit Bitburg by saying that the soldiers there were "victims of Nazism also." Reagan's steadfast determination to honor the Germany of the present, at the expense of the German victims of the past, illustrated the emphasis some were willing to place on the Cold War narrative of the German people.[24]

But at the same time, as this episode illustrates, the power of the Holocaust narrative grew incredibly during the last thirty years of the twentieth century. At the same time that Berlin was regaining—and indeed even building upon—its power to shape American perceptions of the Cold War, the Nazi destruction of European Jewry gradually became the *defining* moment of the Third Reich as well as of the Second World War. Like Berlin, the Holocaust became a powerful moral metaphor in American life. Unlike Berlin, however, which symbolized heroism and ultimately triumph, the Holocaust emerged as the benchmark for victimization in the United States. "The murder of European Jewry," observes Alan Mintz, "became the ultimate standard for speaking of the victimization of peoples in the modern period in spheres that had no necessary connection to the Jews." In focusing on the victims, those persecuted by the Nazis, instead of the perpetrators, the emphasis in popular culture moved from the causes of the Holocaust to its effects, subsuming, in a sense, the Third Reich to its most heinous act. Because the Holocaust lay bare the Third Reich's basest actions and depredations, representation of it became a series of heartrending emotional icons and anecdotes, representing the depths of human suffering and despair.[25]

Mainstream Americans' first significant encounter with the Holocaust came in 1978 with the broadcast of NBC's four-part miniseries *Holocaust*. Produced in a time when Americans were suffering from what President Carter would infamously characterize a year later as a "crisis of confidence," the broadcast ostensibly impressed upon Americans the importance of preventing such an act from occurring again. The universalization of the Holocaust in a low period of American history demonstrated the fear and ambivalence Americans possessed about themselves and their place in the world. In a time of triumphalism fifteen years later, by contrast, Americans reinterpreted the Holocaust through *Schindler's List* and the United States Holocaust Memorial Museum to prove the superiority of American values and actions.

Thus, while acknowledging and concurring with the importance of the Holocaust, Americans, at the same time, largely resisted the efforts of liberals to universalize the Holocaust in another, related way. Beginning with Raul Hilberg and gaining steam with Christopher Browning, American academics in the post-1960s era increasingly argued or implied that the bureaucratic and systemic factors that underlay the Holocaust could be present in most industrialized societies, and thus a similar event potentially could happen anywhere, including the United States. Whereas conservatives used Berlin to celebrate American life and values, liberals used the Holocaust as a cautionary tale to point out the shortcomings of American society.[26]

Intended to rival ABC's wildly popular miniseries *Roots,* an account of the African American experience, *Holocaust* became the most important site of memory regarding the Third Reich in the 1970s. In major markets around the country, at least one-fourth to one-third of Americans were tuned in to at least part of the series, leading to estimates of 120 million viewers in the United States. Because of its widespread popularity and impact, many scholars of the Holocaust view NBC's production as a seminal event.[27]

Sensing a real opportunity, Jewish organizations put on a full-court press to raise awareness of the show and encourage people to watch it, directing their efforts at both mainstream Americans and American Jews. The American Jewish Committee and the Anti-Defamation League each generated and distributed millions of copies of promotional and educational material tied to the program. Other organizations successfully encouraged newspapers to publish parts of the novel adaptation. Jewish organizations also worked with Christian churches to encourage viewership and engagement with the significant issues raised by the miniseries.[28]

Holocaust followed the fortunes of two German families during the rise and fall of the Third Reich. The Weiss clan, a Jewish family, witnessed a steady erosion of its prestige, and eventually the gradual elimination of its members, as the full extent of Hitler's genocidal plans became realized. The Dorf family, headed by the unemployed but ambitious Erik, on the other hand, took advantage of the new regime to move steadily higher in society. Erik Dorf became one of the most important agents of the Holocaust as he trained his considerable analytical powers on making mass murder increasingly efficient. By personalizing the Holocaust in such a way, the screenwriter sought to have a major impact on viewers.

Holocaust was the brainchild of network executives who believed the time was ripe for an extensive exploration of the Holocaust experience. The network spared no expense in promoting the show. With a screenplay written by respected author Gerald Green, the story was serialized in several American periodicals and published as a paperback novel before airing to maximize exposure. Sunday, April 16, the first day of the miniseries, was "unofficially" proclaimed Holocaust Sunday, and several organizations dedicated that week to a remembrance of the Holocaust. NBC published a study guide for the series and encouraged other organizations to do the same. The network also shrewdly timed the event to coincide with a couple of major Jewish events: the final episode aired on the thirty-fifth anniversary of the Warsaw Uprising, one week before the beginning of Passover. As one magazine stated, "For Jews, [viewing the program] has about it the quality of a religious obligation."[29]

Reactions to the series varied, but the greatest debate revolved around the appropriateness of television as a medium for such a horrific historical event. Elie Wiesel led the criticism, arguing that *Holocaust* trivialized and vulgarized the suffering of millions. Others blanched at the juxtaposition of Lysol commercials promising to wipe out germs with images of concentration camps, seemingly symbolic of the efforts of the Aryan race to eliminate the disease of Judaism. While recognizing the shortcomings of the medium, supporters nevertheless praised the miniseries for its efforts to bring the issues of the Holocaust to the forefront of America's consciousness.[30]

But beyond the highly visible debate on this narrative of the Holocaust existed a growing consensus on the nature of the phenomenon itself. Americans' overall interpretive strategy illustrated that during the late 1970s many understood the Holocaust to have universal implications. Unlike the reception of *Judgment at Nuremberg* in August 1961, in which Americans largely identified the Holocaust as a German event, the mainstream reception of *Holocaust* suggested that Americans in the 1970s viewed Nazi crimes against the larger backdrop of the Western world. Recalling the Milgram experiments, one MIT student focused on "the ease [with] which the minds of the German people were manipulated." After viewing the miniseries, a congressional representative from Oklahoma read the Holocaust as a cautionary tale against "big government": "These murders, by the thousands and by the millions, were made possible by . . . governments so large and so powerful that they had the ability to direct the lives of others and to end those lives if they chose." Indeed, the plans for a march by American Nazis in Skokie, Illinois, at the same time of the broadcast of the series reinforced the notion that Nazism was a disease that could infect anyone. Despite the unease associated with watching the series, one congressman believed that the "story needed to be told" in light of the national attention that the heirs of George Lincoln Rockwell were receiving.[31]

The most common reading of *Holocaust* was to view it as one of the many kinds of violence that humans might commit against one another. Everyday Americans as well as several members of Congress found that, in fact, multiple holocausts were happening in their day. One individual wrote to the editor of the *Washington Post* referencing the wrongdoings around the world, in places like Argentina, the Philippines, South Africa, and South Vietnam. While claiming that he could not "offer any judgment of the people that stood by" while the Nazi extermination of the Jews occurred, Senator Orrin Hatch of Utah pointed to Cambodia and expressed his "outrage that we would ever permit such an event to happen again." The president of the Jewish Community Council of Greater Washington wrote that Americans, as they "relived the horrifying history of the Third Reich in our homes," should be aware of the Kurds, Ugandans, and others "threatened by mass hatred and destruction."[32]

Senator William Proxmire was the most vocal in this regard. Proxmire used the occasion of the broadcast to renew his campaign for the passage of the Genocide Convention, legislation drafted to make genocide an international crime. On several different occasions, the senator recounted poignant or telling scenes from the miniseries to drive home the point that such crimes should never be permitted to happen again. He argued that the ratification of the convention would help prevent future atrocities. "My interest in the series is strong," he declared, "because it demonstrates what I have asserted on the floor of the Senate for the last 11 years." Despite the evident moral power of the miniseries and the tirelessness of his crusade, success proved elusive for Proxmire; it was not ratified until the 1980s.[33]

In these ways, Americans during the late 1970s began to appropriate and universalize the Holocaust. Increasingly, the event was no longer tied specifically to German history (or even Jewish history, for that matter). And this was a point that many believed was crucially important. As one American wrote to the *Washington Post,* "If there is a lesson to the Holocaust, it is the depths of good and evil that exist in us all when we separate ourselves on the basis of race or religion, or when we consider other people on any basis except that of our common humanity."[34]

Holocaust aired at a time when the American populace was uncertain of itself. Still experiencing the aftereffects of the revolutionary 1960s, many Americans universalized both the emotions and the causes of the Holocaust, believing that such an event could happen anywhere, including in the United States. By the 1990s, things had changed. Inspired by the conservative ascendancy in the United States and the absence of domestic conflict, the mainstream American public, while still recognizing the Holocaust as the ultimate benchmark for victimization, came to view the destruction of Europe's Jews as a historical event, a past atrocity that was unlikely ever to be repeated, especially in the United States. However, academics, for the most part, remained wedded to the 1960s–1970s understanding of the Holocaust, railing against the American desire to reduce the event to a simple morality tale of Nazi evil against American good.

Holocaust occupies an honored place in Holocaust research in the United States because it was the first substantial cultural encounter many Americans had with the issue. Yet, for all of its novelty, the miniseries was not a cinematic triumph. It was straitjacketed by the limited talents of the producers, the demands of television, and the gross intrusion of commercials. It remained for a celebrated Jewish director of action films to capitalize on the dramatic attributes inherent in the tragic suffering of Europe's Jews and elevate Holocaust representation to art.[35]

Steven Spielberg's *Schindler's List* (1993) captured American attention in such an incredible fashion that it threatened to rewrite all that Americans understood about the Holocaust. Figures from Oprah Winfrey to

President Clinton claimed that watching the film was a necessity. Jeffrey Katzenberg, head of Walt Disney, made the outrageous claim that dissemination of the film could bring "peace on earth." The film won seven Oscars in 1994 and was declared film of the year by *Newsweek*. Needless to say, millions of Americans filed into the theaters to watch it.[36]

Schindler's List offered a redemptive tale of one German's transformation from profligate industrialist to concerned (even emotionally tortured) humanitarian. Oskar Schindler begins the film as an unconcerned Nazi, but by the end he becomes the savior of several of his Jewish employees. His counterpart is the evil Amon Goeth, who tortures and kills Jews out of malevolent boredom. The conflict between the two plays out against the larger backdrop of the Holocaust, and it is through both of their lives that the viewer sees and understands the extermination of the Jews.

The reception of *Schindler's List* in some ways mirrored that of *Holocaust*. Criticism focused on the limited ability of a commercial film to represent a horror of such epic proportions. Several critics believed that Spielberg, like the producers of *Holocaust*, had profaned the Holocaust by subjecting it to Hollywood treatment. They claimed that Schindler's tale did not accurately represent the larger event and suggested that Spielberg was, at base, unwilling to deal with the horror at the core of the Holocaust. Taken together, these criticisms echoed those levied at *Holocaust* in their suggestions that films could never do justice to the unspeakable destruction of European Jewry.[37]

In addition to aesthetic criticisms, many reviewers focused on the content of the film—and here disagreement raged. The debate reflected the growing divide between academic and popular understandings of the Holocaust. For the most part, the moviegoing public found the film mesmerizing and helpful in understanding the destruction of European Jewry. Positive reviewers praised Spielberg for dropping his customary use of artifice and allowing the essential drama of the Holocaust to shine through. They particularly liked his decision to leave Schindler's conversion unexplained, suggesting that heroism is often ineffable. Their greatest compliment, however, was that *Schindler's List* had transcended the status of film and become a moving monument to the destruction of the Jews. Along this line, some reviewers claimed that the film better represented the Holocaust than any other cultural or scholarly document.

The case against *Schindler's List* was made most forcefully by American academics. Many of their substantive criticisms stemmed from their damnation of the film as the "Hollywoodization of the Holocaust." First and foremost, they pointed out that the film provided a happy ending: "Virtually every character in whom the audience has emotionally invested lives!" That all of the primary characters should survive in a situation in which historically the overwhelming majority of Jews most assuredly did not seemed to distort the very nature of the Holocaust, robbing the event of its larger significance. Many academics thus believed that this specific story of the Holocaust was a poor, even untruthful representation of the historical event.[38]

Too, many academics had problems with the focus of the film resting on Oskar Schindler and Amon Goeth. By centering on two Germans, one ultimately good and the other eternally evil, the film reduced the Holocaust to a simplistic morality tale, thus obfuscating the technological and bureaucratic aspects to the destruction of Europe's Jews. In a similar vein, academics despaired at the heroization of Schindler, his characterization as almost a Christlike figure. In focusing on the successful efforts of a single man to save Jews, the film implied that individuals could make a difference, even in something as overwhelming as the Holocaust. Also, in depicting Schindler, a Christian, as savior of the Jews, the film overemphasized the role of Gentiles and minimized that of Jews in resisting the Nazi pogrom. Together, these criticisms suggested that *Schindler's List* missed or glossed over much of the significant import of the Holocaust, while distorting and romanticizing its more tangential aspects.[39]

Even as reaction to *Schindler's List* demonstrated the growing divide between scholarly and popular interpretations of the Holocaust, the film also confirmed the Holocaust as the ultimate benchmark of suffering and victimization in the United States. Other groups appropriated the language of the Holocaust. A leader in the Nation of Islam known for his anti-Semitic remarks, Khalil Muhammed observed after watching the film: "That was a Holocaust but African-Americans pay a hell of a cost." Later, after touring the United States Holocaust Memorial Museum, Muhammed claimed, "We were given swindler's list." Such comments revealed African Americans' years of frustration with the overwhelming attention paid to Jewish victimhood to the exclusion of their own suffering.[40]

The varied receptions given to *Schindler's List* illustrated the hardening divide regarding the nature of the Holocaust. The mainstream reception affirmed a moral understanding of the Holocaust as the ultimate litmus test for suffering, but offered a simple understanding of the cause as a struggle between good and evil. Subscribing to a more nuanced set of interpretations, academics pushed for a more complicated rendering that they believed better represented the causes and course of the Holocaust. This growing divide in interpretations of the Holocaust between popular audiences, who were increasingly affected by the conservative resurgence in American life, and academics, who for the most part remained faithful to the heritage of the 1960s, was evidenced most acutely in the polarizing debate over Daniel Goldhagen's book, *Hitler's Willing Executioners*.[41]

It must be mentioned that the disputation over Goldhagen's book was not the first "historian's debate" over the Holocaust. Indeed, Reagan's visit to Bitburg initiated a wrenching debate in West German society over the nature of the Holocaust. Known as the *Historikerstreit,* it engulfed the German people in a tortuous trial, as German intellectuals fought bitterly over the "normalization" of German history. Some argued that the Holocaust should be placed in proper historical perspective—in comparison to other atrocities committed at other times, they claimed, the Holocaust was not unique. Others, led by Jürgen Habermas, feared that such rationalization downplayed the evils of the Nazi regime and allowed Germans to forget the Third Reich. The debate was followed by American academics but rarely noted by mainstream Americans.[42]

The debate over Goldhagen's book was different. Popular audiences, for the most part, championed the book; academics, for the most part, loathed it. The former found it a stimulating glimpse into the visceral nature of the extermination of the Jews, the latter a hackneyed and fraudulent simplification of the Holocaust. Published in 1997 and thus coming on the heels of *Schindler's List* and the opening of the United States Holocaust Memorial Museum, *Hitler's Willing Executioners* found an America interested in understanding why the Holocaust had happened. The answer Goldhagen provided was simple: the Germans did it because they adhered to an "eliminationist anti-Semitism." In essence, Goldhagen argued that the Germans were programmed by centuries of cultural indoctrination to hate the Jews and desire their destruction. To make his case, Goldhagen sketched a number of vignettes that ostensibly revealed the murderous intent of the Germans toward the Jews.

For Americans, Goldhagen's narrative was comforting because it offered an explanation of the Holocaust that confined it to a German phenomenon. He explained the Holocaust as a function of an abnormal German society, one in which "irrational" values flourished. Jane Caplan has noted that Goldhagen offered American readers a "seductive counterimage of themselves." In positioning the Nazis of World War II against the "we" of contemporary America, Goldhagen invited Americans to "identify themselves as the heirs of Enlightenment values and to distinguish themselves from the Germans about whom [Goldhagen] writes, from their alien values and 'radically different' culture." Omer Bartov has also suggested that Goldhagen's simple assertion of German guilt ignored anti-Semitic traditions in other countries. It also conveniently insisted on the absence of this sentiment in postwar Germany, thus providing an "important safety valve" for "America's loyal ally." In these ways, *Hitler's Willing Executioners* reinforced notions of both Germany and the United States that trumpeted the virtues of American society.[43]

Academics, by contrast, had become more comfortable with a more subtle, multicausal view of the Holocaust. Beginning with Raul Hilberg's *Destruction of the European Jews* (1961) and continuing with Christopher Browning's *Ordinary Men* (1992), scholars began emphasizing other aspects of Nazi Germany besides anti-Semitism. Some focused on the mindless, bureaucratized nature of the Holocaust, while others emphasized the importance of peer pressure. Whatever the focal point, these scholars increasingly implied that the factors that gave rise to the Holocaust could be found in other industrialized states, including the United States. The lesson, forged in the fires of the 1960s, suggested that Americans should maintain a watch not only on the Germans but on themselves as well.

The emergence of Goldhagen's book thus challenged the increasing complexity that surrounded the Holocaust in academic discourse while reaffirming the great morality tale that shaped popular understandings of Nazi Germany. This division was clearly demonstrated at a public symposium at the United States Holocaust Memorial Museum in 1996 attended by Goldhagen and other top historians on the Holocaust. When Goldhagen spoke he received excited applause from members of the audience. When other historians criticized his work, the audience remained silent or murmured angrily.[44]

Scholars have increasingly come to understand the Goldhagen phenomenon as part and parcel of American triumphalism in the wake of the Cold War. Omer Bartov has admirably summed up this viewpoint: "The argument that after the fall of Nazism the Germans became 'just like us,' and that therefore they are as unlikely to perpetrate genocide again as 'we' are, can produce an excessive sense of complacency not merely about postwar Germany but about the rest of 'us.'" When the Goldhagen phenomenon is viewed against the larger backdrop of discourse on Germany and the Holocaust, it becomes clear that this view represents the resurgence of the consensus view of Americans that reemerged after the fractious 1960s.[15]

The official space for commemorating the Holocaust in the United States supports this nationalistic view of the attempted extermination of Jewry. The opening of the United States Holocaust Memorial Museum in 1993 represented the culmination of a decade and a half of tireless working and lobbying on the part of several American organizations. In the wake of the furor created by the *Holocaust* miniseries, President Carter established a commission to examine ways to memorialize the atrocity visited upon Europe's Jews. When the museum was finally completed after fifteen years, it rapidly became one of the most popular tourist destinations in Washington.

The United States Holocaust Memorial Museum portrays Americans as liberators who confronted unspeakable and un-American horrors. According to its director, Michael Berenbaum, the museum narrates the story of the Holocaust as the "violastion of every essential American value." "We must transmit a sense of horror and outrage in a moving experience that from beginning to end addresses and touches the visitor," Berenbaum said while the museum was still in the planning stages. "We must speak to the moral dimension of the history and we must relate the story of the Holocaust to the location of our Museum on the National Mall and to the neighboring institutions of the Smithsonian complex." At the beginning of the exhibit, visitors are invited to adopt the identity of an American liberator as they listen to the recorded testimony of a GI before they encounter the exhibits. The GI describes the concentration camps with great difficulty, stuttering his way through the observation that he has never seen anything like this before and the protestation that nothing of this sort could ever happen in the United States. By identifying visitors with the American liberators, the museum makes the Holocaust part of American history while at the same time insisting that such an event runs counter to everything America stands for.[46]

The location of the museum on the Mall makes the effect even greater. As visitors emerge into daylight after their experience, they are confronted with iconic symbols of American democracy: the Washington Monument and the Capitol. This jarring juxtaposition between "an anti-museum . . . of Nazi racism, intolerance, dictatorship, and persecution" and these treasured hallmarks of "pluralism, tolerance, democracy, and human rights" heightens the contrast and enhances the effect. The result, according to Michael Berenbaum, is an understanding of the Holocaust as the "violation of every essential American value." A visitor more cynically noted that "a proper dose of the Holocaust, the thinking goes, will build up the needed antibodies against totalitarianism, racism, state-sponsored mass murder."[47]

As Jacob Eder has convincingly shown, the Federal Republic under the long reign of Helmut Kohl carefully monitored and debated the release of *Schindler's List,* the publication of *Hitler's Willing Executioners,* and the establishment of the United States Holocaust Memorial Museum. Detailing what he calls "Holocaust Angst," Eder demonstrates that Kohl's government viewed the growth of Holocaust consciousness in America along lines similar to previous West German administrations, seeing in them a potential threat to Germany's reputation in the United States and elsewhere. Following the lead of predecessors also concerned about representations of Germans in the United States but introducing a more explicit linkage between shaping narratives of German history and Federal Republic foreign policy, the Kohl administration sought to counter these narratives through initiatives to strengthen relations with Jewish organizations, influence the final form of the United States Holocaust Memorial Museum, and sponsor new voices for positive portrayals of German history, such as the German Historical Institute, all with varying degrees of success.[48]

The significance and meaning of both Berlin and the Holocaust in shaping American debates about itself and the world in the last decades of the twentieth century demonstrate the enduring power of the framework established for understanding Germany in the early postwar period. The frequent use of both symbols illustrates how central narratives of Germany had become to conversations about American identity and purpose in the world. The use of both also shows that despite their seemingly negative tone at times, narratives of Germany had become an integral part of American consciousness—and thus ensured that present-day Germans were regarded as Americanized and therefore safe.

Conclusion

The Significance of the German Question in the Twenty-First Century

Enemies to Allies illustrates how the meaning of powerful symbols associated with Germany have been contextually determined. Throughout the Cold War, Americans appropriated Germanness for different purposes and drew radically different interpretations from it. Based on extensive archival research in the United States and the Federal Republic of Germany, the book has shown how state and nonstate actors have sought to shape how Americans understood these narratives of Germany. With insights from the study of reception and collective memory, this book has demonstrated the contingent nature of some of the most frequently invoked symbols and images of the last several decades. At the same time, the book has attempted to use the notion of "interpretive communities" to group and generalize American responses to these powerful signs. It has argued that images of Germany and Germans were embedded in Cold War and world war narratives that changed and adapted over the course of the Cold War—and after.

Beginning with the English colonization of North America, notions of Germanness have played a major role in how Americans understood themselves and the world around them. In the first half of American history, Germany and Germans played an essential role in helping define American identity, but the character of this role evolved along with American society. For many years, Germanness was defined largely by the millions of German immigrants coming to the United States who helped shape an American identity rooted in democracy, self-sufficiency, masculinity, and loyalty. Beginning in the late nineteenth century, Americans interpreted Germanness through the new German empire, admiring its technological advances, educational innovations, and economic growth but fearing its antidemocratic behavior and militarism. After an interregnum during the Weimar era, the rise of the Third Reich heightened Germany's role as foil to American values and mission. By the end of World War II, even if Americans could not agree on the nature of the German threat, they all shared an understanding of America's role as liberator and savior of Western civilization.

The ways in which stories of Germanness shaped Americans' attitudes toward themselves and their world during the first two decades of the Cold War established patterns that endured throughout the rest of the twentieth century. In both its past and its present, Germany presented Americans with a comfortable notion of themselves, one in line with traditional Cold War interpretations of the American mission in the world. With the concept of totalitarianism, mainstream America found a schema for understanding the apparently dramatic about-face in Germany during the early Cold War period, and this framework proved an essential part of the Cold War consensus, which continued to resonate powerfully throughout the rest of the era.

But this consensus was not hegemonic. Even during its heyday, a sizable group of Americans clung to a World War II understanding of the Germans. Narratives rooted in America's struggle against Germany in the world wars gained renewed credence in the 1960s, and they became a tool of critics on both the left and the right who sought to use Nazi Germany as an effective metaphor to challenge the status quo in America. But despite the fears of German diplomats and their American allies that these stories about Germany signaled a return to the antideutsche sentiments of the Second World War, the evidence suggests that Americans incorporated these narratives into a larger interpretation of the U.S.-led postwar West. In this context, the Americanization of Germany meant the transformation of Germany's story into a chapter of the larger American tale, a narrative in which Germans were sometimes cast as villains and sometimes as heroes but rarely as an incomprehensible "others" who threatened present-day America—even as these narratives were simplified by the dominant symbols of Berlin and the Holocaust in the remaining decades of the twentieth century.

The first decade and a half of the twenty-first century suggest, however, that the power of narratives of Germany to shape Americans' understanding of themselves and their world may be waning as circumstances change. The attacks of 9/11 and the ensuing "War on Terror" ushered in a new phase of American foreign relations in which previous models rooted in the experience with Germany have proved less useful. Critics rebelled against President George W. Bush's effort to label the WMD-seeking governments of Iran, Iraq, and North Korea as the "axis of evil," drawing several distinctions between contemporary antagonists and the World War II–era Axis powers of Germany, Italy, and Japan. Likewise, attempts to frame Al Qaeda, Hezbollah, Hamas, and the Islamic State as manifestations of "Islamofascism" have been regarded by many as crude, simplistic, and wrongheaded. In instances such as these, invoking time-tested historical memories to frame new threats has largely failed as a rhetorical strategy.

At the same time, evidence suggests that in recent years Americans have not used metaphors of Germany to frame domestic issues to the same degree as their predecessors. The major protest movement of the last five years, the Occupy Wall Street movement, failed to follow in the footsteps of 1960s-era protest groups in engaging symbolism associated with Germany in any significant way. Instead the protestors opted for global symbols of inequality, such as "We are the 99%." In what has emerged as one the chief civil rights issue of the last few years, that of police brutality against African Americans, there has been little reference to the nation's police forces as "totalitarian" or "pigs," comparisons that were drawn constantly a half century earlier during periods of unrest. Instead, there has been a general call to recognize the structural racism that still pervades the country and recognize that "Black Lives Matter."

If we directly compare metaphors from the World War II experience and those from the Cold War, there are indications that the former have a better chance of remaining relevant in the twenty-first century. A basic search of the digitized *Public Papers of the Presidents,* hosted by the University of California–Santa Barbara's American Presidency Project, shows in raw terms the comparative frequency of the terms *World War II* and

Cold War in presidential discourse. Over the period 2001 to 2014, "World War II" appears almost twice as often as "Cold War" in the public utterances of Bill Clinton (briefly), George W. Bush, and Barack Obama, even though the Cold War lasted ten times as long.

This finding is echoed in the major feature films of the last fifteen years. Few have drawn on the Cold War experience (the Indiana Jones franchise changing the primary villains from Nazis to Soviet communists in *Kingdom of the Crystal Skull* [2008] is a notable exception), but interest has remained strong in the Third Reich, with high-profile projects such as *The Monuments Men* (2014), *The Book Thief* (2013), *Valkyrie* (2008), and *Inglourious Basterds* (2009) all doing well at the box office. If Americans have shown signs of forgetting the Cold War, as Jon Wiener has argued, World War II has proved more memorable.[1]

Whatever the relevance of these stories to America's future identity may be, it is clear that they played a central, decisive role in shaping how Americans thought of themselves and their place in the world during the twentieth century.

Acknowledgments

This book has been a long time coming. It has traveled with me lots of places and through many stages of my life. It should go without saying that a book that has taken this long to finish has accrued lots of debts; and if I've forgotten somebody in what follows, please know that it's not intentional—it's just that it's been such a long process that I'm bound to have left somebody important out.

The history department at The Ohio State University offered a wonderfully nurturing environment, and Michael Hogan and Peter Hahn were ideal dissertation advisors. Mike first gave me an idea that became this book; I'm afraid, however, that it has turned out far different from the one he imagined (that book still waits for you to write, Mike!). Other significant mentors included Alan Beyerchen, Steve Conn, and David Steigerwald. My graduate student colleagues formed a wonderful support network: in the field of diplomatic history John Tully, Matt Davis, Nate Citino, Matt Masur, and Jenn Walton; and outside of our clan Brad Austin, Mark Spicka, Laura Hilton, Emre Sencer, Paul Hibbeln, Jack Wells, Nick Steneck, Bill Caraher, Mike Fronda, Doug Palmer, and Greg Wilson. They not only offered valuable insights and perspectives on my work, they made the journey through the doctoral program far more enjoyable than it would have been otherwise.

My first posting at Louisiana Tech University provided me with life-long colleagues and friends. Steve Webre was a model department chair who first helped educate me about "all the things they don't teach you in graduate school." Vice President for Academic Affairs Ken Rea, also a historian, was a great source of support, encouragement, and sage advice. My history colleagues Dave Anderson, Jace Stuckey, Jeff Hankins, Laurie Stoff, Phil Cook, and Elaine Thompson were wonderful supporters. I also had the good fortune to build great relationships with colleagues outside of the history department: Jeremy Mhire, Rick Simmons, Heath Tims, Christian Duncan, and Galen Turner all provided good companionship and valuable counsel.

I have been similarly fortunate at subsequent postings. At the University of Baltimore, excellent colleagues nurtured and sustained me. My boss, Provost Joe Wood, pushed me to finish the manuscript. Good friends and colleagues Betsy Nix, Steve Scalet, Josh Kassner, Jeffrey Sawyer, Nicole Hudgins, Boram Yi, Charity Fox, Cheryl Wilson, Nancy O'Neill, Kelly McPhee, Paul Walsh, Will Hubbard, Danni Fowler, Pete Ramsey, and Lucy Holman all collaborated with and supported me through a variety of initiatives. And although I am still getting settled in my new position, I have already enjoyed the support of colleagues and administrators at Georgia Gwinnett College also.

In this historical profession at large, I have drawn wisdom and inspiration from countless colleagues. At the University of Georgia, Bill Stueck first gave me the confidence to believe that I could do meaningful historical work, and Peter Hoffer was an encouraging but firm mentor who likewise inspired me to forge on in the profession. Ken Osgood, Jeremi Suri, Jason Parker, Todd Bennett, Mitch Lerner, Laura Belmonte, Michael Krenn, Frank Costigliola, Tom Zeiler, Jessica Gienow-Hecht, Hiroshi Kitamura, Frank Schumacher, Andreas Daum, Neal Rosendorf, Giles Scott-Smith, David Snyder, and Nick Cull all encouraged this project along in their own special ways. A good friend and colleague, Andy Johns deserves special mention for encouraging me to submit my project to the University Press of Kentucky. Steve Wrinn and Allison Webster at the press have been a delight to work with, and many thanks go to the two anonymous reviewers who provided thorough and encouraging feedback. A special thank-you goes to Robin DuBlanc for her thorough copyediting of this book.

Conducting the research necessary to write this book required the support and advice of archivists and staff members at several institutions. In the United States, I am grateful for help I received at the American Jewish Archives, the American Jewish Historical Society Archives, the Warner Bros. Archive at the Cinematic Arts Library, University of Southern California, the Hoover Institution Archives, the National Museum of American Jewish Military History, the Margaret Herrick Library at the Academy of Motion Pictures Arts and Sciences, the National Archives

II, the Rare Book and Manuscript Library at Columbia University, the Wisconsin Historical Society, the UCLA Film and Television Archive, the United States Holocaust Memorial Museum, the Winston Churchill Memorial Library, and the YIVO Institute for Jewish History. In the Federal Republic, archivists and staff at the Bundesarchiv in Koblenz and at the Landesarchiv and the Politisches Archiv des Auswaertiges Amts in Berlin deserve special mention for their patience in helping me navigate holdings (here the stereotype is true: they *really are* very organized!). I would also like to thank native speakers Barbara Glenn and Julia H. Ceaser-Bolster for going over and confirming some of my German translations to make sure I got them right.

All this research would not have been possible without the generosity of many organizations. The German Academic Exchange Service (DAAD) supported my research in two ways: first in language training at the Goethe Institute in Berlin through a summer language scholarship, and second through a research grant that enabled me to carry out research in Koblenz and Berlin. Backing from Ohio State included the Phyllis Krumm International Memorial Scholarship, the International Travel Dissertation Grant, the Mershon Center's Study Abroad Grant, the Graduate School Summer Research Award, and the Graduate Student Alumni Research Award. The Society for Historians of American Foreign Relations (SHAFR) supplied travel assistance to do research in Washington, D.C., through the Georgetown Travel Grant. The American Jewish Archive supported research in its holdings through the Lowenstein-Wiener Fellowship. The Garnie McGinty Trust at Louisiana Tech University furnished support for research in California and New York, and Louisiana Tech provided a quarter-long sabbatical through the University Faculty Fellowship. I deeply appreciate their support, and I apologize that it's taken so long for the result to come to fruition.

Most of all, I'd like to thank my family. My parents, who made education a priority, sacrificed to support me through my undergraduate education. They also steadfastly encouraged me as I turned away from more lucrative fields to pursue a degree in history. Without their loving help, I would never have been in a position to write this book.

My sons have been a perpetual source of inspiration. I've been working on this book longer than any of them have been alive, and Grady, Spencer, and Bennett have lovingly lived with and tolerated my many eccentricities as I've tried to finish it. They have also gently prodded and chided me to finish the book, all while serving as a constant reminder of what really matters in the world. I suspect they've put up with me because they have high aspirations that this book will outsell *Harry Potter* (and that can happen only with your help, Gentle Reader). I couldn't ask for a better set of kids.

And that's in large part because of my wife, who brought them into the world and has devoted herself to their development. Through it all there's been Erica, the very definition of a loving, understanding, and supportive spouse. I started graduate school shortly after we were married, and so we've been copilots on this crazy ride from the beginning. In the words of Charles Murray, ours is a start-up marriage, which means we have forged our adult lives together (as opposed to merging our separate lives later in life). This is one of the few things I would agree with Murray about: marrying young can make for the most meaningful kinds of union because we remember "when it was all still up in the air" and we understand and appreciate that we wouldn't be the same without the other. Not that the positive influence and support have been anything close to balanced. Erica worked to put me through graduate school. She supported and moved our family to Ohio, then to Louisiana, then to Maryland, and then back to Georgia again. And that doesn't even begin to scratch the surface. For the few of you lucky enough to have married well, you know that most of the love and encouragement is beyond the capacity of words to describe. All I can say is that without her this book wouldn't have been written—and that the book (close your ears, University Press of Kentucky) is among the least important things her presence has meant to my life. As a small token of appreciation, I humbly dedicate this work to her.

Parts of this book have appeared previously in the following publications: "*The Desert Fox,* Memory Diplomacy, and the German Question in Early Cold War America," *Diplomatic History* 32 no. 2 (2008): 207–38; "*Die antideutsche Welle:* The Anti-German Wave in Cold War America and Its Implications for the Study of Public Diplomacy," in *Decentering the United States: New Directions in Culture and International Relations,* ed. Jessica Gienow-Hecht (New York: Berghahn Books, 2007), 73–106; "In Search of Germans: Contested Germany in the Production of *The Search,*" *Journal of Popular Film and Television* 34, no. 1 (2006): 34–45.

Notes

The following abbreviations are used in the notes:

AJCR   American Jewish Congress Records, American Jewish Historical Society Archives, Center for Jewish History, New York, N.Y.

BAK   Bundesarchiv, Koblenz, Germany

CO-JCRC   Cincinnati, Ohio—Jewish Community Relations Council, American Jewish Archives, Cincinnati, Ohio

CTE   Christopher T. Emmet Papers, Hoover Institution Archives, Stanford University, Stanford, Calif.

FRUS   *Foreign Relations of the United States*

LAB   Landesarchiv Berlin, Berlin, Germany

MHL   Margaret Herrick Library, American Motion Picture Arts and Sciences, Beverly Hills, Calif.

NA   National Archives II, College Park, Md.

NJCRAC   National Jewish Community Relations Advisory Council Records, American Jewish Historical Society Archives, Center for Jewish History, New York, N.Y.

NMAJMH   National Museum of American Jewish Military History, Washington, D.C.

PAAA   Politisches Archiv des Auswaertiges Amts, Berlin, Germany

RG   Record Group

SKP   Stanley Kramer Papers, UCLA Library Special Collections, Los Angeles, Calif.

SPWWIII   Society for the Prevention of World War III, Rare Book and Manuscript Library, Columbia University, New York, N.Y.

USHMMIA   United States Holocaust Memorial Museum Institutional Archives, Washington, D.C.

WBA   Warner Bros. Archive, Cinematic Arts Library, University of Southern California, Los Angeles, Calif.

WHS   Wisconsin Historical Society, University of Wisconsin, Madison

WJCC   World Jewish Congress Collection, American Jewish
                Archives, Cincinnati, Ohio
YIVO   YIVO Institute for Jewish History, Center for Jewish
                History, New York, N.Y.

Introduction

1. For clarification, two points should be made. First, this book is not a study of traditional policy making; nor does it regard as its ultimate aim the explanation of foreign policy. Instead, it in large part examines how memory was instrumentalized by the American and West German governments to achieve foreign policy objectives. Second, for the purposes of this work, West Germany is taken to represent Germany in American memory. This is not to deny the existence of the German Democratic Republic, nor is it to ignore much of the important work done on East Germany in recent years. Instead, it is a recognition of the fact that few in the United States during this period considered the East German government to be a legitimate representative of the German people. Almost all Americans regarded the regime as a puppet of the Soviet Union. In this sense, the relationship of the past to the present in East Germany was not contested in the United States.

2. Jon Wiener has argued that the memory of the Cold War has faded since it came to an end; see *How We Forgot the Cold War*. The literature on German-American relations is voluminous. For a good overview, see Junker, *The United States and Germany in the Era of the Cold War*. For a relative sampling, see Ninkovich, *Germany and the United States;* Eisenberg, *Drawing the Line;* Schwartz, *America's Germany;* Backer, *The Decision to Divide Germany*. On understanding the change in American attitudes toward Germany, Goedde, *GIs and Germans;* and Reuther, *Die ambivalente Normalisierung* are notable exceptions. For the study of American representations of Asia during much of the same time, see Klein, *Cold War Orientalism*.

3. See Halbwachs, *On Collective Memory*. For an excellent discussion of memory and foreign relations history, see Schulzinger, "Memory and Understanding U.S. Foreign Relations." For good discussions of public memory, see Thelen, *Memory and American History;* Kansteiner, "Finding Meaning in Memory"; Bourdon, "Some Sense of Time"; Winter, "Film and the Matrix of Memory"; Hoskins, "New Memory." Important works on memory include Hutton, *History as an Art of Memory;* Kammen, *Mystic Chords of Memory;* Huyssen, *Twilight Memories*.

4. Bourdon, "Some Sense of Time," 7; Bodnar, *Remaking America;* Sturken, *Tangled Memories;* Anderson, *Imagined Communities;* Winter, "Film and the Matrix of Memory," 864.

5. Schulzinger, "Memory and Understanding U.S. Foreign Relations"; McMahon, "Contested Memory"; Rosenberg, *A Date Which Will Live*.

6. Lipsitz, *Time Passages*, 5; Landsberg, *Prosthetic Memory*, 2, 3, 8.

7. Useful works on public diplomacy, past and present, include Hixson, *Parting the Curtain;* Pells, *Not Like Us;* Gienow-Hecht, *Transmission Impossible;* Osgood, *Total Cold War;* Kennedy and Lucas, "Enduring Freedom"; von Eschen, "Enduring

Public Diplomacy"; Critchlow, "Public Diplomacy during the Cold War"; Maack, "Books and Libraries as Instruments of Cultural Diplomacy"; Robin, "Requiem for Public Diplomacy?"; Wagnleitner, *Coca-Colonization and the Cold War;* Taylor, *British Propaganda in the 20th Century;* Ross, "Public Diplomacy Comes of Age."

8. Fish, *Is There a Text in This Class?*; Bourdon, "Some Sense of Time," 8–9.

1. "Tomorrow the World"

1. Quoted in Keller, *Chancellorsville and the Germans,* 2–3, 78, 87. Also see Helbich, "German-Born Union Soldiers"; and Knobel, *America for the Americans,* 159–61.

2. Fogleman, *Hopeful Journeys,* 3, 80–81, 97.

3. Ibid., 5; quoted in Wellenreuther, "Image and Counterimage," 89; Schrag, *Not Fit for Our Society,* 20; Leonard and Parmet, *American Nativism,* 15.

4. Quoted in Leonard and Parmet, *American Nativism,* 115–16; quoted in Eichhoff, "The German Language in America," 227. For more on Franklin's attitudes, see Schrag, *Not Fit for Our Society,* 20; Otterness, *Becoming German,* 146, 150, 157; Leonard and Parmet, *American Nativism,* 15; Fogleman, *Hopeful Journeys,* 151–52.

5. Quoted in Wellenreuther, "Image and Counterimage," 90.

6. Fogleman, *Hopeful Journeys,* 149–53; Schrag, *Not Fit for Our Society,* 20.

7. Otterness, *Becoming German.*

8. Quoted in ibid., 54–55, 59.

9. Ibid., 146–54. Quotes on 146, 147, 154.

10. Quoted in Jones, *The Georgia Dutch,* 60–61, 71–72.

11. Otterness, *Becoming German,* 155, 162; Wellenreuther, "Image and Counterimage," 96.

12. Keller, *Chancellorsville and the Germans,* 11; Moltmann, "Pattern of German Emigration," 15.

13. Leonard and Parmet, *American Nativism,* 53; quoted in Gjerde, "Prescriptions and Perceptions," 119.

14. Quoted in Gjerde, "Prescriptions and Perceptions," 126.

15. Ibid., 128, 129 (quote).

16. Wellenreuther, "'Germans Make Cows and Women Work.'"

17. Levine, *The Spirit of 1848,* 84.

18. Quoted in ibid., 5, 188. For more on the forty-eighters, see Bergquist, "The Forty-Eighters."

19. Quoted in Frizzell, *Independent Immigrants,* 92; quoted in Keller, *Chancellorsville and the Germans,* 13. On being German in America in the nineteenth century, see Conzen, "German-Americans and the Invention of Ethnicity."

20. Keller, *Chancellorsville and the Germans,* 11–14; Knobel, *America for the Americans,* 127.

21. Keller, *Chancellorsville and the Germans,* 13, 15, 20, chapter 5, chapter 7.

22. Conzen, "German-Americans and the Invention of Ethnicity," 134–39; Keller, *Chancellorsville and the Germans,* 13.

23. Rippley, "German Assimilation," 123–24, 129 (quote).

24. Walch, *Immigrant America,* 206; Nagler, "From Culture to Kultur," 149.

25. Nagler, "From Culture to Kultur," 131–34.

26. Ibid., 136–37, 152; Gienow-Hecht, *Sound Diplomacy,* 26–29.

27. Jeismann, "American Observations," 22–23; Günther, "Interdependence between Democratic Pedagogy in Germany and the Development of Education in the United States in the Nineteenth Century," 52–53; Gregory P. Wegner, "Prussian *Volksschulen* through American Eyes: Two Perspectives on Curriculum and Teaching from the 1890s," 57; Derek S. Linton, "American Responses to German Continuation Schools during the Progressive Era," 71.

28. Wegner, "Prussian *Volksschulen* through American Eyes," 59; Nagler, "From Culture to Kultur," 141, 143.

29. Nagler, "From Culture to Kultur," 144.

30. Gienow-Hecht, "Trumpeting Down the Walls of Jericho," 588. The lone exception to this tale of ineptitude, according to Gienow-Hecht, was the diplomacy of music. Trommler, "Inventing the Enemy," 100–104; quoted in Nagler, "From Culture to Kultur," 146, 147.

31. Nagler, "From Culture to Kultur," 150–51.

32. Flanagan, "Woodrow Wilson's 'Rhetorical Restructuring,'" 117.

33. Ibid., 117–27 (quotes from same).

34. Ibid., 131–35 (quotes from same).

35. Quoted in Axelrod, *Selling the Great War,* 130.

36. Ibid., 180, 183–84 (quote from 184).

37. Quoted in ibid., 130, 143.

38. Quoted in ibid., 164–65.

39. Nagler, "From Culture to Kultur," 154; quoted in Schrag, *Not Fit for Our Society,* 85; Axelrod, *Selling the Great War,* chapter 10.

40. On the German American desire to become "white," see Kazal, *Becoming Old Stock.*

41. Hoenicke Moore, *Know Your Enemy,* 38–40.

42. Glaser-Schmidt, "Between Hope and Skepticism," 214–15; quoted in Krueger, "Germany and the United States," 180; Wala, "Reviving Ethnic Identity," 327.

43. Ibid., 326–37.

44. Hoenicke Moore, *Know Your Enemy,* 23 (quotes in ibid., 32, 35).

45. Casey, *Cautious Crusade,* 5–8 (quote on 6); Hoenicke Moore, *Know Your Enemy,* 87 (quote from same).

46. Lipstadt, *Beyond Belief,* 31–36; Hoenicke Moore, *Know Your Enemy,* 42–60.

47. Diamond, *The Nazi Movement in the United States,* 24–29.

48. Ibid., 109–96.

49. Ibid., 204. For more on the Bund and other right-wing activities, see Gary, *The Nervous Liberals.*

50. Karl Lischka, Notes, 1939, Confessions of a Nazi Spy, Production Code Administration Files, MHL; W. W. Dobson to Warner Bros., 16 May 1939, Correspondence 1, WBA; Sylvia Razey to Warner Bros., 1939, Confessions of a Nazi Spy, Correspondence 1, WBA; An American Born to Jack Warner, 1 January 1939, Confessions of a Nazi Spy, Confessions of a Nazi Spy—Notes etc., WBA; Luis De Angelis to Warner Bros., 31 May 1939, Confessions of a Nazi Spy, WBA; Diamond, *The Nazi Movement in the United States,* 22; Adler and Paterson, "Red Fascism."

51. Hoenicke Moore, *Know Your Enemy,* 107, 119–20, 142–50.

52. Ibid., 156–61. See also Koppes and Black, *Hollywood Goes to War,* 122–25; and Dick, *The Star-Spangled Film,* 2–9.

53. S. K. Padover, "War: A German Industry," *American Mercury,* October 1943, 468; Henry Wolfe, "German Plans for the Next War," *American Mercury,* August 1944, 180–81; Thomas Mann, "What Is German?" *Atlantic Monthly,* May 1944, 78–85.

54. Heinrich Fraenkel, "Is Hitler Youth Curable?" *New Republic,* 18 September, 1944, 335; Dorothy Thompson, "Germany—Enigma of the Peace," *Life,* 6 December 1943, 69.

55. Letters to the Editor, *Life,* 23 December 1943, 5; Gallup, *The Gallup Poll,* 356.

56. "Unconditional Surrender of Fascism," *National Jewish Monthly,* September 1943, 1; Eugene Tillinger, "Prussia: Menace to Peace," *National Jewish Monthly,* February 1944, 188.

57. "Tomorrow, the World!" Advertising Campaign, 1944, Previews, Tomorrow the World, Lester Cowan Collection, MHL; Jack Diamond to Rubine, 9 May 1944, Correspondence, Tomorrow the World, Lester Cowan Collection, MHL; Memorandum, 8 August 1944, Advertising, Lester Cowan Collection, MHL.

58. The Democratic versus the Nazi Way of Life: A Report on an Experiment with the Motion Picture "Tomorrow the World," 1945, Correspondence, Tomorrow the World, Lester Cowan Collection, MHL. In referencing the "Nazi" way of life, the study was already slanted in favor of an interpretation that did not read the Third Reich as representative of the German people. Nevertheless, several children voiced interpretations that coincided more with the harsher narrative.

59. The Democratic versus the Nazi Way of Life: A Report on an Experiment with the Motion Picture "Tomorrow the World," 1945, Correspondence, Tomorrow the World, Lester Cowan Collection, MHL.

60. Ibid.

61. List of Main Changes in Treatment, 1944, Hotel Berlin, WBA; 1945 Reviews, 1945, Hotel Berlin, Clippings File, MHL.

2. "Germany Belongs in the Western World"

1. Memorandum of Conversation, 18 December 1950, Central Decimal Files, RG 59, NA.

2. John Stone, Report No. 19, 5 April 1950, Motion Picture Committee, box 51, NJCRAC; John Stone, Report No. 28, 1 March 1951, Motion Picture Committee—John Stone Reports, box 51, NJCRAC; Statement Made by Irving Kane, 22 May 1951, Committee—Germany, box 55, NJCRAC; Jules Cohen to NCRAC Motion Picture Committee, 18 October 1951, Committees—National Motion Picture 51–52, box 49, NJCRAC; Draft Statement re: "The Desert Fox," 18 October 1951, Committees—National Motion Picture 51–52, box 49, NJCRAC; Mulvey to Lewis, 3 December 1951, Central Decimal Files, RG 59, NA; Bonn to Secretary of State, 20 November 1951, Central Decimal Files, RG 59, NA; Paul Ginsburg to Geoffrey Lewis, 30 October 1951, Central Decimal Files, RG 59, NA.

3. Lears, "The Concept of Cultural Hegemony," 572; McAlister, *Epic Encounters,* 6.

4. Bernhard, *U.S. Television News and Cold War Propaganda,* has done an excellent job of illustrating the nature of institutional power in cultural hegemony.

5. A good example would be Drew Middleton, "Vignettes of a Rudderless Germany," *New York Times Magazine,* 8 May 1949, 10, 63–65, in which he attacked the illusion that "the mass of Germans are good little democrats after four centuries of authoritarianism and four years of occupation." Henry Regnery, *Memoirs of a Dissident Publisher* (Lake Bluff, Ill.: Regnery, 1985), 70; Frei, *Adenauer's Germany,* 285–86; Washington Embassy to Lilienfeld, BPA, B 145/775, 21 August 1951, BAK; Krekeler to Auswaertiges Amt, 1 April 1952, B 145/775, BAK; Sulzberger to Emmet, 3 February 1950, Sulzberger, box 100, CTE; Joseph Lichten to ADL Regional Offices, 9 February 1950, folder 10, box 56, CO-JCRC.

6. Baughman, *The Republic of Mass Culture,* 9–16, 21–23.

7. Ibid., 30, 59, 63, 74.

8. Kimball, *Swords or Ploughshares?;* Schwartz, *America's Germany;* Eisenberg, *Drawing the Line;* Trachtenberg, *A Constructed Peace.* Several of the aforementioned episodically discuss the role of historical memory, but Backer, *The Decision to Divide Germany,* is a notable exception in its devotion to memory's role in the division of Germany.

9. Morgenthau to Roosevelt, in *FRUS* (1945), 3:376–77; Backer, *The Decision to Divide Germany,* 34.

10. Kimball, *Swords or Ploughshares?* 4–5; quoted in Schwartz, *America's Germany,* 20.

11. Quoted in Eisenberg, *Drawing the Line,* 44–46; quoted in Schwartz, *America's Germany,* 19. For Roosevelt's World War II beliefs, see Michaela Hoenicke Moore, *Know Your Enemy.*

12. Quoted in Eisenberg, *Drawing the Line,* 45–47; quoted in Schwartz, *America's Germany,* 20.

13. *Harry S. Truman, 1947, Public Papers of the Presidents of the United States* (Washington, D.C.: Government Printing Office, 1963), 269; quoted in Ninkovich, *Germany and the United States,* 50.

14. Trachtenberg, *A Constructed Peace,* 50–51; *Harry S. Truman,* 209. On the formation of the Cold War consensus, see Melanson, *American Foreign Policy,* 14–16.

15. Schwartz, *America's Germany,* 86, 113–294; Ninkovich, *Germany and the United States,* 67, 76 (Truman quote), 82–106. Both of these works have excellent discussions of the concept of "dual" or "double" containment.

16. For more details on this transformation, see Trachtenberg, *A Constructed Peace;* and Schwartz, *America's Germany.* On the Eisenhower approach, see Felken, *Dulles und Deutschland.*

17. Douglas Batson to Mr. Alexander, Assistant Director, Bureau of Prisons, 2 August 1950, Central Decimal Files, RG 59, NA; German Police Leader Program, Evaluation 1952, International Information Administration, Field Program for Germany (IFG), RG 59, NA; Memorandum of Conversation, 6 July 1950, Information Policy—Germany, Subject Files, 1941–1954, Records of the Office of Western European Affairs, RG 59, NA; Arthur Settel to Ralph Burns, 28 January 1952, Central Decimal Files, RG 59, NA; Settel to Henry Kellermann, 29 February 1952, Central Decimal Files, RG 59, NA; Revision of the Public Affairs Program and Conclusion of a Cultural Treaty, 13 March 1951, Public Affairs Program, Subject Files, 1941–1954, Records of the Office of Western European Affairs, RG 59, NA; Henry Byroade, "Comment by Henry Byroade, Director of the Bureau of German Affairs," *Department of State Bulletin,* 28 August 1950, 354.

18. Huebner to War Department, 12 April 1947, Central Decimal Files, RG 319, NA.

19. Huebner to Parks, 1 April 1947, Central Decimal Files, RG 319, NA; King to Frankfurt, 14 April 1947, Central Decimal Files, RG 319, NA; King to Frankfurt, 16 December 1947, Central Decimal Files, RG 319, NA.

20. King to HQ Eucom Frankfurt, 15 May 1947, Central Decimal Files, RG 319, NA; Telegram, Huebner (Frankfurt) to Parks, War Department, 9 May 1947, Central Decimal Files, RG 319, NA; King to Frankfurt, 8 April 1947, Central Decimal Files, RG 319, NA.

21. John Norris, "Army Reluctant to Clarify Inaction on Nuernberg Film," *Washington Post,* 19 September 1949, 1, 8.

22. Ibid.; Office Memorandum, 28 January 1949, Central Decimal Files, 1945–1949, RG 59, NA; Memorandum of Conversation, 4 March 1949, Central Decimal Files, RG 59, NA; Memorandum from Wright to Beam and Fuller, 9 February 1949, Central Decimal Files, RG 59, NA; Edwin McElwain to Henry Kellerman, 28 November 1949, Central Decimal Files, RG 59, NA; Kellerman to McElwain, 13 March 1949, Central Decimal Files, RG 59, NA; Lorentz to Adrian Fisher, 14 May 1951, Central Decimal Files, RG 59, NA; Meeting of Subcommittee of Three, 6 December 1949, 229, AJC Gen-10, YIVO; Barnouw, cited in Clifford Rothman, "Ending the Silence over Nuremberg," *Los Angeles Times,* 2 June 1997, F5.

23. Quoted in Gleason, *Totalitarianism,* 61, 77, 82; Adler and Paterson, "Red Fascism," 1046.

24. Television Broadcast on 20 August 1950, Television Broadcasts, Miscellaneous German Files, 1943–1954, Records of the Office of Western European

Affairs, 1941–1954, RG 59, NA; McCloy, "Assisting Germany to Become a Peaceful Democracy," 63.

25. Information Program on Germany, 6 November 1945, Information Policy—Germany, Subject Files, 1941–1954, Records of the Office of Western European Affairs, RG 59, NA; Projected Information Activities on Germany, 15 February 1946, Information Policy—Germany, Subject Files, 1941–1954, Records of the Office of Western European Affairs, RG 59, NA.

26. Memorandum of Meeting, Reeducation Japan and Germany, 1 May 1946, Information Policy—Germany, Subject Files, 1941–1954, Records of the Office of Western European Affairs, RG 59, NA; Report by Members of Education Mission to Germany, 18 October 1946, Information Policy—Germany, Subject Files, 1941–1954, Records of the Office of Western European Affairs, RG 59, NA; Tentative List of Organizations from Which to Request Comments, 17 April 1952, Public Affairs Program, Subject Files, 1941–1954, Records of the Office of Western European Affairs, RG 59, NA; Proposed Cultural Convention with Germany, 24 January 1952, Public Affairs Program, Subject Files, 1941–1954, Records of the Office of Western European Affairs, RG 59, NA.

27. Schwartz, *America's Germany*, 168. For more on the Landsberg cases, see Schwartz, *America's Germany*, 157–75. Henry Kellermann to Shepard Stone, 19 March 1951, Information Policy—Germany, Subject Files, 1941–1954, Records of the Office of Western European Affairs, RG 59, NA.

28. Bernhard, *U.S. Television News and Cold War Propaganda*, 1–9, 123 (quote), 124.

29. Simon to Breen, 21 November 1949, Chief of Information, Central Decimal Files, RG 59, NA; Breen to Carl Humelsine, 23 November 1949, Central Decimal Files, RG 59, NA.

30. Byroade to Breen, 9 December 1949, Central Decimal Files, RG 59, NA; Breen to Byroade, 14 December 1949, Central Decimal Files, RG 59, NA.

31. Sannebeck to Patterson, 9 August 1951, Central Decimal Files, RG 59, NA; Memorandum of Conversation, 14 August 1951, Central Decimal Files, RG 59, NA; J. M. Fleischer of US HICOG to Dr. Denzer, 17 August 1950, B 145/1202, BAK.

32. Goedde, "From Villains to Victims."

33. For a useful overview of Federal Republic cultural diplomacy, see Aguilar, *Cultural Diplomacy and Foreign Policy;* and Paulmann, *Auswärtige Repräsentationen*. For the treatment of Germany's past within Germany, see Wiesen, *West German Industry;* Moeller, "War Stories"; Bracher et al., *'45 und die Folgen*. The Society for the Prevention of World War III often lodged complaints with the U.S. government over its lenient treatment of Germans. See, for example, C. Monteith Gilpin to Robert Patterson, 22 July 1946, 2, SPWWIII. Many of the organization's fears are publicly expressed in its publication *Prevent World War III*. For the relationship between Germans and American Jews after World War II, see Shafir, *Ambiguous Relations*.

34. Aguilar, *Cultural Diplomacy and Foreign Policy*, 33–35; Krekeler to Aus-

waertiges Amt, 20 August 1951, B 145/775, BAK; Krekeler to Auswaertiges Amt, 28 May 1954, B 90/36, PAAA.

35. Aufzeichnung, 18 July 1951, B 90/71, PAAA; Krekeler to Auswaertiges Amt, 20 August 1951, B 145/775, BAK.

36. Aufzeichnung, 17 January 1951, B 11/297, PAAA; Generalkonsulat New York to Auswaertiges Amt, 12 February 1952, B 11/298, PAAA.

37. Krekeler to Auswaertiges Amt, 18 October 1951, B 145/775, BAK; von Lilienfeld to Walter Gong, 17 October 1951, B 145/775, BAK; Aufzeichnung, 18 October 1951, B 145/775, BAK; Aufzeichnung, 25 June 1951, B 11/297, PAAA; Contract between Federal Republic of Germany and Roy Bernard, 1951, B 145/775, BAK.

38. Report, Krekeler, May 28, 1952, B 145/532, BAK; Marta Erdman, Researcher, Foreign News, to Campbell, Roy Bernard, 31 August 1953, B 145/693, BAK; Vermerk, 2 July 1955, B 145/776, BAK; Kessel to Auswaertiges Amt, 2 October 1957, B 145/773, BAK.

39. Campbell to Moennig, 16 September 1952, B 145/1277, BAK.

40. Ibid.; Thomas to von Lilienfeld, 7 August 1952, B 145/1277, BAK.

41. Roy Bernard to von Lilienfeld, October 1952, B 145/775, BAK; Gong to von Lilienfeld, 31 March 1952, B 145/775, BAK; Gong to von Lilienfeld, 10 April 1952, B 145/775, BAK.

42. Annual Report, April 1957, B 145/9764, BAK.

43. German Embassy to Auswaertiges Amt, 28 January 1951, B 11/298, PAAA; Auszug aus dem Zwischenbericht der Firma Roy Bernard an Dr. Heinz Krekeler, 16 April 1952, B 145/775, BAK; Report, Blumenthal to Gong, 9 June 1952, B 145/775, BAK; Report on Roy Bernard, 19 July 1954, B 145/775, BAK.

44. Annual Report, 1957, B 145/9764, BAK; "Perspective of Germany," *Atlantic Monthly,* March 1957, 102.

45. Auszug aus dem Zwischenbericht der Firma Roy Bernard an Dr. Heinz Krekeler, 16 April 1952, B 145/775, BAK; "Germany: The World's Fate Lies in Its Rubble," *Look,* 26 February 1952, 69–75.

46. Roy Bernard to von Lilienfeld, October 1952, B 145/775, BAK.

47. Sommers to Blumenthal, 5 November 1953, B 145/775, BAK; Mary Hornaday to Campbell, 16 March 1954, B 145/775, BAK; John Scott to Campbell, 5 June 1954, B 145/775, BAK; Kaltenborn to Blumenthal, 11 June 1954, B 145/775, BAK.

48. Roy Bernard's feeble efforts in the film and television media are somewhat surprising, given that Blumenthal for a brief time represented the American Jewish Congress on the Motion Picture and Mass Media Committee of the National Community Relations Advisory Council. See, for example, his participation in the meeting of the Motion Picture and Mass Media Committee, 6 October 1949, 49, NJCRAC; Auszug aus Brief Walter Gong, 15 October 1952, B 145/532, BAK; Krekeler to von Lilienfeld, 16 April 1952, B 145/775, BAK; von Eckardt to Auswaertiges Amt, 21 August 1952, B 145/775, BAK; von Lilienfeld to Campbell, 15 August 1952, B 145/775, BAK; Krekeler to Auswaertiges Amt, 1 April 1952, B 145/775, BAK; Krekeler to von Lilienfeld; Gong to von Lilienfeld, 3 September

1952, B 145/775, BAK; Georg von Lilienfeld to Blumenthal, 13 November 1953, B 145/775, BAK; Krekeler to Auswaertiges Amt, 23 March 1953, B 145/775, BAK; Richard Mönnig to von Lilienfeld, September 1953, B 145/775, BAK.

49. Aufzeichnung, 24 June 1953, B 145/531, BAK; Report, Krekeler to Auswaertiges Amt, 11 February 1954, B 145/531, BAK; Aufzeichnung, Mönnig, 16 July 1953, B 145/531, BAK.

50. Knappstein to Auswaertiges Amt, 3 November 1952, B 106/903, BAK; Riesser to Auswaertiges Amt, 21 July 1952, B 106/903, BAK.

51. On the Atlantik-Brücke, see Kühnhardt, *Atlantik-Brücke.*

52. Agenda for Meeting of Managing Committee, American Council on Germany, 14 March 1952, Knauth, Theodore, box 43, CTE; George N. Shuster to Eric Warburg, 26 June 1952, Knauth, Theodore, box 43, CTE; Eric Warburg to Theodore Knauth, 18 August 1952, Knauth, Theodore, box 43, CTE; Theodore Knauth to Eric Warburg, 20 August 1952, Knauth, Theodore, box 43, CTE; Invitation to Dinner in Honor of Christopher Emmett, n.d., Testimonial Dinner, New York, 9 November 1961—General, box 1, CTE.

53. Theodore Knauth to Eric Warburg, 20 August 1952, Knauth, Theodore, box 43, CTE; Theodore Knauth to Eric Warburg, 28 August 1952, Knauth, Theodore, box 43, CTE. This network can easily be seen through a cursory examination of Emmet's correspondence at the Hoover Institution Archives.

54. Report on the Activities of the American Council on Germany, 15 October 1953, American Council on Germany—Reports of Activities, box 4, CTE; Report on Activities of the American Council on Germany, Inc., 1 January 1954, American Council on Germany—Reports of Activities, box 4, CTE; Secretary's Annual Report of Activities, 1955, American Council on Germany—Reports of Activities, box 4, CTE; Chris Emmet to Louis P. Lochner, 2 May 1956, American Council on Germany, 1952–1961, box 1, Louis Lochner Papers, WHS.

55. Kennan, *Memoirs,* 255.

56. In giving his support to the statement, Louis Lochner recounted that Kennan in wartime Berlin had refused to believe that Hitler would invade the Soviet Union. "Now do you see why I don't think too highly of George as a political prognosticator?" quipped Lochner. Louis Lochner to Christopher Emmet, 20 December 1957, folder 13, box 1, Louis Lochner Papers, WHS; Emmet to Acheson, 24 December 1957, Acheson, Dean, box 60, CTE.

57. "Text of Acheson's Reply to Kennan," *New York Times,* 12 January 1958, Acheson, Dean, box 60, CTE; Emmet to Acheson, 4 January 1958, Acheson, Dean, box 60, CTE; Acheson to Emmet, 30 December 1957, Acheson, Dean, box 60, CTE.

58. Emmet to C. D. Jackson, 31 January 1958, Correspondence—Jackson, box 80, CTE.

59. Emmet to Erik Blumenfeld, 13 September 1954, Blumenfeld, box 63, CTE.

60. Murphy to the Secretary of State, 13 August 1945, in *FRUS* (1945), 3:1039–40; Murphy to Secretary of State, 4 September 1945, in *FRUS* (1945), 3:1047.

61. Murphy to Secretary of State, 26 June 1948, in *FRUS* (1948), 2:919–20.

62. Clay to Draper, 19 July 1948, in *The Papers of General Lucius D. Clay: Germany, 1945–1949,* ed. Jean Edward Smith (Bloomington: Indiana University Press, 1974): 2:745–46.

63. McCloy, "German Problem and Its Solution," 587; Maxwell Taylor, quoted in "Spirit of the Front Line," *Time,* 29 January 1951, 23.

64. Frank Howley to Reuter, 21 February 1950, B Rep. 002/975, LAB; Elmer Cox to Mayor Otto Suhr, 2 May 1955, B Rep. 002/977, LAB; Kellermann to Reuter, 25 March 1949, 002/972, LAB.

65. Secretary of State to the Office of the United States High Commissioner for Germany at Frankfort, 9 February 1950, in *FRUS* (1950), 4:824–25; Memorandum by the Under Secretary of State (Webb) to the Executive Secretary of the National Security Council, 3 May 1950, in *FRUS* (1950), 4:849; Director of the Berlin Element, HICOG, to the Office of the United States High Commissioner for Germany at Frankfort, 9 February 1950, in *FRUS* (1950), 4:824–25.

66. *Dwight D. Eisenhower, 1953, Public Papers of the Presidents of the United States* (Washington, D.C.: Government Printing Office, 1960), 109, 31.

67. Tusa, *The Last Division: A History of Berlin,* 97; Burr, "Avoiding the Slippery Slope."

68. Tusa, *The Last Division: A History of Berlin,* 99; *Dwight D. Eisenhower,* 229.

69. *Berlin—Cross-road of World Politics,* n.d., E Rep. 200-18/16/1, LAB; Abschlussbericht, Berlin-Aktion 1959, 29 July 1959, B 136, BAK.

70. Citron to Hirschfeld, 15 April 1953, B Rep. 002/3129, LAB; Citron to Schlesinger, 21 June 1954, B Rep. 010-01/372, LAB; Report to the City of Berlin (Senator for Economics), B Rep. 002/3129, LAB; Wolf Citron to Schlesinger, 12 January 1955, B Rep. 010-01/372, LAB.

71. Citron to Schlesinger, 29 December 1958, B Rep. 002/4097, LAB; Krueger to Paul Hertz, 27 April 1959, B Rep. 002/4097, LAB; Vermerk, 21 May 1959, B Rep. 002/4097, LAB; Bahr to Schlesinger, 10 June 1960, B Rep. 002/4097/I, LAB.

72. Lawrence Spivak to Reuter, 28 March 1949, 002/972, LAB; Freda Utley to Reuter, 24 March 1949, 002/972, LAB; George Edwards to Reuter, 28 March 1949, 002/972, LAB; Documents on Hirschfeld's Tour of USA in 1955, 13 February 1955, E Rep. 200-18/14/1, LAB; Dr. Hans Hirschfeld, Day-by-Day Itinerary, March 1955, E Rep. 200-18/14/3, LAB; Draft Statement, 1955, E Rep. 200-18/14/4, LAB; Press Release, 1955, E Rep. 200-18/14/3, LAB.

73. Paul Ward Brody to Brandt, 1 December 1958, E Rep. 200-18/14/2, LAB; William J. McCormick to Brandt, 31 December 1958, E Rep. 200-18/14/2, LAB; Henry Rutz to Willy Brandt, 12 December 1958, E Rep. 200-18/14/2, LAB; Walter Kirschenbaum to Brandt, 19 January 1958, E Rep. 200-18/14/2, LAB; Frances Trocaine to Brandt, 6 January 1958, E Rep. 200-18/14/2, LAB; O. J. Keller to Brandt, 29 December 1958, E Rep. 200-18/14/2, LAB; Aufzeichnung, 26 March 1958, B 136/6758, BAK.

74. Brandt to William Chamberlain, 12 April 1958, B Rep. 002/982, LAB; Chamberlain to Brandt, 14 July 1958, B Rep. 002/982, LAB; Goerl to Suhr, 18

April 1956, B Rep. 002/979, LAB; Henry Kissinger to Hans Hirschfeld, 4 February 1959, E Rep. 200-18/13/1, LAB; Report of Conversation, 25 December 1958, B Rep. 002/983, LAB.

75. Gillon, *Politics and Vision,* 1–7 (quote on 7).

76. Ibid., 8–9; Kleinman, *A World of Hope,* 207–10.

77. Gillon, *Politics and Vision,* 9–11; Kleinman, *A World of Hope,* 211–13.

78. Gillon, *Politics and Vision,* 9–11; Kleinman, *A World of Hope,* 215–21.

79. Kleinman, *A World of Hope,* 216–19.

80. Gillon, *Politics and Vision,* 13–21; Kleinman, *A World of Hope,* 222–34.

81. Shafir, *Ambiguous Relations,* 71–178. Peter Novick also discusses this split. See *The Holocaust in American Life,* 63–123.

82. On Jewish identity in the postwar period, see Staub, *Torn at the Roots.*

83. Quoted in Shafir, *Ambiguous Relations,* 141–44.

84. Ibid., 87–104; Novick, *The Holocaust in American Life,* 90–97.

85. Shafir, *Ambiguous Relations,* 105–21.

86. Ibid., 124–27; Minutes of the Meeting of the Executive Committee, 21 March 1948, Committees—Exec 48–49, box 32, NJCRAC; David Petergorsky to Marcus, 16 March 1949, folder 13, box H131, WJCC; Harry Greenstein to John Slawson, Germany Apr–Jan 49, box 23A, AJC FAD-1, YIVO; Harry Greenstein to AJC, AJDC, JAP, WJC, 21 March 1949, folder 13, box H131, WJCC; Maurice L. Perlzweig to Members of the WJC Executive, 28 March 1949, folder 13, box H131, WJCC; Richard Bluestein to Dorothy M. Nathan, 28 March 1949, Germany Apr–Jan 49, box 23A, AJC FAD-1, YIVO; Charles Sonnenreich to New York City Area Divisional Presidents, A.J. Congress and Women's Division, 4 April 1949, Denazification, box 38, AJCR; Maurice Perlzweig to Alex Easterman, 5 April 1949, folder 13, box H131, WJCC; Background Memorandum regarding Picketing of German Industry Exhibit, 7 April 1949, folder 13, box H131, WJCC; Press Release, 7 April 1949, Germany Apr–Jan 49, 23A, AJC FAD-1, YIVO; Abram Becker to Louis Bennett, 7 April 1949, 23A, AJC FAD-1, YIVO; German Industrial Exhibit, 19 April 1949, Apr–Jan 49, box 23A, AJC FAD-1, YIVO; Selma Hirsh to John Slawson, 21 April 1949, Germany Apr–Jan 49, box 23A, AJC FAD-1, YIVO.

87. The arguments for each position were laid out in Memorandum, 14 June 1949, Activities—Denazification, box 68, NJCRAC; Samuel Spiegler to NCRAC agencies, 8 August 1949, folder 9, box 56, CO-JCRC.

88. David Petergorsky to American Jewish Congress and Women's Division Regional, Division and Chapter Presidents, 22 September 1949, Denazification, box H131, WJCC; Minutes of Special Meeting of the Committee on Overt Anti-Semitism, 10 June 1949, Committees—Germany, box 34, NJCRAC; Milton Roseman to Henry Carpenter, 20 October 1949, folder 1, box 9, BNY-BJCC, AJA; Minutes of the meeting of the National Administrative Sub-committee on Denazification, 11 May 1949, Denazification, box 38, AJCR.

89. *Stop the Renazification of Germany!* n.d., Denazification 1949–, box 38, AJCR.

90. Jules Cohen to NCRAC Membership, 21 December 1949, folder 9, box 56, CO-JCRC; Jules Cohen to NCRAC Membership, 5 May 1950, folder 10, box 56, CO-JCRC.

91. The council is briefly discussed in Shafir, *Ambiguous Relations,* 87–104; Cohen to Committee on Anti-Semitism, 30 June 1949, Committees—Germany, box 34, NJCRAC; Summary of Discussions at Informal Conference re: U.S. Policy in Germany, 12 July 1949, Committees—Germany, box 34, NJCRAC.

92. Jay Lovestone to I. M Minkoff, 17 August 1949, Committees—Germany, box 34, NJCRAC; Reinhold Niebuhr, 14 October 1949, Committees—Germany—Coordinating Council for a Democratic Germany, box 32, NJCRAC; Alfred Bingham to Joseph Lichten, 25 August 1950, Committees—Germany, box 34, NJCRAC.

93. Alfred Bingham to Joseph Lichten, 25 August 1950, Committees—Germany, box 34, NJCRAC; American Press Opinion on Rearming West Germany, 1 October 1950, folder 10, box 56, CO-JCRC; Summary of American Jewish Congress Activities in Regard to Post-war Germany and Neo-Nazism, 1951, Denazification 1949–, box 38, AJCR; The German Problem, 6 May 1949, Germany 51, box 22, AJC FAD-1, YIVO.

94. Minutes of Special Meeting of NCRAC Committee on Germany, 22 June 1951, Committees—Germany, box 34, NJCRAC; Minutes of the Meeting of the Executive Committee, 22 May 1951, Committees—Exec 51, box 33, NJCRAC.

95. Minutes of Meeting of Mass Media Committee on Motion Pictures, 24 May 1948, Committees—National Motion Picture 48–50, box 49, NJCRAC; John Stone, Report No. 28, 1 March 1951, 51, NJCRAC.

96. The literature on the Anne Frank film is fairly extensive. See Novick, *The Holocaust in American Life,* 117–20; Lipstadt, "America and the Memory of the Holocaust"; Baron, "The Holocaust and American Public Memory."

97. Shaw, *The Young Lions;* Dmytryk, *The Young Lions.*

98. Material was found by keyword search "The Young Lions" in the online American Film Institute Catalog at http://www.afi.com/members/catalog/. "NY Critics Divided on *The Young Lions,*" *Los Angeles Times,* 23 April 1958; "*The Young Lions,*" *New York Times,* 23 March 1958, SM99.

99. John Stone, Report No. 102, 12 March 1957, Motion Picture Committee, Stone Report 90-, box 51, NJCRAC; John Stone, Report No. 104, 7 May 1957, Motion Picture Committee, Stone Report 90-, box 51, NJCRAC; John Stone, Report No. 107, 8 August 1957, Motion Picture Committee, Stone Report 90-, box 51, NJCRAC; material by Adler found by keyword search "The Young Lions" in the online American Film Institute Catalog at http://www.afi.com/members/catalog/.

100. Robert Disraeli to David Danzig, 8 May 1958, Germany 58-57, box 21, AJC FAD-1, YIVO.

101. McAleer, *Rex Stout,* 265–321; Casey, "The Campaign to Sell a Harsh Peace."

102. McAleer, *Rex Stout,* 265–81.

103. Ibid., 288–300.

104. Quoted in ibid., 294–95.

105. Ibid., 304, 318 (quotes).

106. "Statement of Policy of the Society for the Prevention of World War III," *Prevent World War III*, June–July 1944, inside cover.

107. James Gerard, "There Is Only One Germany," *Prevent World War III*, May 1944, 10–11; Alvin Barach, "The Abnormality in Nazi Germans and in German Tradition," *Prevent World War III*, June–July 1944, 36–37.

108. Louis Nizer, "The Return of the Trojan Horse," *Prevent World War III*, June–July 1944, 3–7.

109. Sigrid Schultz, "Pan-Germans at Work," *Prevent World War III*, May 1944, 4–5; Nizer, "The Return of the Trojan Horse"; "Beware of German Peace Trap," *Prevent World War III*, June–July 1944, 26; Paul Winkler, "Anti-Nazi Doesn't Equal 'Anti-war,'" *Prevent World War III*, September 1944, 35–36; "An Open Letter to Hollywood," *Prevent World War III*, May 1944, 7–8.

110. McAleer, *Rex Stout*, 265–321; Casey, "The Campaign to Sell a Harsh Peace"; Allan J. Winter to Donald Steven, 13 May 1944, 1, SPWWIII.

111. Robert Marcus to Eugene Tillinger, 15 March 1949, B71, WJCC; Tetens, *Germany Plots with the Kremlin;* "The Case of General Draper," *Prevent World War III*, February–March 1946, 28; "McCloy's Speech—A Turning Point?" *Prevent World War III*, March–April 1950, 1–2; "On Moral Principles: An Open Letter to the Hon. John Foster Dulles," *Prevent World War III*, January–February 1953, 5–6.

3. "Your Post on the Frontier"

1. Loew to Acheson, 30 March 1949, Central Decimal Files, RG 59, NA.

2. For a superficial discussion of the film's reception, see Sternberg, "Real-Life References in Four Fred Zinemann Films."

3. For more on the Cold War consensus, see Whitfield, *The Culture of the Cold War;* Henriksen, *Dr. Strangelove's America;* Biskind, *Seeing Is Believing;* Kuznick and Gilbert, *Rethinking Cold War Culture;* Melanson, *American Foreign Policy,* 10–11. In the literature, much has been made of the notion of "containing" difference both at home and abroad. For a recent example, see Klein, *Cold War Orientalism.*

4. For more on sexual containment, see May, *Homeward Bound.*

5. Gallup, *The Gallup Poll,* 501, 506–7; U.S. Opinion concerning Germany, 18 October 1946, Germany, 1944–1946, Office of Public Opinion Studies, 1943–1965, Public Opinion on Foreign Countries and Regions, Germany, 1944–1952, RG 59, NA.

6. American Public Opinion on Postwar Treatment of Germany, October 1944, Germany, 1944–1946, Office of Public Opinion Studies, 1943–1965, Public Opinion on Foreign Countries and Regions, Germany, 1944–1952, RG 59, NA; American Opinion on Treatment of Germany, 29 December 1944, Germany, 1944–1946, Office of Public Opinion Studies, 1943–1965, Public Opinion on Foreign Countries and Regions, Germany, 1944–1952, RG 59, NA; Special Report on

Attitudes toward Germany, 2 June 1945, Germany, 1944–1946, Office of Public Opinion Studies, 1943–1965, Public Opinion on Foreign Countries and Regions, Germany, 1944–1952, RG 59, NA.

7. Gallup, *The Gallup Poll,* 501; "Morgenthau Plan" for the Economic Treatment of Germany, 18 October 1944, Germany, 1944–1946, Office of Public Opinion Studies, 1943–1965, Public Opinion on Foreign Countries and Regions, Germany, 1944–1952, RG 59, NA; Special Report on Attitudes toward Germany, 2 June 1945, Germany, 1944–1946, Office of Public Opinion Studies, 1943–1965, Public Opinion on Foreign Countries and Regions, Germany, 1944–1952, RG 59, NA.

8. U.S. Opinion concerning Policy toward Germany, 31 January 1946, Germany, 1944–1946, Office of Public Opinion Studies, 1943–1965, Public Opinion on Foreign Countries and Regions, Germany, 1944–1952, RG 59, NA; Gallup, *The Gallup Poll,* 582; Joseph Phillips, "Retrospection on Germany," *Newsweek,* 6 December 1948, 34.

9. U.S. Opinion concerning Germany, 26 March 1948, Germany, 1944–1946, Office of Public Opinion Studies, 1943–1965, Public Opinion on Foreign Countries and Regions, Germany, 1944–1952, RG 59, NA; "Our Next Step in 'Cold War,'" *U.S. News and World Report,* 28 November 1947, 16.

10. "'We Are Going Ahead,'" *Time,* 19 July 1948, 29; U.S. Opinion concerning Germany, 16 April 1948, Germany, 1947–1948, Office of Public Opinion Studies, 1943–1965, Public Opinion on Foreign Countries and Regions, Germany, 1944–1952, RG 59, NA; U.S. Opinion concerning Germany, 11 June 1948, Germany, 1947–1948, Office of Public Opinion Studies, 1943–1965, Public Opinion on Foreign Countries and Regions, Germany, 1944–1952, RG 59, NA; U.S. Opinion concerning Germany, 25 June 1948, Germany, 1947–1948, Office of Public Opinion Studies, 1943–1965, Public Opinion on Foreign Countries and Regions, Germany, 1944–1952, RG 59, NA.

11. U.S. Opinion concerning Germany, 25 October 1946, Germany, 1944–1946, Office of Public Opinion Studies, 1943–1965, Public Opinion on Foreign Countries and Regions, Germany, 1944–1952, RG 59, NA.

12. U.S. Opinion concerning Germany, 16 April 1948, Germany, 1947–1948, Office of Public Opinion Studies, 1943–1965, Public Opinion on Foreign Countries and Regions, Germany, 1944–1952, RG 59, NA; U.S. Opinion concerning Germany, 25 June 1948, Germany, 1947–1948, Office of Public Opinion Studies, 1943–1965, Public Opinion on Foreign Countries and Regions, Germany, 1944–1952, RG 59, NA; U.S. Opinion concerning Germany, 2 July 1948, Germany, 1947–1948, Office of Public Opinion Studies, 1943–1965, Public Opinion on Foreign Countries and Regions, Germany, 1944–1952, RG 59, NA; U.S. Opinion concerning Germany, 6 August 1948, Germany, 1947–1948, Office of Public Opinion Studies, 1943–1965, Public Opinion on Foreign Countries and Regions, Germany, 1944–1952, RG 59, NA; U.S. Opinion concerning Germany, 6 August 1948, Germany, 1947–1948, Office of Public Opinion Studies, 1943–1965, Public Opinion on Foreign Countries and Regions, Germany, 1944–1952, RG 59, NA.

13. Popular Attitudes on Occupation Policy for Germany and Japan, 23 July 1948, Germany, 1947–1948, Office of Public Opinion Studies, 1943–1965, Public Opinion on Foreign Countries and Regions, Germany, 1944–1952, RG 59, NA.

14. Popular Sentiment toward "Punishing" Germany and Japan, 1949, Germany, 1949, Office of Public Opinion Studies, 1943–1965, Public Opinion on Foreign Countries and Regions, Germany, 1944–1952, RG 59, NA; Gallup, *The Gallup Poll*, 841; American Public Opinion on Germany, 20 September 1949, Germany, January 1949–July 1950, Office of Public Opinion Studies, 1943–1965, Public Opinion on Foreign Countries and Regions, Germany, 1944–1952, RG 59, NA; Germany and Austria, 11 August 1949, Germany, January 1949–July 1950, Office of Public Opinion Studies, 1943–1965, Public Opinion on Foreign Countries and Regions, Germany, 1944–1952, RG 59, NA; Special Report on American Opinion: Germany and Austria, 6 January 1950, Germany, January 1949–July 1950, Public Opinion on Foreign Countries and Regions: Germany, Office of Public Opinion Studies, 1943–1965, RG 59, NA; Special Report on American Opinion: Germany and Austria, 6 January 1950, Germany, January 1949–July 1950, Office of Public Opinion Studies, 1943–1965, 59, NA.

15. Gallup, *The Gallup Poll*, 914, 932; Germany and Austria, 5 January 1954, Germany, January 1949–July 1950, Office of Public Opinion Studies, 1943–1965, Public Opinion on Foreign Countries and Regions, Germany, 1944–1952, RG 59, NA; Germany and Related Issues, 31 August 1954, Germany, January 1949–July 1950, Office of Public Opinion Studies, 1943–1965, Public Opinion on Foreign Countries and Regions, Germany, 1944–1952, RG 59, NA; Gallup, *The Gallup Poll*, 1273.

16. Germany and Related Issues, 31 August 1954, Germany, January 1949–July 1950, Office of Public Opinion Studies, 1943–1965, Public Opinion on Foreign Countries and Regions, Germany, 1944–1952, RG 59, NA; Germany and Related Issues, 10 August 1954, Germany, January 1949–July 1950, Office of Public Opinion Studies, 1943–1965, Public Opinion on Foreign Countries and Regions, Germany, 1944–1952, RG 59, NA; Gallup, *The Gallup Poll*, 1274–75; Germany and Related Issues, 10 May 1955, Germany, January 1949–July 1950, Office of Public Opinion Studies, 1943–1965, Public Opinion on Foreign Countries and Regions, Germany, 1944–1952, RG 59, NA; Gallup, *The Gallup Poll*, 1377.

17. Adler and Paterson, "Red Fascism."

18. For broad narratives of this phenomenon, see Foner, *The Story of American Freedom;* and Stephanson, *Manifest Destiny.*

19. Quoted in Gleason, *Totalitarianism,* 64; quoted in Adler and Paterson, "Red Fascism," 1051–52; quoted in Lifka, *The Concept "Totalitarianism,"* 1:351.

20. Gleason, *Totalitarianism,* 61; quoted in Adler and Paterson, "Red Fascism," 1063; quoted in Gleason, *Totalitarianism,* 108–10, 122; George Orwell, *Nineteen Eighty-Four* (New York: Milestone Editions, 1949); Arendt, *The Origins of Totalitarianism.*

21. Novick, *The Holocaust in American Life,* 86–87.

22. Quoted in ibid., 86; quoted in Adler and Paterson, "Red Fascism," 1053.

23. Quoted in Gleason, *Totalitarianism*, 64, 67; Rand, *Atlas Shrugged*.

24. Quoted in Goedde, "From Villains to Victims," 16, 19; quoted in Gimbel, *The American Occupation of Germany*, 6.

25. Dorothy Thompson, "Obituary for Germany," *Ladies' Home Journal*, May 1945, 6; "Letter from Germany," *American Mercury*, August 1945, 155, 157; Sidney Olson, "Defeated Land: Germany's Cities Are Crushed, Her People Are Frightened and Servile," *Life*, 14 May 1945, 39.

26. "GI Legacy in Germany," *Newsweek*, 16 June 1947, 48–50; "Letter Home," *American Mercury*, August 1945, 158.

27. J. P. O'Donnell, "Do the Frauleins Change Our Joe?" *Newsweek*, 24 December 1945, 50; Richard Joseph and Waverley Root, "Why So Many GI's Like the Germans Best," *Reader's Digest*, March 1946, 7.

28. Goedde, *GIs and Germans*, 81, 101–8.

29. Quoted in Zinnemann, *A Life in the Movies*, 57.

30. Viertel to Wechsler, 22 June 1946, The Search, Fred Zinnemann Collection, MHL; Viertel to Zinnemann, 19 November 1946, The Search, Fred Zinnemann Collection, MHL; Viertel to Zinnemann, 12 December 1946, The Search, Fred Zinnemann Collection, MHL.

31. Viertel to Zinnemann, 19 November 1946.

32. Viertel to Zinnemann, 12 December 1946.

33. Zinnemann to Viertel, 2 December 1946, The Search, Fred Zinnemann Collection, MHL.

34. Zinnemann to Lastfogel, 24 January 1947, The Search, Fred Zinnemann Collection, MHL.

35. Florence Lowe, "Washington Hullabaloo," *Variety*, 12 March 1947, 6.

36. Viertel to Zinnemann, 12 March 1947, The Search, Fred Zinnemann Collection, MHL.

37. Zinnemann to Viertel, 3 April 1947, The Search, Fred Zinnemann Collection, MHL.

38. Duplication of Report from OMGUS, 18 December 1946, The Search, Fred Zinnemann Collection, MHL; Viertel to Zinnemann, 12 December 1946, The Search, Fred Zinnemann Collection, MHL.

39. "Dick" to Zinnemann, 19 January 1948, The Search, Fred Zinnemann Collection, MHL.

40. Richard Schweizer, *The Search*, ed. Fred Zinnemann (Metro-Goldwyn-Mayer, 1948)

41. "Dick" to Zinnemann, 6 February 1948, The Search, Fred Zinnemann Collection, MHL; Lt. Col. William Rogers to Fred Zinnemann, 24 March 1948, The Search, Fred Zinnemann Collection, MHL.

42. For a more detailed discussion of the production and reception of *The Search*, see Etheridge, "In Search of Germans."

43. "Movie Review," *Time*, 3 May 1948, 93–94; "*Berlin Express*," *Variety*, 6

April 1948, 3; Lowell Redelings, "German Ruins Provide Grim Background to *Berlin Express* Film," *Hollywood Citizen-News,* 1 July 1948, 17; "Movie Review," *New Republic,* 12 April 1948, 21; Philip Hartung, "Movie Review," *Commonweal,* 23 April 1948, 654.

44. "Movie Review," *New Republic,* 31 May 1948; Frank Eng, "Film Review: *Berlin Express,*" *Daily News,* 1 July 1948; "Movie Review," *New Republic,* 12 April 1948, 21.

45. Robert Hatch, "Movie Review," *New Republic,* 15 May 1950, 23; "Movie Review," *Time,* 8 May 1950, 90–91; see also "Movie Review," *Newsweek,* 1 May 1950, 90; Philip Hartung, "Movie Review," *Commonweal,* 5 May 1950, 98.

46. Hatch, "Movie Review"; "Movie on Air Lift Achievement, Too," *Los Angeles Times,* 11 May 1950, Big Lift, Clippings File, MHL; Realistic Romance: "*The Big Lift* Displays a Typical Ambiguity," *New York Times,* 30 April 1950, Big Lift, Clippings File, MHL; "Movie Review," *Time,* 8 May 1950, 90–91.

47. "*Foreign Affair* Cynical, Brilliant, Postwar Comedy," *Los Angeles Times,* 23 July 1948, 14; "Movie Review," *New Statesman and Nation,* 4 September 1948.

48. Quoted in Ralph Willett, "Billy Wilder's *A Foreign Affair* (1945–48): 'The Trials and Tribulations of Berlin,'" *Historical Journal of Film, Radio and Television* 7, no. 1 (1987): 14.

49. Ibid. On the film as isolationist, see Rosenberg, "Foreign Affairs."

50. "'Foreign Affair' Cynical, Brilliant Postwar Comedy," *Los Angeles Times,* 23 July 1948, 14; Bosley Crowther, "Movie Review," *New York Times,* 4 July 1948; quoted in "*Foreign Affair* Delights B'way Critics and Patrons," *Hollywood Reporter,* 6 July 1948, 8.

51. Autobahn, 13 October 1950, Devil Makes Three, Metro-Goldwyn Mayer Collection, MHL; Autobahn, 15 January 1951, Devil Makes Three, Metro-Goldwyn Mayer Collection, MHL.

52. Autobahn—Notes from Jerry Davis, 2 May 1951, Devil Makes Three, Metro-Goldwyn Mayer Collection, MHL.

53. The Devil Makes Three: Original Screenplay, 1952, Devil Makes Three, Metro-Goldwyn Mayer Collection, MHL.

54. *An Oral History with Richard Goldstone,* MHL.

55. Ibid.; A. H. Weiler, "By Way of Report," *New York Times,* 4 May 1952, X5.

56. "Review," *Newsweek,* 15 September 1952, 103; "The Screen," *Commonweal,* 19 September 1952, 583; "Movie Review," *Time,* 8 September 1952, 106; "Movie Review," *Saturday Review,* 20 September 1952; Hertz to Auswaertiges Amt, 8 October 1952, B 106/903, BAK.

57. Frederick Hamwell to Reuter, 24 October 1951, 002/974, LAB; James I. Younger to Reuter, July 1953, 002/976, LAB.

58. Goedde, "From Villains to Victims," 18.

59. Schlesinger, *The Vital Center;* and Hartz, *The Liberal Tradition in America.*

60. Fousek, *To Lead the Free World,* 7.

61. "Germany's Prosperity—And the Man Behind It," *Newsweek,* 5 October

1953, 42; "Germany: From Rubble to Riches in 12 Years," *U.S. News and World Report,* 20 September 1957, 49.

62. "Germany's Prosperity," 34; "Germany: From Rubble to Riches in 12 Years," 49; "Comeback in the West," *Time,* 15 February 1954, 84.

63. "Comeback in the West," 84, 86; "Germany: From Rubble to Riches in 12 Years," 50.

64. "Germany's Prosperity," 44; "Comeback in the West," 84; "No Window-Shopping for the East Germans!" *Saturday Evening Post,* 30 July 1955, 10–11.

65. "Comeback in the West," 86; "The 'Model T' of the Jet Age," *U.S. News and World Report,* 18 May 1956, 68–70. For more about Volkswagen, see Rieger, *The People's Car.*

66. James O' Donnell, "Russian Zone: A German Lenin in Berlin," *Newsweek,* 3 June 1946, 36; J. P. O'Donnell, "Do the Frauleins Change Our Joe? Not a Bit of It, He's All Wised Up: Yanks Fraternize One Way but Think in the Other Direction; Still Blame Nazis for War," *Newsweek,* 24 December 1945, 50.

67. Reinhold Niebuhr, "The Fight for Germany," *Newsweek,* April 1946, 42–43.

68. Emmet Hughes, "Berlin under Siege," *Life,* 19 July 1948, 25–27.

69. "Two Berlins: Photographs," *New York Times Magazine,* 12 June 1949, 8–9; "Journey to the West," *Time,* 23 May 1949, 25.

70. "This Is Berlin: West Sector Shows a Brave Gaiety," *Life,* 4 December 1950, 141–49.

71. "Uncle Joe's Miracle Mile in Red Berlin," *Life,* 22 December 1952, 27–30.

72. "Shadow of Fear Falls on Berlin," *Life,* 9 March 1953, 25–29; "Berlin Reds Get Mean Again," *Life,* 12 December 1955, 36–37.

73. Dr. Martin Gumpert, "Return to Europe," *American Scholar,* July 1950, 319–40. Heinz Guadze, a subscriber to *American Scholar,* claimed that Gumpert was too harsh on regular Germans in his assessment. A former German himself, Guadze wondered whether he and Gumpert would have fared any better than other Germans had they stayed: Heinz Guadze, "Return to Europe: Reply," *American Scholar* 20, no. 1 (1951): 108.

74. Joseph Wechsberg, "Letter from Berlin," *New Yorker,* 5 August 1950, 28–32; Joseph Wechsberg, "Letter from West Berlin," *New Yorker,* 19 March 1955, 122.

75. "West Is Ready for the Test," *Newsweek,* 29 May 1950, 23; "Reds in Berlin Do Not Choose to Fight," *Life,* 12 June 1950, 29–31; "Berlin in the Rain," *Time,* 5 June 1950, 22–23.

76. "Reds in Berlin Do Not Choose to Fight"; "Berlin in the Rain."

77. David Perlman and Seymour Freidin, "Red Plot to Seize Berlin," *Collier's Magazine,* 27 May 1950, 26. The Chargé at Berlin (Page) to the Office of the United States High Commissioner for Germany at Frankfort, in *FRUS* (1950), 4:861–62.

78. "Berlin Surprise Outbreak Jolts a Weakened Kremlin," *Newsweek,* 29 June 1953, 36.

79. "West Berlin Mourns East Berlin's Heroes," *Life,* 6 July 1953, 25–27; "Berlin Will Rise Again," *Newsweek,* 29 June 1953, 38; A. Brun, "How Two Workers

Fought the Reds in Berlin Riots," *Newsweek,* 20 July 1953, 45–46; Thomas Goldstein, "East German Revolt," *New Republic,* 20 July 1953, 9–10.

80. Howard Woodard to Reuter, 4 January 1949, 002/972, LAB; J.M.J. to Brandt, 16 February 1959, B Rep. 002/982, LAB.

81. C. Bentley to Reuter, 10 June 1950, B Rep. 002/973, LAB. Similar letters along these lines include Crippen to Brandt, 7 January 1958, E Rep. 200-18/14/2, LAB; and George Starry to Brandt, 7 April 1959, B Rep. 002/985, LAB.

82. Jane Elligett to Reuter, 31 March 1953, B Rep. 002/975, LAB; Martin Gill to Brandt, 30 December 1958, B Rep. 002/983, LAB; Lowell Edison to Brandt, 29 May 1959, B Rep. 002/982, LAB; Ted Sly to Willy Brandt, Jan 1959 (no specific date), E Rep. 200-18/13/1, LAB.

83. Ken Browne to Reuter, 27 January 1951, B Rep. 002/973, LAB; Calvin Cowden to Brandt, 20 June 1959, B Rep. 002/982, LAB; Edward Gerard Maurice Lynch to Willy Brandt, 18 December 1958, B Rep. 002/984, LAB; Paul Andrews to Brandt, 25 November 1958, B Rep. 002/981, LAB; John Brovaco to Brandt, 24 June 1959, B Rep. 002/981, LAB.

84. John Brovaco to Brandt, 24 June 1959; David H. Blair to Mayor Schreiber, 19 April 1954, B Rep. 002/977, LAB.

85. Lawrence Elbinal to Reuter, 17 December 1950, B Rep. 002/973, LAB; Robert Hansen to Reuter, 24 October 1951, B Rep. 002/974, LAB; Ira Porter to Reuter, 3 May 1953, B Rep. 002/976, LAB; A. C. Hobbie to Reuter, 11 May 1953, B Rep. 002/976, LAB.

86. Gus Petrit to Lindenau and Reuter, 19 August 1953, B Rep. 002/976, LAB; Petrit to Guss and Lindenau, 26 October 1953, B Rep. 002/976, LAB; R. J. Rondorff to Reuter, 27 March 1953, B Rep. 002/976, LAB; John and Lillian Jones to Suhr, 11 June 1956, B Rep. 002/979, LAB.

87. Stanley Mayall to Willy Brandt, 27 December 1958, B Rep. 002/984, LAB; John Smith and Jack Van Vranken, 12 December 1958, B Rep. 002/985, LAB.

88. Charlotte Lehman to Reuter, 23 March 1949, B Rep. 002/972, LAB; Bob Kirkpatrick to Brandt, 28 February 1959, B Rep. 002/983, LAB; Crandall S. Brandt to Brandt, 18 July 1959, B Rep. 002/981, LAB; Rose Martin to Brandt, 23 May 1959, B Rep. 002/984, LAB.

89. Wallace Berning to Reuter, February [date by receipt; none given by author] 1952, B Rep. 002/973, LAB. This letter was annotated in typewritten English: "It seems he hasn't all cups in the cupboard."

90. John Maass et al., "Letters to the Editor," *Life,* 25 December 1950, 5.

91. Lester G. Rees, 27 February 1959, B Rep. 002/984, LAB.

92. B. M. Joffe to CRC's, 16 February 1951, box 57, CO-JCRC; Report of Meeting, 21 March 1955, 67, CO-JCRC; Arnold Forster to Charles Posner, 23 February 1955, box 67, CO-JCRC.

93. Statement Made by Irving Kane, 22 May 1951, box 57, CO-JCRC; Press Release, 2 April 1951, 55, NJCRAC; Jacob Marcus to Louis Schwab, 26 March 1951, 55, NJCRAC; Albert Vorspan to Charles Posner, 26 March 1951, 55, NJC-

RAC; Minutes of the Community Relations Committee Cincinnati Jewish Community Council, 16 March 1951, 55, NJCRAC.

94. Memorandum, Town Affiliation—Cincinnati-Munich, 9 September 1955, Community Participation Alphabetical by American City, box 13, A156, RG 306, NA; Benjamin Stickney to Mr. Needhan, 23 October 1956, Community Participation Alphabetical by American City, box 13, A156, RG 306, NA; "Milwaukee Cool on Ties to Munich," *New York Times,* 28 March 1965.

4. "The Anti-German Wave"

1. Martin Quigley, "An Important Political Event," *Motion Picture Herald,* 27 December 1961, 7–9, *Judgment at Nuremberg* Clippings File, MHL; Address of Governing Mayor Brandt at World Premiere of Judgment at Nuremberg, Publicity—Horwits, Al Correspondence, SKP.

2. Minutes and Assignments of Meeting, 24 October 1961, Berlin Task Force Minutes of Meetings, Records relating to the Berlin Crisis, 1961–1962, Executive Secretariat, RG 59, NA; Minutes and Assignments of Meeting, 30 October 1961, Berlin Task Force Minutes of Meetings, Records relating to the Berlin Crisis, 1961–1962, Executive Secretariat, RG 59, NA; Roeber to Schiffer, 1 December 1961, B 106/903, BAK; Wrasmann to Roeber, 23 November 1961, B 106/903, BAK.

3. The antideutsche Welle should not be confused with Deutsche Welle, the broadcasting arm of the Federal Republic. Deutsche Welle was established in 1953 to combat anti-German sentiment.

4. Baughman, *The Republic of Mass Culture,* 91–92.

5. On changes in the relationship, see Mayer, *Adenauer and Kennedy;* and Schwartz, *Lyndon Johnson and Europe.*

6. Schwartz, *Lyndon Johnson and Europe,* 231–32.

7. Quoted in Mayer, *Adenauer and Kennedy,* 4, 7–8.

8. Ibid., 20 (quote), 21–22; John F. Kennedy, "The President's News Conference," 1 February 1961, in Gerhard Peters and John T. Woolley, *The American Presidency Project,* http://www.presidency.ucsb.edu/ws/?pid=8089; Mayer, *Adenauer and Kennedy,* 22; John F. Kennedy, "Transcript of Interview with the President by Aleksei Adzhubei, Editor of Izvestia," 25 November 1961, in Peters and Woolley, *The American Presidency Project,* http://www.presidency.ucsb.edu/ws/?pid=8459.

9. Quoted in Schwartz, *Lyndon Johnson and Europe,* 24, 41, 44, 45, 89, 154.

10. John F. Kennedy, Television and Radio Interview: "After Two Years—a Conversation with the President," 17 December 1962, in Peters and Woolley, *The American Presidency Project,* http://www.presidency.ucsb.edu/ws/?pid=9060; Lyndon B. Johnson, Address at Johns Hopkins University: "Peace without Conquest," 7 April 1965, in Peters and Woolley, *The American Presidency Project,* http://www.presidency.ucsb.edu/ws/?pid=26877; Lyndon B. Johnson, "The President's News Conference," 17 November 1967, in Peters and Woolley, *The American Presidency Project,* http://www.presidency.ucsb.edu/ws/?pid=28555.

11. Lyndon B. Johnson, "Remarks before Two Groups at the Fifth Regiment Armory in Baltimore," 24 October 1964, in Peters and Woolley, *The American Presidency Project,* http://www.presidency.ucsb.edu/ws/?pid=26647; Lyndon B. Johnson, "Remarks at an Airport Rally in Wilmington, Delaware," 31 October 1964, in Peters and Woolley, *The American Presidency Project,* http://www.presidency.ucsb.edu/ws/?pid=26699.

12. Lyndon B. Johnson, "The President's News Conference," 3 May 1967, in Peters and Woolley, *The American Presidency Project,* http://www.presidency.ucsb.edu/ws/?pid=28233; Lyndon B. Johnson, "'A Conversation with the President': Joint Interview for Use by Television Networks," 19 December 1967, in Peters and Woolley, *The American Presidency Project,* http://www.presidency.ucsb.edu/ws/?pid=28621.

13. Presidential Candidates Debates, "Presidential Debate in Washington, DC," 7 October 1960, in Peters and Woolley, *The American Presidency Project,* http://www.presidency.ucsb.edu/ws/?pid=29401; Presidential Candidates Debates, "Presidential Debate Broadcast from New York and Los Angeles," 13 October 1960, in Peters and Woolley, *The American Presidency Project,* http://www.presidency.ucsb.edu/ws/?pid=29402; quoted in Mayer, *Adenauer and Kennedy,* 36; John F. Kennedy, "Radio and Television Report to the American People on Returning from Europe," 6 June 1961, in Peters and Woolley, *The American Presidency Project,* http://www.presidency.ucsb.edu/ws/?pid=8180; John F. Kennedy, "Radio and Television Report to the American People on the Berlin Crisis," 25 July 1961, in Peters and Woolley, *The American Presidency Project,* http://www.presidency.ucsb.edu/ws/?pid=8259.

14. John F. Kennedy, "Remarks Following the Vice President's Report on the Berlin Situation," 21 August 1961, in Peters and Woolley, *The American Presidency Project,* http://www.presidency.ucsb.edu/ws/?pid=8284; John F. Kennedy, "Letter to Senate and House Minority Leaders on U.S. Information Activities relating to Berlin," 1 September 1962, in Peters and Woolley, *The American Presidency Project,* http://www.presidency.ucsb.edu/ws/?pid=8844; John F. Kennedy, "Remarks in the Rudolph Wilde Platz, Berlin," 26 June 1963, in Peters and Woolley, *The American Presidency Project,* http://www.presidency.ucsb.edu/ws/?pid=9307. For more on Kennedy's famous speech, see Daum, *Kennedy in Berlin.*

15. Memorandum of Conversations, in *FRUS* (1961–1963), 19:81; John F. Kennedy, "Remarks at the La Morita Resettlement Project Near Caracas," 16 December 1961, in Peters and Woolley, *The American Presidency Project,* http://www.presidency.ucsb.edu/ws/?pid=8488; John F. Kennedy, "Address at a Dinner at the San Carlos Palace in Bogota," 17 December 1961, in Peters and Woolley, *The American Presidency Project,* http://www.presidency.ucsb.edu/ws/?pid=8495.

16. President's Consultant on Vietnam (Taylor) to President Johnson, in *FRUS* (1964–1968), 3:712; Department of State to the Embassy in Vietnam, in *FRUS* (1964–1968), 3:741; Chairman of the Joint Chiefs of Staff (Wheeler) to Secretary of Defense McNamara, in *FRUS* (1964–1968), 3:675.

17. John F. Kennedy, "Remarks at the White House to Members of the American Legion," 1 March 1962, in Peters and Woolley, *The American Presidency Project*, http://www.presidency.ucsb.edu/ws/?pid=9083; John F. Kennedy, "Address at Independence Hall, Philadelphia," 4 July 1962, in Peters and Woolley, *The American Presidency Project*, http://www.presidency.ucsb.edu/ws/?pid=8756; John F. Kennedy, "Annual Message to the Congress on the State of the Union," 14 January 1963, in Peters and Woolley, *The American Presidency Project*, http://www.presidency.ucsb.edu/ws/?pid=9138.

18. Lyndon B. Johnson, "Address before a Joint Session of the Congress," 27 November 1963, in Peters and Woolley, *The American Presidency Project*, http://www.presidency.ucsb.edu/ws/?pid=25988; Lyndon B. Johnson, "Remarks at Syracuse University on the Communist Challenge in Southeast Asia," 5 August 1964, in Peters and Woolley, *The American Presidency Project*, http://www.presidency.ucsb.edu/ws/?pid=26419; Lyndon B. Johnson, "Remarks to Committee Members on the Need for Additional Appropriations for Military Purposes in Viet-Nam and the Dominican Republic," 4 May 1965, in Peters and Woolley, *The American Presidency Project*, http://www.presidency.ucsb.edu/ws/?pid=26938; Lyndon B. Johnson, "Remarks to Delegates to the National Farmers Union Convention in Minneapolis," 18 March 1968, in Peters and Woolley, *The American Presidency Project*, http://www.presidency.ucsb.edu/ws/?pid=28741; Lyndon B. Johnson, "Remarks to Delegates to the Conference of the Building and Construction Trades Department, AFL-CIO," 25 March 1968, in Peters and Woolley, *The American Presidency Project*, http://www.presidency.ucsb.edu/ws/?pid=28754.

19. John F. Kennedy, "Statement by the President on the Physical Fitness of Young Americans," 5 September 1961, in Peters and Woolley, *The American Presidency Project*, http://www.presidency.ucsb.edu/ws/?pid=8309; John F. Kennedy, "Remarks at Redstone Arsenal, Huntsville, Alabama," 18 May 1963, in Peters and Woolley, *The American Presidency Project*, http://www.presidency.ucsb.edu/ws/?pid=9220.

20. John F. Kennedy, "Radio and Television Report to the American People on Civil Rights," 11 June 1963, in Peters and Woolley, *The American Presidency Project*, http://www.presidency.ucsb.edu/ws/?pid=9271; Lyndon B. Johnson, "Annual Message to the Congress on the State of the Union," 8 January 1964, in Peters and Woolley, *The American Presidency Project*, http://www.presidency.ucsb.edu/ws/?pid=26787; Lyndon B. Johnson, "Remarks to New Participants in 'Plans for Progress' Equal Opportunity Agreements," 22 January 1964, in Peters and Woolley, *The American Presidency Project*, http://www.presidency.ucsb.edu/ws/?pid=26020.

21. Tusa, *The Last Division: A History of Berlin*, 336–37 (quote).

22. Supreme Allied Commander, Europe (Norstad) to Secretary of Defense McNamara, in *FRUS* (1961–1963), 15:274; Memorandum of Conversation, in *FRUS* (1961–1963), 15:299.

23. Minutes and Assignments of Meeting, 19 September 1961, Berlin Task Force Minutes of Meetings, Records relating to the Berlin Crisis, 1961–1962, Executive

Secretariat, RG 59, NA; Berlin Viability Program, 1962, US Investment in Berlin—1962, Records related to Berlin and Eastern European Affairs, 1957–1968, Bureau of European Affairs, RG 59, NA; U.S. Mission Berlin to Department of State, 30 March 1962, Central Decimal Files, RG 59, NA.

24. Telegram from the Embassy in Germany to the Department of State, in *FRUS* (1961–1963), 15:276; Memorandum of Conversation, in *FRUS* (1961–1963), 15:305; Aufzeichnung, 19 October 1965, B 145/2873, BAK; von Lilienfeld to Diehl, 4 November 1965, B 145/2873, BAK.

25. Sydney Gruson and Flora Gruson, "Have the Germans Learned?" *New York Times Magazine,* 29 January 1961, 8, 13; Richard Lowenthal, "Germans Feel Like Germans Again," *New York Times Magazine,* 6 March 1966, 40.

26. Thomas to Leonard, 5 October 1967, B 145/2873, BAK; Aufzeichnung, 9 January 1968, B 145/3005, BAK.

27. Aufzeichnung, 24 January 1966, B 145/2973, PAAA.

28. Amconsul Hamburg to Department of State, EDX GER W-US, Subject Numeric Files, 22 June 1964, RG 59, NA.

29. Consulate General Boston to the German Embassy, 10 February 1966, B 97/356, PAAA.

30. Thomas to Leonard H. Goldenson, 21 April 1964, B 145/3004, BAK; Consulate General Boston to the German Embassy, 10 February 1966, B 97/356, PAAA; Botschaft Guatemala to Auswaertiges Amt, 3 May 1967, B 145/3003, BAK.

31. Aufzeichnung, Bauer to Thomas, 15 October 1965, B 145/2873, BAK; Graf Schweinitz to von Lilienfeld, 1 December 1965, B 145/2873, BAK.

32. Aufzeichnung, 19 October 1965, B 145/2873, BAK; "German Americans Provoked by Portrayal of Germans on TV," *New York Times,* 25 February 1968, B 145/3005, BAK; Thomas to Leonard H. Goldenson, 21 April 1964, B 145/3004, BAK; Thomas to Hedda Hopper, 19 November 1965, B 145/2140, BAK; Graf Schweinitz to Sellier, 18 January 1966, B 145/2873, BAK.

33. Report, 11 June 1959, B 145/1304, BAK; von Eckardt to Auswaertiges Amt, 3 August 1960, B 145/1304, BAK; Grewe to Auswaertiges Amt, 21 October 1960, B 145/1304, BAK; News Release: "Germany Opens Information Center in New York City," 6 May 1961, B 145/3255, BAK; Botschaft to Auswaertiges Amt, 2 February 1962, B 145/3255, BAK.

34. Amconsul Hamburg to Department of State. Schröder to Dr. Fritz Fischer, 7 March 1964, B 96 (IV 7)/783, PAAA.

35. Vermerk, 25 August 1967, B 145/3003, BAK; Fernschreiben, Krapf, Botschaft in Tokyo, to BPA, 14 February 1968, B 145/3005, BAK; Report, Kramer to Bundestag Ausschuss fuer Petitionen, 28 October 1965, B 145/2873, BAK; Aufzeichnung, 19 October 1965, B 145/2873, BAK.

36. Fehr to Diehl, 23 November 1965, B 145/2873, BAK; Auszug aus einem Brief von Michael Fehr, Salem, Mass., USA, 26 October 1965, B 145/2873, BAK; Fritz F. W. Krohn to Bundeskanzler Georg Kiesinger, 3 January 1968, B 145/3005, BAK; Arthur Sellier to BPA, 10 December 1965, B 145/2873, BAK.

37. Von Lilienfeld to Diehl, 4 November 1965, B 145/2873, BAK; Vermerk, 23 November 1965, B 145/2873, BAK; Aufzeichnung, 19 October 1965, B 145/2873, BAK.

38. Clipping, "Germans Relish Popularity Gain, New U.S. Image," *Inquirer,* 30 June 1966, B 145/9869, BAK; Graf Schweinitz to W. Simon, 16 February 1966, B 145/2873, BAK; Report, Thomas to GIC, 22 July 1969, B 145/6444, BAK.

39. Facts about the American Council on Germany, November 1971, American Council on Germany—Correspondence, box 4, CTE; Report on Activities, 1960–1961, 1961, American Council on Germany—Reports of Activities, box 4, CTE; Report on Activities, 1962–1963, 1963, American Council on Germany—Reports of Activities, box 4, CTE; Report on Activities, 1963–1965, 1965, American Council on Germany—Reports of Activities, box 4, CTE.

40. Report on the Second American-German Conference, 1961, American-German Conference, 2d, Washington, 16–19 February 1961, box 13, CTE.

41. Emmet to James P. O'Donnell, 27 August 1960, Correspondence—O'Donnell, James, box 92, CTE; Emmet to Thomas Dodd, 6 January 1964, Correspondence—Dodd, Thomas, box 69, CTE.

42. Excerpt from *Congressional Record,* Pell, box 94, CTE.

43. Emmet to Javits, 1963, Correspondence—Javits, box 80, CTE; Emmet to Egon Bahr, 1963, Correspondence—Bahr, box 62, CTE.

44. Report on Activities, 1962–1963, 1963, American Council on Germany—Reports of Activities, box 4, CTE; Report on Activities, 1960–1961, 1961, American Council on Germany—Reports of Activities, box 4, CTE; The New Phase of the Berlin Crisis, 1964, Radio—"The New Phase of the Berlin Crisis," WEVD, New York, 8 June 1964, 124, CTE.

45. Report on Activities, 1960–1961, 1961, American Council on Germany—Reports of Activities, box 4, CTE; William H. Chamberlain, "The Revival of Anti-Germanism," *Modern Age,* Summer 1962, 277.

46. Emmet to Mr. and Mrs. Leeds, 1961, American Council on Germany—Fundraising Campaigns, 4, CTE; Chamberlain, "The Revival of Anti-Germanism," 278. Gerhard Krodel took issue with Emmet's support of this interpretation. In a letter to Walter Stahl of the Atlantik-Brücke, Krodel, a professor at the Lutheran Theological Seminary, disagreed with Emmet about the meaning of the anti-German wave. According to Krodel, Emmet believed that "the motive for these revivals is commercial, not political, nor the spirit of revenge." Krodel thought that the persistent anti-German sentiment was fueled by a "steady diet of war movies and programs on Nazism" and a latent hostility against Germans among the media. Gerhard Krodel to Walter Stahl, 1 February 1968, B 145/4913, BAK.

47. Christopher Emmet and Norbert Muhlen, *The Vanishing Swastika: Facts and Figures on Nazism in West Germany* (Chicago: Regnery, 1961), 54; Report on Activities, 1960–1961, 1961, American Council on Germany—Reports of Activities, box 4, CTE.

48. Anti-Semitism Outbreaks in Germany, 5 January 1960, box 126, CTE; Muhlen to Rothschild, 12 February 1960, Muhlen, Norbert, box 45, CTE; Report

on Activities, 1960–1961, 1961, American Council on Germany—Reports of Activities, box 4, CTE.

49. Chamberlain, "The Revival of Anti-Germanism," 281; Norbert Muhlen, "The U.S. Image of Germany, 1962, as Reflected in American Books," *Modern Age,* Fall 1962, 420.

50. Muhlen, "The U.S. Image of Germany," 422; Chamberlain, "The Revival of Anti-Germanism," 281.

51. The Meaning of the German Elections, November 1966, Correspondence— Ball, George, box 62, CTE; Foreign Affairs Roundtable, 12 December 1966, "The German Elections," WEVD, New York, 12 December 1966, 124, CTE; WEVD Broadcast, 1969, "The Impact of the German Elections," WEVD, New York, 6 October 1969, 124, CTE; Report on Activities, 1963–1965, American Council on Germany—Reports of Activities, box 4, CTE.

52. Simon Segal to Irving Engel, 1961, Education—American Council on Germany, 23, AJC FAD-1, YIVO; Paul Freedman to Simon Segal, 16 March 1962, Education— American Council on Germany, box 23, AJC FAD-1, YIVO; Irving Engel to Christopher Emmet, 28 April 1961, Education—American Council on Germany, box 23, AJC FAD-1, YIVO; Eugene Hevesi to John Slawson, 29 May 1961, Education—American Council on Germany, box 23, AJC FAD-1, YIVO; Shafir, *Ambiguous Relations,* 232.

53. Quoted in Shafir, *Ambiguous Relations,* 203–5; Milton Krentz to Irving Engel, 1 April 1959, 1959–1958, box 234, AJC Gen-10, YIVO.

54. *The German Dilemma,* 1959, folder 2, box H140, WJCC; Shafir, *Ambiguous Relations,* 206.

55. Quoted in Shafir, *Ambiguous Relations,* 208; Report on Meeting Held at the Institute of Human Relations, 15 June 1960, Swastika Epidemic—AJC Meetings, box 10, AJC FAD-1, YIVO.

56. Quoted in Shafir, *Ambiguous Relations,* 208–9.

57. Report on Meeting Held at the Institute of Human Relations, 15 June 1960, Swastika Epidemic—AJC Meetings, box 10, AJC FAD-1, YIVO; George Kellman to John Slawson, 21 October 1960, Swastika Epidemic—AJC Reports, box 10, AJC FAD-1, YIVO.

58. Dear Colleague, 27 January 1960, folder 19, box H343, WJCC.

59. Ibid.; George Kellman to John Slawson, 21 October 1960, Swastika Epidemic—AJC Reports, box 10, AJC FAD-1, YIVO; Effect of Publicity on Vandalism, 13 January 1960, Swastika Epidemic—Mass Media, box 10, AJC FAD-1, YIVO.

60. Selected Findings from New York School Study, 1961, Swastika Epidemic— Youth Study, box 10, AJC FAD-1, YIVO.

61. Lawrence Crohn, Louis Rosenzweig, and B. M. Joffe to Officers and Delegates of Council Affiliated Organizations, 14 January 1960, folder 20, box H343, WJCC; Effect of Publicity on Vandalism, 13 January 1960, Swastika Epidemic— Mass Media, box 10, AJC FAD-1, YIVO.

62. Report on Meeting Held at the Institute of Human Relations, 15 June 1960, Swastika Epidemic—AJC Meetings, box 10, AJC FAD-1, YIVO; Dear Colleague, 27 January 1960, folder 19, box H343, WJCC.

63. Philip Klutznick to Monroe Sheinberg, 22 February 1965, folder 15, box H138, WJCC.

64. Shafir, *Ambiguous Relations,* 219.

65. Ibid., 220.

66. Quoted in ibid., 220–21.

67. Report on Meeting Held at the Institute of Human Relations, 15 June 1960, Swastika Epidemic—AJC Meetings, box 10, AJC FAD-1, YIVO; quoted in Novick, *The Holocaust in American Life,* 132.

68. Shafir, *Ambiguous Relations,* 223; Bernstein, *Hannah Arendt,* 157; Novick, *The Holocaust in American Life,* 135. For a somewhat personal account of the maelstrom surrounding the book, see Bergen, *The Banality of Evil,* ix–xii.

69. Arendt, *Eichmann in Jerusalem,* 117, 120.

70. Ibid., 276.

71. Quoted in Novick, *The Holocaust in American Life,* 135–36.

72. For Your Information, May 1961, folder 1, box H126, WJCC.

73. Ibid.; Recent Incidents of Neo-Nazism, August 1962, Swastika Epidemic—AJC Reports, box 10, AJC FAD-1, YIVO.

74. Simonelli, *American Fuehrer,* chapter 6.

75. Shafir, *Ambiguous Relations,* 234–35.

76. Quoted in ibid., 235.

77. Clipping, "A Message for the Conscience of the World from the Jewish War Veterans of the U.S.A.," West Germany 1965, box 24, Joseph F. Barr Papers, NMAJMH; Shafir, *Ambiguous Relations,* 235–36; Department of California—Press Release, 8 March 1965, West Germany 1965, box 24, Joseph F. Barr Papers, NMA-JMH; Memorandum on Meeting at German Embassy, 1964, West Germany 1964–1965, box 24, Joseph F. Barr Papers, NMAJMH.

78. Philip Klutznick to Monroe Sheinberg, 22 February 1965, folder 15, box H138, WJCC; Monroe Sheinberg to Arnold Forster, 8 March 1965, West Germany 1965, box 24, Joseph F. Barr Papers, NMAJMH; Hy Haves to Monroe Sheinberg, 1965, West Germany 1965, box 24, Joseph F. Barr Papers, NMAJMH; Shafir, *Ambiguous Relations,* 236.

79. Report by Dr. Joachim Prinz in CIA Perspectives, n.d., folder 19, box 270, AJCR; Press Release, 1966, folder 2, box 64, WJCC.

5. "We Refuse to Be 'Good Germans'"

1. Individual Audience Preview Cards, 1961, San Francisco, SKP.

2. Martin Quigley, "An Important Political Event," *Motion Picture Herald,* 27 December 1961, Al, Clippings File, MHL; "Germans Are Grim at Preview of *Judgment at Nuremberg,*" *Boxoffice,* 25 December 1961, Clippings File, MHL; David Binder, "World Premiere for *Nuremberg*'" *New York Times,* 15 December 1961, Clippings File, MHL; "Berliners Applaud *Nuremberg* Film," *Los Angeles Mirror,* 15 December 1961, Clippings File, MHL.

3. Quoted in Sitkoff, *King,* 156; Warren Hinckle and David Welsh, "Five Bat-

tles of Selma," *Ramparts* 4 (June 1965): 36; Isserman and Kazin, *America Divided,* 137; *Congressional Record* (1965), 111:4351, 4639.

4. On the breakdown of the consensus, see Melanson, *American Foreign Policy,* 24–25; Suri, *Power and Protest,* 93. For good works on radicalism in the 1960s, see Gitlin, *The Sixties;* Isserman and Kazin, *America Divided;* Foner, *The Story of American Freedom,* 287–93.

5. Williams, *The Tragedy of American Diplomacy.*

6. Shafir, *Ambiguous Relations;* Shapiro, *A Time for Healing;* Novick, *The Holocaust in American Life.*

7. Generalconsulate Boston to the German Embassy, 10 February 1966, B 97/356, PAAA. For more on representations of World War II in postwar America, see Casaregola, *Theaters of War.*

8. Ken Annakin, *The Battle of the Bulge* (Los Angeles: Warner Bros., 1965).

9. Bosley Crowther, "Screen: Fonda in *Battle of the Bulge:* Film Opens at Warner Cinerama Theater; Distortions Mar Story of 1944 Campaign," *New York Times,* 18 December 1965.

10. On general histories and interpretations of the impact of television, see Hoskins, "Television and the Collapse of Memory"; Bourdon, "Some Sense of Time"; Paris, *Repicturing the Second World War.*

11. Quoted in Davidsmeyer, *"Combat!"* 11.

12. Quoted in Royce, *"Hogan's Heroes,"* 3.

13. Quoted in ibid., 21.

14. Quoted in ibid., 5.

15. On Stanley Elkins, see Fermaglich, *American Dreams and Nazi Nightmares,* 24–57 (quote on 26).

16. Ibid., 47–50.

17. On Friedan, see ibid., 58–82 (quote on 58).

18. Quoted in ibid., 70.

19. Quoted in ibid., 72–73.

20. On Milgram, see ibid., 83–123 (quote on 88).

21. Quoted in ibid., 88, 93.

22. Quoted in ibid., 109, 113.

23. Quoted in "The Crusader," *Time,* 22 March 1963, 58.

24. For more on the film, see Shandler, *While America Watches,* 69–79.

25. Souvenir Program from Berlin Premiere, 1961, Berlin, "Judgment at Nuremberg" Clippings File, MHL; Abby Mann, "Judgment at Nuremberg," 1961, SKP.

26. "Recollections by Abby Mann Interviewed by Stephen Farber," *An Oral History of the Motion Picture in America* (Los Angeles: Regents of the University of California, 1969), 24.

27. Stanley Kramer, *Ship of Fools* (Los Angeles: Columbia Pictures, 1965).

28. Sidney Lumet, *The Pawnbroker* (Los Angeles: Allied Artists, 1965). For more on *The Pawnbroker,* see Rosen, "'Teach Me Gold.'"

29. Schwartz, "'No Harder Enterprise,'" 40. Performances by Lehrer and the Mitchell Trio can be found through a keyword search on YouTube.

30. Gitlin, *The Sixties*, 25–26. On the language of protest in the 1960s, see Windt, *Presidents and Protesters*, 204, 230, 233. On young Jews drawn to the movement, see Staub, *Torn at the Roots*.

31. Quoted in Lieberman, *Prairie Power*, 71; quoted in Windt, *Presidents and Protesters*, 233; quoted in Peck, *Uncovering the Sixties*, 188; quoted in Wynkoop, *Dissent in the Heartland*, 14; quoted in Heineman, *Campus Wars*, 201.

32. Quoted in Heineman, *Campus Wars*, 173, 198; quoted in Tollefson, *The Strength Not to Fight*, 26; quoted in Bodroghkozy, *Groove Tube*, 254.

33. Quoted in Margot Adler, "Memories of a Freshman," in Cohen and Zelnik, *The Free Speech Movement*, 124; quoted in Robert Cohen, "This Was *Their* Fight and *They* Had to Fight It," in Cohen and Zelnik, *The Free Speech Movement*, 238.

34. Gitlin, *The Sixties*, 290, 335–36; Stern, *With the Weathermen*, 26–27; quoted in Bodroghkozy, *Groove Tube*, 113–14.

35. Quoted in Kaiser, *1968 in America*, 241; quoted in Isserman and Kazin, *America Divided*, 234.

36. Quoted in J. Anthony Lukas, "Judge Hoffman Is Taunted at Trial of the Chicago 7 after Silencing Defense Counsel," *New York Times*, 6 February 1970, 41; Seale, *Seize the Time*, 60.

37. Seale, *Seize the Time*, 47, 65, 66.

38. Ibid., 306, 303, 404, 431.

39. Quoted in Varon, *Bringing the War Home*, 6, 76, 98.

40. Quoted in Isserman and Kazin, *America Divided*, 207, 208; quoted in Schneider, *Cadres for Conservatism*, 8, 18; quoted in Farber and Roche, *The Conservative Sixties*, 30.

41. Quoted in Andrew, *The Other Side of the Sixties*, 18, 42; Goldwater, *Conscience of a Conservative*, 8; quoted in Farber and Roche, *The Conservative Sixties*, 10.

42. Goldwater, *Conscience of a Conservative*, 101; Iverson, *Barry Goldwater*, 109.

43. Quoted in Perlstein, *Before the Storm*, 506–7; quoted in Andrew, *The Other Side of the Sixties*, 196–97.

44. Quoted in Farber and Roche, *The Conservative Sixties*, 1; Andrew, *The Other Side of the Sixties*, 126; quoted in Schneider, *Cadres for Conservatism*, 118. Young conservatives felt they were oppressed. See Klatch, *A Generation Divided*, 108.

45. Quoted in Donaldson, *Liberalism's Last Hurrah*, 177; quoted in Andrew, *The Other Side of the Sixties*, 178, 198. For more, see White and Gill, *Suite 3505*.

46. Quoted in Perlstein, *Before the Storm*, 375, 438.

47. Quoted in Brennan, *Turning Right in the Sixties*, 78; quoted in Iverson, *Barry Goldwater*, 114; quoted in Schneider, *Cadres for Conservatism*, 84–85; quoted in Donaldson, *Liberalism's Last Hurrah*, 274.

48. Brennan, *Turning Right in the Sixties*, 17.

49. Quoted in Kalk, *The Origins of the Southern Strategy*, 35, 38, 39.

50. For more on oppositional readings of the media in this context, see Dobratz and Shanks-Meile, *White Power, White Pride!* 54.

51. Swastika 1960: The Epidemic of Anti-Semitic Vandalism in America, 1961,

folder 2, box 17, WJCC; Swastika 1960—The Epidemic of Anti-Semitic Vandalism in America, 1960, Anti-Semitism—Swastika Epidemic, box 10, AJC, YIVO.

52. The 1960 Swastika-Smearings: Analysis of the Apprehended Youth, 1962, folder 2, 17, WJCC.

53. Swastika 1960: The Epidemic of Anti-Semitic Vandalism in America, 1960, Anti-Semitism—Swastika Epidemic, box 10, AJC, YIVO.

54. Swastika 1960: The Epidemic of Anti-Semitic Vandalism in America, 1961, folder 2, box 17, WJCC.

55. Swastika 1960: The Epidemic of anti-Semitic Vandalism in America, 1960, Anti-Semitism—Swastika Epidemic, box 10, AJC, YIVO.

56. Ibid.

57. The 1960 Swastika-Smearings: Analysis of the Apprehended Youth, 1962, folder 2, 17, WJCC.

58. Ibid.

59. Stein, Martin, and Rosen, *The Swastika Daubings;* Selected Findings from New York School Study, 1961, Swastika Epidemic—Youth Study, box 10, AJC FAD-1, YIVO.

60. Selected Findings from New York School Study, 1961, Swastika Epidemic—Youth Study, box 10, AJC FAD-1, YIVO.

61. Dobratz and Shanks-Meile, *White Power, White Pride!* 34–88.

62. Simonelli, *American Fuehrer,* 11, 21.

63. Ibid., 26–32.

64. Ibid., 44–50; For Your Information, May 1961, folder 1, box H126, WJCC.

65. Ibid., 33–34.

66. Ibid., 81–95, 50–51.

67. Ibid., 96–105.

68. Ibid., 106–12.

69. Frederick Dutton to Congressman Randall, Subject Numeric Files, EDX 15 GER W, RG 59, NA; John F. Kennedy, "Address at Miami Beach at a Fundraising Dinner in Honor of Senator Smathers," 10 March 1962, in Peters and Woolley, *The American Presidency Project,* http://www.presidency.ucsb.edu/ws/?pid=9090.

70. Quoted in Warren Hinckle and David Welsh, "Five Battles of Selma," *Ramparts,* June 1965, 368; Foner, *The Story of American Freedom,* 267.

71. Paper Prepared in the Department of State, *FRUS* (1961–1963), 23:158; Memorandum of Conversation, *FRUS* (1961–1963), 23:551.

6. "The Hero Is Us"

1. *Congressional Record* (1999), 145:11763.

2. Ibid., 11768. For more on nationalism and commemoration, see Bodnar, *Remaking America,* 13–20.

3. "The Glow of Freedom," *Newsweek,* 22 November 1999, 20; "The Fall of the Berlin Wall: Ten Years Later," *Austin-American Statesman,* 10 November 1999, A1;

Roger Cohen, "For the Wall's Fall, East Germans Are Given Their Due," *New York Times*, 10 November 1999, A3; Werner Renberg to the Editor, *New York Times*, 15 November 1999, A26.

4. Melanson, *American Foreign Policy*, 45; Bundy, *A Tangled Web*. For more on the Nixon administration's approach to Ostpolitik, see Garthoff, *Détente and Confrontation; Richard M. Nixon, 1971, Public Papers of the Presidents of the United States* (Washington, D.C.: Government Printing Office, 1972), 239. On the negotiations of the Quadripartite Agreement itself, see Sarotte, *Dealing with the Devil;* Hanhimäki, *The Flawed Architect*, 86; Hanhimäki, *The Rise and Fall of Detente*, 62–67.

5. *Richard M. Nixon, 1972, Public Papers of the Presidents of the United States* (Washington, D.C.: Government Printing Office, 1974), 1033, 603, 7.

6. Herz to Blumenthal, 27 March 1972, B Rep. 002/8266, LAB; Program Outline 1972, B Rep. 002/8266, LAB.

7. "An End to Berlin Crises?" *Newsweek*, 6 September 1971, 27; "Berlin: Shaping Agreements," *Time*, 30 August 1971.

8. "Crack in the Wall: Easter Passes to West Berliners," *Time*, 10 April 1972; "Hands across the Wall," *Newsweek*, 10 April 1972.

9. Mason, *Richard Nixon and the Quest for a New Majority*, 138–39; Brennan, *Turning Right in the Sixties*, 135–37; Hanhimäki, *The Rise and Fall of Detente*, 77; *Congressional Record* (1974), 120:16185; *Congressional Record* (1973), 119:21003–4.

10. Brands, "The Idea of the National Interest," 24; Hanhimäki, *The Rise and Fall of Detente*, 101–2; *Jimmy Carter, 1979, Public Papers of the Presidents of the United States* (Washington, D.C.: Government Printing Office, 1978), 1293, 1295.

11. Brands, "The Idea of the National Interest," 24; Hanhimäki, *The Rise and Fall of Detente*, 122; Melanson, *American Foreign Policy*, 182; quoted in Fischer, *The Reagan Reversal*, 17.

12. Robert Zimmerman, "V-E Day Widens Berlin's Split," *San Diego Union-Tribune*, 29 April 1985, A-1.

13. William Tuohy, "Barrier to Freedom; Berlin Wall—25 Years of Infamy," *Los Angeles Times*, 12 August 1986, 1; Krista Weedman, "25 Years Later: Peering over the Wall," *New York Times*, 11 August 1986, A19; William Tuohy, "6 Germans Reportedly Killed in Bizarre Attempt to Flee to West," *Los Angeles Times*, 3 July 1986, 15; Jackson Diehl, "3 in Truck Ram through Berlin Wall," *Washington Post*, 29 August 1986, A1; "2 Teen-agers Climb Berlin Wall, Then Swim River to West," *Los Angeles Times*, 10 September 1986, 1.

14. Richard Reeves, "Berlin: The City Is a Message," *San Diego Union-Tribune*, 10 May 1987, C-2.

15. "Let the Wall Come Tumbling Down," *San Diego Tribune*, 15 June 1987, B-6; "Tear Down Berlin Wall, Reagan Asks: Challenge Issued to Soviet Leader in Divided City," *Los Angeles Times*, 13 June 1987, 1. The letters to the editor in the *Los Angeles Times* were critical of Reagan's speech, with most viewing it as a cynical public relations ploy. See John T. Kelly, "Tear Down the Wall," *Los Angeles Times*, 22 June 1987, 4.

16. Kelly, "Tear Down the Wall," 4; Moshe Kam, "Letter to the Editor: Cain's Mark," *New York Times*, 27 August 1986, A22.

17. Stein, "The Politics of Humor."

18. *BusinessWeek*/Harris poll, 27 November 1989; *CBS News* poll, 26 November 1989, http://www.cbsnews.com/news/cbs-news-poll-database/.

19. *CBS News* poll.

20. "Attention, Shoppers, a Piece of the Berlin Wall Can Be Yours to Keep for Just $9.99," *St. Louis Dispatch*, 30 November 1989, 1A; "Deck the Wall . . . Stores Selling Gift Chunks from Berlin," *Washington Post*, 30 November 1989, B3; "Bits of the Wall Bring in Cash," *Guardian*, 29 December 1989.

21. "Letter to the Editor," *Dayton Daily News*, 30 November 1999.

22. William Drozdiak, "Europe's Elusive Unity: Economic and Ethnic Divisions Still Stand," *Washington Post*, 9 November 1999, "Peaceful Revolution," *Boston Globe*, 9 November 1999; "After the Wall," *New York Times*, 9 November 1999.

23. David Hoffman, "Reagan to Go to German War Cemetery," *Washington Post*, 12 April 1985, A1; "Reagan Tells of Respect for War Victims," *Los Angeles Times*, 14 April 1985, 1.

24. "Reagan Likens Nazi War Dead to Concentration Camp Victims," *New York Times*, 19 April 1985, A1.

25. Mintz, *Popular Culture and the Shaping of Holocaust Memory*, 26.

26. Hilberg, *The Destruction of the European Jews;* Browning, *Ordinary Men.* On this tradition, see Bartov, "Reception and Perception," 40.

27. Shandler, *While America Watches*, 163; Richard Shepard, "TV's Story of Nazi Terror Brings High Ratings and Varied Opinions," *New York Times*, 18 April 1978.

28. Novick, *The Holocaust in American Life*, 210.

29. Shandler, *While America Watches*, 163 (quote). See also Sander A. Diamond, "*Holocaust* Film's Impact on Americans," *Patterns of Prejudice* 12 (July-August 1978): 1–9, 19; Meeting concerning the NBC "Holocaust" Series, folder 16, box 67, CO-JCRC; Novick, *The Holocaust in American Life*, 209–10.

30. Shandler, *While America Watches*, 164–75.

31. *Congressional Record* (1978), 124:10988, 12812–13; Shepard, "TV's Story of Nazi Terror Brings High Ratings and Varied Opinions."

32. Dolores Ebert, "Letter to the Editor," *Washington Post*, 23 April 1978, D6; *Congressional Record* (1978), 124:12231; Bernard White, "Letter to the Editor," *Washington Post*, 23 April 1978, D6.

33. *Congressional Record* (1978), 124:12718, 12259, 11929; Shandler, *While America Watches*, 163.

34. Patricia Fulda, "Letter to the Editor," *Washington Post*, 23 April 1978, D6.

35. Consult any work on the "Americanization of the Holocaust" and you will be sure to find heavy discussion of this miniseries.

36. Novick, *The Holocaust in American Life*, 214; Cole, *Selling the Holocaust*, 73.

37. Cole, *Selling the Holocaust*, 73–94.

38. Quoted in ibid., 70; Mintz, *Popular Culture and the Shaping of Holocaust Memory,* 127–49.

39. Ibid.; Mintz, *Popular Culture and the Shaping of Holocaust Memory,* 127–58.

40. Quoted in Loshitzky, introduction, 6–7; Novick, *The Holocaust in American Life,* 9–10, 193–95.

41. Goldhagen, *Hitler's Willing Executioners.*

42. For more on the Historikerstreit, see Maier, *The Unmasterable Past.* A notable exception was Judith Miller, "Erasing the Past: Europe's Amnesia about the Holocaust," *New York Times,* 16 November 1986, 30.

43. Caplan, "Reflections on the Reception of Goldhagen," 159–60; Bartov, "Reception and Perception," 40; Novick, *The Holocaust in American Life,* 137.

44. Caplan, "Reflections on the Reception of Goldhagen," 154.

45. Bartov, "Reception and Perception."

46. Cole, *Selling the Holocaust,* 152–58 (quote on 154); Remarks by Dr. Michael Berenbaum, Content Committee—January 20, 1988—Joint Dev. Meeting, box 1, Michael Berenbaum's Committee Memoranda and Reports, USHMMIA.

47. Quotes and analysis from Cole, *Selling the Holocaust,* 152–58.

48. Jacob Eder, *Holocaust Angst* (New York: Oxford University Press, forthcoming).

Conclusion

1. Wiener, *How We Forgot the Cold War.*

Bibliography

Archival Sources

American Jewish Archives, Cincinnati, Ohio

    Cincinnati, Ohio—Jewish Community Relations Council

    World Jewish Congress Collection

American Jewish Historical Society Archives, Center for Jewish History, New York, N.Y.

    American Jewish Congress Records

    National Jewish Community Relations Advisory Council Records

Bundesarchiv, Koblenz, Germany

    B 106: Bundesministerium des Innern

    B 136: Bundeskanzleramt

    B 145: Bundespresseamt

Cinematic Arts Library, University of Southern California, Los Angeles, Calif.

    Warner Bros. Archive

Hoover Institution Archives, Stanford University, Stanford, Calif.

    Christopher T. Emmet Papers

Landesarchiv Berlin, Berlin, Germany

    B Rep. 002: Der Regierende Bürgermeister von Berlin/Senatskanzlei

    B. Rep 010-010: Senatsverwaltung für Kreditwesen

    E. Rep 200-018: Nachlass Hans E. Hirschfeld

Margaret Herrick Library, Academy of Motion Picture Arts and Sciences, Beverly Hills, Calif.

    Clippings File

    Fred Zinnemann Collection

Lester Cowan Collection
Metro-Goldwyn Mayer Collection
Production Code Administration Files

National Archives II, College Park, Md.

RG 59: Records of the Department of State
RG 306: United States Information Agency
RG 319: Records of the Army Staff
RG 340: Secretary of the Air Force

National Museum of American Jewish Military History, Washington, D.C.

Joseph F. Barr Papers

Politisches Archiv des Auswaertiges Amts, Berlin, Germany

B 11: Laenderabteilung
B 32: USA/Kanada
B 90: Kulturabteilung
B 96: Kulturinstitut
B 97: Kulturreferat

Rare Book and Manuscript Library, Columbia University, New York, N.Y.

Society for the Prevention of World War III

UCLA Library Special Collections, Los Angeles, Calif.

Stanley Kramer Papers

United States Holocaust Memorial Museum Institutional Archives, Washington, D.C.

Michael Berenbaum's Committee Memoranda and Reports

Winston Churchill Memorial Library, Fulton, Mo.

Wisconsin Historical Society, University of Wisconsin, Madison

Goodrich-Hackett Papers
Leo Lania Papers
Louis Lochner Papers
NBC Records
United Artists Collection

YIVO Institute for Jewish History, Center for Jewish History, New York, N.Y.

American Jewish Committee Records

Newspapers and Periodicals

American Mercury
Atlantic Monthly
Life
Look
Los Angeles Times
National Jewish Monthly
New Republic
Newsweek
New York Times
New York Times Magazine
Time
U.S. News and World Report

Published Government Sources

Congressional Record
Foreign Relations of the United States
Public Papers of the Presidents of the United States

Additional Primary Sources

Arendt, Hannah. *Eichmann in Jerusalem: A Report on the Banality of Evil.* New York: Penguin, 1994.

———. *The Origins of Totalitarianism.* New York: Harcourt, 1951.

Dmytryk, Edward. *The Young Lions.* Beverly Hills, Calif.: Twentieth Century-Fox Home Entertainment, 1958.

Gallup, George Horace. *The Gallup Poll: Public Opinion, 1935–1971.* New York: Random House, 1972.

Goldwater, Barry. *Conscience of a Conservative.* Princeton, N.J.: Princeton University Press, 2007.

Hilberg, Raul. *The Destruction of the European Jews.* Chicago: Quadrangle Books, 1961.

Kennan, George F. *Memoirs, 1950–1963.* Vol. 2. Boston: Little, Brown, 1972.

McCloy, John J. "Assisting Germany to Become a Peaceful Democracy." *U.S. Department of State Bulletin,* 9 July 1951.

———. "German Problem and Its Solution." *U.S. Department of State Bulletin* 22 (1950).

Rand, Ayn. *Atlas Shrugged.* New York: Random House, 1957.

Seale, Bobby. *Seize the Time: The Story of the Black Panther Party and Huey P. Newton.* Baltimore: Black Classic, 1991.

Shaw, Irwin. *The Young Lions.* New York: Random House, 1948.

Stein, Mary Beth. "The Politics of Humor: The Berlin Wall in Jokes and Graffiti." *Western Folklore* 48, no. 2 (1989): 101–7.

Stern, Susan. *With the Weathermen: The Personal Journal of a Revolutionary Woman.* New York: Doubleday, 1975.

Tetens, T. H. *Germany Plots with the Kremlin.* New York: H. Schuman, 1953.

Secondary Sources

Abrams, Nathan. "'A Profoundly Hegemonic Moment': De-mythologizing the Cold War New York Jewish Intellectuals." *SHOFAR* 21, no. 3 (2003).

Adler, Les K., and Thomas G. Paterson. "Red Fascism: The Merger of Nazi Germany and Soviet Russia in the American Image of Totalitarianism, 1930's–1950's." *American Historical Review* 75 (1970): 1046–64.

Aguilar, Manuela. *Cultural Diplomacy and Foreign Policy: German-American Relations, 1955–1968.* New York: Peter Lang, 1996.

Allen, Craig. *Eisenhower and the Mass Media: Peace, Prosperity, and Prime-time TV.* Chapel Hill: University of North Carolina Press, 1993.

Allen, Tim. "Civil War, Ethnicity and the Media." *Anthropology Today* 11, no. 6 (1995): 16–18.

Altschuler, Glenn C., and David I. Grossvogel. *Changing Channels: America in TV Guide.* Urbana: University of Illinois Press, 1992.

Anderson, Benedict R. *Imagined Communities: Reflections on the Origin and Spread of Nationalism.* London: Verso, 1991.

Andrew, John A. *The Other Side of the Sixties: Young Americans for Freedom and the Rise of Conservative Politics.* New Brunswick, N.J.: Rutgers University Press, 1997.

Andrews, Geoff. *New Left, New Right and Beyond: Taking the Sixties Seriously.* New York: St. Martin's, 1999.

Annan, Noel. *Changing Enemies: The Defeat and Regeneration of Germany.* Ithaca, N.Y.: Cornell University Press, 1997.

Appy, Christian G., ed. *Cold War Constructions: The Political Culture of United States Imperialism, 1945–1966.* Amherst: University of Massachusetts Press, 2000.

Assmann, Aleida. "Texts, Traces, Trash: The Changing Media of Cultural Memory." In "The New Erudition," special issue, *Representations,* no. 56 (1996): 123–34.

Axelrod, Alan. *Selling the Great War: The Making of American Propaganda.* New York: Palgrave Macmillan, 2009.

Backer, John H. *The Decision to Divide Germany: American Foreign Policy in Transition.* Durham, N.C.: Duke University Press, 1978.

Bailey, Steve. *Media Audiences and Identity: Self-Construction in the Fan Experience.* New York: Palgrave Macmillan, 2005.

Barnouw, Dagmar. *Germany, 1945: Views of War and Violence.* Bloomington: Indiana University Press, 1996.

Baron, Lawrence. "The Holocaust and American Public Memory, 1945–1960." *Holocaust and Genocide Studies* 17, no. 1 (2003): 62–88.

Barthes, Roland. "(I) Operation Margarine; (II) Myth Today." In *Media and Cultural Studies: Keyworks,* edited by Meenakshi Gigi Durham and Douglas Kellner, 121–28. Malden, Mass.: Blackwell, 2001.

Bartov, Omer. "Reception and Perception: Goldhagen's Holocaust and the World." In *The "Goldhagen" Effect,* edited by Geoff Eley, 33–87. Ann Arbor: University of Michigan Press, 2000.

Baughman, James L. *The Republic of Mass Culture: Journalism, Filmmaking, and Broadcasting in America since 1941.* 3rd ed. Baltimore: Johns Hopkins University Press, 2006.

Bender, Thomas. *Rethinking American History in a Global Age.* Berkeley: University of California Press, 2002.

Bergen, Bernard. *The Banality of Evil: Hannah Arendt and "The Final Solution."* Lanham, Md.: Rowman & Littlefield, 1998.

Berghahn, Volker Rolf. *America and the Intellectual Cold Wars in Europe: Shepard Stone between Philanthropy, Academy, and Diplomacy.* Princeton, N.J.: Princeton University Press, 2001.

Bergquist, James. "The Forty-Eighters: Catalysts of German-American Politics." In *The German-American Encounter: Conflict and Cooperation between Two Cultures, 1800–2000,* edited by Frank Trommler and Elliott Shore, 22–36. New York: Berghahn Books, 2001.

Bering, Henrik. *Outpost Berlin: The History of the American Military Forces in Berlin, 1945–1994.* Chicago: Edition Q, 1995.

Bernhard, Nancy E. *U.S. Television News and Cold War Propaganda, 1947–1960.* Cambridge: Cambridge University Press, 1999.

Bernstein, Richard J. *Hannah Arendt and the Jewish Question.* Cambridge, Mass.: MIT Press, 1996.

Berry, Nicholas O. *Foreign Policy and the Press: An Analysis of the New York Times' Coverage of U.S. Foreign Policy.* New York: Greenwood, 1990.

Beschloss, Michael R. *The Conquerors: Roosevelt, Truman and the Destruction of Hitler's Germany.* New York: Simon & Schuster, 2002.

———. *The Crisis Years: Kennedy and Khrushchev, 1960–1963.* New York: Edward Burlingame Books, 1991.

Biskind, Peter. *Seeing Is Believing: How Hollywood Taught Us to Stop Worrying and Love the Fifties.* New York: Henry Holt, 2000.

Biskupski, Mieczyslaw B. *Hollywood's War with Poland, 1939–1945.* Lexington: University Press of Kentucky, 2010.

Bjerre-Poulsen, Niels. *Right Face: Organizing the American Conservative Movement, 1945–65.* Copenhagen: Museum Tusculanum, 2002.

Blantz, Thomas E. *George N. Shuster: On the Side of Truth.* Notre Dame, Ind.: University of Notre Dame Press, 1993.

Blight, David W. *Race and Reunion: The Civil War in American Memory.* Cambridge, Mass.: Belknap Press of Harvard University Press, 2001.

Bliss, Edward. *Now the News: The Story of Broadcast Journalism.* New York: Columbia University Press, 1991.

Bloom, Alexander, and Wini Breines. *"Takin' It to the Streets": A Sixties Reader.* New York: Oxford University Press, 2003.

Boddy, William. *Fifties Television: The Industry and Its Critics.* Urbana: University of Illinois Press, 1990.

Bodnar, John E. *The "Good War" in American Memory.* Baltimore: Johns Hopkins University Press, 2010.

———. *Remaking America: Public Memory, Commemoration, and Patriotism in the Twentieth Century.* Princeton, N.J.: Princeton University Press, 1992.

Bodroghkozy, Aniko. *Groove Tube: Sixties Television and the Youth Rebellion.* Durham, N.C.: Duke University Press, 2001.

Boehling, Rebecca L. *A Question of Priorities: Democratic Reforms and Economic Recovery in Postwar Germany: Frankfurt, Munich, and Stuttgart under U.S. Occupation, 1945–1949.* Providence, R.I.: Berghahn Books, 1996.

Borneman, John. *Belonging in the Two Berlins: Kin, State, Nation.* Cambridge: Cambridge University Press, 1992.

Bornstein, Jerry. *The Wall Came Tumbling Down: The Berlin Wall and the Fall of Communism.* New York: Arch Cape, 1990.

Borstelmann, Thomas. *The Cold War and the Color Line: American Race Relations in the Global Arena.* Cambridge, Mass.: Harvard University Press, 2001.

Bosworth, Richard. *Explaining Auschwitz and Hiroshima: History Writing and the Second World War, 1945–1990.* London: Routledge, 1993.

Bourdon, Jérôme. "Some Sense of Time: Remembering Television." *History and Memory* 15 (Fall/Winter 2003): 5–35.

Bracher, Karl Dietrich, Hugo Borger, Ekkehard Mai, Stephan Waetzoldt, and Fritz Thyssen-Stiftung. *'45 und die Folgen: Kunstgeschichte eines Wiederbeginns.* Cologne: Böhlau, 1991.

Bradley, Mark. *Imagining Vietnam and America: The Making of Postcolonial Vietnam, 1919–1950.* Chapel Hill: University of North Carolina Press, 2000.

Brands, H. W. "The Idea of the National Interest." *Diplomatic History* 23, no. 2 (1999): 239–61.

Braverman, Jordan. *To Hasten the Homecoming: How Americans Fought World War II through the Media.* Lanham, Md.: Madison Books, 1996.

Brennan, Mary. *Turning Right in the Sixties: The Conservative Capture of the GOP.* Chapel Hill: University of North Carolina Press, 1997.

Brinkley, Alan. *Franklin Delano Roosevelt.* New York: Oxford University Press, 2010.

Broderick, Jim. "Berlin and Cuba: Cold War Hotspots." *History Today* 48, no. 12 (1998): 23–29.

Browder, Dewey A. *Americans in Post–World War II Germany: Teachers, Tinkers, Neighbors and Nuisances.* Lewiston, N.Y.: E. Mellen, 1998.

Browning, Christopher R. *Ordinary Men: Reserve Police Battalion 101 and the Final Solution in Poland.* New York: HarperCollins, 1992.

Bundy, William. *A Tangled Web: The Making of Foreign Policy in the Nixon Presidency.* New York: Hill & Wang, 1998.

Burnham, Alexander. *We Write for Our Own Time: Selected Essays from Seventy-Five Years of the "Virginia Quarterly Review."* Charlottesville: University Press of Virginia, 2000.

Burns, Rob. *German Cultural Studies: An Introduction.* Oxford: Oxford University Press, 1995.

Burr, William. "Avoiding the Slippery Slope: The Eisenhower Administration and the Berlin Crisis, November 1958–January 1959." *Diplomatic History* 18, no. 2 (1994): 177–205.

Burr, William, and U.S. National Security Archive. *The Berlin Crisis, 1958–1962.* Alexandria, Va.: Chadwyck-Healey, 1992.

Cahn, Anne H. *Killing Detente: The Right Attacks the CIA.* University Park: Pennsylvania State University Press, 1998.

Cameron, Keith. *National Identity.* Exeter, U.K.: Intellect, 1999.

Canedy, Susan. *America's Nazis: A Democratic Dilemma; A History of the German American Bund.* Menlo Park, Calif.: Markgraf, 1990.

Caplan, Jane. "Reflections on the Reception of Goldhagen in the United States." In *The "Goldhagen" Effect,* edited by Geoff Eley, 151–62. Ann Arbor: University of Michigan Press, 2000.

Carr, Graham. "Rules of Engagement: Public History and the Drama of Legitimation." *Canadian Historical Review* 86, no. 2 (2005): 317–54.

Carter, Erica. *How German Is She? Postwar West German Reconstruction and the Consuming Woman.* Ann Arbor: University of Michigan Press, 1997.

Casaregola, Vincent. *Theaters of War: America's Perceptions of World War II.* New York: Palgrave Macmillan, 2009.

Casey, Steven. "The Campaign to Sell a Harsh Peace for Germany to the American Public, 1944–1948." *History* 90, no. 297 (2005): 62–92.

———. *Cautious Crusade: Franklin D. Roosevelt, American Public Opinion, and the War against Nazi Germany.* Oxford: Oxford University Press, 2002.

Castiglia, Christopher, and Christopher Reed. "'Ah Yes, I Remember It Well': Memory and Queer Culture in *Will and Grace.*" *Cultural Critique* 56 (2003): 158–88.

Chomsky, Noam. *World Orders, Old and New.* New York: Columbia University Press, 1996.

Clark, Suzanne. *Cold Warriors: Manliness on Trial in the Rhetoric of the West.* Carbondale: Southern Illinois University Press, 2000.

Clurman, Richard M. *To the End of Time: The Seduction and Conquest of a Media Empire.* New York: Simon & Schuster, 1992.

Cobley, Paul. *The Communication Theory Reader.* London: Routledge, 1996.

Cohen, Aaron J. "Oh, That! Myth, Memory, and World War I in the Russian Emigration and the Soviet Union." *Slavic Review* 62, no. 1 (2003): 69–86.

Cohen, Robert, and Reginald E. Zelnik, eds. *The Free Speech Movement: Reflections on Berkeley in the 1960s.* Berkeley: University of California Press, 2002.

Cole, Tim. *Selling the Holocaust: From Auschwitz to Schindler; How History Is Bought, Packaged, and Sold.* New York: Routledge, 1999.

Confino, Alon. "Collective Memory and Cultural History: Problems of Method." *American Historical Review* 105, no. 5 (1997): 1386–403.

———. *The Nation as a Local Metaphor: Württemberg, Imperial Germany, and Na-*

tional Memory, 1871–1918. Chapel Hill: University of North Carolina Press, 1997.

Connelly, Matthew James. *A Diplomatic Revolution: Algeria's Fight for Independence and the Origins of the Post–Cold War Era*. Oxford: Oxford University Press, 2002.

Conolly-Smith, Peter. *Translating America: An Immigrant Press Visualizes American Popular Culture, 1895–1918*. Washington, D.C.: Smithsonian Books, 2004.

Conzen, Kathleen Neils. "German-Americans and the Invention of Ethnicity." In *America and the Germans: An Assessment of a Three-Hundred-Year History*, edited by Frank Trommler and Joseph McVeigh, 134–40. Philadelphia: University of Pennsylvania Press, 1985.

———. *Immigrant Milwaukee, 1836–1860: Accommodation and Community in a Frontier City*. Cambridge, Mass.: Harvard University Press, 1976.

Cookman, Claude. "An American Atrocity: The My Lai Massacre Concretized in a Victim's Face." *Journal of American History* 94, no. 1 (2007): 154–62.

Crane, Susan A. "Memory, Distortion, and History in the Museum." In "Producing the Past: Making Histories inside and outside the Academy," special issue, *History and Theory* 36, no. 4 (1997): 44–63.

Critchlow, James. "Public Diplomacy during the Cold War: The Record and Its Implications." *Journal of Cold War Studies* 6, no. 1 (2004): 75–89.

Crofts, Stephen. "Authorship and Hollywood." In *American Cinema and Hollywood: Critical Approaches*, edited by John Hill and Pamela Gibson, 85–102. Oxford: Oxford University Press, 2000.

Cull, Nicholas John. *Selling War: The British Propaganda Campaign against American "Neutrality" in World War II*. New York: Oxford University Press, 1995.

Dallek, Robert. *Franklin D. Roosevelt and American Foreign Policy, 1932–1945*. New York: Oxford University Press, 1995.

Daum, Andreas W. *Kennedy in Berlin: Politik, Kultur und Emotionen im Kalten Krieg*. Paderborn: Schöningh, 2003.

Davidann, Jon. "America's Geisha Ally: Reimagining the Japanese Enemy." *Journal of American History* 94, no. 2 (2007): 640–41.

Davidsmeyer, Jo. *"Combat!" A Viewer's Companion to the WWII TV Series*. Rev. ed. Tallevast, Fla.: Strange New Worlds, 2002.

Davidson, Eugene. *The Death and Life of Germany: An Account of the American Occupation*. Columbia: University of Missouri Press, 1999.

Davis, Kenneth Sydney. *FDR, the War President, 1940–1943: A History*. New York: Random House, 2000.

Dean, Kevin W. "'We Seek Peace—but We Shall Not Surrender': JFK's Use of Juxtaposition for Rhetorical Success in the Berlin Crisis." *Presidential Studies Quarterly* 21, no. 3 (1991): 531–44.

Dean, Robert Dale. "Manhood, Reason, and American Foreign Policy: The Social Construction of Masculinity and the Kennedy and Johnson Administrations." Ph.D. diss., University of Arizona, 1995.

Degens, T. *Freya on the Wall*. San Diego: Browndeer / Harcourt Brace, 1997.

De Grazia, Victoria. *Irresistible Empire: America's Advance through Twentieth-Century Europe*. Cambridge, Mass.: Belknap Press of Harvard University Press, 2005.

Denning, Michael. *The Cultural Front: The Laboring of American Culture in the Twentieth Century*. London: Verso, 1996.

Derderian, Richard L. "Algeria as a Lieu de Memoire: Ethnic Minority Memory and National Identity in Contemporary France." *Radical History Review* 83 (2002): 28–43.

Deshmukh, Marion. "Recovering Culture: The Berlin National Gallery and the U.S. Occupation, 1945–1949." *Central European History* 27, no. 4 (1994): 411–39.

Diamond, Sander A. *The Nazi Movement in the United States, 1924–1941*. Ithaca, N.Y.: Cornell University Press, 1974.

Dick, Bernard F. *The Star-Spangled Film*. Lexington: University Press of Kentucky, 1985.

Diefendorf, Jeffry M. *In the Wake of War: The Reconstruction of German Cities after World War II*. New York: Oxford University Press, 1993.

Diefendorf, Jeffry M., Axel Frohn, and Hermann-Josef Rupieper. *American Policy and the Reconstruction of West Germany, 1945–1955*, Publications of the German Historical Institute. Cambridge: Cambridge University Press, 1993.

Diner, Dan. *Beyond the Conceivable: Studies on Germany, Nazism, and the Holocaust*. Berkeley: University of California Press, 2000.

Dinnerstein, Leonard. *Antisemitism in America*. New York: Oxford University Press, 1994.

Dittgen, Herbert. *Deutsch-amerikanische Sicherheitsbeziehungen in der Ära Helmut Schmidt: Vorgeschichte und Folgen des Nato-Doppelbeschlusses*. Munich: Wilhelm Fink, 1991.

Dobratz, Betty A., and Stephanie L. Shanks-Meile. *White Power, White Pride! The White Separatist Movement in the United States*. New York: Twayne, 1997.

Doenecke, Justus D. *Storm on the Horizon: The Challenge to American Intervention, 1939–1941*. Lanham, Md.: Rowman & Littlefield, 2000.

Donaldson, Gary. *Liberalism's Last Hurrah: The Presidential Campaign of 1964*. Armonk, N.Y.: M. E. Sharpe, 2003.

Dorfman, Ariel, and Armand Mattelart. "Introduction: Instructions on How to Become a General in the Disneyland Club." In *Media and Cultural Studies: Keyworks*, edited by Meenakshi Gigi Durham and Douglas Kellner, 144–51. Malden, Mass.: Blackwell, 2001.

Doubler, Michael D. *Closing with the Enemy: How GIs Fought the War in Europe, 1944–1945*. Lawrence: University Press of Kansas, 1994.

Dudziak, Mary L. "Desegregation as a Cold War Imperative." In *Race and U.S. Foreign Policy during the Cold War*, edited by Michael Krenn, 177–236. New York: Garland, 1998.

Dumbrell, John. *American Foreign Policy: Carter to Clinton*. New York: St. Martin's, 1997.

Durham, Meenakshi Gigi, and Douglas Kellner, eds. *Media and Cultural Studies: Keyworks*. Malden, Mass.: Blackwell, 2001.

Duroy, Stéphane. *Berlin: Portrait of a City.* Boston: Little Brown, 1990.

Dwyer, Owen J. "Symbolic Accretion and Commemoration." *Social & Cultural Geography* 5, no. 3 (2004): 419–35.

Eagleton, Terry. *Literary Theory: An Introduction.* Minneapolis: University of Minnesota Press, 1996.

Eder, Jacob. "Holocaust Angst: The Federal Republic of Germany and Holocaust Memory in the United States, 1977–98." Ph.D. diss., University of Pennsylvania, 2012.

Edgerton, Gary R., and Peter C. Rollins. *Television Histories: Shaping Collective Memory in the Media Age.* Lexington: University Press of Kentucky, 2001.

Eichhoff, Jürgen. "The German Language in America." In *America and the Germans: An Assessment of a Three-Hundred-Year History,* edited by Frank Trommler and Joseph McVeigh, 224–39. Philadelphia: University of Pennsylvania Press, 1985.

Eigler, Friederike Ursula, and Peter Pfeiffer. *Cultural Transformations in the New Germany: American and German Perspectives.* Columbia, S.C.: Camden House, 1993.

Eisenberg, Carolyn. *Drawing the Line: The American Decision to Divide Germany, 1944–1949.* Cambridge: Cambridge University Press, 1996.

Endy, Christopher. *Cold War Holidays: American Tourism in France.* Chapel Hill: University of North Carolina Press, 2004.

Epler, Doris M. *The Berlin Wall: How It Rose and Why It Fell.* Brookfield, Conn.: Millbrook, 1992.

Ermarth, Michael. *America and the Shaping of German Society, 1945–1955.* Providence, R.I.: Berg, 1993.

Ernst, Wolfgang. "Between Real Time and Memory on Demand: Reflections on/of Television." *South Atlantic Quarterly* 101, no. 3 (2002): 625–37.

Etheridge, Brian C. "*Die antideutsche Welle:* The Anti-German Wave in Cold War America and Its Implications for the Study of Public Diplomacy." In *Decentering the United States: New Directions in Culture and International Relations,* edited by Jessica Gienow-Hecht, 73–106. New York: Berghahn Books, 2007.

———. "*The Desert Fox,* Memory Diplomacy, and the German Question in Early Cold War America." *Diplomatic History* 32, no. 2 (2008): 207–38.

———. "In Search of Germans: Contested Germany in the Production of *The Search.*" *Journal of Popular Film and Television* 34, no. 1 (2006): 34–45.

Farber, Dave, and Jeff Roche. *The Conservative Sixties.* New York: Peter Lang, 2003.

Feifer, George. "The Berlin Tunnel." *MHQ: The Quarterly Journal of Military History* 10, no. 2 (1998): 62–71.

Felken, Detlef. *Dulles und Deutschland: Die amerikanische Deutschlandpolitik, 1953–1959.* Bonn: Bouvier, 1993.

Fermaglich, Kirsten Lise. *American Dreams and Nazi Nightmares: Early Holocaust Consciousness and Liberal America, 1957–1965.* Waltham, Mass.: Brandeis University Press, 2006.

Fink, Carole, Philipp Gassert, and Detlef Junker, eds. *1968: The World Transformed.* New York: Cambridge University Press, 1998.

Finklestein, Norman. *The Holocaust Industry: Reflections on the Exploitation of Jewish Suffering.* New York: Verso, 2000.

Finzsch, Norbert, and Jürgen Martschukat. *Different Restorations: Reconstruction and "Wiederaufbau" in Germany and the United States, 1865, 1945, and 1989.* Providence, R.I.: Berghahn Books, 1996.

———. *Reconstruction und Wiederaufbau in Deutschland und den Vereinigten Staaten von Amerika, 1865, 1945 und 1989.* Stuttgart: F. Steiner, 1996.

Fischer, Beth A. *The Reagan Reversal: Foreign Policy and the End of the Cold War.* Columbia: University of Missouri Press, 1997.

Fish, Stanley. *Is There a Text in This Class? The Authority of Interpretive Communities.* Cambridge, Mass.: Harvard University Press, 1980.

Flanagan, Jason. "Woodrow Wilson's 'Rhetorical Restructuring': The Transformation of the American Self and the Construction of the German Enemy." *Rhetoric and Public Affairs* 7, no. 2 (2004): 115–48.

Flanzbaum, Hilene, ed. *The Americanization of the Holocaust.* Baltimore: Johns Hopkins University Press, 1999.

Fleming, Thomas J. *The New Dealers' War: Franklin D. Roosevelt and the War within World War II.* New York: Basic Books, 2001.

Flemming, Thomas, and Hagen Koch. *Die berliner Mauer: Geschichte eines politischen Bauwerks.* Berlin: Be.bra Verlag, 1999.

Fogleman, Aaron Spencer. *Hopeful Journeys: German Immigration, Settlement, and Political Culture in Colonial America, 1717–1775.* Philadelphia: University of Pennsylvania Press, 1996.

Foner, Eric. *The Story of American Freedom.* New York: Norton, 1998.

Fousek, John. *To Lead the Free World: American Nationalism and the Cultural Roots of the Cold War.* Chapel Hill: University of North Carolina Press, 2000.

Fox, Richard Wightman, and T. J. Jackson Lears, eds. *The Power of Culture: Critical Essays in American History.* Chicago: University of Chicago Press, 1993.

Frech, Birgit. *Die berliner Mauer in der Literatur: Eine Untersuchung ausgewählter prosawerke Seit 1961.* Pfungstadt bei Darmstadt: Ergon, 1992.

Freedman, Lawrence. *Kennedy's Wars: Berlin, Cuba, Laos, and Vietnam.* New York: Oxford University Press, 2000.

Freeman, Jo. *At Berkeley in the Sixties: The Education of an Activist, 1961–1965.* Bloomington: Indiana University Press, 2003.

Frei, Norbert. *Adenauer's Germany and the Nazi Past: The Politics of Amnesty and Integration.* Translated by Joel Golb. New York: Columbia University Press, 2002.

Friedman, Murray. *The Neoconservative Revolution: Jewish Intellectuals and the Shaping of Public Policy.* Cambridge: Cambridge University Press, 2005.

Frizzell, Robert W. *Independent Immigrants: A Settlement of Hanoverian Germans in Western Missouri.* Columbia: University of Missouri Press, 2007.

Frohn, Axel, Anne Hope, and the German Historical Institute (Washington, D.C.).

Holocaust and Shilumim: The Policy of Wiedergutmachung in the Early 1950s.
Washington, D.C.: German Historical Institute, 1991.

Fyne, Robert. *Long Ago and Far Away: Hollywood and the Second World War.* Lanham,
Md.: Scarecrow, 2008.

Garthoff, Raymond L. *Détente and Confrontation.* Washington, D.C.: Brookings Institution Press, 1985.

Gary, Brett. *The Nervous Liberals: Propaganda Anxieties from World War I to the Cold
War.* New York: Columbia University Press, 1999.

Gassert, Philipp. *Amerika im Dritten Reich: Ideologie, Propaganda und Volksmeinung,
1933–1945.* Stuttgart: Steiner, 1997.

Gearson, John P. S. *Harold Macmillan and the Berlin Wall Crisis, 1958–62: The Limits
of Interests and Force.* New York: St. Martin's in association with King's College,
London, 1998.

Geitz, Henry, Jürgen Heideking, and Jurgen Herbst, eds. *German Influences on Education in the United States to 1917.* Cambridge: German Historical Institute,
Cambridge University Press, 1995.

Gelb, Norman. *The Berlin Wall: Kennedy, Khrushchev, and a Showdown in the Heart of
Europe.* New York: Dorset, 1990.

Germroth, David S., and Rebecca J. Hudson. "German-American Relations in the
Post–Cold War World." *Journal of Social, Political and Economic Studies* 16, no.
2 (1991): 131–57.

Gidlow, Liette. "Deligitimizing Democracy: 'Civic Slackers,' the Cultural Turn, and
the Possibilities of Politics." *Journal of American History* 89, no. 3 (2002): 922–57.

Gienow-Hecht, Jessica C. E. "Shame on Us?" *Diplomatic History* 24, no. 3 (2000):
465–94.

———. *Sound Diplomacy: Music and Emotions in Transatlantic Relations, 1850–
1920.* Chicago: University of Chicago Press, 2009.

———. *Transmission Impossible: American Journalism as Cultural Diplomacy in Postwar Germany, 1945–1955.* Baton Rouge: Louisiana State University Press, 1999.

———. "Trumpeting Down the Walls of Jericho: The Politics of Art, Music, and
Emotion in German-American Relations, 1870–1920." *Journal of Social History*
26, no. 3 (2003): 585–613.

Gienow-Hecht, Jessica C. E., and Frank Schumacher, eds. *Culture and International
History.* New York: Berghahn Books, 2003.

Giesen, Bernhard. "The Collective Identity of Europe: Constitutional Practice or
Community of Memory?" In *Europeanisation, National Identities, and Migration: Changes in Boundary Construction between Western and Eastern Europe,* edited by Willfried Spohn and Anna Triandafyllidou, 21–35. London: Routledge,
2003.

Giles, Geoffrey J., and German Historical Institute. *Stunde Null: The End and the
Beginning Fifty Years Ago.* Washington, D.C.: German Historical Institute, 1997.

Gillon, Steven M. *Politics and Vision: The ADA and American Liberalism, 1947–1985.*
New York: Oxford University Press, 1987.

Gimbel, John. *The American Occupation of Germany.* Stanford, Calif.: Stanford University Press, 1968.

Gitlin, Todd. *The Sixties: Years of Hope, Days of Rage.* New York: Bantam Books, 1993.

Gjerde, Jon. "Prescriptions and Perceptions of Labor and Family among Ethnic Groups in the Nineteenth-Century American Middle West." In *German-American Immigration and Ethnicity in Comparative Perspective,* edited by Wolfgang Helbich and Walter D. Kamphoefner, 117–37. Madison, Wis.: Max Kade Institute for German-American Studies, 2004.

Glaser-Schmidt, Elisabeth. "Between Hope and Skepticism: American Views of Germany, 1918–1933." In *Transatlantic Images and Perceptions: Germany and America since 1776,* edited by David E. Barclay and Elisabeth Glaser-Schmidt, 191–217. Cambridge: Cambridge University Press, 1997.

Gleason, Abbott. *Totalitarianism: The Inner History of the Cold War.* New York: Oxford University Press, 1995.

Gluck, Carol. "Operations of Memory: 'Comfort Women' and the World." In *Ruptured Histories: War, Memory, and the Post-Cold War in Asia,* edited by Sheila Miyoski Jager and Rana Mitter, 45–77. Cambridge, Mass.: Harvard University Press, 2007.

Godfried, Nathan. "A Shadow of Red: Communism and the Blacklist in Radio and Television." *Journal of American History* 94, no. 2 (2007): 642–43.

Goedde, Petra. "From Villains to Victims: Fraternization and the Feminization of Germany, 1945–1947." *Diplomatic History* 23, no. 1 (1999): 1–20.

———. *GIs and Germans: Culture, Gender and Foreign Relations, 1945–1949.* New Haven, Conn.: Yale University Press, 2003.

Goldhagen, Daniel Jonah. *Hitler's Willing Executioners: Ordinary Germans and the Holocaust.* New York: Knopf, 1997.

Gramsci, Antonio. "(I) History of the Subaltern Classes; (II) The Concept of "Ideology"; (III) Cultural Themes: Ideological Material." In *Media and Cultural Studies: Keyworks,* edited by Meenakshi Gigi Durham and Douglas Kellner, 43–47. Malden, Mass.: Blackwell, 2001.

Graver, Lawrence. *An Obsession with Anne Frank: Meyer Levin and the "Diary."* Berkeley: University of California Press, 1997.

Gray, William Glenn. *Germany's Cold War: The Global Campaign to Isolate East Germany, 1949–1969.* Chapel Hill: University of North Carolina Press, 2003.

Halbwachs, Maurice. *On Collective Memory.* Edited and translated by Lewis A. Coser. Chicago: University of Chicago Press, 1992.

Hall, Stuart. "Encoding/Decoding." In *Media and Cultural Studies: Keyworks,* edited by Meenakshi Gigi Durham and Douglas Kellner, 166–76. Malden, Mass.: Blackwell, 2001.

Hamby, Alonzo L. *For the Survival of Democracy: Franklin Roosevelt and the World Crisis of the 1930s.* New York: Free Press, 2004.

Hampton, Mary N. *The Wilsonian Impulse: U.S. Foreign Policy, the Alliance, and German Unification.* Westport, Conn.: Praeger, 1996.

Hanhimäki, Jussi M. *The Flawed Architect: Henry Kissinger and American Foreign Policy.* New York: Oxford University Press, 2004.
———. *The Rise and Fall of Detente: American Foreign Policy and the Transformation of the Cold War.* Washington, D.C.: Potomac Books, 2012.
Hariman, Robert. *Popular Trials: Rhetoric, Mass Media, and the Law.* Tuscaloosa: University of Alabama Press, 1990.
Harrington, Daniel F. "United States, United Nations and the Berlin Blockade." *Historian* 52, no. 2 (1990): 262–85.
Harris, Richard. "1948: The Berlin Airlift." *American History* 33, no. 2 (1998): 48–58, 60, 62–63.
Harris, Robert L., Jr. "Racial Equality and the United Nations Charter." In *Race and U.S. Foreign Policy during the Cold War,* edited by Michael Krenn, 2–24. New York: Garland, 1998.
Hartz, Louis. *The Liberal Tradition in America.* New York: Harcourt, Brace & World, 1955.
Hasain, Marouf, Jr. "Anne Frank, Bergen-Belsen, and the Polysemic Nature of Holocaust Memories." *Rhetoric and Public Affairs* 4, no. 3 (2001): 349–74.
Heale, M. J. *American Anticommunism: Combating the Enemy Within, 1830–1970.* Baltimore: Johns Hopkins University Press, 1990.
Heimannsberg, Barbara, and Christoph J. Schmidt. *The Collective Silence: German Identity and the Legacy of Shame.* San Francisco: Jossey-Bass, 1993.
Heineman, Kenneth J. *Campus Wars: The Peace Movement at American State Universities in the Vietnam Era.* New York: New York University Press, 1993.
Heins, Cornelia. *The Wall Falls: An Oral History of the Reunification of the Two Germanies.* London: Grey Seal, 1994.
Helbich, Wolfgang. "German-Born Union Soldiers: Motivation, Ethnicity, and 'Americanization.'" In *German-American Immigration and Ethnicity in Comparative Perspective,* edited by Wolfgang Helbich and Walter D. Kamphoefner, 295–325. Madison, Wis.: Max Kade Institute for German-American Studies, 2004.
Henke, Klaus-Dietmar. *Die Amerikanische Besetzung Deutschlands.* Munich: R. Oldenbourg, 1995.
Henriksen, Margot A. *Dr. Strangelove's America: Society and Culture in the Atomic Age.* Berkeley: University of California Press, 1997.
Herf, Jeffrey. *Divided Memory: The Nazi Past in the Two Germanys.* Cambridge, Mass.: Harvard University Press, 1997.
———. *The Jewish Enemy: Nazi Propaganda during World War II and the Holocaust.* Cambridge, Mass.: Belknap Press of Harvard University Press, 2006.
Hersh, Seymour M. *The Dark Side of Camelot.* Boston: Little Brown, 1997.
Hertle, Hans-Hermann. *Chronik des Mauerfalls: Die dramatischen Ereignisse um den 9. November 1989.* Berlin: Ch. Links Verlag, 1996.
Herz, Deborah. *How Jews Became Germans: The History of Conversion and Assimilation in Berlin.* New Haven, Conn.: Yale University Press, 2007.

Hill, John, and Pamela Gibson, eds. *American Cinema and Hollywood: Critical Approaches.* Oxford: Oxford University Press, 2000.

Hixson, Walter L. *Parting the Curtain: Propaganda, Culture, and the Cold War, 1945–1961.* New York: St. Martin's, 1997.

Hoberman, J. *The Red Atlantis: Communist Culture in the Absence of Communism.* Philadelphia: Temple University Press, 1998.

Hodgson, Godfrey. *The World Turned Right Side Up: A History of the Conservative Ascendancy in America.* Boston: Houghton Mifflin, 1996.

Hoenicke, Michaela. "'Know Your Enemy': American Interpretations of National Socialism, 1933–1945." Ph.D. diss., University of North Carolina, 1998.

Hoenicke Moore, Michaela. *Know Your Enemy: The American Debate on Nazism, 1933–1945.* Cambridge: Cambridge University Press, 2010.

Hoffmann, Johannes J. *Adenauer, "Vorsicht und keine Indiskretionen!" Zur Informationspolitik und Öffentlichkeitsarbeit der Bundesregierung, 1949–1955.* Aachen: Shaker, 1995.

Hogan, Michael J. "The Enola Gay Controversy; History, Memory, and the Politics of Presentation." In *Hiroshima in History and Memory,* edited by Michael J. Hogan, 200–232. Cambridge: Cambridge University Press, 1996.

———. "The Next Big Thing: The Future of Diplomatic History in a Global Age." *Diplomatic History* 28, no. 1 (2004): 1–21.

Hogan, Michael J., and Thomas G. Paterson, eds. *Explaining the History of American Foreign Relations.* 2nd ed. Cambridge: Cambridge University Press, 2004.

Hoganson, Kristin L. *Fighting for American Manhood: How Gender Politics Provoked the Spanish-American and Philippine-American Wars.* New Haven, Conn.: Yale University Press, 1998.

Höhn, Maria. *GIs and Fräuleins: The German-American Encounter in 1950s West Germany.* Chapel Hill: University of North Carolina Press, 2002.

Holsti, Ole R. *Public Opinion and American Foreign Policy.* Ann Arbor: University of Michigan Press, 1996.

Hoskins, Andrew. "New Memory: Mediating History." *Historical Journal of Film, Radio and Television* 21, no. 4 (2001): 333–45.

———. "Television and the Collapse of Memory." *Time & Society* 13, no. 1 (2004): 109–27.

Huntington, Thomas. "The Berlin Spy Tunnel Affair." *American Heritage of Invention & Technology* 10, no. 4 (1995): 44–52.

Hutton, Patrick H. *History as an Art of Memory.* Hanover: University of Vermont, 1993.

Huyssen, Andreas. "Present Pasts: Media, Politics, Amnesia." *Public Culture* 12, no. 1 (2000): 21–38.

———. *Twilight Memories: Marking Time in a Culture of Amnesia.* New York: Routledge, 1995.

Iriye, Akira. "A Century of NGOs." *Diplomatic History* 23, no. 3 (1999): 421–35.

———. "Culture and International History." In *Explaining the History of American*

Foreign Relations, edited by Michael J. Hogan and Thomas G. Paterson, 241–56. Cambridge: Cambridge University Press, 2004.

Isserman, Maurice. *Which Side Were You On? The American Communist Party during the Second World War.* Urbana: University of Illinois Press, 1993.

Isserman, Maurice, and Michael Kazin. *America Divided: The Civil War of the 1960s.* New York: Oxford University Press, 2000.

Iverson, Peter. *Barry Goldwater: Native Arizonan.* Norman: University of Oklahoma Press, 1997.

Jaehn, Tomas. *Germans in the Southwest, 1850–1920.* Albuquerque: University of New Mexico Press, 2005.

James, Daniel. "Meatpackers, Peronists, and Collective Memory: A View from the South." *American Historical Review* 102, no. 5 (1997): 1404–12.

Jeismann, Karl-Ernst. "American Observations concerning the Prussian Educational System in the Nineteenth Century." In *German Influences on Education in the United States to 1917*, edited by Henry Geitz, Jürgen Heideking, and Jurgen Herbst, 21–42. Cambridge: Cambridge University Press, 1995.

Jespersen, T. Christopher. *American Images of China, 1931–1949.* Stanford, Calif.: Stanford University Press, 1996.

Johnson, Charles T. *Culture at Twilight: The National German-American Alliance, 1901–1918.* New York: Peter Lang, 1999.

Johnson, Thomas J. *The Rehabilitation of Richard Nixon: The Media's Effect on Collective Memory.* New York: Garland, 1995.

Jones, George Fenwick. *The Georgia Dutch: From the Rhine and Danube to the Savannah, 1733–1783.* Athens: University of Georgia Press, 1992.

Jones, Gerard. *Honey, I'm Home! Sitcoms, Selling the American Dream.* New York: St. Martin's, 1993.

Junker, Detlef, ed. *The United States and Germany in the Era of the Cold War, 1945–1990: A Handbook.* 2 vols. Cambridge: Cambridge University Press, 2004.

Kabir, Ananya Jahanara. "Gender, Memory, Trauma: Women's Novels on the Partition of India." *Comparative Studies of South Asia, Africa and the Middle East* 25, no. 1 (2005): 177–90.

Kaiser, Charles. *1968 in America: Music, Politics, Chaos, Counterculture, and the Shaping of a Generation.* New York: Grove, 1988.

Kalk, Bruce H. *The Origins of the Southern Strategy: Two-Party Competition in South Carolina, 1950–1972.* Lanham, Md.: Lexington Books, 2001.

Kammen, Michael G. *In the Past Lane: Historical Perspectives on American Culture.* New York: Oxford University Press, 1997.

———. *Mystic Chords of Memory: The Transformation of Tradition in American Culture.* New York: Knopf, 1991.

Kansteiner, Wulf. "Finding Meaning in Memory: A Methodological Critique of Collective Memory Studies." *History & Theory* 41, no. 2 (2002): 179–97.

———. "Nazis, Viewers and Statistics: Television History, Television Audience Research and Collective Memory in West Germany." *Journal of Contemporary History* 39, no. 4 (2004): 575–98.

Kaplan, Philip, and Jack Currie. "Night Raid on Berlin: Edward R. Murrow Flies with the RAF." *American History Illustrated* 28, no. 6 (1994): 56–65.

Karwelat, Jürgen, Marcel Munte, and Berliner Geschichtswerkstatt. *Wahnsinn: Erinnerungen an den Berliner Mauerfall vom 9. November 1989.* Berlin: Berliner Geschichtswerkstatt, 1999.

Kazal, Russell A. *Becoming Old Stock: The Paradox of German-American Identity.* Princeton, N.J.: Princeton University Press, 2004.

Kazin, Michael. *The Populist Persuasion: An American History.* New York: Basic Books, 1995.

Keller, Christian B. *Chancellorsville and the Germans: Nativism, Ethnicity, and Civil War Memory.* New York: Fordham University Press, 2007.

Kempe, Frederick. *Father/Land: A Personal Search for the New Germany.* Bloomington: Indiana University Press, 2002.

Kennedy, Liam, and Scott Lucas. "Enduring Freedom: Public Diplomacy and U.S. Foreign Policy." *American Quarterly* 57, no. 2 (2005): 309–33.

Kershaw, Ian. *Hitler, 1889–1936: Hubris.* New York: Norton, 1999.

Khong, Yuen Foong. *Analogies at War: Korea, Munich, Dien Bien Phu, and the Vietnam Decisions of 1965.* Princeton, N.J.: Princeton University Press, 1992.

Kielmansegg, Peter, Horst Mewes, and Elisabeth Glaser-Schmidt, eds. *Hannah Arendt and Leo Strauss: German Émigrés and American Political Thought after World War II.* Cambridge: Cambridge University Press, 1995.

Kim, Jong-pyo. *Image-Behavior Linkage: An Analysis of Soviet Images of America and Detente, 1969–1978.* Chapel Hill: University of North Carolina Press, 1990.

Kimball, Warren F. *Swords or Ploughshares? The Morgenthau Plan for Defeated Nazi Germany, 1943–1946.* Philadelphia: Lippincott, 1976.

Klatch, Rebecca. *A Generation Divided: The New Left, the New Right, and the 1960s.* Berkeley: University of California Press, 1999.

Kleihues, Josef Paul, and Christina Rathgeber, eds. *Berlin/New York: Like and Unlike; Essays on Architecture and Art from 1870 to the Present.* New York: Rizzoli, 1993.

Klein, Christina. *Cold War Orientalism: Asia in the Middlebrow Imagination, 1945–1961.* Berkeley: University of California Press, 2003.

Kleinman, Mark L. *A World of Hope, a World of Fear: Henry A. Wallace, Reinhold Niebuhr, and American Liberalism.* Columbus: Ohio State University Press, 2000.

Klubock, Thomas Miller. "History and Memory in Neoliberal Chile: Patricio Guzman's Obstinate Memory and the Battle of Chile." *Radical History Review* 85 (2003): 272–81.

Knobel, Dale T. *America for the Americans: The Nativist Movement in the United States.* New York: Twayne, 1996.

Koch, Hans-Jörg. *Der 9. November in der deutschen Geschichte: 1918, 1923, 1938, 1989.* Freiburg im Breisgau: Rombach, 1998.

Kondert, Reinhart. *The Germans of Colonial Louisiana, 1720–1803.* Stuttgart: Hans-Dieter Heinz, 1990.

Koppes, Clayton, and Gregory Black. *Hollywood Goes to War: How Politics, Profits, and Propaganda Shaped World War II Movies.* Berkeley: University of California Press, 1987.

Krampikowski, Frank. *Amerikanisches Deutschlandbild und deutsches Amerikabild in Medien und Erziehung.* Interkulturelle Erziehung in Praxis und Theorie, vol. 10. Baltmannsweiler: Pädagogischer Verlag Burgbücherei Schneider, 1990.

Kroes, Rob. *If You've Seen One You've Seen the Mall: Europeans and American Mass Culture.* Urbana: University of Illinois Press, 1996.

Kroes, Rob, Robert W. Rydell, D. F. J. Bosscher, and John F. Sears. *Cultural Transmissions and Receptions: American Mass Culture in Europe.* Amsterdam: VU University Press, 1993.

Krueger, Peter. "Germany and the United States, 1914–1933: The Mutual Perception of Their Political Systems." In *Transatlantic Images and Perceptions: Germany and America since 1776,* edited by David E. Barclay and Elisabeth Glaser-Schmidt, 171–90. Cambridge: Cambridge University Press, 1997.

Kühnhardt, Ludger. *Atlantik-Brücke: Fünfzig Jahre deutsch-amerikanische Partnerschaft, 1952–2002.* Berlin: Propyläen, 2002.

Kutulas, Judy. "'Totalitarianism' Transformed: The Mainstreaming of Anti-communism, 1938–1941." *Mid-America* 77, no. 1 (1995): 71–88.

Kuzdas, Heinz J., and Michael Nungesser. *Berliner Mauer Kunst.* Berlin: Elefanten, 1990.

Kuznick, Peter J., and James Burkhart Gilbert. *Rethinking Cold War Culture.* Washington, D.C.: Smithsonian Institution Press, 2001.

LaFeber, Walter. *Michael Jordan and the New Global Capitalism.* New York: Norton, 1999.

Landsberg, Alison. *Prosthetic Memory: The Transformation of American Remembrance in the Age of Mass Culture.* New York: Columbia University Press, 2004.

Large, David Clay. "The Great Rescue." *MHQ: The Quarterly Journal of Military History* 9, no. 3 (1997): 14–21.

Lauren, Paul Gordon. "First Principles of Racial Equality: History and the Politics and Diplomacy of Human Rights Provisions in the United Nations Charter." In *Race and U.S. Foreign Policy during the Cold War,* edited by Michael Krenn, 25–50. New York: Garland, 1998.

Laurie, Clayton D. *The Propaganda Warriors: America's Crusade against Nazi Germany.* Modern War Studies. Lawrence: University Press of Kansas, 1996.

Lears, T. J. Jackson. "The Concept of Cultural Hegemony: Problems and Possibilities." *Journal of American History* 90, no. 3 (1985): 576–93.

Lee, Susanna. "'These Are Our Stories': Trauma, Form, and the Screen Phenomenon of Law and Order." *Discourse* 25, no. 1 (2004): 81–97.

Leonard, Ira M., and Robert D. Parmet. *American Nativism, 1830–1860.* New York: Van Nostrand Reinhold, 1971.

Lev, Peter. *Transforming the Screen, 1950–1959.* New York: Charles Scribner's Sons, 2003.

Levine, Bruce C. *The Spirit of 1848: German Immigrants, Labor Conflict, and the Coming of the Civil War.* Urbana: University of Illinois Press, 1992.

Lichter, S. Robert, Linda S. Lichter, and Stanley Rothman. *Watching America.* New York: Prentice Hall, 1991.

Lieberman, Robbie. *Prairie Power: Voices of 1960s Midwestern Student Protest.* Columbia: University of Missouri Press, 2004.

Lifka, Thomas. *The Concept "Totalitarianism" and American Foreign Policy.* 2 vols. New York: Garland, 1988.

Lipsitz, George. *Time Passages: Collective Memory and American Popular Culture.* Minneapolis: University of Minnesota Press, 1990.

Lipstadt, Deborah E. "America and the Memory of the Holocaust, 1950–1965." *Modern Judaism* 16, no. 3 (1996): 195–214.

———. *Beyond Belief: The American Press and the Coming of the Holocaust, 1933–1945.* New York: Simon & Schuster, 1986.

Little, Douglas. *American Orientalism: The United States and the Middle East since 1945.* Chapel Hill: University of North Carolina Press, 2002.

Loshitzky, Yosefa. Introduction to *Spielberg's Holocaust: Critical Perspectives on Schindler's List,* edited by Yosefa Loshitzky, 1–17. Bloomington: Indiana University Press, 1997.

Lutzeier, Elizabeth. *The Wall.* New York: Holiday House, 1992.

Maack, Mary Niles. "Books and Libraries as Instruments of Cultural Diplomacy in Francophone Africa during the Cold War." *Libraries & the Cultural Record* 36, no. 1 (2001): 58–86.

MacDonald, J. Fred. *One Nation under Television: The Rise and Decline of Network TV.* New York: Pantheon Books, 1990.

Maier, Charles S. "A Nation among Nations: America's Place in World History." *Journal of American History* 94, no. 1 (2007): 232–33.

———. *The Unmasterable Past: History, Holocaust, and German National Identity.* Cambridge, Mass.: Harvard University Press, 1988.

Maltby, Richard, and Ian Craven. *Hollywood Cinema: An Introduction.* Cambridge, Mass.: Blackwell, 1995.

Marchand, Roland. *Creating the Corporate Soul: The Rise of Public Relations and Corporate Imagery in American Big Business.* Berkeley: University of California Press, 1998.

Mariniello, Silvestra, and James Cisneros. "Experience and Memory in the Films of Wim Wenders." *SubStance* 34, no. 1 (2005): 159–79.

Marks, John. *The Wall.* New York: Riverhead Books, 1998.

Marshall, Barbara. *Willy Brandt: A Political Biography.* New York: St. Martin's, 1997.

Martin, Andrew. *Receptions of War: Vietnam in American Culture.* Norman: University of Oklahoma Press, 1993.

Mason, Robert. *Richard Nixon and the Quest for a New Majority.* Chapel Hill: University of North Carolina Press, 2004.

May, Elaine Tyler. *Homeward Bound: American Families in the Cold War Era.* New York: Basic Books, 1988.

Mayer, Frank A. *Adenauer and Kennedy: A Study in German-American Relations, 1961–1963.* New York: St. Martin's, 1996.

McAleer, John. *Rex Stout: A Majesty's Life.* Rockville, Md.: James A. Rock, 2002.

McAlister, Melanie. *Epic Encounters: Culture, Media, and U.S. Interests in the Middle East, 1945–2000.* Los Angeles: University of California Press, 2001.

McBride, David, Leroy Hopkins, and Carol Blackshire-Belay. *Crosscurrents: African Americans, Africa, and Germany in the Modern World.* Columbia, S.C.: Camden House, 1998.

McCaffery, Robert Paul. *Islands of Deutschtum: German-Americans in Manchester, New Hampshire and Lawrence, Massachusetts, 1870–1942.* New York: Peter Lang, 1996.

McCartney, Paul T. "Americanism: New Perspectives on the History of an Ideal." *Journal of American History* 94, no. 1 (2007): 234–35.

McMahon, Robert. "Contested Memory: The Vietnam War and American Society, 1975–2001." *Diplomatic History* 26, no. 2 (2002): 159–84.

Melanson, Richard. *American Foreign Policy since the Vietnam War: The Search for Consensus from Nixon to Clinton.* Armonk, N.Y.: M. E. Sharpe, 2000.

Merritt, Richard L. *Democracy Imposed: U.S. Occupation Policy and the German Public, 1945–1949.* New Haven, Conn.: Yale University Press, 1995.

Miller, Roger G. "The Berlin Airlift in Pictures." *Air Power History* 45, no. 3 (1998): 1–72.

Mintz, Alan. *Popular Culture and the Shaping of Holocaust Memory in America.* Seattle: University of Washington Press, 2001.

Moeller, Robert G. "Germans as Victims? Thoughts on a Post–Cold War History of World War II's Legacies." *History & Memory* 17, no. 1 (2005): 147–94.

———. "War Stories: The Search for a Usable Past." *American Historical Review* 101, no. 4 (1996): 1008–48.

———. *War Stories: The Search for a Usable Past in the Federal Republic of Germany.* Berkeley: University of California Press, 2001.

———. *West Germany under Construction: Politics, Society, and Culture in the Adenauer Era.* Ann Arbor: University of Michigan Press, 1997.

Moltmann, Gunter. "The Pattern of German Emigration to the United States in the Nineteenth Century." In *America and the Germans: An Assessment of a Three-Hundred-Year History,* edited by Frank Trommler and Joseph McVeigh, 14–24. Philadelphia: University of Pennsylvania Press, 1985.

Murphy, David E., Sergei A. Kondrashev, and George Bailey. *Battleground Berlin: CIA vs. KGB in the Cold War.* New Haven, Conn.: Yale University Press, 1997.

Mutz, Diana C. "Contextualizing Personal Experience: The Role of Mass Media." *Journal of Politics* 56, no. 3 (1994): 689–714.

Nadel, Alan. *Containment Culture: American Narratives, Postmodernism, and the Atomic Age.* Durham, N.C.: Duke University Press, 1995.

Nagler, Jörg. "From Culture to Kultur: Changing American Perceptions of Imperial Germany, 1870–1914." In *Transatlantic Images and Perceptions: Germany and America since 1776,* edited by David E. Barclay and Elisabeth Glaser-Schmidt, 131–54. Cambridge: Cambridge University Press, 1997.

Ninkovich, Frank A. *Germany and the United States: The Transformation of the Ger-man Question since 1945.* New York: Twayne, 1995.

———. *Modernity and Power: A History of the Domino Theory in the Twentieth Cen-tury.* Chicago: University of Chicago Press, 1994.

Noer, Thomas J. "Truman, Eisenhower, and South Africa: The 'Middle Road' and Apartheid." In *Race and U.S. Foreign Policy during the Cold War,* edited by Mi-chael Krenn, 131–60. New York: Garland, 1998.

Nolletti, Arthur, Jr., ed. *The Films of Fred Zinnemann: Critical Perspectives.* Albany: State University of New York Press, 1999.

Nora, Pierre, and Lawrence D. Kritzman. *Realms of Memory: Rethinking the French Past.* New York: Columbia University Press, 1996.

Novick, Peter. *The Holocaust in American Life.* Boston: Houghton Mifflin, 1999.

Nuechterlein, Donald Edwin. *A Cold War Odyssey.* Lexington: University Press of Kentucky, 1997.

Olick, Jeffrey K. "Collective Memory: The Two Cultures." *Sociological Theory* 17, no. 3 (1999): 333–48.

Olick, Jeffrey K., and Joyce Robbins. "Social Memory Studies: From 'Collective Memory' to the Historical Sociology of Mnemonic Practices." *Annual Review of Sociology* 24 (1998): 105–40.

O'Neill, William L. *A Democracy at War: America's Fight at Home and Abroad in World War II.* New York: Free Press, 1993.

Osgood, Kenneth Alan. *Total Cold War: Eisenhower's Secret Propaganda Battle at Home and Abroad.* Lawrence: University Press of Kansas, 2006.

Otterness, Philip. *Becoming German: The 1709 Palatine Migration to New York.* Itha-ca, N.Y.: Cornell University Press, 2004.

Paris, Michael. *Repicturing the Second World War: Representations in Film and Televi-sion.* Basingstoke, U.K.: Palgrave Macmillan, 2007.

Paterson, Thomas G. *On Every Front: The Making and Unmaking of the Cold War.* New York: Norton, 1992.

Paulmann, Johannes, ed. *Auswärtige Repräsentationen: Deutsche Kulturdiplomatie nach 1945.* Cologne: Böhlau, 2005.

Peck, Abe. *Uncovering the Sixties: The Life and Times of the Underground Press.* New York: Pantheon Books, 1985.

Pells, Richard H. *Not Like Us: How Europeans Have Loved, Hated, and Transformed American Culture since World War II.* New York: Basic Books, 1997.

Perlstein, Rick. *Before the Storm: Barry Goldwater and the Unmaking of the American Consensus.* New York: Hill & Wang, 2001.

Phillips, Gene D. *Exiles in Hollywood: Major European Film Directors in America.* Bethlehem, Pa.: Lehigh University Press, 1998.

Philo, Greg. *Message Received: Glasgow Media Group Research, 1993–1998.* New York: Longman, 1999.

Poiger, Uta G. *Jazz, Rock, and Rebels: Cold War Politics and American Culture in a Divided Germany.* Berkeley: University of California Press, 2000.

Pollock, James Kerr, and Ingrid Krüger-Bulcke. *Besatzung und Staatsaufbau nach 1945: Occupation Diary and Private Correspondence, 1945–1948.* Munich: R. Oldenbourg, 1994.

Pommerin, Reiner. *The American Impact on Postwar Germany.* Providence, R.I.: Berghahn Books, 1995.

Quart, Leonard. "There Were Good Germans: Fred Zinnemann's *The Seventh Cross.*" In *The Films of Fred Zinnemann: Critical Perspectives,* edited by Arthur Nolletti Jr., 69–77. Albany: State University of New York Press, 1999.

Radway, Janice A. *Reading the Romance: Women, Patriarchy, and Popular Literature.* Chapel Hill: University of North Carolina Press, 1991.

Reuther, Thomas. *Die ambivalente Normalisierung: Deutschlanddiskurs und Deutschlandbilder in den USA, 1941–1955.* Stuttgart: Franz Steiner, 2000.

Ribuffo, Leo P. "What Is Still Living in 'Consensus' History and Pluralist Social Theory." *American Studies International* 38, no. 1 (2000): 42–60.

Rice, Leland, and Charles E. McClelland. *Up against It: Photographs of the Berlin Wall.* Albuquerque: University of New Mexico Press, 1991.

Rieger, Bernhard. *The People's Car: A Global History of the Volkswagen Beetle.* Cambridge, Mass.: Harvard University Press, 2013.

Rippley, La Vern J. "German Assimilation: The Effect of the 1871 Victory on Americana-Germanica." In *Germany and America: Essays on Problems of International Relations and Immigration,* edited by Hans L. Trefousse, 122–36. New York: Brooklyn College Press, 1980.

Robben, Antonius C. G. M. "How Traumatized Societies Remember: The Aftermath of Argentina's Dirty War." *Cultural Critique* 59 (2005): 120–64.

Robin, Ron Theodore. *The Barbed-Wire College: Reeducating German POWs in the United States during World War II.* Princeton, N.J.: Princeton University Press, 1995.

———. "Requiem for Public Diplomacy?" *American Quarterly* 57, no. 2 (2005): 345–53.

Rosen, Alan. "'Teach Me Gold': Pedagogy and Memory in the Pawnbroker." *Prooftexts* 22, no. 1 (2002): 77–117.

Rosenbaum, Ron. *Explaining Hitler: The Search for the Origins of His Evil.* New York: Random House, 1998.

Rosenberg, Emily. *A Date Which Will Live: Pearl Harbor in American Memory.* Durham, N.C.: Duke University Press, 2003.

———. "Foreign Affairs after World War II: Connecting Sexual and International Politics." *Diplomatic History* 18, no. 1 (1994): 59–70.

———. "Walking the Borders." In *Explaining the History of American Foreign Relations,* edited by Michael J. Hogan and Thomas G. Paterson, 24–35. New York: Cambridge University Press, 1991.

Rosenfeld, Gavriel. "The Reception of William L. Shirer's *The Rise and Fall of the Third Reich in the United States and West Germany, 1960–1962.*" *Journal of Contemporary History* 29, no. 1 (1994): 95–128.

Rosenzweig, Roy, and David P. Thelen. *The Presence of the Past: Popular Uses of History in American Life.* New York: Columbia University Press, 1998.

Ross, Christopher. "Public Diplomacy Comes of Age." In *The Battle for Hearts and Minds: Using Soft Power to Undermine Terrorist Networks,* edited by Alexander Lennon, 251–61. Cambridge, Mass.: MIT Press, 2003.

Rousso, Henry. *The Vichy Syndrome: History and Memory in France since 1944.* Cambridge, Mass.: Harvard University Press, 1991.

Royce, Brenda Scott. *"Hogan's Heroes": A Comprehensive Reference to the 1965–1971 Television Comedy Series with Cast Biographies and an Episode Guide.* Jefferson, N.C.: McFarland, 1993.

Rupieper, Hermann-Josef. *Die Wurzeln der westdeutschen Nachkriegsdemokratie: Der amerikanische Beitrag 1945–1952.* Opladen: Westdeutscher Verlag, 1993.

Sarotte, M. E. *Dealing with the Devil: East Germany, Detente, and Ostpolitik, 1969–1973.* Chapel Hill: University of North Carolina Press, 2001.

Savage, Barbara Dianne. *Broadcasting Freedom: Radio, War, and the Politics of Race, 1938–1948.* Chapel Hill: University of North Carolina Press, 1999.

Schild, Georg. "Die Kennedy-Administration und die Berlin-Krise von 1961." *Zeitschrift fur Geschichtswissenschaft* 42, no. 8 (1994): 703–11.

Schlesinger, Arthur. *The Vital Center: The Politics of Freedom.* Boston: Houghton Mifflin, 1949.

Schmaltz, William H. *Hate: George Lincoln Rockwell and the American Nazi Party.* Washington, D.C.: Brassey's, 1999.

Schmundt-Thomas, Georg. "America's Germany: National Self and Cultural Other after World War II." Ph.D. diss., Northwestern University, 1992.

Schneider, Gregory L. *Cadres for Conservatism: Young Americans for Freedom and the Rise of the Contemporary Right.* New York: New York University Press, 1999.

Schneider, Peter, and Leigh Hafrey. *The Wall Jumper: A Berlin Story.* Chicago: University of Chicago Press, 1998.

Schrag, Peter. *Not Fit for Our Society: Nativism and Immigration.* Berkeley: University of California Press, 2010.

Schultke, Dietmar. *"Keiner kommt Durch": Die Geschichte der innerdeutschen Grenze 1945–1990.* Berlin: Aufbau Taschenbuch Verlag, 1999.

Schultz, Nancy. *Fear Itself: Enemies Real and Imagined in American Culture.* West Lafayette, Ind.: Purdue University Press, 1999.

Schulzinger, Robert D. "Memory and Understanding U.S. Foreign Relations." In *Explaining the History of American Foreign Relations,* edited by Michael J. Hogan and Thomas G. Paterson, 336–52. Cambridge: Cambridge University Press, 2004.

Schürer, Ernst, Manfred Erwin Keune, and Philip Jenkins. *The Berlin Wall: Representations and Perspectives.* New York: P. Lang, 1996.

Schwartz, Thomas Alan. *America's Germany: John J. Mccloy and the Federal Republic of Germany.* Cambridge, Mass.: Harvard University Press, 1991.

———. *Lyndon Johnson and Europe: In the Shadow of Vietnam.* Cambridge, Mass.: Harvard University Press, 2003.

———. "'No Harder Enterprise': Politics and Policies in the German-American Relationship, 1945–1968." In *The United States and Germany in the Era of the Cold War, 1945–1990: A Handbook,* edited by Detlef Junker, 1:29–43. Cambridge: Cambridge University Press, 2004.

Schwarz, Hans-Peter. *Konrad Adenauer: A German Politician and Statesman in a Period of War, Revolution, and Reconstruction.* Providence, R.I.: Berghahn Books, 1995.

Schweizer, Peter. *The Fall of the Berlin Wall: Reassessing the Causes and Consequences of the End of the Cold War.* Washington, D.C.: Hoover Institution Press, 2000.

Scott, Len. "The Spy Who Wanted to Save the World." *Intelligence and National Security* 8, no. 4 (1993): 138–46.

Shafir, Shlomo. *Ambiguous Relations: The American Jewish Community and Germany since 1945.* Detroit: Wayne State University Press, 1999.

———. "The American Jewish Community's Attitude to Germany: The Impact of Israel." *Journal of Israeli History* 18, nos. 2–3 (1997): 237–53.

———. *American Jews and Germany after 1945: Points of Connection and Points of Departure.* Cincinnati: American Jewish Archives, 1993.

Shandler, Jeffrey. *While America Watches: Televising the Holocaust.* Oxford: Oxford University Press, 1999.

Shapiro, Ann-Louise. "Whose (Which) History Is It Anyway?" In "Producing the Past: Making Histories inside and outside the Academy." Special issue, *History and Theory* 36, no. 4 (1997): 1–3.

Shapiro, Edward. *A Time for Healing: American Jewry since World War II.* Baltimore: Johns Hopkins University Press, 1992.

Shepardson, Donald E. "The Fall of Berlin and the Rise of a Myth." *Journal of Military History* 62, no. 1 (1998): 135–53.

Shiner, Linda. "Heroes Welcome." *Air & Space / Smithsonian* 13, no. 2 (1998): 34–41.

Short, K. R. M. "'The March of Time': Time Inc. and the Berlin Blockade, 1948–1949; Selling Americans on the 'New' Democratic Germany." *Historical Journal of Film, Radio and Television* 13, no. 4 (1993): 451–68.

Shull, Michael S., and David E. Wilt. *Doing Their Bit: Wartime American Animated Short Films, 1939–1945.* 2nd ed. Jefferson, N.C.: McFarland, 2004.

Siemon-Netto, Uwe. *The Fabricated Luther: The Rise and Fall of the Shirer Myth.* St. Louis: Concordia, 1995.

Simonelli, Frederick J. *American Fuehrer: George Lincoln Rockwell and the American Nazi Party.* Urbana: University of Illinois Press, 1999.

Sitkoff, Harvard. *King: Pilgrimage to the Mountaintop.* New York: Macmillan, 2009.

Skidmore, David. *Reversing Course: Carter's Foreign Policy, Domestic Politics, and the Failure of Reform.* Nashville: Vanderbilt University Press, 1996.

Smith, Jean Edward. *Lucius D. Clay: An American Life.* New York: H. Holt, 1992.

Southall, Aidan William. *The City in Time and Space.* New York: Cambridge University Press, 1998.

Spigel, Lynn. "Entertainment Wars: Television Culture after 9/11." *American Quarterly* 56, no. 2 (2004): 235–70.

Staiger, Janet. *Interpreting Films: Studies in the Historical Reception of American Cinema.* Princeton, N.J.: Princeton University Press, 1992.

————. *Media Reception Studies.* New York: New York University Press, 2005.

Standifer, Leon C. *Binding Up the Wounds: An American Soldier in Occupied Germany, 1945–1946.* Baton Rouge: Louisiana State University Press, 1997.

Stark, Steven D. *Glued to the Set: The 60 Television Shows and Events That Made Us Who We Are Today.* New York: Free Press, 1997.

Staub, Michael E. *Torn at the Roots: The Crisis of Jewish Liberalism in Postwar America.* New York: Columbia University Press, 2002.

Steege, Paul. "More Than an Airlift: Constructing the Berlin Blockade as a Cold War Battle, 1946–1949." Ph.D. diss., University of Chicago, 1999.

Steigerwald, David. "All Hail the Republic of Choice: Consumer History as Contemporary Thought." *Journal of American History* 93, no. 2 (2006): 385–403.

Stein, Herman, John Martin, and Alex Rosen. *The Swastika Daubings and Related Incidents of Winter, 1960: An Exploratory Study Centered in the New York Metropolitan Area.* New York: Research Center, New York School of Social Work, Columbia University, 1961.

Steinweis, Alan E. "The Legacy of the Holocaust in Germany and the United States." In *The United States and Germany in the Era of the Cold War, 1945–1990: A Handbook,* edited by Detlef Junker, 1:488–94. Cambridge: Cambridge University Press, 2004.

Stephan, Alexander, and Jan van Heurck. *"Communazis": FBI Surveillance of German Emigré Writers.* New Haven, Conn.: Yale University Press, 2000.

Stephanson, Anders. *Manifest Destiny: American Expansionism and the Empire of Right.* New York: Hill & Wang, 1996.

Sternberg, Claudia. "Real-Life References in Four Fred Zinnemann Films." In *The Films of Fred Zinnemann: Critical Perspectives,* edited by Arthur Nolletti Jr., 199–218. Albany: State University of New York Press, 1999.

Stock, Catherine McNicol. "Aryan Cowboys: White Supremacists and the Search for a New Frontier, 1970–2000." *Journal of American History* 94, no. 2 (2007): 654–55.

Stoler, Mark. "A Half Century of Conflict: Interpretations of U.S. World War II Diplomacy." *Diplomatic History* 18, no. 3 (1994): 374–403.

Strong, Robert A. *Working in the World: Jimmy Carter and the Making of American Foreign Policy.* Baton Rouge: Louisiana State University Press, 2000.

Sturken, Marita. *Tangled Memories: The Vietnam War, the Aids Epidemic, and the Politics of Remembering.* Berkeley: University of California Press, 1997.

Suid, Lawrence H. *Guts & Glory: The Making of the American Military Image.* Lexington: University Press of Kentucky, 2002.

Suleiman, Susan Rubin. "History, Heroism, and Narrative Desire: The 'Aubrac Affair' and National Memory of the French Resistance." *South Central Review* 21, no. 1 (2004): 54–81.

Suri, Jeremi. *Power and Protest: Global Revolution and the Rise of Detente.* Cambridge, Mass.: Harvard University Press, 2003.

Svonkin, Stuart. *Jews against Prejudice: American Jews and the Fight for Civil Liberties.* New York: Columbia University Press, 1997.

Tai, Hue-Tam Ho. "Remembered Realms: Pierre Nora and French National Memory." *American Historical Review* 106, no. 3 (2001): 906–22.

Takaki, Ronald T. *Double Victory: A Multicultural History of America in World War II.* Boston: Little, Brown, 2000.

Taylor, Philip M. *British Propaganda in the 20th Century: Selling Democracy.* Edinburgh: Edinburgh University Press, 1999.

Thelen, David. *Memory and American History.* Bloomington: Indiana University Press, 1990.

———. "A Moment in a Scholar's Understanding of America: Attending Rob Kroes's Retirement Talk." *Journal of American History* 93, no. 2 (2006): 414–16.

Tillman, Terry. *The Writings on the Wall: Peace at the Berlin Wall.* Santa Monica, Calif.: 22/7, 1990.

Tollefson, James W. *The Strength Not to Fight: Conscientious Objectors of the Vietnam War—In Their Own Words.* Washington, D.C.: Brassey's, 2000.

Trachtenberg, Marc. *A Constructed Peace: The Making of the European Settlement, 1945–1963.* Princeton, N.J.: Princeton University Press, 1999.

Trommler, Frank. "Inventing the Enemy: Germany-American Cultural Relations, 1900–1917." In *Confrontation and Cooperation: Germany and the United States in the Era of World War I, 1900–1924,* edited by Hans-Jürgen Schröder, 99–125. Providence, R.I.: Berg, 1993.

Tuck, Jim. *The Liberal Civil War: Fraternity and Fratricide on the Left.* Lanham, Md.: University Press of America, 1998.

Tusa, Ann. *The Last Division: A History of Berlin, 1945–1989.* Reading, Mass.: Addison-Wesley, 1997.

Tye, Larry. *The Father of Spin: Edward L. Bernays & the Birth of Public Relations.* New York: Henry Holt, 2002.

Valantin, Jean-Michel. *Hollywood, the Pentagon and Washington.* London: Anthem, 2005.

Varon, Jeremy. *Bringing the War Home: The Weather Underground, the Red Army Faction, and Revolutionary Violence in the Sixties and Seventies.* Berkeley: University of California Press, 2004.

Vaughn, Stephen. *Holding Fast the Inner Lines: Democracy, Nationalism, and the Committee on Public Information.* Chapel Hill: University of North Carolina Press, 1980.

Viertel, Peter. *Dangerous Friends: At Large with Hemingway and Huston in the Fifties.* New York: Doubleday, 1992.

Von Eschen, Penny M. "Enduring Public Diplomacy." *American Quarterly* 57, no. 2 (2005): 335–43.

Wagnleitner, Reinhold. *Coca-Colonization and the Cold War: The Cultural Mission of the United States in Austria after the Second World War.* Chapel Hill: University of North Carolina Press, 1994.

Wahl, Angelika von. *Zwischen Heimat und Holocaust: Das Deutschlandbild der Nach-kommen deutscher Juden in New York.* Frankfurt: Peter Lang, 1992.

Wala, Michael. "Reviving Ethnic Identity: The Foreign Office, the Reichswehr, and German Americans during the Weimar Republic." In *German-American Immi-gration and Ethnicity in Comparative Perspective,* edited by Wolfgang Helbich and Walter D. Kamphoefner, 326–42. Madison, Wis.: Max Kade Institute for German-American Studies, 2004

Walch, Timothy. *Immigrant America: European Ethnicity in the United States.* New York: Garland, 1994.

Walleiser, Gerd. *Die Teilung: Das deutsche Interregnum 1945/49; Eine historische Re-portage.* Berlin: Verlag am Park, 1999.

Weinberg, Gerhard L. *A World at Arms: A Global History of World War II.* New York: Cambridge University Press, 1994.

Weitz, Richard. "Henry Kissinger's Philosophy of International Relations." *Diplo-macy & Statecraft* 2, no. 1 (1991): 103–29.

Wellenreuther, Hermann. "'Germans Make Cows and Women Work': American Per-ceptions of Germans as Reported in American Travel Books, 1800–1840." In *Transatlantic Images and Perceptions: Germany and America since 1776,* edited by David E. Barclay and Elisabeth Glaser-Schmidt, 41–61. Cambridge: Cambridge University Press, 1997.

———. "Image and Counterimage, Tradition and Expectation: The German Im-migrants in English Colonial Society in Pennsylvania, 1700–1765." In *America and the Germans: An Assessment of a Three-Hundred-Year History,* edited by Frank Trommler and Joseph McVeigh, 85–104. Philadelphia: University of Pennsylva-nia Press, 1985.

Wenger, Andreas. *Living with Peril: Eisenhower, Kennedy, and Nuclear Weapons.* Lan-ham, Md.: Rowman & Littlefield, 1997.

Wenn, Stephen R. "A Suitable Policy of Neutrality? FDR and the Question of Ameri-can Participation in the 1936 Olympics." *International Journal of the History of Sport* 8, no. 3 (1991): 319–35.

Wetzel, David. *From the Berlin Museum to the Berlin Wall: Essays on the Cultural and Political History of Modern Germany.* Westport, Conn.: Praeger, 1996.

White, F. Clifton, and William J. Gill. *Suite 3505: The Story of the Draft Goldwater Movement.* Ashland, Ohio: Ashbrook, 1992.

Whitfield, Stephen J. *The Culture of the Cold War.* 2nd ed. Baltimore: Johns Hopkins University Press, 1996.

Wiener, Jon. *How We Forgot the Cold War: A Historical Journey across America.* Berke-ley: University of California Press, 2012.

Wiesen, S. Jonathan. *West German Industry and the Challenge of the Nazi Past, 1945–1955.* Chapel Hill: University of North Carolina Press, 2001.

Wilhelm, Cornelia. *Bewegung oder Verein? Nationalsozialistische Volkspolitik in den USA.* Stuttgart: F. Steiner, 1998.

Willett, Ralph. "Billy Wilder's *A Foreign Affair* (1945–48): 'The Trials and Tribulations of Berlin.'" *Historical Journal of Film, Radio and Television* 7, no. 1 (1987): 3–14.

Williams, William A. *The Tragedy of American Diplomacy.* Cleveland: World, 1959.

Willms, Johannes, Peter Bender, Wolfgang Benz, Hans Mommsen, Fritz Richard Stern, and Heinrich August Winkler. *Der 9. November: Funf Essays zur deutschen Geschichte.* Munich: Beck, 1994.

Willoughby, John. *Remaking the Conquering Heroes: The Social and Geopolitical Impact of Post-war American Occupation on Germany.* New York: Palgrave, 2001.

Windt, Theodore. *Presidents and Protesters: Political Rhetoric in the 1960s.* Tuscaloosa: University of Alabama Press, 1990.

Winkler, Allan M. *Home Front U.S.A.: America during World War II.* 2nd ed. Wheeling, Ill.: Harlan Davidson, 2000.

Winter, Jay. "Film and the Matrix of Memory." *American Historical Review* 106, no. 3 (2001): 857–64.

Wittebols, James H. *Watching "M*A*S*H," Watching America: A Social History of the 1972–1983 Television Series.* Jefferson, N.C.: McFarland, 1998.

Woods, Jeff. *Black Struggle, Red Scare: Segregation and Anti-Communism in the South, 1948–1968.* Baton Rouge: Louisiana State University Press, 2004.

Woods, Randall. *Fulbright: A Biography.* New York: Cambridge University Press, 1995.

Wurm, Clemens A. *Western Europe and Germany: The Beginnings of European Integration, 1945–1960.* German Historical Perspectives 9. Oxford: Berg, 1995.

Wyman, David S. *The Abandonment of the Jews: America and the Holocaust, 1941–1945.* New York: New Press, 1998.

Wyman, Mark. *DPs: Europe's Displaced Persons, 1945–1951.* Ithaca, N.Y.: Cornell University Press, 1998.

Wynkoop, Mary Ann. *Dissent in the Heartland: The Sixties at Indiana University.* Bloomington: Indiana University Press, 2002.

Yinan, He. "Remembering and Forgetting the War." *History & Memory* 19, no. 2 (2007): 43–74.

Young, Andrew. *An Easy Burden: The Civil Rights Movement and the Transformation of America.* New York: HarperCollins, 1996.

Zacharasiewicz, Waldemar. *Das Deutschlandbild in der amerikanischen Literatur.* Darmstadt: Wissenschaftliche Buchgesellschaft, 1998.

Zeiler, Barbie. *Remembering to Forget: Holocaust Memory through the Camera's Eye.* Chicago: University of Chicago Press, 1998.

Zeiler, Thomas W. *Dean Rusk: Defending the American Mission Abroad.* Wilmington, Del.: SR Books, 2000.

Zelikow, Philip, and Condoleezza Rice. *Germany Unified and Europe Transformed: A Study in Statecraft.* Cambridge, Mass.: Harvard University Press, 1995.

Zinnemann, Fred. *A Life in the Movies.* New York: Charles Scribner's Sons, 1992.

Index

BOOKS IN THE SERIES